THE FUTURE OF NORTH AMERICA:

Canada, The United States, and Quebec Nationalism

HARVARD STUDIES
IN INTERNATIONAL AFFAIRS
Number 42

THE FUTURE OF NORTH AMERICA:

Canada, The United States, and Quebec Nationalism

Edited by
Elliot J. Feldman
Neil Nevitte

Center for International Affairs   and   Institute for Research on
Harvard University   Public Policy
Cambridge, Mass.   Montreal, Quebec

Written under the auspices of the Center for International Affairs, Harvard University, and the Institute for Research on Public Policy, Montreal.

The Institute for Research on Public Policy is a national Canadian organization which acts as a catalyst to facilitate informed public debate on issues of major public interest; seeks to stimulate participation by all segments of the national community in the process that leads to decision-making; and tries to find practical solutions to important public policy problems.

The Center is happy to provide a forum for the expression of responsible views. It does not, however, necessarily agree with them.

Harvard University
Center for International Affairs

Executive Committee

Created in 1958, the Center for International Affairs fosters advanced study of basic world problems by scholars from various disciplines and senior officials from many countries. The research of the Center focuses on economic, social, and political development; the management of force in the modern world; the problems and relations of advanced industrial societies; transnational processes and international order; and technology and international affairs.

The Harvard Studies in International Affairs, which are listed at the back of this book, may be ordered from the Publications Office, Center for International Affairs, 1737 Cambridge St., Cambridge, Mass. 02138, at the prices indicated. Recent books written under the auspices of the Center, listed on the last pages, may be obtained from bookstores or ordered directly from the publishers.

CONTENTS

The essays in this book were written originally as papers for presentation at Harvard University's 1977-78 Seminar on Canadian-United States Relations chaired by Elliot J. Feldman and Neil Nevitte at the Center for International Affairs. The seminar was organized around two main themes, tensions within Canadian Confederation and present and potential tensions between Canada and the United States. For each paper an expert commentator was invited to initiate discussion. Every paper but one was presented by a Canadian; commentators for all Canadian papers (save one) were Americans. In many instances the American commentator was chosen not for an expertise in Canadian-American affairs, but rather for an expertise in the subject matter—energy, communications, bureaucracy, foreign investment, and foreign policy—in order to provide a comparative American perspective. With this structure we guaranteed an underlying theme of comparison of experience as well as a contrasting perspective associated with nationality. Only Premier René Lévesque's essay is without a commentator, for the paper was originally presented as the 1978 Jodidi Lecture in Harvard's Sanders Theater.

Scholars from Brandeis, Tufts, and Clark Universities, the Fletcher School of Law and Diplomacy, Boston College, Holy Cross College, Boston State College, Bridgewater State College, and the Massachusetts Institute of Technology participated regularly in the seminar discussions. Diplomats and civil servants from nearly a dozen foreign countries, visiting in the Center for International Affairs' Fellows Program, contributed the experiences of their native lands. Businessmen and bankers from Greater Boston, and representatives of the Canadian Consulate and the Quebec Government Bureau joined our discussions. Every paper was subjected to detailed questioning from this audience.

Following seminar sessions, authors received written responses from the expert commentator. Authors revised their papers on the basis of the commentary and the seminar discussion; commentaries were revised in response to adjustments made in the papers, and authors and commentators exchanged their written remarks at least once more before surrendering the dialogue to the editors. All the authors, moreover, considered all the other papers before writing the final versions of their own essays and comments. Hence it can be said that these essays were not merely presented to the seminar: they are also the product of the seminar, and in their refined form they reflect the quality of our collective discussions and deliberations. They are truly the product of scholarly exchange.

The dialogues in this volume are perhaps scholarly, but the book could hardly be accused of being academic. Of the 27 contributors, 10 are active or retired politicians and civil servants; two are practicing international lawyers, and two others are accomplished professional writers. In other words, fewer than half the authors hold university appointments, and of these, six are regular consultants to various governments. This book juxtaposes scholars and practitioners, Canadians and Americans, in order to highlight different views and interpretations of international relations in North America.

All books have flaws. This book is perhaps the first written deliberately for Canadian and American audiences simultaneously; we have had to compromise, therefore, on language use. The pace of political change in Canada has accelerated since November 1976, and no essay can hope, ultimately, to keep up. Prime Minister Trudeau was invited to speak, and later to write, on the issues raised by the seminar participants. We had hoped Prime Minister Trudeau might contribute to the volume in order to balance the essays of former and present premiers of Quebec and of a highly visible senior member of the Progressive Conservative opposition, but he declined. Flora MacDonald provided some perspective from her native Maritimes, but no essay has been included specifically on the problems of the Atlantic provinces. Two leaders of the New Democratic Party, Canada's third major political force, declined invitations to present papers. Despite these errors of omission, we have been able to assemble a discussion uniquely valuable both to specialists and to people generally unfamiliar with Canadian and Quebec affairs.

The literary, humorous, and ironic exchange between Mordecai Richler and Sylvia Wright which begins the book helps emphasize the institutional seriousness which follows, for even the most comic side of the human condition ultimately is political. Ian McDougall's discussion of natural resources conflict is altogether unusual in its focus. The essay by Robert Bourassa is his first formal statement since the defeat of his Liberal Government in Quebec in November 1976. Gordon Stead's analysis of the Canadian bureaucracy opens an issue never before broached in Canada or in the United States, and Gordon Gibson's analysis of Western alienation from Ottawa is the most comprehensive one available to a general public. Allan Gotlieb's review of Canadian foreign policy is a remarkable *tour d'horizon* in the comparative study of foreign policy.

We do not emphasize these essays in order to diminish the significance of any of the others. Taken together as a collection derived from one continuous discussion, the beginner will discover the drama of North American politics through the eyes of politicians, diplomats, civil servants, political scientists, economists, lawyers, and novelists. The more informed reader will discover the most up-to-date and expansive analysis of Canadian and Quebec problems. There may be no final solutions here, but the agenda for research and discussion is rich and the paths offered are many.

ACKNOWLEDGEMENTS

Because the essays in this book were prepared originally for seminar presentation, there are two groups of people we wish to thank. One group has been essential to the seminar; the other has been crucial to the book production.

The seminar was made possible through the wisdom of former Director Raymond Vernon and former Acting Director Benjamin Brown of the Harvard Center for International Affairs. They each understood the need and value for a special country seminar dealing with Canada and they each gave continuing support to the seminar program. Richard Neustadt appreciated the opportunity presented by the seminar and through the auspices of the Mackenzie King Chair at Harvard provided the initial and necessary financial support.

Both the Consulate General of Canada and the Government Bureau of Quebec cooperated with the design of the program and the participation of spokesmen from their respective governments. Geoffrey Bruce, a Fellow at CFIA and now Canada's High Commissioner for Kenya and Uganda, proved a resource of inestimable value. Lily Gardner Feldman, the seminar's most loyal participant, helped in all the ways only a wife and colleague can. Beverly Davenport, in her capacity as secretary to the seminar, coordinated everything from the reproduction and distribution of seminar papers to the menus for seminar dinners. Sally Cox, former Executive Officer of the Center for International Affairs, and her assistant Jean Allison, sustained the seminar, and later the book, with wise counsel, continuing commitment, and remarkable negotiating skill. Neither the seminar nor the book would have been possible without these contributions.

To convert the seminar papers for publication required another set of skills. Michael Kirby and Bill Stanbury of the Institute on Public Policy Research in Montreal made publication possible by recognizing the publishable potential of the papers and by providing vital financial assistance. Dolores Timbas made her way through the editorial scribblings of three different hands with an extraordinary speed and accuracy, and Deb Forrester, Publications Assistant, coordinated the movement of manuscripts among authors, commentators, and editors; without such coordination we might still be looking for lost copies. Peter Jacobsohn, Publications Editor of the Center, managed the entire publication procedure and contributed an astute final editing to all the manuscripts. If any one person was indispensable to the book project, it was he.

Finally, we would like to thank the many seminar participants from the universities, businesses, and other institutions of the Greater Boston area. The stimulating discussions of active and concerned people made the seminar attractive, sharpened perspectives, and improved the papers immeasurably between first presentation and final publication. Whatever mistakes remain are our fault.

Cambridge   Elliot J. Feldman
December 1978   Neil Nevitte

1_____INTRODUCTION

Elliot J. Feldman

A government seeking independence from Canada has ruled Quebec since November 15, 1976. Whereas the federal government seeks greater power to hold the union together, Western Canada, led by Alberta and British Columbia, demands more freedom from the authority of Ottawa, and the Atlantic provinces worry whether social and economic survival is possible under the present rules of Canadian Confederation. Erstwhile constitutional authors are abundant from sea to sea, as Canada is adrift in its greatest crisis since welding Upper and Lower Canada, anglophone and francophone worlds, into one nation-state 111 years ago.

Canada's population is only one-tenth the population of the United States, but it is the United States' leading trade partner and principal ally. Its standard of living is among the highest in the world, and it is one of the world's most important manufacturing and trading countries. The Automobile Pact of 1965 between Canada and the United States is probably the most comprehensive trade agreement between any two countries, binding the Canadian and United States economies into an encompassing interdependence. The air defense of North America is under unified command, and the partnership of Canada and the United States in NATO is so fundamental that the region is defined as a single area. American security depends no less than Canada's on the world's longest undefended border.

Canada's fate as a nation-state, and the strain in Canadian-U.S. relations generated by American domination and Canadian response, has opened North America to a searching debate unknown since the United States' Civil War. If in the early 1970s the "good neighbor to the north" did not seem as friendly as before, in the late 1970s "gray Canada" is not as boring as once imagined. Instead, Canada has become a laboratory for the development of federalism, a test case for the governance of antagonistic cultural and linguistic groups and an advanced industrial society still struggling with a colonial heritage. Americans are becoming aware that a laboratory failure could destroy all confident assumptions about the future of North America.

The challenge in the late 1970s to Canada's political existence has been generated primarily by internal forces: unequal distribution of wealth by region as well as class; controversial distribution of power between two nations inhabiting the same state. But this challenge has emerged after an earlier challenge, in the 1950s and '60s, from south of the 49th parallel. The United States, the world's most powerful economic and military nation-state, rushed into the vacuum created by British withdrawal from authority in Canada. The impact was so overwhelming that Kari Levitt accused the Canadian government of a "silent surrender" to the American-based multinational corporation,[1] and George Grant "lamented" the passing of Canada as a nation,[2] subsumed into a North American culture and economy.

Canadians were openly hostile to American pressure during this period, but there was little to be done. The insult to any hope of an identity independent of the United States was compounded by direct injury to the Canadian economy. The U.S. denied Canada special treatment in trade arrangements in August 1971, and Canada responded against American culture (in the media) and American finance (in foreign investment). Canadian-U.S. relations deteriorated steadily in the Nixon-Ford years, and Canadian identity fell under an American siege. Preoccupation with the American challenge, however, came from Ontario, and especially from federalist forces in Ottawa.

There was a different preoccupation in Quebec. There, the authoritarian one-party rule of Maurice Duplessis and the Union Nationale was broken with the election of Jean Lesage and the Liberal Party in 1960. French Québécois had lived in Confederation by exchanging economic power (ceded to anglophone capitalists in Montreal) for provincial political power and cultural protection. Francophones controlled the countryside; anglophones controlled urban society. The Catholic Church maintained an hierarchical and essentially authoritarian rural culture. The defeat of Duplessis, however, signalled the great urban migration which was to transform Quebec from a self-contained French society to a population demanding new economic opportunities. While Canada (particularly Ontario) discovered the impact of the American economy and culture, Quebec discovered the impact of the anglophone economy and political structure.

As Canada publicly groped for an identity, Quebec proclaimed an identity all her own. However, Canada's claims assumed Québécois partnership; Quebec's "Quiet Revolution" was marked by a move for independence. In the 1960s, federal Minister of Finance Walter Gordon founded the Committee for an Independent Canada; meanwhile, René Lévesque, Quebec's Provincial Resources Minister, founded the Parti Québécois. Gordon's committee demanded independence from the United States; Lévesque's party demanded independence from Canada. Increased attention to "things Canadian" in the anglophone world was matched by a growing awareness of a French identity in Quebec.

Canada's resources had led Prime Minister Wilfrid Laurier to predict that the twentieth century would be Canada's, and economically, in anglophone Canada, Laurier was not far wrong. But French Canadians—French North Americans, as Robert Bourassa calls them—earned 10% less than other Canadians in the 1960s, even less than new immigrants from Europe. The income gap between Ontario and Quebec was 20%. French Canadians witnessed the benefits of Canadian nationhood without extracting what they thought a fair share; many believed they would be better off on their own.

Thus, as Canada became wealthier it became more endangered; as it became more outspoken towards the United States, it spoke with a less and less unified voice. Canada had made its mark in world affairs; now Quebec demanded its own delegations to francophone countries. As the U.S. front opened, in economic and diplomatic conflict, the home front opened with a cacophony of competing interests and demands. Canada's wealthiest hours were not to be its finest; the U.S., dependent on the outcome of Canadian conflict, could not bring harmony, for the U.S. was consigned to a peculiar spectator's status, witness to events with profound consequence in which its influence would be mostly symbolic.

Challenge and Paradox

Canada may be understood through many images. While enjoying one of the world's highest standards of living, its industry still is heavily protected and its wealth derives primarily from the extraction of natural resources, stimulated mostly by foreign investment. As a resource exporter, Canada is similar to states in the lesser developed world. Although sovereign, Canada's economy and defense are wholly dependent on the United States. Canada is a leading member of the British Commonwealth, but Quebec political leaders are not known for their respect for the Crown—and Quebec is a decisive member of the national polity. Canada is a federal state because it divides power between the central government and the provinces, yet its political institutions are organized around the unitary concepts of Parliament imported from England. Hence, Canada's many images yield paradoxes: a lesser developed member of the advanced industrial world; a North American federal state with grafted English institutions; a sovereign power wholly dependent economically and militarily on its neighbor.

These paradoxes would be challenge enough for the governance of any nation-state. But with the additional challenges directly from the United States and from competing perspectives on unity, Canada's crisis absorbs all of North America. The continent's economy is interdependent, defense is mutual, the societies are kindred. Until recently, Canadians assumed that any breath from the U.S. giant could blow Canada away. In turn, Americans have begun to understand that Canadian breath is more than cold winds of the Montreal express; Canada's breath, too, is essential to the life of North America.

According to Prime Minister Trudeau,

> Canadians feel that the time has come to reconsider what we are and to determine what we want to become...we must assert the Canadian identity, establish once and for all what this identity consists of, and express it more vigorously through our actions, both individual and collective.[3]

The "time for action," as the Prime Minister calls it, has come indeed. The Canadian identity parlor game suddenly matters to people beyond Canada's borders, and it is difficult for a country to give priority to world affairs when its very constitutional existence is in doubt. Despite its wealth, Canada decided in the summer of 1978 to close selected consular offices in order to help the economy at home. Uncertainty has spilled over into the financial world, where the Canadian dollar has fallen 19% in two years against the weakened American dollar. Strikes plague the economy, unemployment holds tenaciously several percentage points above the rates south of the border, and no reassuring voices are heard anywhere. The Canadian consensus is that there is a crisis. It is, all seem agreed, a time to act—but agreement stops there.

Canada's crisis is especially remarkable because, as Mordecai Richler points out, the streets remain safe; the discussion is civil and responsible. The issues are no less divisive because of this civility, but the style of crisis permits a unique and open dialogue. We have brought together in this volume some of Canada's most creative minds with some of the United States' most informed and perceptive critics. In their dialogue they expose the most important issues dividing Canada and affecting the United States. Some are scholars seeking perspective; others are engaged politicians and civil servants and lawyers looking for pragmatic, imaginative, and immediate solutions to conflict. They often disagree, not only over interpretation, but over the "facts" themselves. The essence of crisis, after all, is a contest between legitimate claims. The contest lives in these pages where authorities reveal their discord in the finest democratic tradition. Agreement on what to disagree about is no guarantee of resolution, but there is probably no better place to begin.

"Some countries have too much history. Canada has too much geography."

Prime Minister William Lyon Mackenzie King

All the authors, in their presentations at Harvard, relied heavily on history and geography in their interpretations of Canadian problems. But their different versions of Canadian history, which we have eliminated in their essays and assembled here in order to compare them, contributed to different analyses of the current challenges and to different proposals for solving present conflicts. John Roberts, for example, argued that, "The history of Canada has been the history of trying to overcome the challenge which geography has posed for the country," and Gordon Gibson suggested that, "Canadians would undoubtedly have no current question of unity if we were all mixed up in some 10% fraction of our geography." Frank Peers contended that transportation and communications were "prerequisites to nationhood" because of "a country strung out over so many miles with its centers of population spaced at irregular intervals like beads on a string, with the rock formation of the Canadian shield jutting down from Hudson Bay to separate the western and central provinces."

For Peers, committed to national unity, the history worthy of emphasis is the history binding Canada from sea to sea:

Canada may be the only country in the world in which a promise of a railway was included in its written constitution.

The building and financing of railways was central to the careers of our first great prime ministers, John A. Macdonald and Wilfrid Laurier. The first large publicly-owned corporation was created to operate and manage a transcontinental railway and auxiliary services, including telegraphs and eventually a radio network. When the Depression brought that radio experiment to an end, another public corporation was created to establish a national radio system on a more permanent basis. That corporation exists today as the largest producer of radio and television programs in Canada, operating in French and English, in seven time zones, and with offices and production facilities in Washington, New York, London, and Paris.

Westerners, in contrast to spokesmen from central Canada, see Canada's size and scope less in terms of the task of bringing the country together and more in terms of the opportunities associated with great distances between regions. Thus, Gordon Gibson remarked:

What we call "the West" doesn't even begin for 1,000 miles west of Toronto, and from there to the Pacific we have four provinces spanning the central plains and the mountain Pacific region, with three of them on the prairies being each the size of your largest (Lower 48) state of Texas, and my own province of British Columbia almost 50% larger. This is 50% of the land of Canada south of the 60th parallel, in which area 99.9% of all Canadians live. Quebec, by comparison, is all by itself slightly more than two times Texas in size.

In contrast, when Walter Gordon noted that Canada was "slightly larger than the U.S. (including Alaska)," he added, "but much of it is uninhabitable or more or less so because of the terrain and just as importantly the climate." Gordon wanted his American audience to think of Canada as concentrated in an area, shunning the geography it could not hope to overcome. He wanted the audience to understand Canada in terms of the logic of union and nationalism; Gibson wanted this same audience to understand the practical, geographical obstacles to common identity, and to suggest that they perhaps could not be overcome.

These competing geographic descriptions resound in the history related by John Roberts. He indicated how Canadians were not where they meant to be:

Canada was not somehow discovered as it was stumbled over by explorers trying to get to some place else...The early history of Canada is the history of people trying to *get through* it as quickly as possible. And then when that proved difficult because of its size, they tried to go *around* as quickly as possible.

Once Canadians decided to stay, the story Roberts related is the same one already told by Frank Peers:

> Canada's history, in the first half of the 19th century, reflected an obsession with the building of canals, improving the system of communications, trying to make transportation more economical. The last half of the 19th century is a history of obsession with railways.

This Canadian history, focusing on the means of overcoming geography in order to guarantee union, is the history of central Canada trying to cope with outlying districts. But as Peers and Roberts extolled the railroad, so Gordon Gibson reported on the Western farmer shaking his fist at the sky and yelling, "God damn the C.P.R.!"

Gordon Stead, another Westerner, reported Canada's history in terms more comprehensible to Gordon Gibson, his Western brother, than to Walter Gordon, Frank Peers, or John Roberts, his Ontario-dwelling cousins. They spoke of Canadians as distinct only from French Canadians, reinforcing the concept of Canada as "two solitudes."[4] Stead condemned reliance on this concept. "It ignores developments of the last hundred years," he said, because "English-speaking Canada is not monolithic."

> Newfoundland derives from the English West Country of four centuries ago. Even more deeply rooted, French Canada is an island left behind by the receding tide of empire. The Maritimes developed as a haven for the dispossessed from the Scottish Highlands. Ontario emerged as a refuge for the Tories displaced by the American Revolution. British Columbia, originally settled from around the Horn under the protection of the Royal Navy, was later "tacked on" to a remote Canada. The prairies, first opened up by migrants from Ontario who soon acquired their own outlook, attracted floods of settlers from Middle Europe.

It is this historical view which leads Stead to argue against growing central authority, and it is not surprising that Flora MacDonald, emphasizing her Cape Breton roots to her Harvard audience, wants to save Confederation in a fashion far more congenial to Stead's interpretation of Canada's history and needs than in a fashion satisfactory to her more centrist colleagues. She helps demonstrate that the view *of* the center is similar from the Atlantic and the Pacific. And the view *from* the center is compatible with neither.

It may be that Canada has just enough geography to keep people apart, and too much history to bring them together. Mordecai Richler reminds us of Louis Riel, the French-speaking Métis executed after he rebelled against the broken promises of Canada's anglophone leaders; it is a nineteenth century saga which still generates twentieth century conflict. Walter Dean Burnham insists on the significance of Quebec's history as a French colony conquered by the English, and René Lévesque points to 110 years of "being too often overlooked and neglected and even the object of discrimination." Walter Gordon points to a history of American economic domination while Robert Bourassa praises a history of American investment. Frank Peers emphasizes a history of American media penetration, and Ian McDougall recounts a history of controversial constitutional interpretation which helped provincial leaders sell the national birthright. Peter Gourevitch emphasizes years of decisions which contributed to Quebec's relative decline, and no one manages to discuss Quebec without reference to the Quiet Revolution and the history of industrialization and development. Though none of our authors is an historian, each constructs an argument around the experiences of a particular historical framework; and it is the combination of these competing histories which amplifies their disagreements. As much as any other force, the long memory is eroding whatever incentives once were perceived for compromise.

Studying the Canadian Crisis: The Struggle for Identity

Neil Nevitte explains in the concluding essay in this book that a sense of nation often is shaped by cultural elites of a society—writers and artists, and musicians. We begin, then, by undertaking Prime Minister Trudeau's charge, "to reconsider what we are and to determine what we want to become...to establish once and for all what this Canadian identity consists of." Mordecai Richler is one of the most distinguished writers to emerge from Canada, and to write about Canada, in our time. He writes humorously and somewhat tragically of Canadian writers whose greatest aspiration was to escape from Canada—to make their literary fortune where it would matter. They wanted to be writers, not Canadian writers. To have come from Canada as a Jew, Richler says, was to come out of the ghetto twice; if he has returned to the ghetto it is in part because Canada has taken its place in the world as a positive, effective, humane force, and Canada is no longer the ghetto of Richler's formative years.

Sylvia Wright responds to Richler's comments with equal irony. She shares Richler's impatience with the quest for identity: "I sometimes wonder if we really have time for this sort of thing," she writes, adding, "Perhaps, if we just went on working, when we took a breather, we would find that a nice discrete identity had been there all along." Wright and Richler agree on the value of competition, and both hope their artistry can be judged without reference to their nationality. Foreign critics, Wright points out, gave great stimulus to American literary development. Although she "stops short of suggesting that Canadians should, for their own good, spend some time writing books about the United States," because it would enhance their consciousness of a "romantic other," she hopes that "since they are a nice people, perhaps they would be willing to do it for our good." Richler and Wright agree that Canadian and American writers ought to pay more attention to each other because it would help each literary tradition to grow.

The theme of cultural competition is echoed in René Lévesque's approach to identity. He contends that the effort to make one nation out of two exacts too great a price. Quebec, he argues, consists mostly of French speakers descendent from the oldest settlements in North America. Québécois have only one problem with their identity—the absence of a political independence necessary to fulfill national ideals. The anglophone and francophone identities cannot produce one nationality, Lévesque says, and everyone would live more happily if the ideal of a binational state were abandoned.

Canada's Postwar Challenge: Relations with the United States

Anglophone Canada's identity crisis derived mostly from sharing the North American continent with the United States. The cultural problem, moreover, has an economic and political face. Walter Gordon proposes a program for the compulsory purchase of major American companies in Canada in order to secure Canada's economic independence from the United States. Without economic independence, Gordon asserts, there is little hope for the survival of a distinct Canadian identity. The former Minister of Finance accuses the United States, and more particularly the multinational corporations, of a concerted effort to monopolize Canadian economic decision-making.

Willis Armstrong, former Assistant Secretary of State for Economic Affairs, accuses Walter Gordon of proposing the nationalization of American corporations in Canada (something Gordon explicitly denies). Armstrong contends that just compensation is impossible in a forced sale, and he suggests that Canadian nationalists seek to turn their back on the very thing which has made them prosperous—American money. Gordon's proposal for Canada to buy out leading American companies operating north of the forty-ninth parallel is, according to Armstrong, a fundamental breach of faith.

The dialogue between Frank Peers, Canada's foremost scholar on Canadian communications policy, and Joel Rosenbloom, a Washington attorney with Buffalo television station clients, is more specific than the Gordon-Armstrong exchange, but no less contentious. Peers accuses American magazines (especially *Time* and *Reader's Digest*) and American broadcasting (especially border television and cablevision) of a desire to seek profits in Canada at the expense of Canadian culture. He assigns economic motives to American interests and cultural and nationalist motives to Canadian interests; and he defends Canada's legal response (taxing advertisers in magazines which are "non-Canadian;" deleting commercials on some American programming beamed into Canada) as the inevitable product of a country seeking independence—and an independent identity—from its neighbor.

Joel Rosenbloom denies Professor Peers' suggestion that "all the non-commercial motives seem to reside north of the border." He compares the Canadian and American philosophies governing communications, and then he compares what Canada has done *vis-à-vis* the American media with what Canada could have done in defense of her own interests. Peers acknowledges the Canadian desire to enjoy the best of both worlds—American entertainment and Canadian non-commercial public service programming; Rosenbloom accuses Canada of piracy in pursuit of this objective. Like Armstrong, Rosenbloom suggests that the cloak of Canadian nationalism cannot cover a "naked desire for commercial gain."

The Gordon-Armstrong and Peers-Rosenbloom exchanges delineate the essential misunderstandings between Canadians and Americans which dominated relations in the early 1970s and especially frustrated Canadians in their desire to develop a distinctive identity. But the multinational corporation and communications are old issues dividing Canada and the United States. There are newer issues which pose a potentially greater challenge. And as communications and corporate investment are also central to Canada's unity (the provinces trying to wrest greater control over both from the federal government), so, too, these newer issues link Canada's postwar challenge of relations with the U.S. to the new challenge of national unity.

The two newest and most prominent issues affecting Canadian-United States relations involve foreign policy and energy and national resources. Confronted with apparent change in the American treatment of Canada, marked by the Connally economic measures of August 1971, Canada undertook a full-scale review of its relations with all foreign countries, including the U.S. It hoped to exercise a "Third Option," beyond the traditional ties to Great Britain and the U.S., in which an independent Canada would make its own impression in world affairs. This foreign policy would help Canada distinguish itself from the U.S., and also permit it greater flexibility in aid programs and trade.

Allan Gotlieb, as Under-Secretary of State for External Affairs, is a leading architect of Canada's Third Option. In his essay here he sets out the key differences between Canadian and American approaches to world affairs, tracing different histories, attitudes, and responsibilities. He offers specific examples of Canadian policy in Latin America, Sub-Saharan Africa, and Asia, as well as Canada's position in the Law of the Sea Conference and its role in the New International Economic Order. Gotlieb calls Canada a "middle power," weakened by the power of the provinces to shape foreign policy outside the control of Ottawa, and he suggests that Canada's foreign endeavors reflect its moral commitments as a people. Canada and the U.S. do not disagree, Gotlieb says, but in foreign policy they have different interests and tend more and more to go their separate ways.

Alan Henrikson, of the Fletcher School of Law and Diplomacy, disputes Gotlieb's claim of moral behavior by asking, "What, besides the overarching U.S. strategic deterrent, allowed this?" Henrikson says, "Canada's influence abroad during the last several generations has depended upon, and derived from, the massive size and strength of the United States." Canada's independent foreign policy, according to Henrikson, is an illusion because of the impact of the U.S. "Stop fighting it," Henrikson counsels Canada, for, "In more instances than now appreciated, the interdependence of the two great industrialized countries of North America, even if unbalanced and asymmetrical, works to the advantage of both."

If the Gordon-Armstrong and Peers-Rosenbloom exchanges

highlight the disagreements of the early 1970s, the Gotlieb-Henrikson dialogue symbolizes relations in the last half of the decade. As Gotlieb points out, "The realm of foreign policy provides little or no evidence of conflict between our two countries." He talks, instead, of "lively contrast." The atmosphere of 1972, when the Third Option was proposed, no longer determines Canadian foreign policy.

The Unity Crisis

Conflict with the U.S., some foreign policy analysts observe, has declined as problems have increased on the home front.[5] Issues of foreign policy and energy constitute in this book a critical bridge between old and new challenges of identity and unity. Richard Simeon, Director of the Institute on Intergovernmental Relations of Queen's University, introduces the discussion of Canada's unity crisis with a broad analysis of federal-provincial relations and the various proposals now offered, especially by the federal government, to resolve conflict and save Confederation. Simeon contends that Canada's key cleavage is regional and territorial and that resolution of the crisis will depend upon a power-sharing formula which will satisfy the provinces without debilitating central authority.

Simeon is pessimistic about a solution. None of the proposals confronts the demands of Quebec, the immediate cause of the unity crisis. Moreover, Simeon does not see a clear path to the preservation of power among provincial premiers consonant with continued central authority. Efforts to bring the competing levels of power together, such as the tri-level meetings of federal, provincial, and municipal officials, have all failed.

Jerome Milch of the University of Pittsburgh concurs with Simeon's concerns about the distribution of power but does not believe a new institutional arrangement, satisfactory to all parties, will solve Canada's problems. Milch says, "The current crisis is as much a product of bureaucratic failure as of a breakdown in representative institutions." Since the regions are calculating whether Confederation pays, inept government can hardly keep them content.

Milch suggests that there are many problems on the government agenda; Ian McDougall, Professor of Law at Osgoode Hall, argues that one such problem in particular—energy and natural resources—is fundamental to Canada's survival. McDougall explores the history of Canadian resource management, especially with respect to the provincial tendency to sell out Canada's energy future to American interests. According to McDougall, "the energy crisis is perhaps the best of all national unity projects. Here Canada has the opportunity to demonstrate in a tangible fashion that federalism cannot only work, but in the long run is worth literally billions of dollars in economic benefits." The energy crisis affords the federal government the opportunity to demonstrate that Canada's independence from the United States can only be achieved through strong central institutions, and McDougall criticizes the provinces for squandering resources—for failing to appreciate the requirements of a national vision.

Whereas Richard Simeon proposed some shift in power from the center to the periphery, Ian McDougall calls for a stronger central government. Stewart Udall, former United States Secretary of the Interior, supports McDougall's assertions of federal weakness by revealing that during his cabinet tenure he had thought Canadian provinces owned and controlled resources (ownership, McDougall has explained, does not mean control); the Canadian federal government was not regarded in this area as an important negotiating partner. If Canadians fared poorly in negotiations with the United States, Udall suggests, it was their own fault, especially because the parliamentary system gives greater opportunity for central control than does American federalism with divided executive and legislative functions. Udall and McDougall agree that both countries need a national energy policy, but Udall is not as sure as McDougall that Canada's need surpasses the policy requirements of the United States.

Robert Stein, former legal counsel to the Canadian-United States International Joint Commission (IJC) and Director of the North American office of the International Institute for Environment and Development, opens a new dimension in his comment on Ian McDougall's analysis of natural resources. Stein points out that natural resources do not always involve power (e.g. oil, gas, water for hydroelectricity). In particular, Stein predicts difficult times between Canada and the United States over water for drinking, irrigation, and other uses. Canada has an abundance of water; the United States, especially in the West, will look to these Canadian waters for some sharing arrangement. In the discussions at Harvard, McDougall acknowledged Stein's concern, but he also described Canadians' "spiritual attachment" to their water. Americans, Stein warned, will need Canadian water; Canadians, McDougall demurred, will not discuss the matter.The McDougall-Stein dialogue reveals the likelihood of a continuing clash between Canadian and U.S. interests, even if national energy policies were to emerge and Canada and the

U.S. were to resolve differences over resources for power.

Resolution of the energy problem, according to McDougall, requires resolution of power relationships between the federal and provincial governments. Gordon Stead shares the Simeon and McDougall diagnoses of regional cleavage and power distribution in the Canadian unity crisis. But Stead prefers Simeon's approach to McDougall's. For twenty-one years a top level civil servant in Ottawa, Stead knows the Ottawa bureaucracy well enough to be wary of its capacity to solve problems efficiently and equitably. He traces the expansion of the upper ranks of the civil service and argues that it has acquired a regional bias protecting the interests of the Ontario core. The center, Stead contends, has no national vision; why entrust it with so much control? Stead looks to bureaucratic reorganization in addition to institutional reform, contradicting McDougall's prescription for greater authority in Ottawa.

Stead's analysis of Ottawa, according to Professor Robert Art of Brandeis University, could be applied in several important respects to Washington. Art compares Washington's impact on the United States with Ottawa's impact on Canada and concludes that "Canada has come of age," a technological society with bureaucratic arrogance and declining political control. Whereas, "the Washington bureaucracy at its best reinforces and at its worst does little if any harm to the national cohesiveness," Art adds, "the Ottawa bureaucracy reinforces the distintegative trends rampant in Canada today." Art confirms Stead's conclusions that the Ottawa bureaucracy must be counted as a separate and significant factor in Canadian disunity.

The unity crisis may derive from a territorial or regional cleavage, requiring greater or lesser central authority, but the catalyst to the crisis clearly is Quebec. And as Simeon observes that most proposals avoid Quebec's demands, so Gourevitch insists that Quebec's case is more serious than most separatist and nationalist movements in the world; it must be tackled by responsible Canadian authorities with more imagination and understanding.

Professor Gourevitch, an American at McGill University, explains Quebec's separatism in the framework of economic and political power. The Quebec challenge does not stem merely from cultural or linguistic differences. Quebec's political and economic status has declined relative to Ontario, and French Canadians have fallen further behind economically than Quebec anglophones. Quebec separatism is comparable, Gourevitch implies, to Scottish nationalism, and the key similarity lies in the economic viability of a potentially independent state. Quebec could, Gourevitch argues, go it alone, thereby posing the single greatest challenge of all to Canada's existence. If the debate over Quebec remains functional, Gourevitch warns, then Ontario will be the net loser when Quebec establishes independence.

Professor François-Pierre Gingras, of the University of Ottawa, agrees with Professor Gourevitch's perception of a viable Quebec state, but he adds a class dimension to Gourevitch's economic analysis. Gingras denies the Simeon and McDougall assertions that the principal cleavage in the system is territorial. Rather, Gingras contends, francophones have suffered as an economic class. A gap has developed between their aspirations and their expectations. Not only is there no congruence between political and economic power, as Gourevitch demonstrates; there is also no congruence between what people hope to have and what they expect to have. Gingras sees no way for the federal government to close this gap. The hopes of Québécois now lie, he says, with the Quebec state.

Competing Solutions to the Unity Crisis

In the end, Canada's problems, and the problems of political arrangements in North America, will be determined in the political arena. The authors here are among the political arena's most important actors.

Gordon Gibson, Leader of the Liberal Party in British Columbia, assesses the alienation of the Western provinces from Confederation. Acknowledging Quebec's leadership in challenging institutional arrangements, Gibson declares Western separatism a latent sentiment now finding a sympathetic audience. Confederation was little more than a business deal; if it no longer pays, it should be abandoned. But, Gibson adds, there are values attached to Canadian nationhood, and he sets out a detailed program for settling the differences which threaten national survival.

Gibson's complaint is concrete: it is cheaper to ship live than processed beef; the ferries connecting the mainland of British Columbia with the provincial capital on Vancouver Island are taxed by the federal government; the Canadian Radio-Television and Telecommunications Commission, and the Canadian Broadcasting Corporation, are insensitive to Western culture; the Canadian Development Corporation, with promises of commitments in the West, is based in Toronto in service to the core; Ottawa is a remote tax collector that imposes irritating regulations on the use of tax dollars returned into Western hands. In sum, there are institutional ways to sweeten the pot, and if Ottawa does not ante up, British Columbia and other Western provinces just might opt out of the game.

David Smith, Chairman of the Economics Department at Queen's University in Ontario, does not calculate the federal deal according to Gordon Gibson's economic formula. Smith considers "regional cost-benefit measurements of membership in and separation from Confederation extraordinarily difficult to make," and he doubts whether different arrangements could be demonstrated, in advance, to be of greater economic benefit to the West. Nor is he persuaded by Gibson's constitutional proposals inasmuch as they would involve protracted negotiations with provincial power brokers. "The constitution is not toothpaste or soap powder," Smith remarks; there is no reason to think consensus will form around one new brand or another.

Robert Bourassa, former Premier of Quebec, shares David Smith's view of Confederation. Quebec, Bourassa insists, is entitled to cultural sovereignty—to a recognition of special status as a unique culture in North America. But, he adds, Quebec's economic prosperity depends on Confederation. He emphasizes the moderation of the Parti Québécois towards business and he rejects accusations that the PQ jeopardizes the future of foreign investment in the province. But he also rejects a Quebec demand for independence.

Bourassa applauds the policy of René Lévesque which keeps provincial doors open to foreign investment, but political scientist Michael Parenti warns the former premier that the impact of foreign investment on dependent economies follows a pattern: a financial alcoholism intoxicates the local economy, and areas rich in resources are populated, paradoxically, by the poor. Whereas Premier Bourassa believes an important solution to Quebec's economic plight may be found in increased foreign investment, Parenti cautions that "such investments do not solve and usually worsen economic conditions."

Gibson and Bourassa state the cases of the West and Quebec largely in financial terms. Flora MacDonald, in contrast, appeals to Canadians more in terms of the idea of nationhood. Her concern, as the Progressive Conservative Party's spokesperson on federal-provincial relations and constitutional reform, is to discover institutional formulas for the resolution of conflict in order to preserve union. She does not make a case in behalf of one region or another, and she insists that ideological concerns must take precedence over economic and geographic considerations. Canada must remain committed, she argues, to "regional equalization." Union, according to MacDonald, is vital in order to withstand the impact of foreign investment (attacked already by nationalist Walter Gordon and Marxist Michael Parenti). Like Simeon, she details the development of a House of the Provinces which would replace the Senate; provincial representation and power would be institutionalized at the federal level.

Flora MacDonald's proposals win the applause and the skepticism of Professor Walter Dean Burnham of the Massachusetts Institute of Technology. Professor Burnham detects similarities in the provincial attacks on Ottawa with the trend to run against Washington in the United States. He perceives a Canadian crisis without Quebec, and he reckons Quebec, in the end, will have to solve its problems internally. That being so, constitutional tinkering is a risky business. Burnham sees in the proposals to replace the Senate a move toward American congressional arrangements, and he warns that institutional changes cannot be isolated; once change is in motion, the outcome is unpredictable. Although he thinks MacDonald brave to try, he is not optimistic about the results.

The position of the Liberal Government is articulated by the Canadian Secretary of State, John Roberts. He rejects demands for a devolution of power towards the provinces, and he claims Quebec has upset an otherwise smooth-sailing ship of state. Solutions, Roberts thinks, may be found in a renewal of old guarantees to Quebec, enshrining language rights, codifying human rights, enhancing provincial representation in Ottawa. He firmly dismisses criticisms of the Ottawa bureaucracy and establishment, and he rejects challenges to Confederation from provinces other than Quebec.

Elliot J. Feldman expresses disappointment with the Secretary of State's view of the unity crisis. The other authors, he says, have perceived Ottawa as central to Canada's problems and have played down the significance of Quebec in stimulating the present challenge. Roberts has not addressed the central concerns of Canadians, according to Feldman; his proposals fall far short of the needs of the day. Confederation, if dependent only on proposals such as these, may not be saved.

Assessing the Analyses

The logic governing the order of these essays is not strict, and the reader may prefer to read essays according to other themes not emphasized in the preceding summary. For example, some of the authors take a predominantly economic view of Canada's problems: Walter Gordon and Willis Armstrong both discuss the economics of natural resources, and their exchange may be read profitably alongside the McDougall-Udall dialogue. Armstrong offers a strong defense of multinational corporations, in sharp contrast with his countryman Michael Parenti.

The definition of Canada's problems varies among the authors. Gordon Stead, Richard Simeon, Flora MacDonald and Jerome Milch all perceive failure in Ottawa as central to the present crisis. Stead and Milch and Robert Art look especially to the role of the bureaucracy. René Lévesque, Gordon Gibson, and Peter Gourevitch adopt an instrumental view in which they doubt whether Confederation is a paying proposition for all members. David Smith, Robert Bourassa, and Ian McDougall insist Confederation is economically sound. Gourevitch and Burnham predict that Ontario will be the net loser if Confederation fails; Smith, Bourassa and McDougall are confident Ontario will suffer least. Whereas Simeon, MacDonald, Gibson, and Gourevitch stress regional cleavages, Burnham, Parenti, and Gingras emphasize class differences, with Burnham amplifying Premier Lévesque's historical account of the conquered French. Burnham, in fact, calls the demand for independence "primordial," perceiving the deep roots which instrumental analyses, such as that of Premier Bourassa, tend to neglect.

Different interpretations of Canada's problems have led to different categories of solutions. For a variety of reasons, Gibson, Peers, Gotlieb, Henrikson, McDougall, Udall, Smith, and Roberts all desire strengthened federal institutions. In different degrees, all the other authors (save Richler, Wright, Stein, Rosenbloom, and Parenti) favor greater provincial power, or greater Quebec autonomy, or both. The universe of choice is small, and the authors are all pragmatic. Canada must undergo a spiritual change (hoped for by the Secretary of State) or an institutional change. There are few, if any, defenders of the *status quo*. Institutional change means an alteration in power relationships. Some units must come out winners, and some losers, if there is to be any change at all.

Numerous other themes run through these essays, but the most notable, probably, is the theme of nationalism. All the authors discuss nationalism, but none pauses to define terms or to develop the concept. In his concluding essay, Neil Nevitte suggests that nationalism may be the main organizing framework necessary for a broad appreciation of Canadian, United States, and Québécois concerns. He differentiates the concepts of nation and state and he traces the discussion of nationalism, nationhood, and statehood as it weaves through these essays. In the final analysis, Nevitte observes, the United States and Canada represent two states—but how many nations? Here, perhaps, is the heart of North America's crisis. Different nations often prefer their own peculiar statehood, their own form of governance. It is not yet clear whether in North America such expression for all parties is possible.

Quebec, Canada, and the United States

The New Democratic Party, Canada's socialists, were never successful in Quebec. The Parti Québécois did not win in Quebec because of social democracy. Instead, in the absence of social democratic traditions, Quebec and the PQ are decidedly *étatiste*. The government apparatus of the Province of Quebec has been the one domain of undisputed francophone control, and this vehicle of the nation has pioneered health and welfare programs for all of Canada. The Quebec government, doggedly interventionist in the economy, improved employment and opportunity for the French, sometimes even at the expense of minority groups. It is not surprising that most Québécois see their future more in the champion role of Quebec City than in anglophone-dominated Ottawa.

There is a clear contrast between French and English styles of government. French government, in Europe as well as in Quebec, has always been more interventionist, and French citizens have always expressed greater confidence in the public sector than the English. Different cultures have educated people into different attitudes toward government and the state; Québécois have had the benefit of more than one hundred years of direct comparative experience, governed simultaneously by English and French philosophies. The philosophies contradict one another, and the confrontation today—the conflict which commands so much attention in this book—constitutes a challenge to make compatible competing philosophies and cultures. In the United States, such a confrontation of cultures was settled only by an ultimate conquest in the Civil War. Although one of Canada's founding cultures was conquered, it was not subdued, and now, in an era of greater tolerance, the authors here look for ways to assure peaceful coexistence within Canada's divided house.

To many, a divided Canada would be of ultimate benefit to the

United States, for Canadian human energies and natural resources would turn, at a disadvantage, to the U.S market. So recently resolute and apparently united against the American challenge, supplicant provinces might be far more attractive to American business than a tough federal government. Yet, no one here advocates the break-up of Canada. Even René Lévesque, this volume's only fully committed separatist, foresees a united Canada (to be sure, without Quebec). Lévesque stresses his good wishes for a Canada more united because the "foreign body," Quebec, will have been removed. Some of the authors here see the U.S. as a threat to Canada; others imagine the U.S. to be a great benefactor. No one sees the U.S., however, as an instigator. Canada's problems are its own, of its own making. And everyone involved in this book hopes it will find its own solutions with justice and with peace.

NOTES

1. Kari Levitt, *Silent Surrender: The Multinational Corporation in Canada* (New York: St. Martin's Press, 1970).

2. George Grant, *Lament for a Nation: The Defeat of Canadian Nationalism* (Toronto: McClelland & Stewart, 1965).

3. Pierre E. Trudeau, *A Time for Action: Toward the Renewal of the Canadian Federation* (Government of Canada, Minister of Supply and Services, 1978), p. 4.

4. Hugh MacLennan, *Two Solitudes* (Toronto: W. Collins Sons & Co., 1945).

5. Elliot J. Feldman and Lily Gardner Feldman, "The Special Relationship Between Canada and the United States." Paper presented to the Duke University Summer Seminar, Kingston, Ontario, June 1978.

Part One

THE STRUGGLE FOR IDENTITY

2_____CANADIAN IDENTITY

Mordecai Richler

In 1965, when Mike Pearson was prime minister of Canada, he visited L.B.J. in Texas. His party landed on a runway right on the ranch. "The rambling old ranch house," Pearson wrote in his memoirs, "was surrounded by planes, jeeps, trucks, communications towers, and security people, with the Pedernales River running past the front door. President Johnson and Lady Bird were awaiting our arrival. As we mounted a little podium before a battery of TV cameras, the President...welcomed me very warmly and greatly enlivened the ceremony by ending his remarks: ...and we are so happy to have Mr. Wilson with us."

Two years later, during Canada's Centennial Year, L.B.J. repaid the visit, stopping at the prime minister's summer residence at Harrington Lake. When he arrived ahead of the President, Pearson has written, security people were all over the place, "on rowboats, and in the bushes with their walkie-talkies....I went into the house and up the stairs. At the top a hard-faced chap said: 'Who are you? Where are you going?' I replied, 'I live here and I'm going to the bathroom.'"

In larger terms, it's some room upstairs, in the North American attic, a place to be ourselves, that Canadians are after these days. But, because many of us feel culturally pressured by the United States, this seems increasingly difficult. As a consequence, some have turned to nationalism, and the more militant among the nationalists to an unfortunate anti-Americanism.

To begin with, I must remind you of the obvious. Canada, of course, is a two-headed culture. The French is cocooned by language, the English isn't. We English-speaking, but not necessarily Anglo-Saxon, Canadians are a very touchy bunch. We have, mind you, reason to be touchy. From the beginning, Canada's two founding races, the English and the French, outdid each other in scornfully disinheriting us. A few arpents of snow, Voltaire wrote contemptuously of Canada;

and Dr. Johnson described the dominion as "a region of desolate sterility....a cold, uncomfortable, uninviting region, from which nothing but furs and fish were to be had."

Since then Canadians have endured the disdain of Oscar Wilde, Samuel Butler, Wyndham Lewis, and even J.B. Priestley. In 1963, W.H. Auden wrote, "The dominions...are for me *tiefste Provinz,* places which have produced no art and are inhabited by the kind of person with whom I have least in common."

Whilst only yesterday, it seems, General de Gaulle, stirring the nationalist pot, flirted with Quebec, sending André Malraux as an emissary ("France needs you," Malraux told the sapient aldermen of Montreal City Council. "We will build the next civilization together."), the truth is French intellectuals, stirring the nationalist pot yet again today, were not always so enamored of Quebec, a province which was largely pro-Vichy in sentiment during World War II. When Gomez, the Spanish republican in Jean-Paul Sartre's novel, *Iron in the Soul,* finds himself in New York on the day that Paris has fallen, he sees only grins and indifference on Seventh Avenue. Then, on 55th Street, he spots a French restaurant, 'A La Petite Coquette,' and enters, hoping to find solace. "Paris has fallen," Gomez says to the bartender, but he only gets a grunt for a reply. Gomez tries again. "Afraid France is a goner." Finally the barman says, "France is going to learn what it costs to abandon her natural allies." Gomez is confused until the barman adds, "In the reign of Louis-the-Well-Beloved, sir, France had already committed every fault there is to commit." "Ah," said Gomez, "you're a Canadian."

"I'm from Montreal," said the barman.

"Are you now?"

A Montrealer myself, I have had my own problems in New York.

On a recent trip, driving into town from LaGuardia airport, a taxi driver asked, "Where are you from?"

"Montreal," I said.

"That," he allowed, beaming, "is my favorite city in the United States."

However ignorant too many Americans remain of most matters Canadian, I have never subscribed, as do many embittered Canadian intellectuals, to the widely self-flattering theory that there is an anti-Canadian cultural cabal common to London and New York. What I do believe is even more depressing. The sour truth is just about everybody outside of Canada finds us boring. Immensely boring. Bob Gottlieb, my editor at Knopf, told me that one afternoon he and his associates compiled a list of twelve deserving but ineffably dull books with which to start a publishing firm that was bound to fail. Leading the list of unreadables was *Canada: Our Good Neighbor to the North.*

Well now, Canada is no longer your good neighbor to the north. It's your fulminating neighbor. And we are only ostensibly boring.

Consider, for instance the seemingly bland prime minister of my boyhood, William Lyon Mackenzie King. The truth is, far from being a bore, King was somewhat loopy. A perfectly appalling man. When he built his country estate, Kingsmere, on the outskirts of Ottawa, he was careful to buy the surrounding hundred acres lest there be, and I'm quoting from his diaries now, "a sale to Jews, who have a desire to get in at Kingsmere and ruin the whole place." Possibly by opening a delicatessen.

In our day we also mistakenly took King for a resounding bore. We didn't realize, that taking a crystal ball for his Kissinger, he rapped with his mother's spirit nightly. Or that, following the disclosures about John F. Kennedy's philandering, we would learn through King's diaries, that he actually did it too. With the hookers of turn-of-the-century Toronto and Chicago. Forking out as much as a dollar twenty-five a trick.

I am indebted to C.P. Stacey, author of *A Very Double Life,* for the further revelation that our prime minister, while still a 19-year-old student, was already a confirmed Gladstonian. Which is to say, bent on the salvation of prostitutes by day he did in fact bend over them by night and later, in his years of maturity, did enjoy a relationship with his "little angel" dog Pat ("the truest friend I ever had") which, put plainly, was just this side of sodomy. Pat died in his arms in the summer of 1941, as King, ever the campaigner, making promises he couldn't fulfil, sang aloud to him, *Safe in the Arms of Jesus.*

During World War II, when Roosevelt and Churchill met in Quebec City, wee Mackenzie King was not allowed into any of the conferences, but, as a special concession, he was allowed to be photographed with the real leaders. Looking big.

Only fifteen years later our continuing fight for recognition had reached beyond politics. The battle for Canada's cultural integrity had begun.

In the fifties, Pierre Berton revealed in his book, *Hollywood's Canada,* there was a government-sponsored film group in Ottawa, the Canadian Co-operation Project, comprised of a group of grown men who actually compiled an annual list of film mentions of Canada they had pried out of obdurate Hollywood. Such dialogue gems as, from *Red Skies of Montana*, "We tie in with the authorities north of the border in Canada," or from *The Tanks Are Coming*, "The Canadians were on our left and although taking a terrific pounding were holding magnificently." In fact, the C.C.P. was so effective they were even responsible for the occasional dialogue change. Originally a line in *New York Confidential* read: "They caught Louis Engelday in Detroit." But a rare combination of Canadian imagination and muscle got it altered to read: "They caught Louis Engelday on his way to Canada."

It sometimes seems to me that to be a Jew and a Canadian is to emerge from the ghetto twice, for self-conscious Canadians, like some touchy Jews, tend to contemplate the world through a wrong-ended telescope, as witness what is still my most cherished Canadian newspaper headline, from the Toronto *Globe and Mail*: "1960 WAS A GOOD YEAR FOR PLAYWRIGHTS FROM OUTSIDE OF CANADA." Like Jews again, Canadians are inclined to regard with a mixture of envy and suspicion those who have forsaken the homestead or *shtetl* for the assimilationist fleshpots of New York or London.

It is easy to poke fun at some of Canada's more paranoid cultural concerns, but our problems are real, nevertheless.

My good friend Robert Fulford, the editor of *Saturday Night*, once observed that the trouble with those who preceded today's nationalists, my generation of Canadians, the cultural internationalists of the fifties, was our conviction that the only thing for the talented to do was "to graduate from Canada."

Let me put the case for my Canadian generation this way.

Elsewhere—that was the operative word. The built-in insult. Canadians of my generation, sprung to adolescence during World War II, were conditioned to believe the world happened elsewhere. You apprenticed for it in Canada, on the farm with a view, and then you packed your bags and lit out for the golden cities: New York, London, Paris. Home was a good neighbourhood, but suburban, even bush, unless you happened to be a hockey player. Of all our boyhood heroes, from Joe DiMaggio to Humphrey Bogart, only hockey players were Canadian *and* undoubtedly the best, at least until they ran into the nefarious Russians. While we did have other indigenous heroes, they were badly flawed by being pint-sized versions of an altogether larger British or American presence. They were world-famous—in Canada. Put plainly, any candidate for excellence was bound to be suspect unless he proved himself under alien skies. The

American kid who wanted to grow up to be president was enjoying a dream of glory, but the Canadian kid who wanted to be prime minister wasn't thinking big, he was setting a limit to his ambitions rather early.

History, for us, was a spectator sport. Revolution, earthquakes, civil war, racial strife, famine—all were other people's miseries. We had never withstood a Spanish Armada. Or overthrown a tyrant. Why, we even lacked an Alamo. After nearly a hundred years of confederation, we remained a fragmentary country, yet to be bound by nationhood, a mythology of our own.

I am speaking of the forties now, but, as late as 1971, Prime Minister Pearson said to me: "We have never fought for our freedom and we have no independent political history." He recalled that when he was a young man, "We were Canadians, yes, but in a British sense; our foreign policy was made on Downing Street. We emerged from World War I with newfound pride and confidence, but just at a time when we could have built up something especially our own, we fell under U.S. economic imperialism. Once more we failed to stand on our own feet."

One thing that distinguishes us from Americans—one of our least fortunate characteristics, perhaps—is that we are not a nation of chance-takers. We are a decent people, yes, but altogether too timorous, I think.

In the late forties, when we were students, we were also embarrassed to be Canadians. Charged with it, we always had a self-deprecating joke ready. In those days, I was a student at Sir George Williams College in Montreal, where I survived for two years, experiencing, among other illuminations, a class on the Modern Novel. Come examination time, we were asked if *Sons and Lovers* by (H.G. Wells, D.H. Lawrence, or Ellery Queen) was a (thriller, psychological, or comic) novel.

I should point out—hastily—that Sir George Williams was a far from typical Canadian educational institution, and that standards at Sir George, now a recognized university, called Concordia, have improved immensely since 1949, but at the time it was a pathetic place. We were taught grammar (English 101) by superannuated high school teachers and poetry by good-natured but inadequate ladies who flushed at the mention of Keats. The university was, and still is, run by the YMCA and, in those days, taking time out to pee in any toilet higher than the second floor was to risk your heterosexual integrity.

However, it was at Sir George, as neophyte writer, that I was sufficiently intrepid to submit to a battery of intelligence tests, these
designed to determine what, if any, natural aptitudes I possessed.

The question I still remember, because it was so cunningly
composed, asked if, given a choice, would I rather have dinner with

a four-star general
a Hollywood starlet
or a Nobel Prize-winning writer.

No fool, I could see what they were getting at, but I had to be
honest. Appetite, always, before ambition.

Bent glumly over the results of my tests, the guidance counsellor
asked me, "What, exactly, do you want to do?"

"I want to be a writer," I said, and in order to fill that office with
integrity it seemed to me at the time that I had to put picayune
Canada, and all it stood for, behind me.

At Sir George Williams, when we began to read the *New Republic*
and the *New Statesman*, and one or perhaps two of us dared to
venture out loud in a tavern, "I'm going to be a writer," the immediate
and crushing rejoinder was, "What? You're going to be a *Canadian*
writer?"

Sir George, in this sense ahead of its day, actually had a course on
Canadian writing. We did not, I must admit, have a text; in fact it was
our pioneering venture to develop a Canadiana bibliography. We
were supposed to scan the libraries for Canadiana, any Canadiana,
listing the books, dimensions, number of pages, and whether or not
there were illustrations. I do hope this bibliography is not still in use
anywhere. For, at the time, we found it easier, and much more fun, to
invent titles and authors rather than hunt them down.

After classes, we used to divert ourselves playing the Canadian
Identity Game, trying to trap that elusive nuance that made us
different from the other Americans. A friend came closest. If, he
ventured, it had been a Canadian marine who had broadcast the last
ringingly defiant message from Wake Island in the darkest days of
World War II, he would not have dared, "Send us more Japs," but
instead, "No offense intended to any ethnic group, but would you
allow us more Japanese, please."

In those days, there were several Canadian little magazines, but we
would have considered it a stigma to have our stories published in any
one of them. We also, on scrutinizing the fiction published in
Canadian Forum, took it for granted that it had already been turned
down by *The Atlantic Monthly* and *Harper's*. And the most shattering

criticism you could make of another man's poetry was to say, "Ryerson is publishing it in Toronto."

We did not want to conquer Toronto. London and New York were the places we looked to for all our excitements. We had never had, in the literary history of our own country, a magazine that young intellectuals might have responded to, like *Partisan Review, Horizon, Story,* or *Penguin New Writing.* Perhaps what really bound us together in those days was a shared sense of how comic our country was. A political party called *Progressive*-Conservative. The cult of ice skater Barbara Ann Scott. Hunt balls *en Montréal, Québec.* The Imperial Order of the Daughters of the British Empire, and so forth. Though, to be fair, we had not yet been saddled with a *Canadian*-born governor-general. In the absence of real linen, our own drip-dry monarchy symbol.

Now no country, including your own, is without its buffoons, inanities and outlandish conventions, but what seemed to make ours different was that only the most private and isolated voices were raised in protest. Here a professor, there a poet, and, between, thousands of miles of wheat and indifference. And so, putting Canada behind me in 1951, I sailed for Europe without regrets. Like most of my intellectual contemporaries, I was mistakenly charged with scorn for *all* things Canadian. If we were indeed hemmed in by the boring, the inane, and the absurd, we foolishly blamed it *all* on Canada, failing to grasp that we would suffer from a surfeit of the boring, the inane, and the absurd, wherever we wandered.

This is one of the themes I tried to cope with in my novel, *St. Urbain's Horseman,* and if you'll pardon me I'd like to lean on that novel and quote from it very briefly now.

"Jake, Luke, and others of their generation were reared to believe in the cultural thinness of their own blood. Anemia was their heritage. As certain homosexuals pander to others by telling the most vicious anti-queer jokes, so Jake, so Luke, shielded themselves from ridicule by anticipating with derisive tales of their own. Their only certitude was that all indigenous cultural standards they had been raised on were a shared joke. No national reputation could be bandied abroad without apology.

"Adrift in a cosmopolitan sea of conflicting mythologies, only they had none. Moving among discontented commonwealth types in London, they were inclined to envy them their real grievances. South Africans and Rhodesians, *bona fide* refugees from tyranny, who had come to raise a humanitarian banner in exile; Australians, who could allude to forebears transported in convict ships; and West Indians, armed with the most obscene outrage of all, the memory of their grandfathers sold in marketplaces. What they failed to grasp was the ironic truth in Sir Wilfred Laurier's boast that the twentieth century would belong to Canada. For amid so many exiles from nineteenth century tyranny, heirs to injustices that could actually be set right politically, thereby lending themselves to constructive angers, only the Canadians, surprisingly, were true children of their times. Only they had packed their bags and left home to escape the hell of boredom. And find it everywhere."

Nevertheless, what many expatriates felt on return visits to Canada in the sixties was that those in the arts who had stayed behind were faint-hearted, and middle-aged before their time, settling for being big fish in a small pond.

Well yes, possibly, but not quite.

Naturally, there are many who still appear to be whales because they have discreetly limited their splashing to the shallow standards of the Canadian pond, but as a Canadian who lived in London for almost two decades, I must admit that nobody has made himself artistically indispensable there. We have not surfaced with a Conrad or a Joyce. And, meanwhile at home, we have always had such as Northrop Frye, Morley Callaghan, and Robertson Davies, among others.

Others in the arts who stayed at home did so out of necessity, not without self-apology, promising themselves that next year, or the year after, they would try New York or London, testing their talents against the larger world. Alas, next year or the year after never came, and a decade later they felt themselves compromised, self-condemned, a big bat in the minors forevermore, until, with hindsight, they redeemed themselves in their own eyes by becoming the most impassioned of today's nationalists, declaring that for all seasons there is nothing like home, which, I fear, was often no more than self-justification. Or, looked at another way, where once we tended to suspect any artistic achievement if it was Canadian, now—overcompensating—we defiantly clapped hands for it so long as it was Canadian.

Since the fifties there have been changes in the Canadian cultural climate, enormous changes: some of them very hopeful indeed, others mind-boggling. Which is to say, we now boast, among other things, a Committee for an Independent Canada, which publishes a bimonthly journal called *The Independencer*. This journal not only deals in ideas, it also publishes poetry. Once, memorably, a two-page verse which was the group inspiration of the Lorna Mayfield Chapter. Called "The Canadian Children's Plea," it began:

> Please, Mr. Prime Minister,
> don't sell us out to the USA!
> Please, Mr. Prime Minister,
> don't give our heritage away!
> When we are grown and take
> our place as men and women
>   of our race,
> We want to be FREE—to control
> —to decide; not to the will
> of a giant tied."

Shortly after my return to Canada, in 1972, it was my good luck to hear from the Committee directly. Their letter, which actually sprung from the Committee's cultural think-tank, began: "Dear Author, You have been chosen along with seventy-nine other major contemporary Canadian authors to present your views..."

Actually, I happened to be right on the spot when the Committee for an Independent Canada first proclaimed itself to the nation.

Toronto, September 1970.

Only three hours after I had landed in the city, still woozy from a trans-Atlantic flight, I found myself in the thin frontline of the newly joined battle for Canada's soul, at a press conference in the Royal York Hotel. I had come to hear the spiritual great-grandsons of the Fathers of Confederation. "We believe," they declared, "that Canadians today share a surging mood of self-awareness...A society has evolved, unique in its quality of life—a kind of civilized resistance to the similarly blessed but much more violent land to the south of us."

Immediately the statement was made, a sagacious reporter bobbed out of his chair. "What," he asked, "does Washington think of your plans?"

Under the television lights sat co-chairman Jack McClelland, the country's leading publisher, and Claude Ryan, then the distinguished editor of *Le Devoir*. After more than a hundred years Canada's two founding races, the English and the French, had got off the fence and finally decided they liked the country well enough to stay and now, understandably, they wanted the freehold back. A second chance for indigenous, rather than foreign, capitalists to exploit the rest of us.

I fail to see how the populace can be roused to do anything about it. In my demonstrating days, revolutionaires argued for a fairer distribution of the wealth, not the virtues of being exploited by home-bred capitalists over one who was a foreigner. An issue which I, being old-fashioned, still consider a matter of indifference to the working man. After all, it I were repairing lines for the telephone company, it would not exercise me whether the Bell tolled for Canadian or American shareholders, but rather which group of coupon-clippers was willing to offer a better deal to the workers. Mind you, the nationalists *are* on to something when they protest that ours is a branch-plant economy. Too many of our natural resources are rail-roaded south to be refined, creating no jobs here. Decisions involving our industries are made outside the country, the head office's priorities, not a community's dependency on the branch-plant, being the primary consideration. Beyond that there is the question of pride. We are not, as the Québécois once put it so eloquently, *maîtres chez nous*. And this applies culturally as well for we are also, in the nature of things, a cultural branch-plant. Canadian publishers, good or bad, suffer from an impossibly small market base, so that a singularly well reviewed literary novel that sells anything over 2,000 copies in Canada is doing very well indeed. As well, I'd say, as a novel that sells 20,000 copies in the United States. Then, to add intellectual insult to economic injury, the going depends largely not on the blessings of Toronto or Montreal newspapers, but, as any bookseller will tell you, on the verdict of the *New York Times Book Review, Time,* or *Newsweek,* should they deign to notice. The continuing need for New York to make it real has, understandably, caused many resentments. It is, of course, humiliating that foreign critics should ordain what's good, and what isn't, in Canadian letters, but in this imperfect world it's only fair to say—one—New York critics didn't sue for that office—and two—New York reviewers are generally more perceptive than all but a few people who write about books in our own newspapers. It should surprise nobody that the average Toronto or Montreal reviewer is no more prescient than his equivalent in, say, Cleveland or Denver or, come to think of it, Leeds or Newcastle. But it does surprise Canadians. Surprise them and make them angry.

Come 1970, there was a new sense of self-awareness in Canada, and the spirit of nationalism was raging over the land.

Look out.

Canada's English-speaking writers are now a largely discontented, even fulminating lot, the most militant bitterly anti-American, given to cultural paranoia, a fire sometimes stoked by real, if not necessarily malign, fatuity, as witness a review of Margaret Laurence's last novel,

The Diviners, in the *New York Times Book Review*. I do not quarrel with the reviewer's assessment of Mrs. Laurence's novel, which is, after all, her prerogative. But, once having admonished Mrs. Laurence for her sloppy prose, the reviewer sails on to place her novel in Ontario, when it is deeply rooted in the prairie soil of Manitoba, and has the author dealing with the meti when in fact the half-breed character in question, whose grandfather fought in the Riel rebellion, a seminal Canadian uprising, was a Métis.

Such blithely insulting ignorance of your once quiescent neighbor, exacerbated by certain economic facts, has created enormous resentments in Canada.

Attention must be paid.

Look here, we not only boast a magnificent and distinctive geography, a little history of our own, singularly honorable politicians, and an emerging, if still fragile, indigenous culture, but, to come clean, we have long been infiltrating your culture high, low, and middle.

Saul Bellow is a Montrealer born and has written splendidly about his Napoleon Street boyhood in *Herzog*. Kenneth Galbraith is also one of ours and, indeed, one of his most engaging books, *The Scotch*, is a celebration of his formative years in rural southern Ontario. Marshall McLuhan, mercifully only one season's guru, is another Canadian. We have also—shrewdly, I think—dumped Guy Lombardo on you, as well as Paul Anka, the Washington Capitols, and Lorne Green, the insufferably ponderous big daddy of El Ponderosa. Why, even the makers of the Hollywood dream, Samuel Goldwyn, Louis B. Mayer, and Jack Warner came out of Canada. Failed maritime scrap dealers, the lot. And, while we're at it, please remember that it was our steadfast rum and whisky runners who saw you through the darkest days of prohibition.

O, our relationship with the United States is both tangled and touchy. Irretrievably so.

Going back to my student days, the U.S. has always been something we both loved and resented. Loved, because the novels and films we consumed with appetite, as well as the pop culture that shaped us, were largely American. Resented, because to visit New York, brimming with goodwill, and to proffer a Canadian dollar bill was to be told, "What's that, kid, monopoly money?" And to introduce the subject of Canadian politics to socially concerned American friends, fascinated by all things African, was to witness their eyes glaze over with boredom.

Then, in 1968, a year when I was writer-in-residence at Sir George Williams University, I was to witness yet another variation of the theme of our American dependence. That was, if you remember, the time of so much student unrest in the United States, but, in Montreal, where we had no racial strife or war in Vietnam, it was also the wasteful year of the great computer fire. To recap briefly. In the winter of '68 a handful of West Indian students, doing badly in biology, charged they were the victims of racial discrimination, which was nonsense. Investigations fumbled on, then faltered, activists rallied, and the upshot was occupation and ultimately destruction by axe and fire of the Sir George Williams computer, the damage being estimated at more than two million dollars.

It was an ugly business, disheartening too.

I happened to be in Ottawa the night of the fire and only found out about it when I read the morning newspapers. An hour or so later, seated in the gallery of the House of Commons, I watched the doyen of our politicians, old Johnny Diefenbaker, rise to deliver one of his vintage one-liners. He wanted to know whether in view of the fact that many of the Sir George Williams students had been found with copies of *Quotations From Chairman Mao* on them, should the government reconsider its policy of recognizing communist China.

Two things struck me most forcibly about the tragedy. Where there was no black problem whatsoever, the students had superimposed one out of issue-envy of the country to the south of us. And then, a few days later, there was the student who brandished a copy of *Time* magazine at me, gleefully pointing out the full-page article. "Look," he exclaimed, "we made the American section. Now, when I go down to New York, nobody will ask me again what is Sir George Williams."

We want to impress you, all right, but we don't want to be dominated by you.

Quebec, as I have already reminded you, is a special case, cocooned by language. Increasingly cocooned by language these days, one might say. But the English-speaking Canadian's "American problem" is much more complex. Obviously, for all our complaining, as we come grudgingly of age, we are Americans too.

North Americans.

Ours, if you like, is the enormous attic, where, as lip-smacking, energy-starved Washington knows, so many, many riches are stored and, furthermore, have been mismanaged for years.

True, we have always suffered from a shortage of development capital, and have resented those who lent it to us, looking for a good return.

Our real problem, however, unique in the Western world, perhaps, was not an indigenous buccaneering capitalist class, indifferent to those whom they exploited, yet bold and imaginative. Nation-builders. Our problem was the Scots: the most inept and cautious capitalists in the West. Not builders, but sellers. If the pre-World War I American boy, at the age of sixteen, was dreaming of how to conquer and market the rest of the world, his Canadian equivalent, at the same tender age, was already looking for a position with an unrivalled pension scheme.

Looking for the quick and safe profit, we have, to some extent, become tenant farmers on our own estate, both culturally and economically, and faced with the bill we are unwilling to pay.

Building something essentially our own, hammering out a mythology, however self-consciously, is the obsession of today's young Canadian intellectuals. Their nationalist ardor has been fed by some heartening changes on the cultural scene and, to give them their due, their anger has made others possible. There is, for openers, the Canada Council, its largesse so fabled that no Canadian writer, toilet-trained or a good speller, need want for a sustaining grant. There is also a National Arts Centre in Ottawa, which, certainly to my surprise, has transmogrified our nation's capital, now no longer merely a cowtown. There's the Canadian Film Development Corporation, armed with the renewable stake of ten million dollars with which to help finance a fledgling industry. There's Stratford and a lively theatre scene in Toronto. While it's true that the Canada Council, the Film Development Corporation, and the National Arts Centre cannot, with all their money, actually create a uniquely Canadian culture, they do make for immensely favorable conditions. All the same, we are a mere twenty-two million, you are more than two hundred million. We share more than grievances. We share a language and a literary tradition. Short of sawing the continent apart at the 49th parallel, we will continue, no matter what, to be enormously influenced, if not dominated, by the culture to the south of us, a culture of a daunting vitality. I'm told that ninety percent of the books sold in Canada originate with foreign-controlled publishers and over eighty percent of the books Canadians buy are written and published outside the country. This makes the nationalists seethe, but I cannot see how it could be different. We are dependent on American or British publishers not only for their own literature, but also for all

the European or Asian books we read in translation. And so, naturally
enough, it is these publishers who provide the majority of the books
we read for pleasure, rather than as a patriotic duty. Which is not to
say there isn't a real Canadian literature, worthy of any serious
reader's attention.

Our nationalists, however, refuse to live with these facts which are
obvious to me, and they have fostered a good deal of embarrassing
chauvinistic nonsense. Again and again, they go too far. If, for
instance, Canadian literature was once beyond the academic pale, not
studied in any of our universities, now courses on Canlit abound. A
good thing in principle, actually. The trouble is suddenly everything
has been declared usable, or so it seems. Unreadable 19th century
writers, their talents clearly inadequate, have surfaced overnight as
Canadian classics. A poor thing, but our own. And many a journey-
man contemporary novelist finds himself declared a set book only
months after publication, being force-fed to innocent students across
the land.

Worse news. Nationalists are lobbying for the imposition of
Canadian content quotas in our bookshops and theatres. Canadian
content quotas would oblige bookshops and those who maintain
paperback racks to legally display or offer as much as twenty percent
Canadian content. In our theatres, the nationalists are after fifty percent content quotas. In a word, largely second-rate writers are
demanding from Ottawa what talent has denied them, an audience,
applause.

Content quotas, already imposed on Canadian television, have
made for some talmudic conundrums. If, for instance, our southern
crackers play yours, that is to say, the Montreal Expos take to the field
against the Dodgers in L.A., and this is broadcast on CBC-TV, is it
100 percent Canadian content or 50? Or does it depend on the final
score? Similarly, if a *bona fide* Canadian publisher were to bring out a
book on the Boston Bruins, Canadian roughnecks to the man, is this
Canadian or American content?

Increasingly, our more militant nationalists remind me of your own
one-time Un-American Activities Committee.

In 1970, typically, an incensed Ottawa professor protested against
Pierre Elliot Trudeau's right to escort Barbra Streisand to the
Manitoba Centennial Party at the National Arts Centre. "Since it is a
Canadian birthday," he wrote in a letter to the *Citizen*, "one might at
least have expected him to appear with a Canadian. But Pierre-baby is
a realist. He knows where it's at...when you're prime minister of a

colony, you appear with one of the princesses of the empire. It's called pragmatism, baby."

Which philosophy, admittedly yet another dirty foreign influence, possibly explained why Trudeau, venturing north later in the same year in the hope of establishing our jurisdiction over the Arctic seas, shlepped Elizabeth II with him, not Barbra. Looked at another way, you can sweet-talk a nice Jewish princess into a weekend in Ottawa, but you can't lead her into the black fly country. With the Queen, however, it's duty above all.

Nationalism is also running riot in many of our book pages. In a review of Robertson Davies' *Fifth Business* in the *Canadian Forum*, the author was adjudged a rotter because, in his novel, he was nasty to Canadian ladies. "Why," wrote the reviewer, "should the beautiful girl whose idea of love is 'a sweet physical convulsion shared with an interesting partner' be South American? Why must all those book subscribers know contemporary Canadian women under forty only as two school girls, one pimply, the other spoiled? And why oh why, dear school master, when you even date your last page as recently as 1970, must you still locate the simian androgyne and the big spiritual adventures outside of Canada? Canada, while you've been expiating, has come to abound in a passionate pagan temperament."

Oh dear oh dear.

What we had here, at last, was a new critical direction. The Canadian school. Its strictures, if applied to British or American letters, would oblige us to repudiate E.M. Forster for writing about shenanigans in a Malabar cave when, as we all know, there are just as many holes in the British Isles, and it would utterly dismiss Hemingway, a loutish cosmopolitan, for setting *The Sun Also Rises* in Paris when it is just as easy to lose a generation in Milwaukee.

We now even have a pop novelist all our own, much beloved by some of the nationalists, and his subject matter should be of interest to you.

I speak of Reserve Air Force General Richard Rohmer, *our* Steve Canyon, whose recent novel, *Exxoneration*, was a Canadian bestseller. *Exxoneration* began where Rohmer's earlier political fantasy, *Ultimatum*, ended, with the American president, at 6:30 P.M., Oct. 7, 1980, announcing the annexation of Canada, and our Governor-General seeing no alternative but to "follow the instructions of the President," even as U.S. Air Force planes are landing at all Canadian air bases to begin the occupation of the country. But wait, wait, the imperialists' fascist bullies hadn't counted on *Exxoneration's* hero, the incomparable Pierre Thomas de Gaspé, of whom our Prime Minister says, "There is something I didn't know about, that is that de Gaspé, as well as being president of the Canada Energy Corporation, is also your Toronto District Commander and is running Operation Reception Party at Toronto International Airport. God, how versatile can a man be!"

Even the Texan President of the U.S.A. respects us, thanks to de Gaspé. "Sure the United States owns most of the country. But those people have a fighting record in the first world war and the second world war like you wouldn't believe."

De Gaspé's Operation Reception Party totally defeats the superior American invading force, and the crushed U.S. Air Force general, just possibly a Southerner, is moved to comment: "Ah gotta hand it to you all, you sure gave it to us good. Ah didn't know you Canadians had that much gumption, but ah sure know it now and ah take my hat off to you."

Rohmer is also a master of the Jewish idiom. Ultimately, the Texan President is defeated in an election by none other than David Dennis, the first Jewish President of the U.S.A., who says of his trip to Israel: "Such a welcome. For a Jewish boy from Detroit, a boy who's come up the hard way..."

Enough.

Nationalists notwithstanding, the fundamental Canadian dilemma remains unchanged over the years. Namely, is it possible to operate a decent but cautious small corner grocery of a country on the same continent as one of the most voracious of supermarket nations? Is the corner grocery worth defending? Is there anything on the shelves, but wheat, iron ore, oil, and yearning? Is there a tradition to cherish and pass on, a culture evolving, something more than a reputation for honest trading?

Sometimes, to come clean, I wonder if the culture is worth defending.

In the sixties, it was my privilege to drive to Brandon, Ontario, to pay tribute to the poet Pauline Johnson, who had been born there a hundred years earlier and was now to become the first Canadian writer to appear on a five cent stamp.

The program got off to a fine start with some tribal dances by Chief Red Cloud, a most engaging man, and his grandson, Little White Bear; and a Miss Rosalie Burnham, who was in Indian costume, treated us to her own rendition of Tommy Dorsey's arrangement of "Indian Love Call." Then the Deputy Minister of Citizenship and

Immigration, a Dr. Davidson, rose to speak. "Though highbrow critics tilted their noses high in the air," he said, "Pauline Johnson was the most truly Canadian poet of them all. It's not high-class poetry," he allowed, "In fact I don't know if it's great or good or what, but ordinary plain Canadians, like ourselves, like it. Miss Johnson," he concluded, "wrote for our boyish enjoyment. Like William Shakespeare."

And only in 1977, in Montreal, the literary critic of our evening newspaper died. In a tribute to him in the *Star's* Saturday edition, the editor wrote, "John Richmond was a poet, both in his own right and in translation, and at his death was busy translating Auden into contemporary Greek. It is difficult to imagine "The Wasteland" in Greek. It clashes intellectually with the language of Sophocles, but Richmond would have made it work..."

But the truth is I do believe there is a tradition evolving at last and that it is worth defending. Hysteria, however, is no shield, chauvinism an unacceptable armor. Canada, Canada, count your blessings.

Because we are Canadian citizens, we have never had to acquiesce to a Suez conspiracy, on the one hand, or the obscene war in Vietnam, on the other. Somebody else's government bears the guilt-load for the suppression of freedom in Czechoslovakia. Rhodesia's not our shame, neither is Watergate. We are the progeny of a thinly populated country, basically decent, with no compromising say in the world's calumnies. This, I should think, is a moral pleasure that far outweighs any artistic shortcomings. And the same, if you like, could also be said of Sweden, Norway, and Denmark, with one crucial difference. They are culturally sheltered by language; we, English-speaking Canadians, are not. Neither are we quite so independent.

Providing we are willing to pay the price, which I strongly doubt, we can legislate more rigorous laws on foreign ownership, but—but—Canada cannot quite so easily pass a bill declaring indigenous pap to be soul-food, pronouncing second-rate novelists to be as necessary as Melville, Faulkner, or Fitzgerald. "There is no Canadian writer," Northrop Frye reminds us in the *Literary History of Canada*, "of whom we can say as we can say of the world's major writers, that their readers grow up inside their work without ever being aware of a circumference."

But I would like to add—no, emphasize—that there is more good and honest writing being done in Canada today than there was twenty years ago. Or, put another way, there is no need to apologize, or be ashamed for the neighbors. If, twenty years ago, Canadian writers suffered from neglect, what we now must guard against is over-praise at home. The largest insult. The dirty double standard. One test for Canadian writers, another, more exacting litmus applied to foreigners. I don't know, I can't be sure, but I hope I speak for every-body else in the Canadian literary house when I say either we are talented enough to pass muster, or we are not. We do not stand in need of a nationalist's dog license. We don't want to be read in our country as village gossip because Canadians recognize the street names in our novels or can nod over the weather conditions. We wish to be read at home, and abroad, because we have something fresh to say about the human condition—or not to be read at all.

For your part, you might show more curiosity about the culture of your good neighbor to the north, and eschew the tendency to treat anything coming out of Canada as if it had emerged out of off-off Broadway. We are not the only ones guilty of parochialism.

And my quarrel with the nationalists at home is that they—obviously thinking very little of us—would put barriers above all, erecting a great cultural wall of Canada, jamming the airwaves, sealing off the frontier, sheltering us from all things American, in the slender hope that something better, something distinctly our own, would emerge from the airless land we would be left to linger in.

Self-indulgent cultural nationalism, lashing out at all things American is ultimately a futile exercise. We do share a larger tradition and will go on being culturally entwined for years to come. If we could only graciously come to terms with this—rejecting the shoddy, be it American, Canadian, or whatever—absorbing excellence wherever it springs from—then it is fair to say Canadian writers, film-makers, and other artists are in the most enviable position.

Such is the cultural yearning that the advantages and the money are out scouring the woods for us. Myth-makers are urgently needed; and, furthermore, applicants needn't be unduly inhibited. The young writer, for instance, who is settling down to a novel in the Maritimes, hasn't the ghost of Faulkner peering over his shoulder. Henry James didn't come before. Or Twain. Or Fitzgerald. If the literary house is haunted, it is only by the amiable Leacock, the dispensable de le Roche. For the rest, the tradition is yet to be made. It's virgin land up for grabs.

In conclusion, I would like to say something about the question of a Canadian identity. Even during my twenty odd years abroad, I was never confused about who I am or where I came from. Our continuing neurotic concern with the question of an identity baffles me. It also makes me impatient. After all, Americans are not asked to define themselves, neither are the British.

Years ago, the British critic Ron Bryden said to me, Canadians are nice, very nice, and they expect everybody else to be very nice; and I have yet to come up with a better or more succinct definition.

We are, if you like, a reticent people, nicely self-deprecating, and we are fortunate enough to live in a country where the small civilities are still observed, whatever its present problems. Like most well-behaved people we are also, to some extent, happy hypocrites. Which is to say, the pleasures of living in a branch-plant country, largely those of a kibbitzer, are not to be sneezed at. If, for instance, there is a war in Vietnam, we can, even while we profit from doing piecework for the aggressors in private, plead for peace in public. And we delight in lecturing the other America on its treatment of blacks, even as we do our best to keep them out of our own country.

But the streets of presently troubled Montreal, where I live, remain not only enjoyable, but also safe. The quarrel between English and French Canadian, however heated, is still remarkably civil.

Years ago, Northrop Frye, attempting to pinpoint what is peculiar to the Canadian psyche, alluded to a painting inspired by the prophecy of Isaiah, "The Peaceable Kingdom," which illustrated a treaty between Indians and Quakers, and a group of lions, bears, oxen, and other animals. Frye wrote that the Canadian tradition as revealed in literature might well be called a quest for the peaceable kingdom.

2_____CANADIAN IDENTITY

COMMENT

Sylvia Wright

I, too, like Mr. Richler, am doubtful about identity. To achieve one you must stop working on whatever you are working on, and concentrate on who you are. This necessary identity-intensive interval has been institutionalized by Erik Erikson, who calls it a "moratorium." Obviously it presents a problem if you are a busy person. As an American (U.S. variety), and therefore in a rush for results, and as a woman with, in these days almost as bedeviling an identity problem as Canada's, I sometimes wonder if we really have time for this sort of thing. Perhaps, if we just went on working, when we took a breather, we would find that a nice discreet identity had been there all along crying to get out, or, if the identity was less nice, slouching somewhere to be born.

However, I will not subvert the topic of Mr. Richler's essay. For, in fact, Americans, too, have had identity problems. One way they addressed them was to confront Europe.

Throughout the nineteenth century, almost every major American thinker or writer spent time observing Europe, writing about Europe, and publishing books about Europe. This was usually England: we got away with taking France less seriously because the French had loose morals which they flaunted in French novels young Americans shouldn't have been reading anyway.

In his preface to his *Discovery of Europe*, a collection of American writing about that continent, Philip Rahv points out that there were in fact two poles of American culture. Against Europe, the rich past, was set the frontier—open space, action, the future. Canada is also stretched between these two poles, but, as Mr. Richler has shown, this is complicated by that third element, the United States, which intervenes, like an overbearing elder brother, who gets everything first and leaves only hand-me-downs. We were lucky, with only two poles.

In our confrontation with Europe we have had other lucky breaks.

One was Benjamin Franklin, who, with his characteristic good sense, managed to be already a typical American before the United States existed. At the same period we were confusing Canada by cluttering it up with all those discarded loyalists.

Europe loved Franklin, and in the process got used to the idea and the presence of Americans watching how they did things. They reciprocated by sending all sorts of writers—de Tocqueville, Mrs. Trollope, Harriet Martineau—to the U.S. to make disapproving comments designed to provoke self-assertive American rebuttals. Oscar Wilde was just as mean to us as he was to you. If we had done the same and sent some critical Americans north to make provocative comments about Canada, it might have served the cause of Canadian identity. Mr. Richler is right in blaming us for not being more curious. This, however, was not totally from parochialism: we didn't realize Canadians were so nice. We simply assumed they were like us, only more impervious to cold.

Franklin was followed by Washington Irving, the *Sketch Book*, in 1819; James Fenimore Cooper, *Gleanings in Europe*, 1837; Melville, *Redburn*, 1849; Emerson, *English Traits*, 1856; Hawthorne, *Our Old Home*, 1863; Mark Twain, *Innocents Abroad*, 1869; and so on down to Henry James, whose career as a writer encompassed the confrontation and who, when he set Daisy Miller in Europe, made her on the spot more clearly American than she could possibly have appeared elsewhere.

Perhaps the process reached its peak in Paris with the expatriates of the twenties and Gertrude Stein, who concluded that all creative artists had to have two civilizations because "if you are you in your own civilization you are apt to mix yourself up too much with your civilization but when it is another civilization a complete other a romantic other another that stays there were it is you in it have freedom inside yourself which if you are to do what is inside yourself and nothing else is a very useful thing to have happen to you..."

This explains why we have not managed to be the romantic other for Canada. We do not stay there where we are, but swarm economically and culturally into Canada.

Shocked as they often were by class differences and poverty in Europe, American writers responded by celebrating American virtues and advantages. When Carlyle told Emerson that the English had much to teach the Americans, Emerson countered that "we play the game with immense advantage...and...England, an old and exhausted island, must one day be contented like other parents, to be strong only in her children." Hawthorne was less polite. "It has required nothing less than the boorishness, the stolidity, the self-sufficiency, the contemptuous jealousy, the half-sagacity, invariably blind of one eye and often distorted of the other, that characterize this strange people that is, the British, to compel us to be a great nation in our own right…"

In any case this activity served to identify and encourage one important facet of the developing American character, a weakness for self-examination, pleasure in self-analysis, which runs persistently through our society.

This combination of self-examination and self-assertiveness is not sympathetic to Canadians. I can understand that to them it appears not only outré, but bumptious. So I stop short of suggesting that Canadians should, for their own good, spend some time writing books about the United States. But, since they are a nice people, perhaps they would be willing to do it for our good.

For it would help us. As an American who has spent some time in Greece, I have come to feel that one thing we desperately need today is a much more distinguished—a higher quality of—anti-Americanism, expressed with more elegance, developed with more logic, and elaborated with more humor. It is time, I think, for Americans to be rigorous about the sort of anti-Americanism they will accept. Canadians in the main have not been good enough at this. Until recently, they have produced nothing of the high rhetorical quality of, for instance, Hawthorne's comments on England.

But things are changing and looking up. A number of very gifted Canadians are quite capable of first-rate criticism of the U.S. Consider Anna Russell in her fine work "The Prince of Philadelphia," admittedly a period piece. A more contemporary note has been struck by Marshall McLuhan, perhaps revving up for another season guruwise, in an article in *The Canadian Imagination*, edited by David Staines. Mr. McLuhan has reshuffled the whole question of Canadian and American identity into what amounts to a superior put-down. He argues that "Since the United States has become a world environment, Canada has become the anti-environment that renders the United States more acceptable and intelligible to many small countries of the world." He goes on to describe "lands long blessed by strong identities" (by which I hope he means the U.S.), as "bewildered by the growing perforation and porousness of their identity image in this electronic age." This is masterly: what could be more devastating than to force 200 million Americans, already wracked by self-analysis, to worry about being at one and the same time full of holes and sopping up everything. It calls to my mind a fine image: an IBM punch card made of blotting paper. The United States?

If I were a Canadian, I am not sure I would accept being an anti-environment. But if, out of an anti-environment, a writer can produce such a really cool anti-Americanism, it might be worthwhile.

In this area Mr. Richler is the best thing that has happened to date. In the first place, he clearly knows the United States as only someone who has grown up with its culture can. Better, in fact; he is careful not to allow us to appropriate anything not rightfully ours: in pointing out that Superman (as well, of course, as his meatball double Clark Kent) was created by a Canadian. All that is necessary is for Richler to write his next novel about the United States.

Mr. Richler says Canadians are too polite to say, "Send us more Japs," but he is having us on. He himself has a literary effrontery few Americans can approach. I am thinking of his corrupt Eskimo in *The Incomparable Atuk*. No American writer would dare be so free with an American Indian. But when Atuk, who is a self-taught Eskimo poet, begins to make the cultural scene in Toronto and changes his poetic style accordingly, he does so in a wholly American tradition. "I have seen the best seal hunters of my generation putrefy raving die from tuberculosis," he recites. Similarly, when Atuk argues with Rory, the bourgeois Zionist about the Eskimos' right to repossess the lands of their ancestors and tells him not only that "to us, you're all Arabs," but worse, "Jewish, Protestant, you're all white to me," it is clear that this is much too sweeping a satire to be appropriated by one relatively unpopulated northern country. Mr. Richler means us, too, whether he admits it or not.

3_____QUEBEC INDEPENDENCE

René Lévesque

After the Seven Years' War and the conquest of New France, Old England was particularly strapped for money and went after it with a vengeance in the colonies. The Boston Massacre followed in 1770, and then, even more decisive, the Boston Tea Party, which opened the door in 1773 to the ultimate demand of independence—a demand for which one of the greatest advocates and international salesmen was that illustrious son of Boston, Benjamin Franklin, who tirelessly, from one capital to another, pleaded, negotiated, charmed, and intrigued for the cause, until finally it was recognized by all in 1783.

Thus, the collective liberty of a small nation of three million people, small even when compared with contemporaneous major European countries, was imposed on the greatest power of all. And it showed the way to others: France in 1789; South America in the early 19th century.

So the American example, begun in Boston, inspired many people on their own path to national emancipation. And it still does, remaining one of the greatest proofs of the validity of national existence for the progress of nations and the evolution of mankind.

I am confident, therefore, that here in Boston, here at Harvard, there will be, if not necessarily agreement, a basic understanding of our aspirations. And here, too, I know that among many there is a solid knowledge of Quebec, just a few hundred miles away, and of its Canadian environment; of the uncertain perspectives arising out of very rapid change over the last generation or so, particularly in our Quebec society, and the way the fallout affects the whole of Canada.

Some Vital Statistics

I was warned, before my visit, that some Americans may suffer slightly from that minor visual defect bred by proximity, a sort of farsightedness that makes a situation blurred, even uninteresting, when it is too close. China is more exotic, or Africa, than good gray Canada (as it is usually called), even when it works itself into a small turmoil. So let me offer a few vital statistics about Quebec.

First: with 636,000 square miles (most of it a northern vision, but nevertheless there), Quebec is the equivalent of about 18% of the United States land mass. Physically, it is rather visible. Quebec's population of 6-1/4 million people, however, is only about 3% of that of the United States. Still, we are in a world where 78 of the now 155 recognized sovereign states have less than 5 million people. Quebec counts among the top 77 in population. That is the second important statistic.

Third: our Gross Provincial Product for 1977, for the first time, crossed the 50 billion dollar mark. And the year before, 1976, per capita production was over $7,400 (U.S.), putting Quebec's production ahead of all but a handful of the most economically advanced national societies in the world. Quebec is highly industrialized and solidly based on hydroelectric power, on forest and mineral resources, and even more so on the human society. Our society for a long time was considered, justifiably, to be behind the times. It has mostly caught up, is as competent, well trained, and educated as other industrialized societies.

The Roots of Quebec's Discontent

The picture of our society is not one of misery or persecution comparable to many parts of the world. But everyone is familiar with the perception of unfairness, or inequality, or injustice, which is tied to one's environment. You compare yourself with others, with people in your neighborhood, and with your peers. That is where the feeling grows.

The results of over 110 years of Canadian federal institutions, with their consistent preferences in economic and development policies, have led Quebec to build a strong feeling of being too often overlooked and neglected and even the object of discrimination. The feeling is essentially one of a colonial people (although no doubt a well-fed colonial people). As in other countries where an important segment, though smaller than the majority, feels more or less cooped up, depending on circumstances, in institutions that are controlled outside themselves, we in Quebec are an inner colony. The feeling of being cooped up inside the Canadian structure, inhibited, basically dependent, has been growing in Quebec over many years, and it is based primarily on the following statistic.

More than 80% of Quebec's people are French, and that is not folklore or museum French. It is a language with its own accent, its own quirks, its North American flavor (we are old North Americans). It is not only a living language; it is also vibrantly alive because it is the essential tool of communication, of cultural expression. It is the tool of everything: work, play, love, for practically each and every one of five million people.

The central fact of language makes Quebec the one Canadian province out of ten which is radically (in the root sense of the word) different from the rest of Canada. It makes Quebec the home base, the homeland, of a compact, very deeply rooted, and rapidly evolving cultural group: a cultural group—there should be no mistake—which sees itself as a national group. Democratic control of provincial institutions in Quebec supplies the Quebec people with a powerful springboard for self-affirmation and self-determination. And self-determination is rooted in the tradition of democracy, in bills of rights internationally recognized, in the rights of different peoples to choose their own institutions.

Since the French people in Quebec are surrounded by a continental ocean of English-speaking people both in Canada and in the United States, the question is often asked: "Why don't you just give up the ghost? What is the use of holding on and going on, more and more insistently in recent years, having all that noise and that confrontation and tension about your century-old and eminently respectable political structure? After all, all of us in North America—the United States, Canada, even Mexico—we are all under federal systems, federal institutions and structures. Nobody has been complaining all that much until now; why not go on? If it has been good for the United States, and not so bad for Canada, apparently, why are you guys in Quebec raising such a ruckus, such a lot of sound and fury about the whole thing—even talking about opting out of such a good deal?"

These questions make it look as if we came from the same mold, but words can be misleading. The vocabulary is basically the same, but I want to emphasize how false is the impression. The federal system, modern style, was invented by Americans; it was a free people, recently emancipated, that invented its own set of institutions. In our case, the story was not exactly the same. In Canada, one hundred years later, there was not much debate, nor much consultation. There was certainly no great interest except among Canadian Pacific lawyers and other railroad builders. It started with four colonies, which were still colonies, and which were resigned to remaining colonies for some time to come.

Those four colonies, Quebec included, were the starting point of federal Canada. They were still tied closely to the imperial parliament in London and all of them worried about American expansionism. America was talking about manifest destiny and flexing its muscles all over the place. To try to hold on to the bits north of the United States that were left to the British realm and to cement them together, a colonial adaptation of the federal system was devised. It was established by a decree of a European parliament.

There is an even more basic contrast. Two hundred years ago, the unity of the United States was firmly established on a uniform basis of language and culture; English was the one and only vehicle for a tradition built from the Pilgrim Fathers to the Puritan tradition. That was strong enough to sustain the melting pot, integrating immigrants from all over into an organized and essentially united nation.

In Canada, when our federal system developed, some 40% of the population was French. More than 25% still is, with a language, tradition, cultural outlook, and aspirations different from those of the English-speaking majority. I believe that the most essential ingredient determining whether a political structure works, whether it has staying power, does not depend on it being federal or unitary. It depends, rather, on cultural and national homogeneity.

And that is the story of Quebec. Not only are we a different cultural body, a different society in many ways, but among all European settlers we were the first on this continent (excluding Mexico). We were the first discoverers, the first pioneers, the first settlers, and now our roots go back a bit further than those of Boston, 370 years. We have worked the same land. We were born on it in the Valley of the St. Lawrence; all our forefathers are buried there. The tradition is tied also to a language which made us different; it is not our fault, but we keep going on. It is tied to the fact that there is this will, with the ups and downs we shared throughout the generations, of staying together. And now it is also tied to something which ties up with the central misunderstanding of our federal institutions.

A nation is made in 370 years. Nationalism often has a bad connotation, but it can be either positive or negative. Quebec nationalism, the tie to home, and the driving aspirations, the urge for development, is not anti-anyone; it is pro-us. I think it is positive, a national feeling of a national group deeply rooted, durable for the future. There lies the central misunderstanding of the whole Canadian structure.

Two Solitudes

From the very start, Canadian federalism has been a dialogue of the deaf. To the English majority in Canada, we are nothing. The feeling has not been hidden very well through history. We are little more than a conquered and dependent minority. The English hoped this relatively small group would dwindle and eventually fade away like old soldiers.

When Canada was devised structurally, the main effort on the English-Canadian side was to develop federal institutions as central and powerful as possible. The French view was exactly the opposite. The federal system was looked upon as decentralization, enhancing, in American parlance, a state power, state rights, and a better chance for the future. And the French dreamt a normal dream for any cultural, national group—that somewhere, sometime, the nation would achieve self-government.

This competing vision of the founding explains, in a nutshell, the century of two solitudes. More recently, since World War II and especially since the "Quiet Revolution" of the 60s, Quebec at a dizzying speed has come of age; what used to be called "cheap-labor Quebec," "priest-ridden," a folkloric society, is growing by leaps and bounds.

We are entitled, like all societies, to this growth, but the structures have become a constraint on our development. Quebec and Ottawa have been at loggerheads practically on a permanent basis for the last 35 years. Quebec citizens have been caught up in a schizophrenic tug-of-war between the two levels of government for which they pay, with an incredible waste of energy, of time, of resources and, more worrisome, with an evergrowing danger of bad blood between the two communities.

The Growth of the Parti Québécois

It is in the context of two solitudes and federal-provincial discord that the *Parti Québécois* (PQ) grew from a few hundred members in 1967 to 23% of the voters in the first election three years later, in 1970. We polled 31% in 1973 and we emerged as the official opposition. In 1976 we became the government with a 41% plurality.

The *Parti Québécois* is the first political party in the Western world, as far as I know, to rise from nothing to become the government while refusing, year after year, any money from any group—either corporate on the right or union on the left—because groups do not vote. We made it a basic principle to keep them at arm's length. No slush funds. With thousands of canvassers all over the place, door to door, we solicited citizens' money, which is not supposed to be, of course, a serious factor in politics. It was serious enough to build a party into the government of a society of six million people. And our government has passed Bill No. 2, the legislation of which I am proudest, requiring all parties to open their books.

When people start, subtly or otherwise, to give us lessons in basic democracy, they should come to see how democracy now works in Quebec. We are in a very imperfect world where democracy has never quite been a reality, but we are the most staunchly dedicated to democracy of all parties anywhere in the Western world. We were elected promising good government, and over the last 16 months we have tried to do the job. We intend to keep government clean.

Sovereignty-Association and the Referendum

We were elected for good government. We were also elected on a platform of sovereignty with association. Those are two key words, "sovereignty" and "association," and we are committed to a democratic referendum about them before the next election. The enabling legislation is passing laboriously, for the wheels of parliament turn slowly, but the referendum will be held as promised.

Many people say the referendum creates uncertainty in Canada and in Quebec. In fact, uncertainty has been with us because of the many misconceptions and misunderstandings, grown in like barnacles, around our federal structures. Uncertainty has been with us for 35 years. It has shaken Canada's structures and the relationship between Quebec and Canada. For the first time, we are offering a chance to get rid of uncertainty, to get rid of it democratically, when people have had a chance to make up their minds, to be consulted, to get information. It is up to Quebecers to decide what they want. It will be the first chance ever for our people to decide for themselves about their institutions and about the whole future of their community.

If Quebecers vote as we hope, then soon afterwards we will acquire sovereignty, self-government. To use a good phrase of basic democracy, there would be no more representation of Quebec in

Ottawa because no more taxation would go to Ottawa from Quebec.

The trend is universal. There were 50 recognized sovereign countries when World War II ended. Now there are 155, and many are comparable to Quebec. Denmark and Norway each has 4 million people; there are 6 million in Switzerland and 8 million in Sweden. These countries are leaders, not just in standard of living, but also in many other accomplishments. No fraternal counsels, no propaganda, will convince us that 6 million should give up the ghost and not pursue democratically normal accomplishments. It is the trend of the last half century.

In addition to sovereignty, we have been proposing from the beginning what we call "association." It is inspired by another universal trend; it is not contradictory. We are convinced that it is just as inevitable as sovereignty. Whatever its eventual shape—whether as a customs union or a common market—it will require still further research and study. The most open-minded people in the rest of Canada, however, are now giving it serious consideration, even though the present climate is hostile. Those courageous enough to look are becoming convinced that some form of association is common sense, responding to the real, hard facts of the situation.

Consequences of Sovereignty-Association

Politically, Canada without Quebec, a lot of people say, would disintegrate. It is the old domino theory, and after all the pieces go, the huge maw next door (that's you) will just gobble it up. I think Canada has a lot of staying power. I know Canada well, both because I have lived there and because I am a former newspaperman. Without the foreign body, which more and more we are, Canada would have more coherence and a chance to reorganize according to its own views and its own preferences. Quebec is a roadblock now because Canadians fear that any change must pose the question, "What the hell is going to happen to Quebec?"

We propose association, first, in order not to "pakistanize" Canada between the Maritimes to the east of Quebec and Ontario and the rest to the west. It is not to build walls of hostility that would take years to break down again. We care about Canada. We do not care about the structures, but we care about the people. We care about the common things we have, many of them, with the Maritimes, with practically as long a tradition as ours and the same kind of outlook in many ways. We care for the fruitful relationships, very mutually profitable, between Quebec and Ontario mostly, and growing with the rest of Canada. But we also care about our own identity. There is no reason why there should be any contradiction, except for people who think that institutions become sacred because they are old. You do not change them like you change your shirt, but not because they are old do you hang on to them when they have passed their day and become obsolete, when they have become like straitjackets.

For political reasons, then, we have proposed a new association, if and when Quebec democratically decides to opt out. There is no reason why it should not be arranged on a free-flow basis. When Alaska became a state of the Union, with some 1100-1200 miles between the state of Alaska and the continental United States, I did not hear any voices of doom. Two civilized countries made arrangements about the free flow of communications and goods. In our case, it would be good for Canada, and so we should do it.

There are also economic reasons for association, recently spelled out by one of those serious minds in English Canada, in Toronto itself, a well-known and reputed economist, Abraham Rotstein, not a party member of ours. He demonstrated that 105,000 jobs next door in Ontario are tied directly to the Quebec market, and there is more or less the equivalent in Quebec facing Ontario. Western beef, with some protection, finds its major market in Quebec. The existence of the Maritimes is tied to a new rapport with Quebec. Newfoundland needs Quebec as a buyer or transmitter of its enormous undeveloped energy resources. We are initiating negotiations with Newfoundland on that subject. Prince Edward Island needs to sell potatoes to the voracious Montreal market.

The Western European Union is our inspiration. It finally gave the French and the Germans the first chance, for centuries, to bridge a chasm of blood and of world wars. Adapted to our own needs, sovereignty-association will give our two societies what we think is terribly needed leeway—breathing space—to protect us from the dangerous risk of growing too far apart.

The Challenge of Major Change

Almost everybody, even staunch federalists, even Mr. Trudeau, are at long last admitting publicly the need for a rethinking and a revamping of our political and constitutional arrangements. The temptation is always present, and I can see it in Mr. Trudeau's eyes when we meet occasionally, for the true believers of the *status quo*, for the hangers-on and the careerists, to try to sell or con people into accepting superficial arrangements, mere plastic surgery. But we are convinced that it would not work. There are too many generations of more solitudes facing each other. There is a danger of bad blood. And all the cosmetic constitutional operations over the last 25 or 50 years have failed to give Canada a truly new face.

The only true solution, from our point of view, for our two peoples, has to lie somewhere in the direction we are indicating. And there, also, lies the first chance for real understanding, the only base for mutual respect and equality and cooperation. Maybe, at long last, there is a promise of real friendship between our peoples which up until now we have not really found.

Quebec's Future with the United States

There are three to six million people with French Quebec roots all over New England. The ties are still very strong in many quarters. They still hang on to the French language because they still have relatives.

I was an habitué of Boston and Cape Cod for years and years. My three children were practically brought up for summers on end around Cape Cod. They learned English and they got warmer water. I was a working newsman for many of those years; when I wanted an instant poll, I needed only to call all the Lévesques in the phone book in practically any town of any importance in New England.

In the hometown paper is Mr. Labbé from Trois-Rivières in Quebec who has come down for the wedding of Mrs. St. Germain, blessed by Reverend Poirier, somewhere in Woonsocket; Sergeant Lemay has just come back from a tour of duty in Korea. Many of you ski in the Laurentians in Quebec, and many of you go to the Gaspé during the summer season. Like migratory birds, depending on the season, we become the majority in Ogunquit, Old Orchard, and a lot of places on Cape Cod; when the winter comes, we could elect a mayor in Miami. And it is true that Quebec investment is booming in Florida, but not because Quebec is going down the drain. The flight of capital is neither new nor exclusively Québécois. It is tied to climate.

There are other serious economic relationships besides tourism. In addition to the traditional trade in pulp and paper, iron ore, asbestos, and other slightly more sophisticated products, a new link for energy between the Power Authority of New York and Hydro Quebec will produce substantial contractual exchanges. Three and two tenths percent of all U.S. imports already come from Quebec, and that trade is growing. We get from you cars, machinery, electrical equipment. In fact, the United States, after the rest of Canada, is Quebec's most important trading partner. There is a solid base of knowledge between us, and there is, I think, mutual trust.

We know that change, especially next door, is always disturbing. When it is painted as a secessionist (we know what that brings back to mind) kind of change, it brings suspicions; it creates a favorable climate for propaganda and for distortion about what is going on in Quebec. But after all, we have to accept that we are in a world of change. When you look back 25 years, you cannot recognize the world. Who would have thought, a few years back, that the Panama Canal would have been the subject of a new treaty. It is a changing world and we have to adapt to it.

We need not necessarily agree with the present changes, but you need to understand them by finding out about them yourselves, not trusting too much those sources that are too easily available. The two sources that are most familiar to you for information about Canada, except if it is firsthand, are English-speaking Montreal, the great congregation of our minority English-speaking fellow citizens with their powerful media, who now feel they are in the eye of change, and the Ottawa federal establishment with its consulates and embassies. It, too, is hanging on for dear life to things as they are, as all establishments do. These perspectives are predictable, but they are also distorted.

You are not so far away—an hour's flight, six or seven hours' driving to Quebec or Montreal. Come in, find out for yourselves what kind of a process is going on. Is it democratic? I say it is. I say it is more than it has ever been.

You must make up your own minds, but I would like to suggest that your attitude might come close to a saying coined in France about us last year: "We follow what is going on with non-indifference, but strictly non-interference." I think you will appreciate and understand what we seek to accomplish.

Part Two

CANADA'S POSTWAR CHALLENGE:
RELATIONS WITH THE UNITED STATES

4___CANADIAN INDEPENDENCE

Walter Gordon

Two central issues concern Canada today, one domestic and one foreign. The domestic issue is the "Quebec problem"; the foreign issue is economic, especially foreign ownership of Canadian companies and resources.

The Current Canadian Economy

Let me begin with the foreign problem. The annual merchandise trade between our two countries is the highest of any two countries in the world. Adding imports and exports together, it amounted to over $50 billion last year. However, Canada's exports to the United States (more than two-thirds of Canada's total exports) are to a large extent made up of industrial raw materials, whereas U.S. exports to Canada (close to one-quarter of total U.S. exports) are largely in the form of manufactured goods. In other words, the United States has a considerable advantage in the labor content of exports.

When we take into account such invisible items as interest and dividend payments on U.S. investments in Canada, freight and travel charges, etc., Canada has incurred a deficit in its current account transactions with the United States in every year over a very long period. These deficits have been reduced to some extent by surpluses with some other countries and, much more importantly, by the capital that has come to Canada, largely from the United States.

The Canadian economy is extremely sluggish at the present time; Canada is, in fact, on the verge of a recession:

1. The Gross National Product in real terms dropped in the second quarter of 1978.
2. Unemployment is running at a seasonally adjusted rate in excess of 8%, the highest it has been since the days of the Great Depression.

3. Wage rates in many manufacturing industries are higher than in the United States, despite the fact that productivity in Canada is much lower than in the U.S.
4. The rate of inflation has been rising again and is presently said to be about 7.5%.
5. For the first half of 1977, the deficit on current account in the Canadian balance of payments was running at an annual rate of $6.5 billion. In U.S. terms, this would be the equivalent of a current account deficit of more than $65 billion in a full year.

It is true that all the oil-importing countries, including the United States, have had balance of payments problems since the oil-producing countries (OPEC) raised their prices so dramatically in 1973, but that does not make the Canadian problem any easier. It is not much wonder that the Canadian dollar, which in 1976 was at a premium in terms of the U.S. dollar, was in July 1978 down to about 88 cents U.S.

Foreign Control of the Economy

There is no doubt that foreign capital (mostly American) helped to develop the Canadian economy much more rapidly than would otherwise have been the case. (By foreign capital, I mean a package that apart from money, included management, scientific and technological know-how, and in many cases an assurance of markets for the raw materials or goods to be produced.) The economy of the United States was developed in much the same way with the aid of foreign capital in the nineteenth century (mostly from Britain). But in those days, the capital came in the form of bonds and other fixed-term securities which the United States was able to pay back out of profits.

In Canada's case, the capital came in the form of equity which ensured continuing control in the future to those who put up the funds (mostly enterprising American corporations). It is this continuing foreign control of the most dynamic industries that concerns Canadians, especially as these industries continue to expand. Many Canadians believe that non-residents control too much of their resources and their business enterprises. Foreign control accounts for approximately 60% of all manufacturing companies, 70% of all mining enterprises, 99% of petroleum refining, 80% of the oil and gas industry (including exploration and development), 95% of the automobile industry, 90% of the rubber industry, 80% of the chemical industry, three-quarters of electrical apparatus, and so on.

In an article in the August 1977 issue of *Fortune*, entitled "Why the Multinational Tide is Ebbing," it is asserted that "some kinds of American corporations are still powerhouses abroad, but the basic attractions of overseas investment have vanished." The article suggests that the urge for U.S. corporations to make direct investment abroad is declining.

In a reference to Canada, the article states:

> Ironically, Canada, which among advanced nations is perhaps the most rabidly opposed to American investment, may have the most to lose from discouraging this investment. It can be argued that the more foreign investment a country has, the more it is likely to benefit from additional investment. The inflow of foreign capital raises the productivity of domestic labor by increasing the amount of capital per worker. Hence real wages rise. At the same time, the new foreign investment should increase domestic competition, driving down prices and thereby lowering the returns to capital. If the capitalists are mostly Americans, which is overwhelmingly the case in Canada, then additional U.S. foreign investment would logically transfer income from American business to Canadian labor and consumers—a circumstance that most Canadians should applaud.

I have three comments to make about these assertions:

1. If Canada is "rabidly opposed to American investment," it is surprising that nothing of substance has been done to restrain it.
2. If "inflow of foreign capital raises the productivity of domestic labor...," why is productivity in Canada so very much lower than it is in the United States?
3. If "the new foreign investment should increase domestic competition...," why has this not been the case?

The article reads like an apologia for U.S. multinational corporations. It is unconvincing to a Canadian like myself. There are many reasons why I believe excessive foreign control of the Canadian economy is not in Canada's best interests. But here I will concentrate on only two of them.

As I have said, some 60% of all Canadian manufacturing is controlled abroad. A typical Canadian subsidiary may be encouraged or directed by its parent corporation to import parts or materials from its parent or the latter's associates instead of developing alternative sources of supply in Canada. Moreover, a typical Canadian subsidiary frequently is not permitted to develop export markets for its products, including markets in the United States, in competition with its parent. While this prohibition is quite understandable, it tends in both cases to reduce job opportunities in Canada and to increase the deficit in the balance of payments.

The largest manufacturers in Canada, as in the United States, are the automobile companies whose operations come under the U.S.-Canada auto pact. According to a recent review of the financial statements of General Motors Corporation (worldwide) and General Motors Canada, the Canadian subsidiary assembled 8.3% of all the vehicles produced by the corporation. However, it does considerably less actual manufacturing than is done in the United States. Consequently, it accounts for only 4.2% of worldwide employment and 4.5% of worldwide payrolls. The Canadian company's payroll represents only 12.5% of the manufactured cost of a car in Canada compared to 33.9% worldwide. It follows that while General Motors is assembling a large number of vehicles in Canada, it is not doing a satisfactory job in terms of employment opportunities.

Consider also the influence of the principal oil companies in Canada, most of them subsidiaries of large U.S. corporations. Prior to 1970, Canadians were informed that they had conventional reserves of crude oil and natural gas that would last 900 and 400 years, respectively. Then, some four years later, new estimates warned of shortages. While both sets of estimates were announced by the Canadian government authorities, inevitably they were based on data supplied by the oil companies. The earlier estimates presumably were based on optimistic expectations of the amount of oil that would prove available in the Alberta basin. They came at a time when the oil companies were urging the Canadian government to persuade the United States to accept more imports from Canada. However, the hopes about the quantities of oil available in Alberta were not substantiated by drilling results. By the time the much lower estimates were announced, and with the new information available, the objectives of the oil companies had changed. By that time, they were urging the Canadian government to approve very substantial price increases, ostensibly to provide them with additional funds with which to step up their exploration activities in Canada.

Perhaps Canadian officials were naive in accepting data supplied to them by the oil companies; they at least might have told the public of the assumptions on which the estimates were based and the uncertainties surrounding such assumptions. Such caution regarding the accuracy of the estimates was of particular importance, as in both cases the reserve estimates supported the objectives of the oil companies at the time; in the first place, to justify increased exports to the United States, and in the second, to justify substantial increases in prices in order to stimulate exploration in the light of serious shortages. This may have been only a matter of coincidence. If so, it was a remarkably favorable coincidence for the oil companies.

Solutions to the Problem of Foreign Ownership

There are several alternatives for dealing with the foreign control problem. The one I have suggested from time to time is that members of the Canadian Parliament should express by resolution the view that the foreign owners of the larger Canadian subsidiary companies should gradually over a period of years sell out to Canadians. By "larger" I mean foreign-controlled companies with assets in excess of $250 million. At the end of 1973, there were only 32 of them, which would make the problem manageable. The seven or eight thousand other foreign-controlled Canadian companies would be left alone unless and until their total assets reached the $250 million mark.

I have suggested that the transfer of ownership should take place in stages over a period of years, beginning with companies in the oil and gas and other resource fields. An estimate of the total cost of the 32 companies in question would come to perhaps as much as $15 billion to be paid by Canadian investors (not the Canadian government) over a period of 10 years. This amount would be well within Canada's financial capabilities.

It would be up to the owners to decide how the changes in control should be accomplished. In many cases, it would simply be a matter of selling the shares of their Canadian subsidiaries for cash through underwriters. In some cases, the Canada Development Corporation or some new federal or provincial agencies established for the purpose might buy control. In still others, it might be necessary to sell control not for cash but for some form of debentures redeemable over a period of years.

The advantages of this proposal would be that:

1. No legislation would be required and there would be no need for sanctions.
2. Only 32 companies would be affected.
3. The companies would not be nationalized.
4. It would be left to the foreign owners to decide how to go about

selling the shares of their subsidiaries to Canadians. They would have plenty of time to work things out.

I should make it quite clear that the Canadian government has shown no disposition to do anything along the lines suggested. Nevertheless, the American Ambassador to Canada, Thomas Enders, has explained United States policy regarding such possible changes as follows:

The United States believes the free flow of private investment capital between countries can make a major contribution to the prosperity of each country, and should be interfered with as little as possible.

However, should a foreign country nationalize or buy into U.S. enterprise for an authentic public purpose, the United States would not oppose the transaction provided full, effective and prompt compensation is made.[1]

Specific Causes of Tension

Let us consider some other specific matters that are now, or could in the future become, the cause of tension between our two countries.

There are no very serious or basic differences between Canada and the United States in the fields of defense and foreign policy at the present time. The U.S. government would have liked Canada to take an active part in the war in Vietnam and no doubt would like Canada to spend more money on defense. But from a Canadian point of view, this would not make sense.

Occasionally, Canada has taken initiatives in its foreign policy, which at the time may have appeared to be contrary to the then current posture of the United States. For example, after long negotiations, Canada established diplomatic relations with the People's Republic of China in 1971. As things turned out, this was a useful prelude to the wholly identical relations that now prevail between the United States and China. However, in this world of superpowers, there are decided limits to what a country like Canada can do. Moreover, as your closest friends and neighbors, we think it fair to say that, as a rule, Canadian and American views and objectives are much the same. I do not expect serious tensions to arise in this general field.

There is the question of a common energy policy for North America which, from time to time, your government authorities have suggested. Canada has not thought this would be desirable from its standpoint. The amount of our conventional reserves of oil and gas is limited, and, even if Canada were to increase exports to the U.S., it would have only a marginal effect on U.S. requirements. Canadians who have any knowledge of the subject will expect their government authorities to safeguard Canada's reserves for domestic use.

A recent issue of *The Canadian Forum* was devoted to a discussion of a gas pipeline from Alaska to the "lower 48," i.e., to the central United States, through Canada. All the contributors opposed the construction of the pipeline at the present time. The reasons included the fact that, as far as Canada is concerned, only a disappointing amount of natural gas has been discovered so far in the Canadian Arctic; the prospects seem to be for greater discoveries in the south, in Alberta itself, than in the Mackenzie Delta. Other reasons for not proceeding with the project now are the desirability of settling the land claims of the native peoples before, not after, the construction of a pipeline, and the supposed damage the construction would do, both to the ecology of the region and the social mores of the natives. I have not agreed with these conclusions and, in a newspaper article published in June 1977, expressed my own views in the following terms:

> An early decision on the pipeline issue is both necessary and desirable because the United States desperately needs the natural gas that has been discovered in large quantities in Prudhoe Bay, Alaska. From the point of view of the Americans, the best way of transporting this gas to the markets is by a pipeline through Canada.
>
> Only limited quantities of Canadian gas have been discovered in the Beaufort Sea area (of Canada) so far, and the potential for further discoveries in the high Arctic may be less than in Alberta itself. It follows that Canadian requirements for natural gas can be taken care of from existing and potential reserves in the south for a good many years during which time the native land claims could be settled.
>
> But the Americans are our friends and neighbors and surely it would be unthinkable for Canada to refuse them access to their gas in Alaska even if approval for a pipeline at an early date may complicate the settlement of native Canadian land claims.
>
> While it would be quite wrong for Canada to refuse permission for a gas pipeline to be built, we would be foolish not to point out to the U.S. the disadvantages to us in proceeding immediately rather than later and to make certain conditions to giving the necessary approvals.

In the first place, it should be agreed that any Canadian gas exported to the United States from now on under existing contracts should be repaid by equal quantities of Alaskan gas, at the same prices, as soon as the pipeline is completed.

Secondly, we should point out the effect a huge inflow of capital needed to finance the line would have on Canada's balance of payments and the exchange rate for the Canadian dollar. This would be an ideal time to offset this inflow of capital by an equivalent outflow represented by the cost of acquiring control of some of the large foreign-owned companies in this country.

And thirdly, in the light of our present unemployment problem, we should insist that priority be given to Canadians and Canadian manufacturers in connection with all phases of the pipeline construction. There is no doubt that under present conditions, the construction of a pipeline from Alaska could do much to relieve the unemployment problem.

Finally, we should insist on measures to protect and safeguard the lives and social habits of the native peoples near the areas to be traversed by the pipeline.

Recently, President Carter and Prime Minister Trudeau announced that they had agreed upon the construction of a natural gas pipeline from Alaska through Alberta along the route of the Alaskan Highway. In doing so, they did not spell out the conditions as specifically as I for one might have thought desirable. However, it is now decided the pipeline will be constructed if it is approved by Congress and the Canadian Parliament. This removes what might have caused serious tensions between our countries.

Canada will be exporting large amounts of electric power to the United States when the huge development in James Bay is completed. Canadians do not seem to object any longer to the export of water power in the form of electricity. But any suggestion that Canada should consider the export of fresh water itself, even if at present it is being wasted in rivers or glaciers emptying into the Arctic or Pacific Oceans, would have Canadians up in arms. This may not seem logical to Americans. But then the United States' tremendous arms exports to the Middle East and, formerly, Iran may seem to others to lack a certain common sense. In other words, the human animal is not always very rational in its thoughts or actions.

I suppose there will always be issues that affect particular industries in particular sections of the country and, therefore, provoke individual Senators or Congressmen to speech, if not to action. The recent row over Canada's decision to disallow as deductions for income tax purposes payments to U.S. television stations for advertising beamed at Canadian audiences is a case in point. Two others that come to mind are disagreements over fishing rights and the question of pollution in the Great Lakes. But such issues are not of very serious proportions.

Conclusion

In conclusion, I always ask my American friends to keep in mind that, by and large, Canadians are your friends, your neighbors, and your allies. We are probably the best friends you have in this dangerous and troubled world.

But please remember that Canada is a separate, sovereign nation and wants to remain that way. We do not like it when American businessmen—sometimes with the best will in the world—treat Canada as if it were just another state of the Union.

I am not exaggerating when I say that we have great admiration for the United States and for all that Americans have accomplished. We acknowledge that we rely on the United States for our defense. We have no alternative, of course, in this age of superpowers.

But this does not mean we would like to become the fifty-first state of the Union. And it does not mean that the United States would wish to have us, even if we did.

The best solution, I submit, is for each of us, Canadians and Americans, to respect one another's independence—to try to understand each other's problems—but whatever happens, to remain good friends.

NOTES

1. Personal conversation between the Hon. Thomas Enders and the author.

4___CANADIAN INDEPENDENCE

COMMENT

Willis Armstrong

Mr. Gordon's chief point concerns investment in Canada by American firms or individuals—what he calls "foreign control of the economy." His specific proposal is the purchase by Canadians of some 32 companies which are foreign-controlled and which represent the biggest chunk of foreign equity in Canada. Such a requirement would result in the public sale of these companies under conditions which would be prejudicial to the owners; i.e., the sale would be a forced one, and the bids would consequently not be as large as those which a free market would produce.

Mr. Gordon has set forth correctly the official U.S. position on nationalization: if undertaken, it should be for a public purpose and should be followed by prompt, adequate, and effective compensation. Putting companies on a proscribed list, thereby reducing the value of their shares, does not meet the criterion of effective compensation. He would say his proposal is not nationalization. I would call it creeping nationalization of the kind in which many developing countries engage.

More important, however, is the fact that the U.S. investments of which he disapproves were made with the full and often vigorous support of Canadian governments, national and provincial. (He admits that Canada experienced rapid growth as a result of the influx of this foreign capital.) Changing the rules for investment after the fact is very common these days and has produced a negative attitude toward future investment.

Mr. Gordon never mentions the fact that Canada already has acted in protectionist fashion without nationalization. The Foreign Investment Review Act, passed some time ago, has resulted in the screening of foreign investment. The criteria in the act are reduced to one very simple test: Is the investment "good for Canada?" The administrator of the act must decide. Clearly the test is one which will invite differences of opinions among Canadians, depending upon the particular investment and the attendant circumstances.

Economic Difficulties and Foreign Investment

There can be no disagreement with Mr. Gordon's analysis of the state of the Canadian economy. Our two countries face much the same problems—inflation, insufficient sound growth, unemployment, and an inability to formulate policies which will produce the necessary economic adjustments. Perhaps the problems are more intense in Canada because it is a less diversified and smaller economy. But one should not overlook the fact that Canada is a very rich country with a high standard of living, which has had an extraordinary growth rate since World War II. The current stagnation may only be a temporary pause, since Canada has great resources which the world needs.

Mr. Gordon states that productivity in Canada is much lower than in the United States, which may well be the case. But it might be still lower if there had been no investment from the United States. Furthermore, U.S. productivity figures in recent years include increases in agricultural productivity which have been extraordinary. Mr. Gordon asserts that domestic competition has not been increased in Canada as a result of foreign investment. I flatly disagree.

Mr. Gordon complains of the strictures placed by American parent companies on their subsidiaries in Canada—i.e., they may not export, often must buy parts from the parent company, etc. Certainly these rules are limiting, but less so in terms of employment than if the investment had not been made at all. Further, the American establishment of a subsidiary in a market protected by a high tariff is simply a response to Canadian government policy dating from John A. Macdonald.

Consequences of the Gordon Proposals

Mr. Gordon's proposal for the sale to Canadians of all major U.S. companies in Canada would tear up the Canada-U.S. automobile pact, which has resulted in an enormous transfer of economic activity from the United States to Canada, to the detriment, in the opinion of many, of the U.S. economy. His drastic measure would disrupt all sorts of industrial relationships for companies, resulting in questions of supply and marketing, patent rights, and access to basic technology. The U.S. companies might well sell under pressure, but there would be no guarantee of any continuing relationship between the present company and its former subsidiary in technology or business or finance. The orphans might not survive.

Canadian Resources and the United States

Mr. Gordon is unhappy about the unreliability of forecasts made by oil and gas people regarding Canada's reserves. Oil is where and when you find it, and sometimes people are disappointed. The fact is that the oil companies and their natural gas counterparts, providing their own financing, gave Canada a great deal of cheap energy and even made Canada a major exporter for a fair period of time. Would such a result have been obtained if the oil and gas companies had not been welcomed by Canada's provinces, which are in charge of natural resources?

Mr. Gordon's comments on the oil companies sound like President Carter's. Oil companies' rates of profit are in fact about average for all industry and are nothing very extraordinary, in Canada or the U.S. There has been a decline in investment in oil and gas in both countries, attributable in large part to adverse government policies. On occasion, government authorities in the U.S. have spoken of a common energy policy with Canada. In fact, what has occurred tends to be a rational use of resources by two independent sovereignties, although both are sufficiently negative toward oil companies to limit the potentialities of the business.

Mr. Gordon's support for a trans-Canada pipeline to bring gas from Alaska to the "lower 48" is welcome. But this altruistic gesture has a string attached. He would use the U.S. need for its own gas as a lever to force the sale of U.S. private entities in Canada—a condition to which one must reply: "Not one cent for tribute!" Such attitudes as Mr. Gordon's illustrate the wisdom of putting the Alaska oil pipeline beyond Canadian reach. His insistence on a "Buy Canadian" requirement for equipment for a gas pipeline in Canada is really unnecessary; Canadian business, being on the spot, has a built-in advantage which needs no reinforcement through discriminatory rules.

I agree with Mr. Gordon that the export of water from Canada is an emotional issue, whereas the export of electric power made from falling water is not. Only a Canadian could understand why.

Conclusion

We are confronted, in Mr. Gordon's presentation, with the face of economic nationalism, which is an authentic and genuine trend in today's world. It leads to highly uneconomic and senseless actions which make employment less available, and goods and services more expensive, for the people whose emotions are meant to be assuaged by the actions taken. Economic nationalism comes easily to people who are themselves comfortable, and who do not take account of the impact their proposals might have on the farmer, the wage earner, the consumer and average citizen. The world is increasingly global in its economic activity, and the most efficient possible arrangements in capital, labor, and resources will be necessary if the doubled world population is to obtain its minimum requirements in the year 2000.

Canada can make a great contribution and become even more wealthy and successful in the process if it follows open market principles, instead of cutting off its nose to spite its face, as Mr. Gordon proposes. The issue he raises is one of political versus economic values in an area where these values share little or no common ground. Nationalism can be a stimulus to economic activity, or it can be counterproductive. To propose that scarce capital in Canada be used to acquire what would become inefficient industries without necessary international connections, in an era when ownership is an obscure and relatively unimportant issue, is no service to the people of Canada. Such problems as would be created for Americans would probably be less significant, but the atmosphere between our two countries would certainly be soured if his proposal were to be implemented.

5_____TENSIONS OVER COMMUNICATIONS

Frank W. Peers

Every nation must provide within itself the means of maintaining stability. In North America today this function is largely directed and exercised through the communications media....

Communications are the thread which binds together the fibers of a nation. They can protect a nation's values and encourage their practice. They can make democratic government possible and better government probable. They can soften sectional asperities and bring honorable compromises.... The communications of a nation are as vital to its life as its defences, and should receive at least as great a measure of national protection....

The tremendous expansion of communications in the United States has given that nation the world's most penetrating and effective apparatus for the transmission of ideas. Canada, more than any other country, is naked to that force, exposed unceasingly to a vast network of communications which reaches to every corner of our land; American words, images and print—the good, the bad, the indifferent—batter unrelentingly at our eyes and ears.

Report of the Royal
Commission on Publications
1961

To many Americans the issue of communications, as it affects Canada and the United States, is merely a struggle for advertising revenues. To argue that the issue is cultural more than economic, some say, is clearly specious.[1] To a Canadian observer, however, the purely economic interpretation seems exceedingly narrow, its emphasis misplaced. It does not take into account Canada's preoccupation with the instruments of transportation and communication as prerequisites of its nationhood. To a country strung out over thousands of miles, with its centers of population spaced at irregular intervals like beads on a string, with the rock formation of the

Canadian shield jutting down from Hudson Bay to separate the western and central provinces, the maintenance of transportation and communication links is vital.

Throughout Canada's history, the means of providing transportation and communication could not be developed or considered without reference to the United States. Canadian rail links dominated nineteenth century concerns, and in the twentieth century, the creation of radio and television networks had explicit national purposes.[2] For the early proponents of a publicly-owned broadcasting service, it was a case of "The State, or the United States,"[3] and ever since the creation of the Canadian Broadcasting Corporation (CBC), Canada has struggled to sustain a communications system independent of the United States, a struggle which frequently has contributed to conflict and misunderstanding. In the 1970s, conflict has focused especially on television and magazines.

American Influence on Canadian Broadcasting

Despite the British model which led to the creation of the CBC, Canada remained a North American country with a political ideology and market ethos resembling that prevailing in the United States. Political leaders were unwilling to oppose the private ownership of the majority of radio stations or, later, television.

The public enterprise was given chief responsibility to produce Canadian programs and to ensure that all sections of the country were provided with a suitable variety of radio and television services. The cooperation between public and private broadcasters needed to make the system work required a strong coordinating and regulating body. The Canadian Radio-Television and Telecommunications Commission (CRTC) corresponds roughly to the American FCC, but it has more specific responsibilities to ensure that all stations and networks fulfill the purposes laid down in the Broadcasting Act. Accordingly, and because Canada lacks any constitutional equivalent of the First Amendment, the CRTC is expected to be vigilant in assessing the program performance of licensed stations and networks, and in ensuring that "the programming provided by each broadcaster should be of high standard, using predominantly Canadian creative and other resources."[4]

For stations and networks that operate as commercial enterprises the temptation to use as much program material from American sources as the CRTC will tolerate is irresistible. American television programs, for example, can be imported at a fraction of the cost that it would take to produce even the simplest Canadian equivalent. American producers recover their costs through sales to their domestic market; any further distribution is gravy. A Canadian buyer, therefore, can purchase rights to release programs at very reasonable rates. Most programs have been pretested to assure their mass appeal, and the program tastes of a Canadian audience tend to be very similar to those of an American audience, particularly in English-speaking Canada. Indeed, the popular taste may well be conditioned by the program fare that customarily has been made available. Because there are no physical barriers to radio signals crossing national boundaries, a similar conditioning affects Canadians and Americans alike. Furthermore, the strong American influences on the popular culture of most western nations is well known; they are particularly evident in Canada.

Many Canadians share American values and tastes; they like American entertainment; as measured by audience ratings, Canadians prefer light entertainment programs of American origin. Quebec is exceptional, for French-speaking Canadians, on the whole, prefer their own programs to those imported from France or other French-speaking countries. American programs dubbed into French are popular, but do not have the impact of the series that are produced in Montreal.

Without government intervention, American advantages associated with economies of scale, common language, and similar tastes would lead to an American domination of broadcasting in Canada. Canadian policy, however, is the deliberate product of the Broadcasting Act. The defense of independent communications is central to Canada's nationhood.

Cable Television and Expanded American Influence

Cable television increased Canada's vulnerability to the United States. The principal reason for the rapid growth of cable television in the 1960s in Canada was that distant American signals could be brought to many new viewers. In the larger cities, where cable provided more choice and clearer pictures, the television audience is fragmented among many more stations and channels.

There have been two main effects. First, local Canadian stations cannot promise to deliver the same size of audience to their advertisers, and thus their income and profitability are threatened.

Second, since viewers now have more American choices, the proportion of the audience that will be watching Canadian productions at any given time is much diminished. Canadian broadcasting stations have responsibilities imposed on them by statute and by the CRTC. To the extent that their revenues are cut by cable competition, the announced objectives for the Canadian broadcasting system are also threatened.

The CRTC has warned that the unbridled growth of cable television is such a threat, but attempts to curb the importation of distant American signals have been thwarted by the public outcry, a sign that by now the reception of American network service is regarded by many Canadians as a right rather than a privilege.

The CRTC realized, after assuming office in 1968, that unless cable television were regulated closely, as an instrument of national policy, the broadcasting system laboriously developed in the preceding 35 years might come tumbling down. Canadian viewing by cable has grown from 15% of viewers in 1968 to 50% a decade later.

As early as February 1971, Pierre Juneau, the CRTC chairman, warned, "The danger to the Canadian broadcasting system is real and immediate.... A solution must be found if the Canadian broadcasting system is to survive."[5] Two years later, he told the Association of Canadian Advertisers, "If we can't maintain and develop a broadcasting system, Canada may remain some kind of trading mechanism but I doubt it will remain a country."[6] The same year, in a speech before the Canadian Association of Broadcasters, he was more specific:

> In some communities like Thunder Bay...Canadian audiences have diminished by over 20%. In Vancouver, American channels had more than 50% of all viewing as early as 1970. Averaged nationally, the audience loss is 6%. If this loss is directly related to advertising revenue, it can be mathematically calculated at a loss of 11 million dollars per year for Canadian stations. While this appears small, it represents almost twice what the CTV network (private Canadian TV) can afford to spend annually on the purchase of Canadian content programming.[7]

In April 1975, when Mr. Juneau spoke, the full impact of cable was yet to come. A number of important centers, such as Calgary, Edmonton, and Halifax, had only recently been licensed for cable. In the first year Calgary received television by cable, a station in Spokane, 275 miles away, set up a sales office in Calgary to attract Canadian advertisers.

Strong ill-feeling and resentment developed against the commercial competition of American TV stations in cities close to the border, especially where Canadian population exceeded the neighboring American towns. A station had long been established in Bellingham, Washington (population: 35,000), with a transmitter in Puget Sound, obviously situated to reach most of the population of British Columbia. The station maintained a sales office and a studio for making commercials in Vancouver. In Buffalo, similarly, three commercial stations were selling advertising in Toronto and Hamilton, grossing perhaps one-third of their total revenues—about $10 million annually. United States border stations were free to compete in Canadian markets, yet FCC policy protecting stations in cities 100 miles apart from commercial competition over cable effectively limited those same stations from penetrating markets of some neighboring United States cities. In an article in the Toronto *Globe and Mail* ("The border TV war from the other side," 21 November, 1975) the managers of the three Buffalo stations explained the different technique employed in the United States to limit TV competition:

> In the United States, when the Federal Communications Commission determines that stations in one market should be protected against competition from stations in another market, it does so by preventing reception of the "foreign" signals.

In Defense of a Distinct Canadian System

Under the Broadcasting Act, the CRTC must insure the existence and satisfactory performance of our Canadian system. This policy has had considerable popular support; nevertheless, the CRTC is facing its greatest challenge from cable television.

Although English-speaking Canadians are particularly receptive to American programs, they are also determined to maintain a distinctive broadcasting system. Some contend that this feeling in support of a distinctively Canadian system belongs only to a minority of Canadians, an elite, or a group of self-conscious Canadian nationalists. There is clear evidence, however—in the public inquiries of royal commissions and of advisory and parliamentary committees, and in public opinion polls—that a majority of Canadians, both English- and French-speaking, want their own broadcasting stations and networks to offer a good measure of Canadian programming.[8] A 1973 poll, conducted on behalf of a weekend supplement to a chain of

English-language newspapers, found 47 percent of respondents thinking there was too much American cultural material in Canada, compared with 8 percent who thought there was too little.[9]

Many of the same people who like to watch American television also express concern about too much American influence on Canadian life. There is no necessary inconsistency. All but the most intellectually rigorous like to be entertained by undemanding programs some of the time, but also seek, perhaps less frequently, programs that bear more directly on deeper concerns. A broadcasting system that chooses its programs and arranges its schedules by commercial criteria is less likely to have many programs that serve other than entertainment interests, and American programming will also, of course, not address concerns peculiar to Canada.

The desire of Canadians to have the best of both worlds, Canadian and American program services, and the penetration of cable television, has not made it easy for the Canadian government and the CRTC to fashion a logical and consistent structure for Canadian broadcasting. Both public and private networks include American programs in their regular schedules—both because viewers want them and because they are more profitable. Cable, however, threatened to eliminate the Canadian choice.

To protect Canadian stations, the CRTC ordered Canadian cable systems in 1971 to carry only Canadian commercials whenever a program was being released simultaneously over an American and a Canadian station. In other words, if "Happy Days" was available on Channel 7, with American commercials, and on Channel 5, with Canadian commercials, the cable viewer would receive only Channel 5 service. The American stations were distressed, but they could hardly protest, since they had bought no *recognized* rights to distribute the program to Canadian audiences in the first place.

A second step was more controversial. The Commission allowed several cable companies, notably in Calgary and Toronto, to delete some commercials from American TV stations more or less at random, and to substitute public service announcements (CRTC Decisions 74-100 to 74-102). Although it was assumed that only a fraction of all commercials would be deleted, the theory was that Canadian advertisers, accustomed to advertising on American stations, could not be sure their messages would be seen on Canadian cable; they might be induced to patronize Canadian TV stations.

American Response to Canadian Defense

Although only one cable company in Toronto began such deletions, the three Buffalo stations—used to gathering in Canadian advertising dollars and Canadian markets—protested. They regarded the cable relay of their programs without their commercial messages as simple piracy. The Buffalo stations argued against the proposed regulation before the CRTC. When that failed, they challenged the CRTC's decision before the courts and sued the offending cable company in Toronto for making deletions.

While awaiting court judgments, the three Buffalo stations reportedly asked American networks to "lean on" Hollywood production agencies to demand higher purchase prices from Canadian stations and networks.[10] The National Association of Broadcasters (NAB) asked Secretary of State Henry Kissinger to intervene, and he did.[11] The NAB also asked United States networks to prevent Canadian broadcasters from receiving U.S. programs before they were shown in the United States. The border stations lobbied both in Washington and Ottawa, engaging former United States Senator Charles Goodell as a spokesman. In July 1976, 18 U.S. senators, mainly from border states and including such heavyweights as Hubert Humphrey of Minnesota, Henry Jackson from Washington, Jacob Javits from New York, as well as Howard Baker from Tennessee, and Hugh Scott from Pennsylvania, addressed a letter to Secretary Kissinger protesting the unfair treatment accorded American broadcasters.

The legal action placed before Canadian courts by the Buffalo stations to prevent the random deletion of commercials by a cable company was not successful. The Federal Court of Appeal in Ottawa unanimously held that the CRTC was within its powers in authorizing a cable company to make such deletions. One of the judges wrote that American broadcasters had "no right to have their signals received in Canada in either the original or altered form."[12] The Buffalo stations appealed to the Supreme Court of Canada, which in November 1977 split 6 to 3 in dismissing the case.[13] The Supreme Court held that the CRTC had acted with due process under the powers given it by the Broadcasting Act.

Magazines in Canada

The CRTC's policy of commercial deletion disturbed U.S. border television stations. During the same period changes in Canadian tax provisions for advertising deductions also involved the defense of Canadian media, and this time the U.S. magazine industry reacted most virulently.

Canadian publishers have long contended that they faced unfair competition from the overflow of American magazines circulated in Canada. The government was reluctant to act on their complaints, not wishing to interfere with the free flow of information, and not wishing to make popular American magazines more expensive for Canadian readers. However, by 1955 the Canadian editions of *Reader's Digest* and *Time Magazine* had over one-third of Canadian magazine advertising revenues, and only one-fifth of the consumer magazines read in Canada were Canadian. Previously well-established magazines were going broke, and the number of general circulation periodicals was declining.

The Liberal government in 1956 introduced legislation to impose a 20 percent tax on advertising contained in Canadian editions of foreign periodicals.[14] A Conservative government after taking office in 1957 removed the tax, but in response to protests from the Canadian magazine industry, in 1960 the government appointed a three-man Royal Commission on publications to inquire into the plight of Canadian periodicals.

In the Commission hearings, the largest consumer magazines published in central Canada maintained that *Reader's Digest* and *Time*, in particular, were a threat to their economic viability. They sought tariff protection for their industry. The report of the Royal Commission recommended that advertisers not be allowed a deduction in income tax for the cost of advertising placed in a foreign periodical, wherever it was printed. The Commission also recommended that a periodical printed outside Canada with advertisements placed there by Canadian advertisers be excluded under the Customs Act.

The Liberal government, in 1965, legislated to exclude split runs of foreign periodicals containing advertising directed specifically at the Canadian market, and of any foreign magazine if over 5 percent of its advertising content was directed at Canadians. In a second move, the Income Tax Act was amended to prohibit tax deductions for advertising placed in non-Canadian periodicals but directed at the Canadian market. Yet, the government decided to exempt *Time* and *Reader's Digest* by excluding from the definition of "non-Canadian periodical" any periodical that for a period of a year or more was being edited, in whole or in part, printed, and published in Canada. Canadian publishers thought the foxes were locked in with the chickens.[15]

To win exemption from the 1965 legislation, *Time* had opened an editorial office in Montreal in 1962—one year after the Royal Commission had made its report. Henry Luce and his representatives enlisted the support of the United States government and made vigorous representations before the Royal Commission and successive ministers of finance. According to Walter Gordon, a Minister of Finance during the period, the U.S. representatives indicated that if Canada did not grant an exemption to the two magazines, the Canada-U.S. Automotive Agreement was unlikely to be ratified in the U.S. Senate.[16] The government agreed to the exemptions, despite the initial recommendation of the Minister of Finance.

During the decade following the report of the Royal Commission, *Time* and *Reader's Digest* increased their hegemony in the Canadian magazine field. *Reader's Digest*, including its French-language version, *Sélection du Reader's Digest*, increased its circulation from about 1 million to 1.5 million copies. The circulation of *Time* in the same ten years doubled—from 215,000 to 440,000 copies in 1969. The share of advertising revenues absorbed by the two American publications climbed from 41 to 56 percent.[17] Almost all other general circulation consumer magazines were in financial trouble. The best-known Canadian-edited publication, *Maclean's*, had to be supported by other magazines published by its owners, especially trade journals. One of the oldest and most respected English-language magazines, *Saturday Night*, was floundering by the time a special Senate Committee on the Mass Media reported in 1970. It soon suspended publication.

The advantages that *Time* and *Reader's Digest* enjoyed were obvious. For them, the basic magazine costs were absorbed by the U.S. operation. Most extra costs were for the relatively small number of pages devoted to Canadian materials (except for the translations into French in the case of *Sélection*). Therefore, according to one writer, in 1969 *Time Canada* would charge an advertiser only $2700 for a full-page advertisement, whereas *Maclean's* had to charge $4600 a page to meet its costs of operation.[18]

The Senate Committee in 1970 again concluded that—as a result of the competition of *Time* and *Reader's Digest*—the Canadian magazines faced extinction. The committee urged the Canadian government:

Remove the present exemptions from Section 12A of the Income Tax Act. Somehow or other, we've arrived in the peculiarly Canadian position where our most successful magazines are American magazines, and we're moving inexorably toward the day when they'll be the *only* magazines we have. This may make sense in terms of economics; on every other basis it's intolerable.[19]

Bill C-58 in 1975 responded to the Committee's plea. It disallowed business deductions for Canadian companies' advertising costs for space in a non-Canadian newspaper or periodical, or for advertising directed primarily to a Canadian market but placed in a foreign broadcasting undertaking. A Canadian periodical was defined as one with 75% equity control and "substantially" different content from foreign periodicals. The decision as to what "substantially different" meant was to be decided by the Minister of National Revenue.

Time and *Reader's Digest* returned to Parliament Hill, arguing in effect that they had become honorary Canadian citizens and that removal of their Canadian status violated previously negotiated understandings. Both magazines planned to share ownership with Canadian investors, but *Time* wanted to know how much Canadian content was necessary for a magazine to be regarded as "substantially different" from its American counterpart. *Time Canada* thought it had assurance that "substantially different" meant anything over 50 percent, but the Minister of National Revenue later announced that, in the case of magazines, the phrase meant 80 percent different.

Reader's Digest approached the problem differently. Compared to *Time Canada's* 58 full-time staff in Canada, *Reader's Digest* boasted 450 employees. Furthermore, the French-language publication gave it a politically influential base in the province of Quebec. Like *Time*, *Reader's Digest* appealed directly to its readers; in addition, members of the Quebec Liberal caucus intervened on its behalf.[20]

The government decided that the stories in *Reader's Digest*, edited and condensed in Canada, would count as Canadian content, regardless of origin. *Reader's Digest* and *Sélection* met the necessary test. *Time* dropped its Canadian edition, but continued Canadian circulation from Montreal. Both continued to accept Canadian advertisements, although they became more costly for the advertisers. *Reader's Digest* sold a majority of its shares to Canadians. Nothing else changed.

In their letter to the United States Secretary of State in July 1976 protesting commercial deletion, the 18 U.S. senators also expressed concern over Bill C-58; they attached a copy of their own bill threatening retaliation against any nation that the FCC found to be discriminating against United States broadcasters. The Administration asked for formal talks with the Canadian government on both subjects, but the Canadian Foreign Minister insisted that Bill C-58 was purely a tax measure for determination by the Canadian Parliament and refused to allow the bilateral discussion.[21]

The original 1965 legislation and the 1976 amendment have had important results for Canadian magazines. *Saturday Night*, which had suspended publication, revived and now has close to the largest circulation in its 90-year old history. The Magazine Association of Canada reported that magazines in 1977 increased their advertising revenue by 34 percent over 1976; *Maclean's*, two or three years before in the red, by 1977 was the top revenue-earner. *Maclean's* plans to publish weekly instead of semimonthly and to enter into direct competition with *Time* and *Newsweek* as a Canadian newsmagazine. *Reader's Digest* is still growing.[22]

Economics or Nationhood?

Can one conclude that the Canadian discussion of the mass media was mainly a struggle between different economic interests, with governments on each side of the border enlisted to protect the positions of the several competitors? Certainly there is this element. However, decisions were taken after a lengthy process of investigation, report, debate among Canadians themselves, and enunciation of objectives that related to the national interest in maintaining or encouraging intra-societal communications. The majority of changes were incremental, partly because of American resistance; and American interests could complain justifiably about uncertain ground rules. Nevertheless, the inconsistencies of Canadian communications policy derive from the ambivalence of Canadians themselves, and from the continuing influence exerted on them by American institutions, American values, American culture, and American success.

Any self-respecting people that seeks to maintain its national identity will sympathize with the objective of controlling prime agencies of communication. The particular measures chosen to prevent indigenous communications systems from being swamped by influences and messages from an adjoining country are more problematic. Public support for public agencies, such as the CBC, is probably more reliable than regulatory measures (such as the commercial-deletion policy initiated by the CRTC). Aside from the dangers of inducing a chain of retaliatory actions, there is the likelihood that Canadian private interests may enlist government or regulatory authority on their behalf, with minimal resulting benefit to the public weal. The Canadian magazine industry has been an endangered species and probably needed the support of governmental action. Canadian cable companies and the larger television stations, however, have been uncommonly profitable; their contributions to Canadian communications have certainly not kept pace with the return to their investors. While Canadian TV stations have a case against the competition emanating from border stations, a broadcasting policy to benefit Canadians as a whole demands positive measures: a more rational regulatory structure, continued independence from the executive branch of government, support from the Canadian people for their own stations and production sources, and above all, financial means for the CBC to produce and to distribute Canadian programs.

The several measures of the Canadian government discussed here were designed to protect the Canadian nation. These measures are incomplete and perhaps uncertain in their effects, but the motives behind them should not be oversimplified or mistaken.

NOTES

1. Such an argument was presented, for example, by Willis Armstrong in a background paper prepared for the fourth Lester B. Pearson Conference on the Canada-U.S. Relationship, held in September 1976. His remarks do not appear in the book reporting the conference, *Canadian Cultural Nationalism,* ed. Janice L. Murray (New York University Press, New York, 1977). However, another conference participant, Roger Frank Swanson, wrote (p. 61): "There is a temptation for U.S. officials to misread the overall phenomenon of Canada's cultural retrofitting by interpreting it as a simple case of economic protectionism."

2. F. W. Peers, "The Nationalist Dilemma in Canadian Broadcasting," in Peter Russell, ed., *Nationalism in Canada,* McGraw-Hill, 1966, pp. 252-67.

3. Margaret Prang, "The Origins of Public Broadcasting in Canada," *Canadian Historical Review.* XLVI (March 1965); and F.W.

Peers, *The Politics of Canadian Broadcasting, 1920-1951,* University of Toronto Press, 1969, p. 441.

4. Canada, Broadcasting Act. R.S.C. 1970, c. B-11, sec. 3(d); originally enacted as S.C. 1967-68, c. 25.

5. CRTC Public Announcement, 26 Feb. 1971.

6. Blaik Kirby, "Juneau wants more Canadian TV," Toronto *Globe and Mail,* 18 Oct. 1973.

7. Quoted by Keith Davey, in "Border Impact: The Mass Media and Canadian Identity," Proceedings of the Association for Education in Journalism Convention Plenary Session, Ottawa, 18 Aug. 1975, p. 31.

8. The most complete survey of public attitudes toward broadcasting objectives was carried out in 1962 by Canadian Facts Limited, and reported under the title, *What the Canadian Public Thinks of the CBC* (CBC publication). About 90 percent of respondents considered that six objectives listed for the CBC were "important" or "very important."

9. "Canadians feel American influence is increasing," *Weekend Magazine,* 4 Feb. 1973, p. 3; the cultural power of the U.S. was seen to be increasing in Canada by a margin of 46%-21%.

10. Jack Miller, "There's a lot of distortion in border TV picture," *Toronto Star,* 6 Oct. 1975.

11. CP dispatch, Washington, in *Toronto Star,* 13 Sept. 1975, under title, "Kissinger is asked to protest 'unfair' Canadian TV rules." The efforts of the U.S. State Department to change the commercial-deletion policy of the CRTC are recounted by Roger Frank Swanson, *op. cit.,* pp. 68-71.

12. *Re Capital Cities Communications Inc. et al. and Canadian Radio-Television Commission,* 52 DLR (3rd), pp. 415-25. The quotation from Mr. Justice Thurlow is on p. 416.

13. *Capital Cities Communications Inc., Taft Broadcasting Company and WBEN, Inc. v. Canadian Radio-Television Commission.* Supreme Court of Canada, Nov. 30, 1977, Judgment (mimeo.)

14. I.A. Litvak and C.J. Maule, "Interest-Group Tactics and the Policies of Foreign Investment: The Time-Reader's Digest Case Study," *Canadian Journal of Political Science,* Dec. 1974, pp. 616-29. See also Litvak and Maule, *Cultural Sovereignty: The Time and Reader's Digest Case in Canada* (New York, 1974).

15. *The Uncertain Mirror* (Report of the Special Senate Committee on Mass Media), Vol. I (Ottawa, Information Canada, 1970), p. 164.

16. Walter Gordon, *A Choice for Canada* (Toronto, 1968), p. 97;

Peter Newman, *The Distemper of Our Times* (Toronto, 1968), p. 225.

17. *The Uncertain Mirror, op. cit.*, pp. 155, 158.

18. Gary Dunford, "Why Are This Magazine's Measurements Now 8¼ Inches Wide by 11¼ Inches High?" *Toronto Star*, 11 Jan. 1969.

19. *The Uncertain Mirror, op. cit.*, p. 257.

20. Information from Senator Keith Davey in personal conversation.

21. The Canadian tax legislation led to retaliatory action on the part of some members of the U.S. Congress. In 1976 the U.S. Tax Reform Act was amended to restrict the deduction of expenses by Americans attending conventions outside the United States. Recognizing the harm this change would do to the Canadian hotel and restaurant industry, Barry Goldwater introduced legislation to exempt Canada, Mexico, and the Caribbean countries from the new tax law. The Goldwater amendment was narrowly defeated in the Senate, and several senators linked their opposition to dissatisfaction with Canada's Bill C-58. See Donald K. Alper and Robert L. Monohan, "Bill C-58 and the American Congress: The Politics of Retaliation," *Canadian Public Policy*, Spring 1978, pp. 184-92.

22. "Magazines' advertising revenue increases by 34 percent from levels of a year ago," Toronto *Globe and Mail*, 1 Feb. 1978.

5_____TENSIONS OVER COMMUNICATIONS

COMMENT

Joel Rosenbloom

Candor and courtesy alike compel not only agreement with Professor Peers on the motivations behind Canada's recent treatment of American broadcasting and print media, but denunciation of the opposite view. At a minimum it is inaccurate, unfair, and obtuse to accuse the Canadians of being motivated wholly or primarily by commercial considerations. Much deeper concerns about national identity, cultural sovereignty, and self-confidence are obviously at the core of the matter.

But candor also compels some questions as to whether Professor Peers has proved very much, and indeed whether the Canadian government has not so identified its own concerns about cultural independence with the profit motives of some of its broadcasters and publishers as to explain a belief by the superficial observer that nothing but money is at stake.

One may question, in addition, whether the motivational picture that Professor Peers draws is not rather one-sided. In the perspective he offers, all the non-commercial motives seem to reside north of the border. There, statesmen, administrative agencies, and Royal Commissions, while perhaps influenced to some degree by the commercial interests of Canadian broadcasters and publishers, have been engaged primarily in a struggle to save Canada's cultural soul, while satisfying at the same time its ambivalent desire to remain—to paraphrase slightly the excerpt from the Report of the Royal Commission on Publications—naked to the battering of American words, images, and print. Here, in contrast, American businessmen summon the aid of powerful senators and ex-senators, as well as high officials of the Executive Branch, in crude but ultimately ineffectual efforts to forestall Canada's hesitant attempts to protect herself—all without much more than a fig leaf of principle to cover (if I may use the word again) their naked desire for commercial gain.

Different Philosophies

One of the bedeviling aspects of this problem is the extent to which the differences between the two societies—which somehow persist, notwithstanding the supposed homogenizing influence of the mass media—distort each side's perception of the other's motives and intentions. As Professor Peers points out, for example, Canada lacks the equivalent of the First Amendment. It is not so much that Canadians lack a comparable devotion to freedom of thought and expression as that they trust their government more to carry out its duties while respecting those freedoms. Picture, however, the United States Internal Revenue Service sitting in judgment on whether the content of an American magazine is sufficiently different from that of foreign magazines to qualify as indigenous. That is the function that Canada's Department of National Revenue undertook when it declared that Canadian purchasers of advertising in the Canadian edition of *Time Magazine* would not qualify for an income tax deduction under the new Canadian law—even if that edition were, as a business enterprise, sold to and owned by Canadians— unless 80% of the magazine's content could be found to be "substantially different" from the content of *Time Magazine's* American edition. Who can doubt that any such governmental venture in the United States would be met with appeals to freedom of the press and a settled determination to fight the issue in every legislative, judicial, or other forum available? And, if you were an American publisher confronted with such treatment by a foreign government, would you not feel that there was an issue of principle involved that transcended any question of commercial advantage?

Again, Canada has until recently lacked any very effective antitrust laws, and it has historically lacked the kind of commitment to the concept of freely competitive markets as the only truly right and moral kind that is so prominent a feature of American thought on the way things economic should be organized and conducted. When the Canadian Radio-Television and Telecommunications Commission licenses a new Canadian television station, it conceives itself as assigning that station to a particular geographical market, the potential revenues of which it deems adequate to support an appropriate service by the new station as well as existing stations. The CRTC may, and sometimes does, forbid a Canadian station to seek revenues in an adjacent market that it actually serves, on the ground that those revenues in some sense "belong" to the stations which the CRTC has assigned to that market.[1]

It is very different in the United States. A policy of maximum feasible competition by no means always prevails, either in fact or in regulatory policy. The FCC is sometimes persuaded that the addition of a new competitive television service to a given market (over-the-air or via cable reception) would not be a good thing for the public and should be prevented on that ground. But the burden of persuasion is clearly on those who urge the protectionist course. The so-called "public interest" bar, the Department of Justice, the courts, Congressional committees, and the academic community that concerns itself with FCC regulation are increasingly and stridently hostile to protectionist action. And the FCC has never taken the view that a station which actually serves a given community and attracts an audience should refrain from selling time to advertisers who wish to reach that audience.

The Deeper Problem

I do not suggest that differences in underlying philosophies about the proper roles of competition, government, and the media are the central or only cause of the border communications problem. Canada might have sought to protect its cultural independence by limiting or preventing Canadian reception of American broadcasting stations. It could have located its own stations with less concern for the risk that they may interfere (electronically) with Canadian reception of American stations. It could have forbidden its own cable systems to carry the signals of American stations. If it had taken this course, there would have been grumbling from American broadcasters and calls for "free trade." But the issue would have been one of relatively minor and parochial interest. The Canadian treatment of *Time* and *Reader's Digest* has not provoked any major eruption. For all our statements of commitment to free competition (and often sincere efforts to live up to that commitment), Americans have always recognized that there are other values worth seeking—in broadcasting and elsewhere. There is plenty of sympathy in the United States for the desire of other countries to maintain their own independence—cultural, economic, or political. And there are a fair number of vocal people in the United States who are not entranced with the service produced by American commercial broadcasting—people who would agree instinctively with the efforts of any foreign government to combat what they perceive as the pernicious influence of that service.

That, however, is not what Canada has done. The Canadian government has encouraged Canadian reception of American stations. In the 1960s, the Canadian government refused to permit a Barrie, Ontario, television station to move its transmitter south, in part (at least) because of concerns that it would interfere with the reception of Buffalo stations in Toronto.[2] The CRTC has licensed scores of Canadian cable systems in all parts of the country, not only to carry American signals but, where necessary, to reach out for those signals, by means of microwave relays, over hundreds of miles. Then, having opted for an all but unlimited battering of Canadian eyes and ears by Archie Bunker, Kojak, Laverne and Shirley and their friends, it has defended Canadian culture by attempting to bar American stations that are received in Canada from competing in Canadian advertising markets.

The means chosen for this purpose have included the CRTC's policy of first encouraging and then seeking to force Canadian cable operators to delete commercials from the services of the American stations they carry. Professor Peers' account of this policy is far too modest. In a 1971 policy statement,[3] the CRTC sought to encourage voluntary deletion and substitution, not merely of public service announcements but of full-blown ads, that would be sold to Canadian firms by local Canadian broadcasters and inserted in the services of American stations by the cable operators (who would, inferentially, have received part of the boodle in compensation). When it got no takers from Canadian cable operators or broadcasters, who generally perceived the practice as immoral, if not illegal, it retreated to the substitution of public service announcements and forced the practice on a Calgary cable operator as the price of authority for him to import the signals of Spokane, Washington, stations.[4]

Subsequently, a Toronto cable operator voluntarily began to delete commercials from the service of Buffalo stations, substituting ads for his own FM station and for new features of his cable service which he offered at a price. Threatened with suit by the Buffalo stations, he asked the CRTC for some form of license authority to cover his practices, a request that was granted on condition that he limit himself to the substitution of public service announcements. It was this CRTC action that was upheld by Canada's Supreme court as within the agency's statutory and constitutional power.

The CRTC has never abandoned its hope of securing the full deletion and substitution of commercial matter. And, not content with the pace of voluntary compliance, it has by now attached conditions to the licenses of every substantial Canadian cable system requiring the cable operators to prepare the necessary equipment and to await its order to commence deletion. That order has been held in abeyance temporarily, after strenuous protests by the U.S. government, pending a study of alternative means to the same end.

The major such alternative is Bill C-58, which substantially doubles the cost to a Canadian advertiser of purchasing time on an American station. Although this legislation did not become fully effective until September 1977, the Canadian revenues earned by American border stations in calendar 1977 were less than half of those they had earned in 1975. The prospects for 1978 and future years are considerably bleaker,[5] and it appears that the Canadian government will largely succeed (by means of this tax device) in eliminating American stations as competitive factors in its advertising markets while retaining (and, indeed, actively distributing) the service of those same stations throughout Canada.

The Basis of the American Complaint

The Canadian government has steadfastly refused discussion with the United States on Bill C-58, yet it has lobbied vigorously for relief from the provisions of U.S. tax law that restrict the deductibility of expenses incurred by Americans in attending conventions held in foreign countries.[6] It is this pattern of action that has produced an emotional response in the United States. American senators and congressmen respond to the interests of their constituents, as do politicians in other democratic societies. But any notion that they are the puppets of this or that "lobby" is generally a product of overheated imaginations. They have responded, in this instance, to a perception that Canada is treating American interests in a fundamentally arbitrary and unfair manner.

From an American perspective, it seems wholly inconsistent for Canada to seek relief from the efforts of American tax measures on Canadian tourism, while refusing to discuss the effects of Canadian tax measures on American broadcasting. It is difficult to understand, moreover, how any threat to Canadian culture created by the exposure of Canadians to American border television service can be met by deleting or taxing out of existence the one element in that service that is plainly Canadian—advertising messages from Canadian businessmen directed to Canadians. The traditional answer has been that protection of Canadian stations from American commercial competition will enhance their financial resources, and that greater resources will enable them to spend more on Canadian programming, thus giving Canadian program producers a better opportunity to compete with the products of New York and Hollywood. But this argument pays little attention to such questions as which Canadian stations will gain or how much they might gain,[7] how much of that amount might actually be applied to the production of Canadian programs, or how much is needed to give Canadian producers the chance which they deserve. The assumption is simply that every additional dollar earned by a Canadian station or network is a contribution to the vigor of Canadian culture.

This is the point at which Canadian cultural motives become so thoroughly identified with the commercial motives of Canadian broadcasters as to make it understandable why foreign observers tend to confuse the two. The identification rests on an extraordinarily crude and simplistic view of the relationship between money and culture. No conceivable diversion of advertising from American to Canadian stations could add more than a pittance to the program budgets available to Canadian producers of entertainment programs. In an appearance before the CRTC on January 19, 1978, Mr. Murray Chercover, President of Canada's CTV Network, made this point explicit:

> The issue is not now in Canada in any economic sense whether the Buffalo stations are marketing. Or able to market in Canada. In fact, if you will recall over the whole dialogue surrounding the issue of C-58 (the tax legislation) and/or the commercial deletion and substitution involved the absolute maximum total of twenty million dollars ($20,000,000). That won't even pay for our Canadian programme service on one channel. So that it is insignificant.

Thus the connection between Canada's policies on this subject and the cultural goals those policies are designed to serve is tenuous, at best. The real motives at play have much more to do with a feeling that it is simply wrong for foreign stations to compete in Canadian markets, no matter what use Canada may make of the program services those stations provide. And that view squarely poses the ultimate issue, as American broadcasters see it.

The Ultimate Issue

Canadian citizens enjoy American television, and Canadian cable operators exploit it for profit-making purposes. In 1976, according to *Statistics Canada*, the Canadian cable industry had gross revenues of $199 million, before-tax profits of $36 million and after-tax profits of $19 million. Not a penny of those revenues came back to the American stations that made them possible. In Canada, as in this country, television broadcasters are expected basically to earn compensation for their services by selling time to advertisers. And the $18-20 million in gross Canadian revenues that American stations once earned—the net revenues after commissions paid to Canadian agencies and sales representatives were closer to $14 million—was surely not an extortionate charge.

The principle for which American border broadcasters contend is older and more fundamental than ideas about the desirability of competition and free trade: those who render a service should be permitted to earn fair compensation. Canadian policy-makers very naturally take offense when it is suggested that they are violating so basic a rule in human affairs. Other Canadians, however, have been quick to see what is at stake. The Toronto *Globe and Mail* called the CRTC's commercial deletion policy "shabby, sleazy, immoral, beneath contempt—but not beneath the CRTC." The temporary halt in the implementation of that policy came, I suggest, not so much in response to American pressure (naked or otherwise) as in recognition that a country's national and cultural identity is defined no less by the fairness with which it treats its neighbors than by the affluence of its media.

It is therefore heartening to find Professor Peers turning, in conclusion, to a more positive approach to the fostering of creativity in Canadian broadcasting. The chances to sustain a vibrant Canadian program production industry, responsive to Canadian needs and capable of commanding the attention of the Canadian public, depend far more on Canada's own efforts than they do on attempts to fence out American commercial competition while ambivalently enjoying the benefits of American television programming. Certainly, the course Canada's policy-makers are now following is not well calculated to allow a sharing of telecommunications opportunities and services among countries on this continent on terms of mutual respect.

NOTES

1. *See* Decisions CRTC 73-501 and 73-502, December 14, 1973.

2. *See* LaMarsh, *Memoirs of a Bird in a Gilded Cage,* p. 259 (Pocket Book edition, 1970).

3. CRTC, *Policy Statement on Cable Television,* July 26, 1971.

4. *Decision CRTC 72-364,* December 21, 1972.

5. *Policies Affecting Services of United States Television Licensees* (Brief submitted to the Trade Policy Staff Committee, Office of the Special Trade Representative, February 13, 1978).

6. *See, e.g.,* the February, 1977 release from the Canadian Government Office of Tourism, concerning the Canadian government's official note to the U.S. government on this subject.

7. The elimination of American stations as vehicles by which Canadian advertisers can reach Canadian viewers will not automatically make weaker Canadian stations (with low audiences) more attractive to advertisers, who may turn to other media or forms of advertising or simply reduce their advertising expenditures. Moreover, as the stronger Canadian stations (with larger audiences) raise their rates, smaller Canadian advertisers are driven out of the medium and larger advertisers are given substantial incentive to concentrate their purchases on stations in the largest cities—skimping or eliminating altogether purchases on stations in small communities.

6__POWER AND VULNERABILITY

CANADIAN AND AMERICAN PERSPECTIVES ON INTERNATIONAL AFFAIRS*

Allan E. Gotlieb

In contrast, perhaps, to the views of some observers of Canada and the United States, the realm of foreign policy provides little or no evidence of conflict between them. What it does provide is some evidence of lively contrast, as well as broad evidence of common values, shared interests, and parallel or cooperative action in dealing with fundamental issues of world affairs.

If their respective foreign policies do not provide the drama of conflict, I hope that they reveal the more subtle theater of two independent nations defining and seeking their own foreign policy objectives. As I shall try to explain, even where these objectives appear similar, they are sometimes based on a different rationale. Where objectives differ, they may in fact flow from an underlying similarity in philosophy and attitude. Where objectives and approaches are much the same, which is usually the case, there remain differences of scale and quality that illuminate the contrasting and complementing global roles of a North American middle power and its North American superpower neighbor.

In essence, Canada is a country that can neither afford to isolate itself from the world, nor ignore the challenges to sovereign national interest that are the natural consequence of an active and varied international life. Despite Canada's considerable economic and political power, its vulnerability to external political and economic forces gives it an unusually keen interest in strengthening the process of conciliation required for a stable world order. Though Canada has excellent relations with the U.S.A. and shares in many ways its vital culture, powerful economy, and cornerstone role in Western security, it has to delineate with care those essential—and literal—boundaries

---

* The views expressed in this essay are those of the author and not necessarily those of the Canadian Government.

that distinguish it from other societies and nations. This paradox has its roots in Canada's geographic and economic vulnerability, and it has occasionally had to take strong national and international action in order to minimize its costs. In this essay I will bring out some examples of how Canada deals with the challenge of its exposure to outside forces.

History and Structure

Let me turn first to some of the obvious, generic factors which may determine Canadian and U.S. attitudes to the world at large. The United States took shape in a heady matrix of philosophy and rebellion, a movement for national liberation whose republican ideology and libertarian spirit remain vital forces at work in the world. The Northern English- and French-speaking colonies of British North America remained loyal to the crown despite political and military advances made in the direction of Canada by the young republic to the south. Indeed, many Americans, United Empire Loyalists, chose to walk away from the Revolution and come north. The Northern colonies, through choice and circumstances, arrived at independence through the evolution of the British colonial system, and through regional political arrangements between Maritime, Central, and Western provinces. This was a slow and complicated process, but one which appeared to suit the linguistic and religious compromises the two founding cultures required. The process also suited Canada's geographic and economic situation, as well as guaranteeing its security from any American military threat.

While successive governments in Washington throughout the nineteenth century articulated their philosophy of liberty and equality, Canada for its part developed a distrust of proselytizing and of ideology. Canadians respected the idealism which underlay American society, but they also had no little experience of the economic expansionism which could be clothed in that rhetoric. Canada's preoccupations were the search for political accommodation between French and English, and its own expansion westward. In Canada's push to the Pacific, it should be noted that central and regional governments took an increasing part. Public sector activity was henceforth to be one of the distinguishing marks of Canadian economic development. Canada's small population, vast territory, and harsh climate dictated new techniques of mobilizing capital and human resources. This factor plays a significant role in the country's domestic and international character today. I could cite, for example, the contrast in international wheat sales between the activities abroad of the Canadian Wheat Board and of United States private sector traders in the respective relations of the two nations with communist countries.

Against this background, the Canadian-American contrast is further illuminated by the federal constitutions of the two countries. The initial, relatively loose, American federal system was transformed by civil war, judicial interpretation, Roosevelt's New Deal, and global obligations into a highly centralized arrangement. This is particularly true in the conduct of United States foreign relations. Canada's British North America Act, drafted in 1867 with the American Civil War very much in mind, was originally intended to provide for a strong central government. Today, after more than a century of Canadian political reality, abetted by and reflected in judicial interpretation, the country's federal system provides for distinct areas of exclusive provincial jurisdiction, areas where jurisdiction is shared between federal and provincial governments, and areas of exclusive federal responsibility. There are, of course, similarities with the evolution of states' rights in the American system. Constitutional experts have, however, described the Canadian system as being, in practice, one of the most decentralized federal systems in the world. The implications for foreign policy are considerable. For example, participation in many international activities in the fields of education, culture, and civil and human rights requires the active involvement of the provinces, as do the formation of delegations to international conferences in these areas and the negotiation of some international agreements. In addition, many of Canada's provinces maintain respresentational offices abroad.

Canada's physical situation is a decisive factor in foreign policy terms. The United States and the U.S.S.R. are Canada's only significant neighbors in a geographic sense. When the two superpowers face each other over the North Pole, they are staring across Canada. The nuclear debris Canada collected in the north, from a crashed Soviet satellite, is a dramatic vignette of its geopolitical location. Canada's three oceans (Atlantic, Pacific, and Arctic) give it a particular concern for maritime issues, as well as its own perspectives on, and links with, Europe, Asia, and the Soviet Union. The variety and extent of the Canadian landmass pose important environmental challenges. The relative isolation of a portion of Canada's population, combined with considerable urbanization, imposes on governments a responsibility to weigh carefully the social impact of resource development—a preoccupation Canada shares with developing countries and with the United States.

The structural contrast between the two economies is profound. The American economy is ten times the size of the Canadian, but Canada's foreign trade is a much larger proportion of its national product. Fully half the goods Canada produces are exported. Our interest in world trade is fundamental. Though Canada is a major industrial and trading power in its own right, its station beside the world's largest economy has been a central factor in its domestic economic development. Canadian governments have tried over the years to strengthen Canadian secondary industry and construct coast-to-coast economic institutions within Canada, partly as a way of limiting its long-term vulnerability to the shaping force of the U.S. economy.

Canada endeavors both at home and abroad to deal with the natural tendency to export raw materials and import manufactured goods resulting from its position relative to the American economy. Though the two countries are, of course, each other's largest—and best—partners in the exchange of goods, services, and capital, Canada aggressively seeks trading partners in other parts of the world. Its special hopes and concerns at the Multi-Lateral Trade Negotiations (MTN) also flow from its differing industrial and tariff structures. In these negotiations, Canada is trying for new arrangements that will open markets abroad to "further. processed" primary products from Canada, while offering to lower its own tariffs as a way of strengthening and rationalizing what some call Canada's "branch plant" manufacturing sector.

There is also, of course, a fundamental political contrast between the U.S. and Canada: the quantitative and qualitative difference between a superpower and a middle power. Beyond the respective histories and forms of government of the two countries, and beyond the many elements which they have in common, this contrast explains much that is different in their foreign policies.

Middle Power: Illusions and Interests

Though the concept of a middle power is an elusive one, I think it helps explain how Canadians see themselves. Canada first came to worry about its rank, rather than simply its autonomy within the international political order, towards the end of World War II. The war greatly accelerated Canada's economic and political development and marked the end of its gradual passage from colony to nation. In foreign affairs, it put Canada in a new position to make its interests known and gave it new responsibilities.

In trying to ensure that the Great Powers did not entirely dominate the U.N. Security Council after the war, Prime Minister Mackenzie King said, in what was in effect a warning, that selection of states for membership

> should in some way be related to a dispassionate appraisal of their probable effective contribution to the maintenance of security.

King said, for the benefit of the British and Americans:

> You will...appreciate how difficult it would be for Canada, after enlisting nearly one million persons in her armed forces and trebling her national debt in order to assist in restoring peace, to accept a position of parity with the Dominican Republic or El Salvador."

Canada emerged in this spirit from the war as a major middle power, not only because of its own economic development, but because of the destruction visited upon other powers by the war. Canada made the most of its strength in helping to shape the U.N. and NATO and assisting in the rebuilding of Europe in the late forties. According to some, this was the peak of Canadian influence.

The world has become more complex, multi-polar, and interdependent over the last 30 years, and Canada's place in it has changed, though not in my view diminished. Canada's history and character—bilingual, pragmatic, distrustful of complete and final answers—has prepared it rather well for the demands of interdependence. Canada is, for example, as comfortable as any other state with the compromises of multilateral forums, instinctively joins forces with like-minded nations, and trades in the commodity of influence rather than power. Canada's interest in a peaceful and prosperous world causes it to be pragmatic and continuously outward-looking. For a middle power, lately a colony, and located next to a superpower, it was no surprise that other countries had to be taken into account. Canada's federal constitution provided further education in the art of the possible.

Canada had always looked far afield for political counterweights and trading partners: its European, Commonwealth, and francophone connections, for example, gave a set of stabilizing linkages in the global mosaic. But the idea of trying to shape on its own the destiny of nations far from its shores was and is, from Canada's point of view, a luxury and burden best left to others. Traditionally, Canada has perceived military force as something to be used collectively—whether through the Empire, NATO, or the United Nations. Canada's early understanding of the costs of dependency, and its inability to make world realities more congenial to its interests, propelled it into a major role in building and supporting international organizations.

Though its interests are worldwide—like the U.S.A.'s—Canada's power to influence major events unilaterally is limited. This geopolitical fact, as well as their inclinations of national character, made the role of conciliator a natural one for Canadians. They had a respectable influence in the 20 years after the war in setting up that stabilizing web of international organizations and customs which are now taken for granted in the global community.

However, Canadians, sometime during the sixties, may have appeared preoccupied by "helpful fixing" for its own sake, irrespective of Canadian interests, and of external factors which seemed to limit the effectiveness of initiatives by many middle powers. Since Canada's review of foreign policy in the late 1960s, it has adjusted to the times and taken a more realistic view of the essential national goals that must underlie, for a country like Canada, an effective and responsible foreign policy. This realistic view has not made Canada less active internationally, nor any less conscious of its dependence on external economic and security realities. But it has helped Canada to discriminate between illusions and interests in looking at the world, and to plan and carry out independent national action when required.

Superpower: Challenge and Response

To set these issues in perspective we should look for a moment at what we customarily mean by the United States as a superpower. There is no question that there was a difference of quality rather than simply of degree in the power and global responsibility thrust upon Canada and the United States after 1945. While the immediate postwar period brought a major middle power role to Canada, it resulted in a colossal expansion of the geographic and strategic frontiers of what the United States judged to be relevant to its vital national interests. The Western European and Japanese competitors of the United States had been demolished. The United States alone had the resources to establish and defend an area of influence that included Western Europe, Japan, and much of Asia.

The main postwar threat to the peaceful evolution of liberal-democratic political and economic institutions in these areas was seen as coming from the Soviet Union. By the early fifties, it was the only power with the military and industrial potential to challenge the U.S.A.'s position in Western Europe and Asia, and to threaten the United States with nuclear weapons. A gulf of mutual suspicion widened between Soviet and American visions of the future, and a contest for allies—and clients—on a global scale crystallized into the central reality of world power politics.

Canada shared America's concern over Soviet expansionism. It helped to establish NATO and with the U.S. formed NORAD, which are essential to their collective defense efforts. Canada assisted in the implementation of the Marshall Plan, and Canadians fought in Korea to help restore a stable balance on the peninsula. But after that, the paths of Canada and the U.S. diverged to some degree. The United States set up a network of alliances in Central and Southeast Asia that Canada did not see as vital to its interests, though it understood the geopolitical rationale for their existence. Some substantive Canadian reservations about self-perpetuating processes in the Cold War existed as well. There was, for example, the risk that too much outside support for Third World countries dealing with the threat of communism could distort their national political and economic development. Such distortions might well increase their long-term vulnerability to revolution.

But on most security matters Canada and the United States agree. They continue, of course, to be partners in the key organizations of continental and Western defense, NORAD and NATO, and consult and cooperate as freely and closely as any two nations in the world.

The View from Ottawa

This distinction between superpower and middle power, and the shaping character of the Canadian nation, help to clarify how some parts of the world look when seen from Ottawa. The fact of two founding peoples, French and English, determines to a large extent Canada's approach to old and new elements in international affairs. Canada's nineteenth-century ties with England and the resulting similarity of outlook might have led to a distrust of Europe. In fact, they ensured Canada's early participation in both World Wars, and an affinity with Europe which has been challenged occasionally but never seriously weakened by isolationist sentiment. Canada's positive approach to the emerging nations of Africa reflected ties developed within the British colonial system and within the community of francophone states. I should like to explore these three elements—Western Europe, the Commonwealth, and *la francophonie*—in somewhat greater depth.

Western Europe

Canada's ties with Western Europe are wide-ranging and deep-rooted. They demonstrate Canada's French and English background, and the influence of waves of immigrants from many European countries. They reflect mutual security, economic interdependence, and shared political tradition. Although there is much in Canada's policies that is similar to the American approach, Canada does not stand in a superpower relationship to Europe. Nor does Canadian civilization threaten theirs with what J.-J. Servan-Schreiber has called *le défi américain.*

Canada has invariably had a different perspective on its relations with postwar Europe, as demonstrated at an early stage by Article 2 of the North Atlantic Treaty. That article, which advocates the use of NATO as an instrument of consultation on political, economic, and social issues, was a Canadian initiative neither understood nor appreciated by the U.S. authorities of the time. For Canada, in the late 1940s, the article embodied its interest in a true Atlantic Community which would reinforce a Canadian relationship with Europe beyond that of junior partner in a security system, and ensure an American interest in Europe which would extend to the issues of peace as well as war.

NATO is, of course, primarily a defensive military alliance. It has not over the years been able to devote much attention to non-strategic economic, social, and political questions. I would like to suggest, however, that the early Canadian impulse towards a more comprehensive postwar re-engagement between Europe and North America has borne fruit in other institutionalized consultative arrangements. The intentions of Canada's approach to Article 2 were finally realized not so much in NATO as in the emergence of the OECD, and in a variety of other organizations reflecting transatlantic partnership. The OECD owes its existence to the need for a consultative mechanism among the industrialized countries of Europe and North America and now Japan. The Canadian participation in the OECD, in summit meetings, in NATO and in other forums, represents for Canada an essential component in managing the community of advanced industrial countries and marking out its place within it. In noting the importance to Canada of such multilateral arrangements, I want to stress how much middle powers need to work to ensure that their interests are taken fully into account—something which the United States can generally take for granted.

The Canadian attitude to European economic integration is also revealing. After some initial reservations about the implications for Canadian and Commonwealth trade of British entry to the E.E.C., Canada set out to establish a contractual link with the new Europe that would institutionalize the relationship, preserve existing economic ties, and open new opportunities. Although Canada did not declare a Year of Europe like the U.S., the period leading up to signature of the Canada-E.E.C. Framework Agreement in 1976 was for Canada a very active one. Canadians reassessed their ties with Europe, on occasion skeptically. What emerged was a reaffirmation of Canada's commitment to Western Europe, and to the pursuit of new political, economic, and cultural arrangements with the European Community and with its member states.

Why is a contractual link with the European Community essential to Canada but of less importance to the U.S.? I think it is middle-powermanship at work, combined with the special features of the Canadian economy which I have already touched on. Canada requires a diplomatic instrument in order to be assured that it shall be consulted on those issues of foreign trade so vital to its economy, such as European agricultural policies. The United States will be consulted with or without such a link. As in NATO, there is a sense in which Canada must oblige others to take its interests into account.

In this review of Canadian relations with Europe, the United States was and remains something of a *deus ex machina*. The decision to negotiate a contractual link with the European Community of necessity took into account Canada's relations with the U.S, as set out in a policy document of late 1972. That document set out three options for Canada in its relations with the U.S.: first, the mixture as before; second, closer integration with the U.S.; third, and I quote, "a comprehensive, long-term stategy to develop and strengthen the Canadian economy and other aspects of our national life and in the process to reduce the present Canadian vulnerability." The matter of vulnerability had been brought home during 1971 by measures taken by Washington to improve the U.S. balance of payments situation; measures which, it seemed to Canada then, betrayed a misunderstanding of the Canada-U.S. economic relationship, and posed a serious threat to our integrity as a nation.

Thus the current era in Canadian relations with Europe, and I might add with Japan, reflects a dimension of Ottawa's relations with Washington, and Canada's determination to diversify its foreign portfolio, as well as the resonances of its long-standing ties with Europe itself. The Third Option has not implied any downgrading of the importance of the U.S.A. for Canada, nor has it delayed the development of steadily closer links with the United States. Canada's policies of developing relations with the U.S. on the one hand, and selected countries and regions of concentration on the other, are complements, not alternatives.

The Commonwealth

The Commonwealth, formerly called the British Commonwealth, is surely one of the most baffling associations for an outsider to comprehend, yet it has been for years one of the cornerstones of Canadian foreign policy. What the Commonwealth offers its 36 members is not colonial nostalgia. On the contrary, the organization has developed into a remarkably forward-looking forum for consultations which continues to welcome new members. Although the English language and the British connection may have brought all the members together, the organization now has its own 20th-century rationale. It spans Asia, Africa, the Caribbean, the Pacific, and North America. It includes states of widely different racial backgrounds, forms of government, and levels of economic development. It provides a network of contacts between heads of government, ministers of finance, parliamentarians, and officials of all kinds. The Commonwealth experience has been a decisive one for Canada, one for which there is no parallel in the context of American foreign policy.

Commonwealth membership has played a part in determining the pattern of Canadian representation abroad and in framing our early inclination towards generous development assistance. It has given Canadian heads of government regular and privileged access to the views of leaders from around the world, and thereby exposed Canada to influences from, for example, New Delhi, Kingston, and Dar-es-

Salaam. Summit meetings of Commonwealth leaders represent a unique high-level political forum which cuts across geographic, economic, and racial lines. As one of the senior leaders of the Commonwealth, Prime Minister Trudeau has played a particularly active role in strengthening these consultations in recent years. One of the more serious attempts to find common ground between developed and developing countries on which to approach reform of the international economic order emerged from the work of a Commonwealth Group of Experts in 1975.

La Francophonie

If the Commonwealth is the international reflection of Canada's British heritage, similar contacts with francophone countries reflect the country's French inheritance. These include membership in, and a key role in the creation of, the "Agence de coopération culturelle et technique," intensified bilateral relations with former French colonies in Africa and with French-speaking states elsewhere. The concept of *francophonie*, articulated in the 60s by President Senghor of Senegal, now embraces 29 countries with a total population of approximately 250 million. Canadian policies in this field have responded not only to national priorities but also to the interests of Quebec and other provinces.*

Contacts among francophone states are clearly different in nature from those among the anglophone Commonwealth. To some extent, this difference reflects the different historical course of French imperialism as compared to British. What is uniquely Canadian in the current relationship is Canada's ability to offer to the new nations of French Africa access in their own language to the social and technological benefits of a North American industrial society where these can promote local development. A relationship of this kind, with a middle power such as Canada, appears to be welcomed by these states. Moreover, Canadians welcome it themselves as a concrete demonstration abroad of the bilingual nature of their country, complementing its established relations with France herself. Canada also benefits from the exchange of views among francophone states, and from the perspectives expressed to Canada, for example, in

---

* I have referred earlier to the shared jurisdictional competence of the Canadian provinces in certain fields.

Abidjan, Yaoundé, and Dakar. Canadian development assistance funds to Africa are now allocated in approximately equal shares to English- and French-speaking nations. Canadians were at one point serving simultaneously as Secretaries-General both of the Commonwealth and the Agence de coopération.

Some Case Studies

I would now like to review the policies of Canada and the United States towards three quite distinct parts of the world—China, Sub-Saharan Africa, and Latin America, and two representative functional issues: the Law of the Sea and the New International Economic Order. These cases make clear some important distinctions in the way Canada perceives its national interest, and the action that it has seen as appropriate to serve that interest. They sharpen contrasts, but also assist in defining similarities.

China

The U.S. recently established full relations with the PRC, but Canada probably already has as close a relationship with China as is possible for a Western country to have. Canada's good relations are based on several factors:
1. Its negotiation of a mutually acceptable recognition formula in 1970 that provided a model for many European and Third World countries;
2. Its support for the PRC's seating in the U.N.;
3. Its subsequent enthusiasm for building a substantive bilateral relationship;
4. Its lack of an "imperialist" past;
5. Its massive wheat sales at a time of economic disaster in China in the early 1960s, despite U.S. reservations.
Ottawa believes that its ties with China over the past few years have not only served Canada's own interest but helped establish a more stable and congenial relationship between China and the world community.

I think there is a revealing distinction in the logic underlying Canadian and U.S. moves towards China in the early 1970s. For Canada, the reasons were in part domestic, an independent assertion by Canadians given substance by the Trudeau government, that the reality of China had been ignored too long. Canada was ready to reciprocate China's new interest, for its own strategic and economic reasons, in establishing relations with the West, including the U.S.A. Recognition was seen by Canadians as a long-term investment in a more stable world order, and a pragmatic consolidation of an already profitable trading relationship.

But the concerns and interests of the United States were rather different. The dynamics of the Cold War and the position of the U.S. as a superpower deeply committed in Asia had locked the U.S. and China into a posture of confrontation for many years. Thus, Washington's motivation to seek improvement of relations was perhaps more strategic, with the opening towards China perceived, in part, as a counterweight to the Soviet Union, with benefits in East/West strategic terms. As well, there was a possibility during the later stages of the Vietnam war that China would limit to some degree North Vietnam's activities in South Vietnam and encourage North Vietnam to negotiate. There was of course long-term reasoning much like that of Ottawa, reflecting the common interests of the two countries in good relations with the PRC, but this reasoning was overlaid with a set of priority tripolar concerns.

Sub-Saharan Africa

Many of the same forces can be seen at play in the policies of Canada and the United States towards Sub-Saharan Africa. It is an area where Canada has a relatively high profile, but where the United States, because of strategic priorities elsewhere, until quite recently has had a relatively low-key involvement.

Canada's relations with the countries of black Africa are primarily guided by what it sees as the need for fostering economic development in the region as a condition for successful nation-building. Canada channels a large part of its bilateral assistance—around 30 percent of its global bilateral disbursements—to Sub-Saharan Africa, while the U.S. figure is more like 5 percent. This heavy involvement can be explained by the priority given to the poorest countries of the world in Ottawa's aid program and by special Commonwealth and franco-phone ties that have brought Canada closer to Africa.

Canada's British and French roots shared with the emerging states of Africa were one important factor. But its lack of imperial background—or ambitions—was perhaps the main element in the success of Canada's involvement. In general, Canada's political relations with most African states have been good and it has not asked much in return from Africa in political or economic terms.

The United States' interest in Africa has been traditionally less than its interests in Europe, the Middle East, and Asia. This is understandable, but slightly paradoxical, given the continent's potential. For example, Americans may not know that Canada's bilateral aid program of over $150 million per year to Sub-Saharan Africa is nearly the same size as that of the U.S. While Canada's interest in Africa has been rather constant and pragmatic, American interest seems perhaps more linked to crisis with possible global consequences. One thinks of the Congo, Angola, or current problems in the Horn and Rhodesia. There has perhaps also been a perceptual problem between the U.S. and the new black African states that Canada has not encountered. No one there really suspects that Canada has ulterior motives in promoting relations with the continent, nor does Canada have any difficulty in dealing with strongly nationalist and socialist regimes such as Tanzania.

The United States has already shown a new and constructive interest in African affairs, where its powerful and positive influence can play a valuable role. Canada and the U.S. are sharing in efforts to work out a peaceful resolution to dangerous tensions in Southern Africa. One only hopes this work is successful, given the potential risk to both North/South and East/West relations which collapse would entail.

Latin America

The relations of Canada and the United States with Latin America illustrate some of the contrasts and parallels that I have touched upon in previous examples.

As usual, geography and history tell us a good deal. The United States looks south upon Mexico, the Caribbean, and Central and South America, while Canada looks south upon its vast and only significant neighbor within thousands of miles, the U.S.A. In the late 19th and early 20th century, while Canadians were building railways and provinces in the West, the dynamic force of American private enterprise and government filled not only the vacuum of its own vast spaces, but overflowed to many other parts of the world. America's expanding frontiers of interest and influence created something close to empire in parts of Latin America.

In contrast to this very considerable U.S. involvement, Canada had little wide-ranging interest in Latin America until quite recently. Canada was a constitutional monarchy and a loyal part of the British Empire long after the Latin Republics to the south had severed their links with Europe. Though Canada was partly francophone, the tie of Latin language and Catholicism made only a limited contribution to developing relations with a continent much of which is physically as far away from Canada as East Asia or West Africa.

Canada's interest in Latin America and its contacts with that continent expanded considerably following World War II. Canada became, and continues to be, enthusiastic about building relations with the region and is active in several important regional organizations. Latin America has been an area of special interest to Canada since the review of foreign policy in the late 1960s which saw opportunities in Latin America and the Pacific for enriching Canadian contacts and reducing the preponderance of other ties. Canada now has a deep and growing interest in Latin America, particularly in the economic area. About half of Canada's exports to the developing world go to Latin America, with excellent prospects for further growth.

Canada's relations have developed in a relatively pragmatic way. As is often the case, ideological and strategic perspectives have been of less interest to Canada than to the U.S. Canada's goal—shared with the United States—has been the development of productive bilateral relations and effective regional institutions. Canada's membership in such organizations as the Inter-American Development Bank reflects its commitment to regional economic development. The thought of too deep involvement in local issues and regional conflicts in Latin America holds little attraction for Canada. For these and other reasons, the question of O.A.S. membership has been a source of continuing debate in Canada. Ottawa now follows closely the development of the Organization but does not consider full membership a precondition of effective participation in the affairs of the hemisphere.

There are some rather crucial footnotes here that I should add. Canada has normal and useful relations with Cuba. Canada's trade and tourist links are extensive, and it has a small aid program there, though there are aspects of Cuba's foreign policy with which Canada of course disagrees strongly. As in the case of China, Canada believes the pressure of isolation does not contribute to the growth of a commitment to global order. I should also mention the very close relationship between Canada and the countries of the Caribbean. Centuries of trading and other historic ties have given Canada a special prominence there, and it is particularly interested in the successful development of these small nations.

In the broadest picture, I think one can identify some convergence in Canadian policy towards Latin America. Canada has an increasing interest in the rapidly developing economic powers of the continent, and has had close contacts with a number of countries in the hemisphere with respect to Law of the Sea and North/South issues. For its part, the U.S. is showing a renewed sensitivity to its southern neighbors: the Panama Canal treaty, an effort to meet Cuba halfway, perhaps a more pragmatic, case-by-case approach to dealing with the countries of Latin America. The fundamental aims of Canada and the United States there are now much the same: a structure of intensified relations with the southern tier of the hemisphere. And the means both nations are now employing to bring about these relations are not that dissimilar.

Law of the Sea

Canadian and American attitudes to the ongoing U.N. Conference on the Law of the Sea (UNCLOS) offer a revealing set of policy comparisons and contrasts, and reflect fundamental differences between the two countries. I should hasten to add that there are, as well, many basic similarities in their positions borne of their long-standing political and economic relationship. Canada is a coastal nation, and it has taken an active part in the Coastal State Group at UNCLOS. But Canada's navy is small, and its blue-water ambitions are modest. Although Canada is a major ship user for its exports and imports, it does not possess an extensive ocean-going merchant fleet. The United States, on the other hand, is a global maritime power and necessarily construes one of its major objectives at the Conference as the preservation of traditional navigational rights and freedom of the seas.

If freedom of the high seas is critical for the U.S. and of relevance to all Western countries that benefit from America's naval strength, Canadians have felt strongly about the management and control of their coastal resources and the protection of the marine environment. Canada has, for example, taken national action in recent years, such as unilaterally extending to 100 miles its authority to control Arctic pollution. It also took action to define its immediate coastal area by fisheries closing lines, drawn point-to-point, to ensure proper fisheries management of bodies of water such as the Gulf of St. Lawrence and Queen Charlotte Sound. In early 1977, Canada extended its fisheries zone to 200 miles. It is essential to note, however, that these steps were taken only after an exhaustive search for international agreement or sanction for such action or, as in the case of the Arctic, where international law had not developed sufficiently to meet the environmental challenges. This international dimension to Canadian policy continues at the UNCLOS.

The U.S.A. has taken similar action to protect the environment and living resources of its coastal areas. The Ports and Waterways Authority Act of 1970 and, most recently, the Clean Water Act, testify to a determination to adopt national measures to meet the threat of vessel-source pollution in territorial waters and the new 200-mile fisheries zone the U.S. declared early in 1977.

While both countries share a deep concern for the protection of their coastal environments, there have been differences at the UN-CLOS negotiations over how the threat of marine pollution can be most effectively controlled or prevented. Canada believes that coastal states should have the power to inspect, and bring proceedings against, vessels polluting or threatening to pollute areas of 200-mile jurisdiction. Canada also asserts the coastal states' right to set national standards, in some respects more stringent than international regulations, for controlling vessel-source pollution in the 12-mile territorial sea. The strategic and economic interests of the U.S. cause its authorities to have reservations about conferring such enforcement powers on coastal states.

There are points of agreement, of course. Both countries hope for a successful outcome to the Conference, and for a stable order of the oceans with an equitable regime for preserving marine resources. In bilateral terms, the differences have not so far seriously impeded bilateral arrangements to combat the threat of marine pollution in adjacent waters. Canada and the U.S. agree that coastal states should enjoy the sovereign right to exploit mineral resources to the edge of the continental margin, and share common objectives at UNCLOS in this regard.

It is on the question of mining of manganese nodules on the deep seabed and its relationship to land-based production, however, that Canadian-U.S. differences surface once more. The nodules contain cobalt, copper, and nickel, as well as manganese, but the major interest is in the nickel content. Canada is the world's major exporter of nickel. The United States is the world's largest importer. Nickel mining provides considerable economic activity for Canadians, and the current depressed state of the international nickel market has caused severe dislocation and lay-offs at mines in several parts of the country.

The Law of the Sea Conference has before it a proposed international regime for the mining of nickel on the deep seabed—the first case in history of international management of an international resource as the common heritage of mankind. Canada believes that this regime must take into account the impact of offshore mineral production on land-based producers and ensure that, as a result of direct or indirect subsidization of seabed production, land-based producers are not harmed. Thus, Canada is advocating a ceiling on seabed nickel production, to guard against such potential disruption of the world nickel market, as well as to ensure sufficient scope for the commercial production of nickel from the deep seabed.

The United States, pursuing its interests as a nickel importer, has argued against any restriction on seabed nickel production. This position is designed to ensure maximum benefit to U.S. national interests, particularly U.S. corporations which have developed the potential to conduct seabed mining operations. The American position is nuanced, and I shall not risk distorting it by a brief summary. But the bottom line is expressed in a January 18, 1978, speech on seabed mining by their chief negotiator, Elliot Richardson, speaking of the current conference:

> Rather than accept outcomes which we consider wrong for the United States and, we believe, would be wrong for the world community as well, we would reluctantly choose to forego a treaty. The United States does not need a comprehensive treaty more than other nations. Seabed mining can and will go forward with or without such a treaty. We have the means at our disposal to protect our oceans' interests if the Conference should fail, and we shall protect those interests if a comprehensive treaty eludes us.

That is undeniably the voice of a superpower protecting its interests.

As I have mentioned, Canada has on occasion acted to extend sovereign rights over fisheries and to protect its offshore environment, but its purpose has been not only to regulate exploitation and to protect its environment but also to safeguard the oceans for future generations as a common heritage for mankind. And Canada has acted within what it regarded as a climate of international acquiescence and in harmony with principles of international conduct emerging at the UNCLOS. The issue of seabed mining plots clearly the respective locations of Canada and the U.S. on the grid of power and vulnerability.

The New International Economic Order

I shall not attempt to define in detail the various elements, often as political as they are economic, of the North/South dialogue on the New International Economic Order (NIEO). I shall also slide off such questions as whether there is an old order, or indeed any order at all. But I would draw your attention to the relative standpoints of Canada and the U.S.A. in the continuing debate on changes in the economic relations between developed and developing countries, and to some of the policy implications for the respective futures of the two countries.

The advocacy of economic changes has been with us for many years and, I suppose, first began to take definitive shape with the establishment of the United Nations Conference on Trade and Development (UNCTAD) in 1964. The Sixth Special Session of the United Nations General Assembly, in 1974, first called specifically for a new international economic order and for action to achieve it. The Conference on International Economic Cooperation (CIEC) grappled with the issues through 1976 and the first half of 1977. A Common Fund Conference has held two sessions—the second one adjourned in an atmosphere of muted frustration (spring 1978). The U.N. General Assembly has decided to create a mechanism to provide a review of North/South issues through the U.N. system.

The agenda for debate is formidable; the multipolar style of diplomacy is unique and complex. The process of negotiation is clearly an element of the new order itself, and getting the process right would be no small accomplishment.

The NIEO concept has its roots in the conviction that global economic development, and its presumed benefits, can be achieved by transfer of technology, resources, and capital; equitable terms of trade; reform of the international monetary system; and greatly increased aid. The Third World is demanding, in addition, a greater voice in the management of the global economic system. CIEC pursued these broad objectives in separate commissions devoted to energy; raw materials and trade; development assistance; and money and finance. What are the views of Canada on this broad issue and how do they differ from the American views?

Although Canada is a comparatively wealthy, technologically advanced country, it has in fact much in common with many developing countries. With a population of only 23 million against its size and identified resources, it may be considered a developing country. Canada's experience of foreign ownership of its resources, its global trade in basic agricultural and mineral commodities, and its dependence on foreign markets for its manufactured goods, have over the years been instrumental in shaping a peculiarly Canadian perspective on the world. It has only recently become a net importer of petroleum products and its long-term energy outlook is promising. Canada imports investment capital, technology, and human expertise to a much greater degree than does the U.S. It has the highest level of foreign participation in its economy of any OECD country. The country's economic strengths and weaknesses give it a stake in international economic arrangements which, I suggest, is proportionally greater than that of the United States.

I would add that Canada's long-standing ties with many developing countries and the experience of its own regional disparities have imposed a further sensitivity to the concerns of the emerging nations. Canada's official development assistance program now adds up to more than one billion dollars annually, disbursed through bilateral and multilateral channels. Against this background, and in view of its own interests in seeing better management of the world economic system, Canadian co-chairmanship of CIEC appeared as an entirely logical task to take on when Canada was invited to do so in late 1975.

The U.S. position on the New International Economic Order took some time to evolve, even after helpful intervention in the Seventh Special Session. The United States is, after all, one of the prime movers of the world economy, with a particularly large stake in free market forces. Canada's more vulnerable position determined a somewhat different response. The U.S.A. understandably adopted positions at CIEC rather similar to those adopted by West Germany and Japan, while Canada, in the work of the Commissions, frequently found like-minded positions among a mixture of developed and developing countries.

The United States will also, perhaps, continue as the target of a disproportionate share of the rhetoric which North/South encounters invariably generate. As the only superpower at the table, this may be inevitable. The American nationality of many multinational corporations is a further complicating factor. What is also unique to the American position is that the United States may be perceived as the last line of resistance to the proposals of the developing countries.

Delays may serve the purposes of other industrial countries, but the resentment will, rather unfairly, focus on the United States. On the other hand, American concurrence ends debate.

How, in the evolution of the North/South relationship and of the changing world it reflects, will Canada and the United States pursue their respective interests? The solidarity of the Third World Group of 77 is by no means eternal, any more than is the solidarity of the industrial countries on all issues. New leading nations are emerging, armed with resources and skills. Regional groupings are emerging with special roles to play, such as the Association of South East Asian Nations. Coalitions of producer and consumer nations have been formed successfully in some commodity areas. For Canada, the message is clear that it must play its part in working with these new forces, and shape policies which will fit a changing world.

Forecast and Conclusion

I have struck a number of themes: the different histories of Canada and the United States, their different windows on the world, the difference in scale of their strategic and security preoccupations, their slightly different perceptions of communism and nationalism in the Third World, the network of influence and associations which a middle power must continually promote and perfect. I have compared Canada's relative freedom to take risks, such as deciding not to build nuclear weapons, and exploratory initiatives such as aid to Cuba, with America's responsibilities which make some risks seem an uncertain luxury. Those contrasts established, I come to some final questions which I think I am obliged to pose.

First, is this Canadian difference, or freedom of action, only made possible by an American security umbrella which also shelters Canada? I think the simple answer is no. Canada's relatively comfortable security situation is but one important factor explaining the evolution of its foreign policy. Like other Western countries, however, it benefits from America's role as the ultimate guarantor of stability in the central power balance. In this context, Canada and the U.S. are close allies in NATO and NORAD. Just as Canada pulls its weight on what it sees as the key questions of Western security, Canadian troops saw action in Korea and in peacekeeping ventures under international auspices in corners of the globe where troops from the superpowers would have been unwelcome. Canadian diplomats and military advisers spent 20 years, at the request of the international community, in a painstaking but unproductive effort to promote a peaceful resolution to the conflict in Indochina. But Canada disagreed bilaterally over many aspects of U.S. policy in Vietnam and it admitted draft evaders. On this, I do not think history and most Americans will judge Canada harshly.

I would not deny, however, that Canada's proximity to the U.S.A. may influence foreign perceptions of it, nor that the global policies of the U.S. help to shape an international environment which is generally congenial to Canada's interests. Nevertheless, Canadian policies flow from the country's own calculus of interests and resources and are intended, as are those of the United States, to encourage a stable evolution of the world system. Independent Canadian initiatives have not been stalking horses for the U.S.A., nor is Canada driven to artificial initiatives in order not to be mistaken for a satellite. Canadians like to think that they have done what they ought to do, for example, when in the early 1970s they increased their aid program at the temporary expense of their defense budget. That was Canada's reading of the way to achieve stability in the world system.

In conclusion, there is another hard question relating to the chances for convergence and divergence in Canadian and U.S. views of the world over the years ahead. I think that the end of America's trial in Vietnam and the spectacular growth of functional interdependence in the global economic and political system during the 1970s may increase the number of parallels in Canadian and U.S. interests abroad, and expand the potential for concerted action in the two countries' approach to global issues.

There can be little quarrel with the statement that the international ground has been shifting under our feet in recent years. The energy crisis, the emergence of leading powers among what had for so long been regarded as an indeterminate group of developing countries, the diffusion of political and economic power, advances in transport and communications—these are just a few of the indicators.

Of equal importance is a trend towards special multilateral diplomatic instruments to deal with newly identified clusters of functional or economic issues. These include the Conference on International Economic Cooperation, the Conference on Security and Cooperation in Europe, the Nuclear Suppliers Group, and OPEC. These organizations and interlocking negotiations are retooling an international system that from time to time seems to transcend narrow national and ideological pursuits.

In this new world, the dialectic of power and vulnerability will continue to unfold, and Canadians and Americans will, I am sure, play their own parts—for their own good reasons—in seeking solutions.

6__POWER AND VULNERABILITY

COMMENT

Alan K. Henrikson

Contrary to the thesis implicit in Mr. Gotlieb's title and skillfully elaborated in his essay, I would submit that Canada, far from being deficient in "power," should be prospectively grouped with the powerful states of the earth. Instead of seeing itself as "vulnerable," Canada should appreciate the senses in which it is one of the least vulnerable of states. The result of a more bullish reassessment of Canada's international situation could be an even bolder and more ambitious, if not necessarily a more "independent," Canadian foreign policy.

How can one, bearing in mind the disparity between "middle power" and "superpower" (a categorical distinction which Mr. Gotlieb and other Canadian diplomatists stress), offer such a paradoxical proposition? It is possible when one recognizes that, where its relations with the outer, or extracontinental, world are concerned, Canada not only draws upon its own resources and reputation but partakes of the potency and prestige of the United States as well. Canadian foreign policy, to be *truly* "realistic," should be planned as much with this circumstance in mind as it is reckoned upon the basis of Canada's strictly internal assets. In other words, Canada's "power" should be seen as relative as well as absolute.

From the vantage of peoples outside North America, the images projected by Canada and the United States are often indistinguishable. Both nations are considered to inhabit a kind of *Insula Fortunata.* Their ample space, abundant resources, hard-working and generally prospering populations and, not least, their amicable relations with each other, set them apart from the majority of mankind. It is not surprising, therefore, that to Europeans, Asians, and Africans, Canada and the United States sometimes appear more "identical" than "individual." Since the Canadian and U.S. governments are unlikely to be able to reduce this perceived identification, they might try more effectively to exploit it—to the advantage of each, and both.

To an American reader, this suggestion of a "North American" foreign policy may be easily accepted, for it implies merely the magnifying or the complementing of the U.S. image. To the Canadian reader, however, the idea may be suspect as another version of "continentalism." There is hardly a more deeply held Canadian belief than the assumption that Canada's nationhood is incomplete without a demonstrably autonomous foreign policy. It has often been in the sphere of diplomacy, where the constraints are least, that Canada has striven to realize distinct ideals ("a bilingual society") and to assert a distinctive role ("conciliator") that have not been, and perhaps cannot be, fully realized at home. This internal concern is reflected clearly in Mr. Gotlieb's reference to Canada's "approximately equal" assistance to English- and French-speaking African countries and also, perhaps, even in his description of the world system as a "global mosaic."

Ironically, given Canadians' preoccupation with distinguishing their role in the world from those of others, Mr. Gotlieb's essay, like the Department of External Affairs' *Foreign Policy for Canadians* (1970) and even the "Third Option" paper (1972), does not appear to rest on a careful discrimination, admittedly difficult, between what Canada can achieve on its own and what it can only accomplish in partnership with the United States. A case could be made that it is in Canada's interest to leave this issue blurred. Nonetheless, Canadian officials themselves, in order to act, must know when and where they must have U.S. support, and in precisely what measure. Without advance assurance of American help, or at least non-hindrance, few Canadian initiatives can in the long run succeed. With American influence augmenting Canadian moves, however, "leadership" is possible.

Mr. Gotlieb, rather than describing the workings of the Canadian-American relationship in his comparison of outlooks, refers to the United States as a *deus ex machina*. The metaphor is significant. It reflects the postwar Canadian image of the United States as an entity of altogether different magnitude on an altogether different plane, capable of providential intervention in Canada's affairs but essentially unpredictable and, therefore, incalculable. Such willful, Jovian behavior on the part of the U.S. was, to be sure, evident in the Nixon Administration's 1971 economic "shocks." But can this episode accurately be taken, as it appears to be, as a precedent on which to base long-term Canadian policy?

Thus, Mr. Gotlieb acknowledges Canada's general dependency

upon the United States but leaves the specific dependencies—the relationships that determine what Canada can and cannot do in certain classes of circumstances—underscribed and therefore not analyzed. As a consequence, there is a certain fluidity, or arbitrariness, in Mr. Gotlieb's argument—and to the extent that this arbitrariness is symptomatic, perhaps also in Canadian foreign policy. He seems to dissociate and reassociate Canadian and U.S. attributes at will, according to the Canadian interest. On the one hand, he denies that Canada exerts any superpower sway over Eruope and that its civilization forms part of le défi américain. On the other hand, he proudly emphasizes Canada's ability to offer the developing nations of French Africa—non-imperially and in their own language—the social and technological benefits of "a North American industrial society." But he cannot have it both ways: either Canada is implicated in the Military-Industrial Complex or it is not.

Canada's and the United States' positions in the world, if not to the same degree their "perspectives" on it, are very much alike. The "windows," to borrow Mr. Gotlieb's metaphor, may be different, but the "house" is the same. The structural unity of the North American habitat and system, more apparent from the outside looking in than from the inside looking out, powerfully determines the policies of both nations. My principal criticism of Mr. Gotlieb's subtle contrasting is that he minimizes the extent to which Canada's foreign policy, even in its most far-flung manifestations, is a function of Canada's proximity to and reliance upon the United States and, more generally, North America.

I do not deny that Canadian foreign policy is autonomous, nor that it is perceived as such. Mr. Gotlieb's assurance that "independent Canadian initiatives"—e.g., recognition of Communist China, trade with Castro's Cuba, the 200-mile fishing limit—have not been "stalking horses for the U.S.A." and that Canada does not take "artificial initiatives in order not to be mistaken for a satellite" may be accepted. Nonetheless, it is clear that Canada's course in foreign policy is to a high degree due—in causation, if not in motivation— to the road the United States has since World War II taken in world affairs.

The simplest form of the argument that Canadian diplomacy depends on the position of the United States is, as Mr. Gotlieb himself expresses it, that the "Canadian difference, or freedom of action," is "only made possible by an American security umbrella which also shelters Canada." Surely, there is some truth even in this primitive contention. Witness Mr. Gotlieb's admission, while affirming

Canada's moral autonomy ("Canadians like to think that they have done what they ought to do"), that "in the early 1970s they increased their aid program at the temporary expense of their defense budget." What, besides the overarching U.S. strategic deterrent, allowed this?

The "security umbrella" argument is not the precise form of the U.S.-dependency thesis I would wish to make, however. Sheer physical safety has never been the only vital consideration even for the most extreme American cold warrior. Moreover, such an interpretation explains too much. To assert that all Canadian foreign-policy decisions are shielded, and therefore facilitated, by the American nuclear cover would be to explain none of them.

Not least among the deficiencies of the defense-shelter argument is that it does not differentiate between direct and indirect influences. The protection immediately afforded to Canada by NORAD is probably less important, in explaining the character of Canadian diplomacy, than the scope provided by the nearly worldwide policing role of the United States. Canadian foreign policy bears the imprint of the American global commitment. Other factors, including the Commonwealth inheritance and the cultural bond with *la francophonie*, have also shaped Canada's activity abroad. None of these other factors, however, has shaped so powerfully the very international context in which Canada has operated.

Mr. Gotlieb hints at the importance of Canada's proximity to the United States when he observes that Canada trades in the commodity of "influence" rather than "power." Although influence in diplomacy is composed of many ingredients (moral standing, habit of fairness, negotiating skill, and the like), its dominant element, as Hans Morgenthau and other realist writers remind us, is the reputation for power. Canada's influence abroad during the last several generations has depended upon, and derived from, the massive size and strength of the United States—or, as I would prefer, the aggregate power of North America as a whole. Let us briefly consider a number of illustrative cases, discussed by Mr. Gotlieb.

Canada's relations with Western Europe have been informed by a broad "Atlantic Community" concept having political, economic, social, and military dimensions. Hence, Canada sponsored the non-military Article 2 of the NATO Treaty. The practical value of this provision, which American authorities allegedly "neither understood nor appreciated," derived from, more than anything else, the commitment of the United States (and of course Canada) to Article 5 ("The Parties agree that an armed attack against one or more of them in

Europe or North America shall be considered an attack against them all").

Canada's relations with the People's Republic of China, which Mr. Gotlieb characterizes as probably as close "as is possible for a Western country to have," is no doubt largely attributable to the various factors he cites, including Prime Minister Trudeau's personal interest in China. Its success is also due, however, as he admits, to China's interests—in particular, its interest in breaking up the iceberg of North American hostility. To some degree, Ottawa has been viewed by Peking as a way station to New York (United Nations membership) and Washington, D.C. (permanent embassy status). By the time of the Trudeau government's October 13, 1970 recognition of the PRC, the Nixon Administration's interest in exploring a new relationship was also well known to Peking (if hardly anywhere else). There is no doubt that Canada was the North American forerunner and direction-setter in this field. Its pace and lead, however, would appear to be governed by the until recently slower progress of the United States.

Canada's relations with sub-Saharan Africa are also dependent on the power of the United States, as well as, of course, Canada's Commonwealth and francophone associations. Canada's freedom to play a consistently humanitarian role in Africa owes much to the fact that the United States has long held the ring around Africa with its naval forces and, of late, aided African governments against external subversion. It hurts slightly, whatever the essential justice, for the United States to be credited with showing "a new and constructive interest" in African affairs. One of the United States' fondest wishes has been to keep superpower influence out of Africa.

Canada's relations with Latin America are an even clearer case of the technical, case-by-case, and sometimes opportunistic "pragmatism" Mr. Gotlieb ascribes to Canadian statecraft. Consider, for example, the Canadian government's sharing in certain of the specialized activities of the Organization of American States without accepting the more thankless political responsibilities. This pragmatism, if not specially admirable, is from a U.S. viewpoint understandable. Canada's close ties with revolutionary Cuba—beyond regular diplomatic and limited trade relations—are more difficult to comprehend, unless one relaxes one's refusal to suspect deliberate Canadian foiling of U.S. policy. It is conceivable, of course, that Canada's "divergent" course was in this case, as in that of Communist China, intended to bring about an eventual North American convergence in policy. Possibly, had not Castro sent troops to Africa, this Canadian "exploratory initiative," too, would have succeeded. In any case, the episode demonstrates the importance of Ottawa's knowing whether it is leading the United States toward a path it is willing to follow.

The two functional areas Mr. Gotlieb analyzes—the Law of the Sea Conference and New International Economic Order (NIEO) discussions—also indicate the heavy weight of Canada upon the American position. Would it be possible for Canada to identify so closely with the "Coastal State Group," leaving the United States to uphold traditional navigational rights, were it not for the fact that the United States Navy defends the sea lanes through which third-party ships bearing Canadian wheat and nickel pass? In the NIEO debates, too, Canadian diplomats may be seen behind the broad target of their American counterparts. Canada is not a developing country. Even Mr. Gotlieb does not seem really convinced of the claim. As he candidly acknowledges, "American delays may serve the purposes of other industrial countries, but the resentment will, rather unfairly, focus on the United States."

In sum, it is clear that in many fields Canada's international role depends, both positively and negatively, on the larger and more central role of the United States. What advice might be given to Canadians naturally concerned about the long-term effects of this relationship? Stop fighting it, and make the most of it. In more instances than now appreciated, I suggest, the interdependence of the two great industrialized countries of North America, even if unbalanced and asymmetrical, works to the advantage of both. Just as the United States relies, for external purposes, on Canada's solidarity, so Canada can use the U.S. "cornerstone" as a fulcrum. A carefully thought-out partnership in diplomacy need not detract from the identity of either; it may even engender a greater sense of equality between them.

A more systematically developed "North American" diplomacy need not involve direct or formal U.S.-Canada cooperation. The differences in the geographical, cultural, and organizational makeups of the two countries, well described by Mr. Gotlieb, suggest continued and perhaps even increased diplomatic specialization. Nonetheless, greater coordination is implied. American as well as Canadian diplomacy may thereby be made more reliable and, in consequence, more effective.

One cannot deny the risk in the suggested program to Canada's wonted freedom of action, her "distinctiveness." Canada's faint image as a neutral, a natural participant in international peacekeeping operations, may disappear altogether. If, however unlikely, this be a consequence of a more integrated North American foreign as well as domestic policy, so be it. The vistas opened to Canadian-American concerted action, which Mr. Gotlieb foresees as a result of a Canadian and American paralleling of perspectives following the Indochina tragedy and growing functional interdependence in the global economic and political system, may be broader than any hitherto envisaged by either country. Canada, rather than standing alone as a moderating, modulated middle power, may then step to the front as a leading power.

Part Three

THE UNITY CRISIS:
THE NEW CHALLENGE

7_____THE FUTURE OF FEDERAL-PROVINCIAL RELATIONS

Richard Simeon

For a long time after the 1976 Quebec election English Canadians seemed to be paralyzed. There were urgent calls for national unity, lots of flag-waving and fervent declarations of a will to survive, but little in the way of concrete suggestions about what to do. To the old question: What does Quebec want? was added another: What does English Canada want?

Now there are some signs of movement. The federal government has made limited constitutional proposals; and it has also introduced its own referendum law, designed in the first instance to hold the Parti Québécois to the outcome of its own referendum, but with obvious broader application in any federal strategy to promote constitutional change.

Several premiers are beginning to put proposals on the table. The Conservative Party has issued a discussion paper on constitutional change, as did the Ontario Advisory Committee on Confederation. After a very slow and rocky start, the Task Force on Canadian Unity, led by Jean-Luc Pépin and John Robarts, is actively searching for what it calls a "Third Option," apparently something between the present federal arrangements and an independent Quebec.

Moreover, since this essay was first prepared the pace of political debate and the level of conflict on constitutional change have increased.

In June 1978, the federal government issued a White Paper, "A Time for Action," and the Constitutional Amendment Bill. It proposed to enact a number of changes with respect to individual rights, language rights, the Supreme Court, and the Second Chamber, by July 1979. A second phase, focused mainly on the division of powers among governments, was to be completed by 1981. In August, a Joint Committee of the Senate and House of Commons began hearings on the Bill and related constitutional questions. In August, too, the provincial premiers held their annual conference, at which they expressed their willingness to engage in constitutional discussions but rejected both the two-phased federal approach and its suggestion that if no agreement was reached, Ottawa could move unilaterally to make changes in national institutions such as the Senate and Supreme Court. They also argued that the division of powers should be brought forward.

The outcome of the partisan and intergovernmental divisions on both the procedure and content of constitutional revision is unclear. This essay, however, restricts itself to the situation as it existed in the spring of 1978.

Meanwhile, federalists in Quebec, who were leaderless and stupefied for months after the election, are getting organized. With Claude Ryan as Liberal leader in Quebec, a third way, which challenges Mr. Trudeau's vision just as much as it does Mr. Lévesque's, now has a powerful spokesman. The alternatives for Quebec are now defined by an equilateral triangle. The provincial Liberals have made a sharp recovery in opinion polls. They are now running neck-to-neck with the Parti Québécois, which is perhaps partly a result of the wide exposure given to the recent Liberal leadership campaign. In the bitter Quebec-Ottawa clash over federal moves to pressure the provinces to lower their sales tax, the position of the PQ was supported by the Quebec Liberals and the Union Nationale. While Claude Ryan has welcomed some aspects of the federal proposals, he has joined other provincial governments in sharply criticizing the federal procedure, and in arguing the proposals do not go far enough.

There are also other, less hopeful, signs. The declining economy, itself partly a result of the political crisis, saps the country's ability to deal with it, and exacerbates regional and other tensions. Ironically, it also keeps separatist support down, at least in the short run. In a sense, therefore, the price of independence is being paid in advance. Deep prejudices and old hatreds and stereotypes are never far from the surface. They may easily flare up in the heat of the referendum campaign or dramatic events like the Sun Life* affair. There is much potential for real bitterness.

Morevoer, Canadians do not have a very good record in past constitutional discussions. After all, pressures from Quebec for more or less fundamental revisions in political arrangements have been

---

* Sun Life Insurance decided early in 1977, over the objections of the federal government, to move its large corporate headquarters from Montreal to Toronto rather than to accept Bill 101.

around since 1960. An intensive series of federal-provincial discussions between 1968 and 1971 did produce a limited package of changes, but it was rejected by Quebec. The dilemma then is the dilemma today. Because there is no consensus, the constitution must be changed; because there is no consensus, it cannot be changed.

Rewriting the Constitution: Some Basic Questions

Today, defenders of the *status quo* are few and far between. Virtually everyone speaks of the need for a "new constitution." One should be skeptical of all this clamor. Existing institutions may be further discredited without having anything to put in their place. In many cases there is little understanding of what the *status quo* actually is, or of the flexibility of the existing constitution. One should also be skeptical of the efficacy of constitutional engineering: it seldom works the way the engineers expect, and no constitution can create a consensus where none has existed before. It will not change social and economic realities: it can only reflect them. It cannot end the tensions in Canadian life: it can only provide a framework within which to manage the conflicts and maintain a creative dialogue between them. The causes of the current crisis lie much deeper than any inadequacies of the existing constitutional documents. Constitutional engineering has narrow limits. Yet dissatisfaction has become so profound and widespread that to refuse change is to endanger the survival of the country. The most basic feature of any constitution—its legitimacy in the eyes of those governed by it—has been eroded. Once the constitutional question has been raised, it cannot simply be forgotten.

In thinking about change several underlying issues must be kept in mind. First, the contemporary Canadian crisis is multidimensional. It is simultaneously a question of the relationship between *language groups*; of the relationship between regional *societies* and the national society; and of the relationship between *governments*. Which aspect the observer considers most important will greatly influence the recommendations he makes.

Second, a variety of causes of the current crisis may be advanced. It may be located at the level of culture, in the attitudes and identities of Canadians and their feelings about the country and each other. Or it may be located in economic forces, focusing on inequalities and uneven development between central Canada and the peripheries of east and west, or between English and French Canada. Or, it may be located in political institutions. The institutional focus, in turn, can stress either the failure of integrative mechanisms within the national government, or the failure of the mechanisms of conflict resolution and policy-making between the federal and provincial governments. Obviously, all three elements are involved—and indeed the crisis lies in the mingling of all three sets of factors. But here, too, prescriptions depend greatly on how the analyst perceives the causes of crisis.

Third, there is a tension between realism and idealism in constitutional change. What may be desirable in some abstract sense may be completely utopian. Proposals must therefore be evaluated in terms of their political feasibility. They must reflect not only existing economic, social and cultural realities, but also the views of the power centers—notably the federal and provincial governments—whose consent is essential to agreement. It is not hard to write any number of "ideal proposals"; what is hard is to get them accepted. In the short run, the constitution cannot change realities, it must accommodate itself to them.

The criterion of feasibility, moreover, directly involves the question of the procedures to be followed in arriving at agreement and of who will participate. Whose agreement is necessary? In some general sense, any new settlement must be acceptable to the public in general. But, the primary vehicle we have developed in Canada for debate on such matters is the federal-provincial conference, involving direct negotiations between the executives of federal and provincial governments. Both interest groups and legislatures have been largely frozen out of this process. This executive-dominated pattern will not likely be broken. The agenda of questions for debate will be limited, with little room for consideration of matters not of direct interest to the eleven governments. Proposals for constitutional guarantees of freedom of information, for example, are unlikely to get very far. "Realism" dictates a general acceptance of the *status quo*, a realization that no fundamental changes will be considered, and that no proposal which threatens greatly to weaken or to undercut any of the power centers in federal or provincial governments is likely to succeed.

Finally, three different sets of criteria must be borne in mind in assessing proposals for change. There is the question of community: how to reconcile the tensions between French and English, center and regions? Most proposals are addressed to this problem. But proposals must also bear in mind a functional criterion: What are the implications of proposals for the ability of Canadian governments to manage the economy and respond to diverse social and economic interests which are not themselves regionally defined? And there is a democratic criterion: What implications do proposals have for citizen effectiveness and governmental responsiveness? Difficult trade-offs must be made among all these perspectives.

The Constitutional Challenge

Causes of Constitutional Disagreement: Quebec

The roots of the crisis lie in the diversity of Canada itself, and in the always uncertain and tentative character of Canada as a national community. Is it a union of two nations, or of ten provinces; of two great cultures, or of many?

More specifically, the current crisis is caused by the growth of regionalism, provincialism, and Quebec nationalism on the one hand, and the decline in the strength, legitimacy, and effectiveness of the federal government on the other. It is above all a crisis not so much of language, culture, or even economy, but a political crisis—a crisis of political communities and their institutions.

The immediate cause, of course, lies in Quebec, and in the growth of a new secular nationalism which sees the state as the primary instrument of national development, as the one primary lever which Quebecers unequivocally control. Hence, for the first time, this nationalism has come to take the form of a widespread demand for *political* independence. Every Quebec government since 1960 has expressed this nationalism in one form or another, and has sought more or less fundamental changes. The Parti Québécois is thus a logical evolution from past developments.

The reasons lie primarily in the mobilization of Quebec society after 1960. Traditional nationalism had emphasized the need to protect the language and the faith; it was hostile to government and the state. It sought to isolate Quebec from the North American world of commercialism and industrialism. It was, in short, a demand to be left alone; and despite occasionally bitter conflict, it did not fundamentally threaten English-Canadian interests.

This traditional nationalism, however, became increasingly anachronistic as Quebec became an urban industrial society, and as a new working class and a new middle class were created. The logjam broke after 1960 and the Quiet Revolution followed. As Quebec emerged into the modern economy several things became evident to Quebecers. The federal government was dominated by the English-Canadian majority; French Canadians were virtually frozen out of positions of power in the federal bureaucracy. French Canadians were hemmed into Quebec; to leave the province was to lose one's culture, because education, government, business, and everything else outside was English.

Most galling of all, the provincial economy itself was dominated by English-speakers; French-speakers were at the bottom of the economic heap, even in their own province. That condition had to be challenged and the one instrument which Quebecers unequivocally controlled was the provincial government. It could be the instrument for Quebec to modernize its society and economy, the tool to protect the language and to force English-owned business to open its doors. Thus, it required more resources and more powers.

The paradox is that as Quebec modernized—indeed became in some senses more like English Canada—English and French Canadians would be in direct competition for the same things—whether it was jobs in Montreal or power in Ottawa.

So economics, culture, language, and politics became intertwined in Quebec's expansionist, outward-looking nationalism. The federal government emphasized the language dimension and responded by attempting to redress the imbalance through its policies to promote bilingualism and biculturalism. Ottawa asserted that it, as much as Quebec, represented francophone interests. French-Canadians must be at home anywhere in the country; "Quebec" and "French Canada" were not synonymous. But Quebec nationalists argued that these policies were too little and too late. Quebec and French culture could develop only within the context of its own national state. Sociological nations should be political nations too. At the same time the federal language policies provoked resentment among many English Canadians.

More important, developments in Quebec helped trigger widespread expression of other regional tensions in Canadian society. If Quebec is a distinctive, self-contained community, people in other regions tended to say, "We are too." The reaction to the Quebec election in English Canada was not to rally around Ottawa but rather to put a whole range of other regional grievances and aspirations on the table. As with Quebec, this resulted from a sense of grievance against federal policies and Ottawa's failure or inability to represent and respond to regional interests, as well as from a more positive sense of regional aspiration and identity.

Causes of Constitutional Clamor: Regional Grievances

The federal failure was in large part a failure of representation. Ottawa was no longer able to be the arena in which all regions and national interests would be expressed and reconciled. The classical brokerage model of Canadian politics has broken down. The large national parties are unable to win support across the country. The weakness of the Liberals in the West—greatly exaggerated by the electoral system—has meant that Westerners have felt left out, over a very long period, from any real influence in the governing party and caucus—surely a major cause of Western alienation. The same theme, in reverse, applies to the Tories in Quebec.

Traditional brokerage politics no longer integrate the country. The British parliamentary model, with its strict party discipline, greatly weakens the federal parliament as an arena of accommodation for regional differences. The growth in the scope and the stakes of government .activity and the shift to party leadership based on the character of the party leader, rather than on regionally powerful provincial spokesmen, reinforce the federal weakness. As a result the provincial governments have become the primary vehicle for expression of regional grievances. The regional/territorial cleavages have become organized into politics, and, correspondingly, other cleavages have been minimized.

Not only have federal parties and institutions been unable to act as vehicles for accommodation at the center, but also discontinuities between national political life and politics in each of the provinces have reinforced sharp differences between federal and provincial governments. Federal and provincial parties lack unified ideologies, have differing electoral coalitions, have different party organizations and sources of financial support, and so on. In some cases the major parties at the provincial level, such as the New Democratic Party and Social Credit in British Columbia, are only minor parties at the national level. There is little mobility of leadership between levels. Similar discontinuities between national and provincial politics appear to exist at the level of bureaucracies and interest groups. Thus, instead of a complex interweaving of politics at each level, as is the case—in different ways—in Germany and the United States, we find in Canada relatively isolated subsystems, which deal with each other primarily through their respective political executives.

The weakness of integrative institutions at the federal level is reflected in grievances against federal *policy.* In every area, feelings

that federal policies exploit some areas to benefit others and that
Ottawa is remote and insensitive are widespread. Some of these
perceptions concern recent policies, but there is a remarkable con-
continuity going back to Confederation itself. Thus, Westerners argue
that Confederation was mainly a device for economic elites based in
Toronto and Montreal to create for themselves a hinterland to be
exploited for raw materials and as a captive market—leading to
grievances over transportation, the tariff, energy, banking, and
others. Most profoundly in the West, there is a demand for political
power to go along with growing economic power and a self-
confidence based on vast resources.

In the Maritimes, the grievances are of a different order. Maritimers
also feel that Confederation oriented development to the West,
leaving them a backwater. They now benefit from many federal
programs designed to relieve economic disparities and promote
regional development, but there is little significant growth. They see
themselves ever more dependent on federal largesse. Their grievances
stem from a loss of power and from the frustration of dependency.

Listing all the grievances leaves the impression that every region is a
loser from Confederation. They ignore the many successes of the
Canadian political economy. It is also extraordinarily difficult to
compile a "balance sheet" of federalism, or to measure exactly how
much federal policies benefit or hurt different regions, though many
are now being produced. The expansion of government activity has
acted to politicize these grievances and attach higher political stakes to
them.

This analysis of representational and policy weaknesses suggests
one possible avenue for constitutional change. That is the search for
ways to restore the capacity of federal institutions to reflect and
accommodate within their own processes the various aspects of
regional and ethnic cleavage.

It may be, however, that the problem lies less with the institutions
and policies than it does with the breadth of the diversity which they
must try to bridge. Modernization and development appear to have
widened, not narrowed, these differences.

Moreover, the development of provincialism and regionalism
appears to be more than simply grievances and frustration against a
federal government believed to be unfair and unrepresentative. It is
also rooted in a strong sense of regional community and identity, and
in a desire for provincial societies to be free to develop themselves, to
pursue their own interests and to retain their natural wealth for their

own benefit. In this sense, for many Quebecers, independence itself is an important value, irrespective of grievances against Ottawa.

Provincial governments have provided a powerful institutional expression to this development. They have become in recent years much larger, more confident and aggressive, and more effective. It is in areas of provincial jurisdiction or responsibility that many of the most important new activities of government have developed. Their control over natural resources has provided them considerable fiscal clout, as has the progressive decentralization of taxing powers. Some political scientists, indeed, see the competition between empire-building political elites, locked in a struggle for status and power, as providing the real dynamic of Canadian federalism. Alan Cairns, for example, argues that the roots of intergovernmental conflict lie not so much in the support of distinctive regional societies, or in different economic and ethnic interests, but in the capacity of governmental elites to mold their environment to their own purposes.[1]

While this approach seems to underestimate the importance of the economic and social bases of governmental power, it underlies another important diagnosis of Canadian problems, which leads to its own set of prescriptions. Thus, the politics of region and ethnicity are *governmentalized*. Politics take the form of competition between federal and provincial governments, each speaking for a different constituency, each seeking to control the levers of public policy across many issues, and each possessing formidable political and organizational resources. This view leads to proposals for reordering the relationship between governments so as to reduce conflict and enhance their collective capacity for making policy which responds to both national and regional needs. Hence, attention turns from change in central government institutions to changes in the division of powers and in the machinery of intergovernmental relations.

Three Competing Drives

These cultural, economic, and governmental dimensions of regional conflict combine in three images of culture, society, and economy whose interplay—sometimes creative, sometimes destructive—has shaped Canadian history. They are country-building, province-building, and Quebec nation-building. These models have an empirical dimension and provide a useful way of organizing information on various aspects of regionalism. But they also have a very important normative dimension: they constitute different concepts of community and identity.

Each of these conceptions has powerful support in the country, and each has a strong institutional base—in Ottawa, the provinces, and Quebec City. Unfortunately, we know little about the support for each in the general population. Each implies a different sense of community, of who "we" are. Each, moreover, suggests a different direction for change for the Canadian system and a different set of solutions to the current crisis. At the same time, each is too strong to be defeated. No set of proposals which enshrines one to the exclusion of the others has much chance of success. Hence, the challenge for constitution-makers is to find a framework which represents and reconciles all of them, allows for shifts as needs and desires change, and encourages the debate among them to be creative rather than destructive.

Country-building is the impulse to develop a strong, integrated, independent pan-Canadian society and economy. It seeks to build a common loyalty and consciousness, to redistribute wealth from rich to poor regions, to maximize overall economic growth, to promote mobility, and to insure that Canada remains a common market. Country-building emphasizes the need for common social programs and standards across the country. It argues that the issue of language should be dealt with primarily by bilingualism at the national level.

Politically, country-building sees the federal government as the primary expression of the national interest. Ottawa should take the initiative and has the responsibility for economic policy. National and regional interests should be reconciled in Ottawa.

Country-building was the impulse behind Confederation itself and the National Policy of Sir John A. Macdonald, which was, in the words of one participant in the Confederation debates, "to redeem Canada from provincialism" and create a "new nationality" built around a dominant federal government.[2] It flowered again during and after World War II, as Ottawa established fiscal dominance and policy leadership in the context of the growth of the welfare state and Keynesian economic management. Its continuing strength can be seen in many current policies.

Most observers believed after World War II that in the modern world the trend towards centralization was irreversible. They believed that the provinces would be reduced to little more than overgrown municipalities, that regional/cultural cleavages were obsolete and would be replaced by functional or economic cleavages centered on the federal government. That, of course, did not happen. Instead, we witnessed what D.V. Smiley has called the "attentuation of federal power."[3]

The province-building impulse was reasserted. It defines the province as the most important community. The provincial governments should be the primary instruments of regional development. They should be free to choose their own priorities, pursue their own goals, and exploit their own resources. They can plan for their own needs and can do it better than Ottawa bureaucrats.

Quebec nation-building really is just one step—a big step—beyond province-building, adding difference to the other elements. The drive for Quebec nation-building also provided an example which helped stimulate the growth of the province-building impulse elsewhere. Few province-builders elsewhere, however, go as far in asserting provincial primacy as do Quebec leaders, even those who are federalists.

Federal-provincial conflict is largely a result of tension among the three impulses. Ottawa continues to pursue its vision of the national interest—as in the anti-inflation program, resource policy, competition policy, etc.—leading to provincial complaints of intrusion into provincial jurisdiction. At the same time, the provinces seek to control the levers of policy in order to promote their own development. They "intrude" on Ottawa. The result is rival state-building, in which each government seeks to occupy the whole policy space. We have seen not so much decentralization, as expansion of both levels of government. And, of course, one man's "intrusion" is another's "national interest."

One result is the complex process of federal-provincial negotiations which have evolved in Canada, with massive overlapping and duplication of activities and responsibilities, with an elaborate network of federal-provincial conferences and much contradiction and inconsistency in policy. Effective policy-making on many issues must be joint policy-making, since instruments necessary to deal with them are shared and since each level has the capacity to frustrate the other. Federal-provincial conflict has not reduced federal-provincial interdependence.

In Search of New Arrangements

Alternative Directions for Change

What about the solutions each model suggests? Country-builders argue that we should strengthen Ottawa, even give it more power, especially in economic and cultural affairs. But they recognize, too, that if Ottawa must be strengthened politically, it must somehow better represent, within itself, Canada's regional diversity. They suggest, therefore, changes in federal institutions to make them more representative—for example, by altering the electoral system to produce a better regional fit between seats and votes, or by changing the procedure in the House of Commons so as to allow members greater freedom as spokesmen for regional interests.

Province-builders argue for more provincial power: more provincial autonomy, greater fiscal resources, and a decentralization of responsibility. They want to restrict Ottawa's abilty to impose itself on the provinces, forcing them into programs they do not want, or limiting their freedom of action. Thus, the federal power to spend in areas of provincial jurisdiction should be limited, as should its ability to challenge provincial control of natural resources. Province-builders also want to give the provinces a much stronger voice in the making of federal policies which affect them, especially in fields like transport and tariffs.

Finally, Quebec nation-builders offer a range of solutions. They all assert, in Claude Ryan's words, "the unique, special and inalienable position of Quebec as the principal and immediate political expression" of the francophone community.[4] Their options range from outright independence to sovereignty with association to various forms of special status.

Each of these strategies represents a powerful reality in contemporary Canada, but each has equally strong opponents. In the present atmosphere, few can imagine actually increasing Ottawa's powers. A strong country-building model would be anathema to many Quebecers, since they would see themselves as a permanent minority.

Decentralizing power has many attractions. It not only responds to provincial demands, but also fits in with the general hostility to bureaucratic government and with the view that governments closer to the people are more responsive. But country-builders raise many objections. Would Canada not become even more fragmented than it is now and approach a state of balkanization? Decentralization might make it impossible to develop any coherent national economic policy which was not simply the lowest common denominator of provincial interests. It might become very difficult to insure the redistribution of wealth from richer to poorer areas, quite apart from the possibility that

Canada might become even more vulnerable to American and world economic forces. In addition, destructive interprovincial competition for investment might arise. And last, but not least, national standards in areas like social and health services might deteriorate. After all, it was federal power which initiated the welfare state.

What would a province-building strategy offer Quebec? It would not recognize Quebec's distinctiveness, and might mean even less recognition of French language rights in most provinces.

Of special status, even of a moderate kind, country and province-builders ask: "Would it not lead down a slippery slope, with independence the eventual outcome anyway?" Could one accept that Quebec representatives in Ottawa would vote on legislation which did not apply in their own constituencies? How could the English-speaking majority accept equal weight with a minority on some key issues? Would not the other provinces want to exercise all the powers available to Quebec? Would there not be, not special status for Quebec, but special status for all, as Premier Lougheed of Alberta has suggested?

In many ways, then, these drives seem to be mutually exclusive and to lead in different directions. Can they be reconciled? It is relatively easy to imagine frameworks for the accommodation of country and province-building; it is very much harder to integrate these with Quebec nation-building. Any reconciliation will require reconsideration of several different factors. First are the institutions of the central government itself—most important, the federal House of Commons and Executive. Second are the institutions of federalism itself—those which were to maintain the intergovernmental relationship and the federal bargain. They include the appointment powers of the Supreme Court, the mechanisms of intergovernmental relations and the division of powers.

The House of the Provinces

I will not explore all these aspects here. One possible mechanism for representing and reconciling the three competing drives and for improving intergovernmental relations, however, is to convert the Senate into a new second Chamber. This "House of the Provinces" would be a legislative and deliberative forum in which the provincial governments would be represented directly by delegates appointed by and responsible to them. Variants of this proposal, which bears some similarity to the German *Bundesrat*, have recently come from the

Ontario Advisory Committee on Confederation, the Province of British Columbia, the federal Progressive Conservatives, and others.[5]

Such a House might have several powers: to debate and to propose amendments to federal legislation, and to have a suspensive veto over federal actions which have significant regional impact; it could have a permanent veto over federal use of those powers, such as the spending power, which now allow Ottawa to occupy areas of provincial jurisdiction.

The House could also approve federal appointments to agencies like the Bank of Canada, the National Energy Board, the Canadian Radio Television and Telecommunications Commission, and the Canadian Transport Commission. These regulatory agencies have become very important in recent years and their decisions often affect provincial and regional interests. It could play a similar ratification role in appointments to the Supreme Court. However impartial the court has been in practice, its legitimacy is eroded by the appointment of its members by the federal government alone. Quebecers have often argued that the court leans to Ottawa, and similar complaints by the other provinces have grown in response to recent decisions which have enhanced federal power. In addition to these legislative roles, the House would be an arena for deliberation between governments on matters of joint concern, such as economic development, overall levels of public spending and borrowing, and the like.

Virtues

A House of the Provinces has two principal virtues. First, it provides a framework for a continuing public dialogue among representatives of each of the three drives. The debate among them can be carried out in a national forum. The federal government would be forced to take account of provincial interests in advance of legislation; provinces will be sensitized to the national dimensions of what they do. It is also a compromise in which each side gains something and loses something. For the country-builder it says: Ottawa can retain overall responsibility for such things as national economic policy and can retain its capacity to move into provincial areas in the national interest; but the price is to give the provinces a direct voice in the making of those policies. For the province-builder it offers a greater influence over national policy, but grants less in the way of new power.

Second, the House could provide a means of institutionalizing federal-provincial relations. No conceivable redistribution of powers can eliminate interdependencies or restore "watertight compartments," in which each government operates independently in clearly delineated spheres. Indeed, while much overlapping can, no doubt, be reduced by administrative action, the likelihood is that there will be more rather than fewer areas of concurrence in a revised constitution. Given the inevitable interpenetration of federal and provincial activity, the nature of citizen demands, the continual emergence of new policy concerns, the interconnectedness of most policy issues, and the Canadian pattern of competitive state-building, effective national policy can only be developed through joint, cooperative activity.

The existing intergovernmental machinery has many defects. It is not mentioned in the constitution; it has no firm decision rules; it often goes on far from public scrutiny; there are often few incentives to agree.

A House of the Provinces, then, could replace a large part of the existing process of intergovernmental negotiations. It moves them into the center and makes them a permanent and formally recognized part of the constitutional structure. The House, indeed, could be seen as a permanent federal-provincial conference, a government of governments. Since these conferences are already one of the primary features of contemporary Canadian government, the proposal is less radical than many others, for it is an extension of what already exists. It recognizes Ottawa and the provinces as the two primary power centers.

Criticism

As a compromise proposal, the House will be attacked by provincialists because it looks like a way to hold on to federal dominance, and by centralists because they see it as a device to hamstring Ottawa. At the same time, it does give each something of what it wants.

It may also be argued that a Provincial House with real power provides a recipe for deadlock and frustration; it could block action by complicating the decision-making process. Three replies are possible. First, the existing *ad hoc* federal-provincial process already poses these problems with no satisfactory means for overcoming them. Second, it is hard to see any solution to the present Canadian difficulty which would not complicate matters even more. And third, while government everywhere is complex, the Canadian system is today, despite the federal-provincial division, less fragmented than either Britain (where so much power is shared with interest groups) or the United States (with its division of powers).

A more serious objection is that this House would be undemocratic—that it would reinforce both the emphasis on territorial cleavage and the dominance of the political executives. Indeed it would, though the confrontation of federal and provincial governments in an arena which was open and publicized would be an improvement on the existing negotiations. Moreover, an elected Senate, while perhaps more democratic, would render Cabinet government more difficult and would lead to even more complication, since it would not reduce the demands of the provinces for more power and voice in national decision-making. Federalism, in any case, fits uneasily with British cabinet government. Under the provincial House proposal, however, the federal cabinet would remain responsible to the House of Commons and the provincial cabinets to their legislatures. Members of the House of Provinces would be accountable through their own provincial governments.

Some valuable functions of the present Senate would be lost with this proposal—notably the detailed scrutiny and improvement of legislative draftsmanship, and the ability to constitute wide-ranging committees to explore matters of general public interest. One response is to suggest that a strengthened House of Commons, with greater independence for members and a stronger committee system, may be able to perform these roles. It is also through reform in the federal and provincial legislatures that progress may be made in limiting the dominance of cabinets and executives.

The role and powers to be given to the House of Provinces are closely related to decisions about the division of powers. The two questions will have to be discussed simultaneously. The most likely direction for change here is for a greater degree of concurrence, which will, in turn, require clearer rules about who will prevail in case of conflict. By introducing more areas of concurrent jurisdiction, and by permitting a province to opt out of some federal programs, as Quebec has been able to do in the case of many shared-cost programs, it should be possible to respond to Quebec's desire for special status without actually using the term.

The Challenge of Change

There are many other issues to discuss in a full-scale constitutional review—civil rights, language rights, the Supreme Court, and so on. The major gap in the proposals which have come from English Canada so far—and in those I have sketched—is that they do not directly come to grips with the Quebec challenge. They are limited and they respond more to grievances elsewhere than to those arising in Quebec. English Canadians have had great trouble in accepting the idea of Quebec as a distinct nation. It is even more difficult for them to accept that relations between English Canada and French Canada should be on the basis of parity, of two equal partners. Hence, the gap between the two conceptions of the country remains vast, and one cannot be optimistic about the outcome.

Mechanisms for Change

Traditional Methods

The question of what changes can be made in the federal system is also deeply intertwined with the question of how to go about making them, and who should participate in this process. The accepted mechanism for constitutional change, as for many other policy matters in Canada, is the federal-provincial conference. While there have been proposals to establish some extraordinary body, such as a constituent assembly, to write a new Constitution, it is virtually inconceivable that in Canada's executive-dominated system, the leaders of the eleven governments would so delegate their authority. Accommodation in Canada has always been an elite affair.

Under the current Constitution, Ottawa can make some constitutional changes unilaterally—it could make some changes in the Senate or the electoral system, for example. But it is unlikely that the provinces would allow Ottawa much freedom of action to enact general constitutional change without their agreement.[6]

Another possibility is that the provinces would take the initiative and would agree among themselves, leaving Ottawa aside. There has been considerable development of provincial coordination in major national issues. In 1976, the provinces adopted a joint position with respect to proposals for amendment and patriation of the Constitution and more recently developed a joint position concerning changes in federal-provincial fiscal arrangements. Following introduction of the Quebec Language Bill, which would require immigrants to Quebec from English Canada to attend French-language schools, the Quebec government proposed "reciprocal agreements" by which mutual access to minority language education could be worked out. While the provinces rejected such agreements on a province by province basis, there was some acceptance of the possibility of a general agreement, in opposition to the federal view that minority rights should be guaranteed in the Constitution. Nevertheless, it is impossible to imagine that Ottawa could be pushed aside in the review process.

Referenda

A major innovation in constitutional change has recently been introduced—the referendum. It was the device used by the PQ to separate the issue of electing a new government from that of independence itself. All decisions on constitutional change now depend on the outcome of this referendum, which will, in effect, allocate the bargaining chips among the players. The Parti Québécois now clearly would like to put it off as long as possible and to make the question as vague as possible, because every indication at the moment is that it would lose.

The federal government, in turn, has introduced its own referendum bill. It purports to involve more democratic procedures than the PQ law. Its first purpose is apparently to keep the PQ honest—to insure its question and its campaign rules are fair. But it also has been suggested that if the PQ delays its vote too long, Ottawa will use its law to preempt the Quebec vote. Moreover, the referendum device could also be used to preempt the other provinces—to win public support for constitutional changes even if they were opposed by the provincial governments. Ottawa has suggested the possibility of building the referendum mechanism directly into any new amendment formula. We do not yet know what role it will play in the adoption of any package of constitutional changes, but it clearly adds an important new dimension to the politics of constitution-making.

The Interpretation of Results: Quebec and Canada's Future

The immediate burden of explaining what a "federalist" vote means falls on the Quebec federalists. Their chief spokesman is likely to be Claude Ryan, the Liberal leader, well known as the conscience of French Canada and a moderate nationalist. Ryan traditionally has argued for special status for Quebec in Confederation, recognizing that the Quebec government is the primary expression of French Canadian interests. This position accepts federal supremacy in some areas and argues for entrenched language rights at the national level.

Ryan has moderated his position, but in the past all versions of special status have been rejected by Prime Minister Trudeau and many English Canadians. Conservative leader Robert Stanfield was criticized in 1968 for his alleged support, and the option has been ruled out of public debate ever since. There may be some change now, especially in a willingness to have some form of *de facto* special status, or a system whereby powers may be available to all provinces yet taken up only by Quebec.

The possibility that the chief federalist spokesmen in Quebec will advocate a position quite different from that advocated by the federal government, or by other provincial governments, poses an acute dilemma. Indeed, M. Ryan and Premier Lévesque share a common problem. Each, in the context of the referendum, will be offering Quebec voters something which he alone cannot deliver. Both require the acceptance of English Canada.

It would be tragic if rival federalist options were put forward in the referendum, or if a successful federalist campaigner in Quebec found his program rejected by Ottawa or the other provinces. A coordinated federalist position is important but difficult, not only because of existing differences between Quebec and federal Liberals, but also because, lacking governmental power, the former cannot participate in the intergovernmental discussion. By the same token, the present Quebec government cannot be excluded from them; precedent suggests Quebec would have a veto over important constitutional amendments (which explains Ottawa's consideration of a referendum and its asserted right to change the Senate and Supreme Court unilaterally). Thus, the procedure for registering agreement remains controversial and complex. Canada is paying a heavy price for past failure to agree on an amending formula.

These difficulties loom larger as the Quebec referendum debate approaches. The federal government would like to have wide agreement on a set of changes before it is held, but it is unlikely to receive such consensus. Nevertheless, it is vital for all other governments to think carefully through not only what they want for themselves, but also what they will accept for Quebec—and to convey enough signals to Quebec voters to convince them that change is possible within the federal system. Given the competing views outlined in this essay, and the limited progress made in the two years following the Quebec election, one cannot be optimistic.

NOTES

1. Alan Cairns, "The Governments and Societies of Canadian Federalism," *Canadian Journal of Political Science*, X:4 (December 1977), p. 700.

2. Quoted in F.R. Scott, *Essays on the Constitution* (Toronto: University of Toronto Press, 1977), p. 34.

3. D.V. Smiley, *The Canadian Political Community* (Toronto: Methuen, 1967), pp. 45-55.

4. Quoted in William Johnson, "Together But Special," *The Toronto Globe and Mail*, 14 February 1978, p. 7.

5. A Committee of the Canadian Bar Association has recently made a similar proposal. The federal government in Bill C-60 has proposed a "House of the Federation," half of whose members would be appointed by the federal legislature, in proportion to party strength in each province at each federal election, and half by provincial legislatures in proportion to the results of provincial elections. It thus combines regional, government, and party representation.

6. In the fall of 1978, the issue of what changes Ottawa could make unilaterally under the existing constitution became a matter of intense controversy between Ottawa and the provinces and within the federal Parliament. Ottawa asserted a broad power to act on its own, especially with respect to the Senate and Supreme Court; others disagreed.

7____THE FUTURE OF FEDERAL-PROVINCIAL RELATIONS

COMMENT

Jerome E. Milch

Richard Simeon's analysis of the crisis of Confederation reflects the views of a growing number of Canadian academics and political figures, including several distinguished contributors to this volume. The problem, according to Professor Simeon, can be traced in large measure to a decline in the strength, legitimacy, and effectiveness of the federal government. The intensification of nationalist sentiments in Quebec, of course, provoked the current challenge, but the crisis stems from the inability of Ottawa to fashion policies which respond to the needs of the provinces. This failure, Professor Simeon argues, is a product of the breakdown in representative institutions. Neither Parliament nor the political parties serve any longer as effective mechanisms to accommodate regional differences, and the specific grievances of the provinces, many of which can be traced back to the nineteenth century, remain unresolved if not entirely ignored.

The failure of national political institutions to deal with conflicting regional interests is undeniable. At the same time, however, the federal government has not demonstrated the capacity to resolve problems of common interest to the provinces. Accusations of insensitivity, remoteness, and inequity have been leveled against Ottawa for decades, but the current situation is exacerbated by the perception that federal policies are also ineffective. Increasingly, in recent years, problem solving has devolved upon the bureaucracy. Hence, the current crisis is as much a product of bureaucratic failure as of a breakdown in representative institutions.[1]

The growing disillusionment with the ability of the federal government to resolve common problems is particularly ironic in light of recent efforts to reform the policy process in Ottawa. Following the report of the Glassco Commission, the federal government began to recruit technical experts and managers to staff the executive agencies and to introduce modern, rational planning techniques into government. The process accelerated in the latter part of the 1960s with the efforts of the Trudeau government to restructure the bureaucracy and to make it "responsive, innovative, and effective." Old-line operating agencies established policy planning staffs to rationalize and systematize their programs; new agencies were created to deal with new problems and to coordinate federal activities in areas such as regional economic expansion, environment, and urban affairs.

These efforts were undoubtedly successful in improving the ability of agencies to analyze problems and formulate solutions, but the reform, as a whole, was unsuccessful in increasing the effectiveness of the federal bureaucracy. Problems of coordination within individual ministries remained unresolved.[2] Cooperation among departments was even more difficult; despite its mandate to "coordinat[e] ... and promot[e] national urban policies among federal departments and agencies," the Ministry of State for Urban Affairs was unable to achieve coherence in federal programs affecting the cities.[3] The frequency and severity of conflict, both within the federal bureaucracy and between Ottawa and the provinces, appeared to increase. Most damaging of all was the failure of carefully conceived and planned federal initiatives in the provinces. For example, Montreal's new Mirabel airport was designed by the Ministry of Transport to keep Canada "one step ahead"; it has proven instead to be a white elephant, which the Ministry has admitted officially and literally, adopting a picture of a white elephant as the airport's emblem.

Why have these reforms failed to improve the performance of the federal government? In some cases, the failure of federal policy was a product of faulty planning and the misapplication of new techniques. The reorganization of the bureaucracy and the recruitment of specialists, after all, provide no guarantee that the new planning tools will be employed effectively in the pursuit of rational policies. A more significant problem, however, stems from the political context in which rational planning and administrative reorganization were introduced. Programs designed by technical specialists were often altered in response to political demands, their final versions emanating, at least in some instances, from the provinces themselves. The plans which emerged from the process were not particularly distinguished by their technical rationality, for the policy planners often proved incapable in many instances of altering other programs to compensate for these politically induced changes.

Even if the new techniques had been employed properly, the reforms would not have increased significantly the effectiveness of the bureaucracy. The essential difficulty resides in the theory of the reform, i.e., the application of rational analysis to functionally discrete agencies. Although governments everywhere are organized along sectoral lines, real problems overlap boundaries and require coordination among functionally discrete units. Rational planning techniques might be useful in facilitating the analysis of problems, but they are destined to produce partial solutions when employed by individual agencies with narrow mandates. Unfortunately, they also generate the conviction that the policies are "correct," thereby complicating the process of coordination; no agency will compromise voluntarily if persuaded that its solution, produced through rational analysis, is appropriate for the problem. The result is predictable: increasing conflict among units of government with different political objectives as well as among agencies with different mandates. In cases where conflict cannot be resolved through brute force, paralysis sets in; on the other hand, agencies or units of government which are sufficiently potent to overcome resistance often implement partial, and too frequently ineffective, policies.[4]

These problems with the reform of the bureaucracy are hardly unique to Canada, and policy analysts in many advanced industrial societies have lamented the increasing ineffectiveness of government. The consequences, however, are particularly significant in Canada, where ineffectiveness is compounded by inequitable distribution and where there are few countervailing institutions to offset bureaucratic tendencies. Moreover, Canadian politicians are less inclined than their American counterparts to intervene in the bureaucracy in order to protect regional interests. One could imagine, for example, that the Department of Transportation (DOT) in Washington might seek to provide assistance for airport development strictly according to a rational development plan for aviation infrastructure. What one could not imagine, however, is that Congress would ignore the implications of such a proposal and allow DOT to allocate funds without regard to regional balance. Indeed, the Airport and Airway Development Act of 1970 specifically requires airport development funds to be distributed to the states and territories largely in accordance with area, population, and passengers enplaned. No similar provision exists in Canadian legislation.

The creation of a House of the Provinces, as advocated by Professor Simeon, would not resolve the problem of the bureaucracy, but it might well provide the necessary counterbalance to it. Such an institution would allow the provinces to choose their own representatives in Ottawa and would provide a permanent forum for the expression of regional grievances. Proponents hope that a House of the Provinces would increase the sensitivity of the federal system with respect to regional interests while, at the same time, enhancing the commitment of the provinces to the maintenance of a national system. And, as Professor Simeon suggests, it might accomplish these desirable objectives without requiring radical changes in the other institutions of government or alterations in the fundamental power relationships in the country.

Is this type of solution adequate to cope with the current tensions in Canada and to assure that the country will emerge from its trials intact and healthy? No one, of course, can be certain, and Professor Simeon himself is not particularly optimistic about the outcome. Moreover, foreign experiences provide little basis for optimism. The threat of dissolution rarely has been dissipated without major structural changes or the application of force. Americans, for example, have been faced with a similar problem twice before in their history. On one occasion, in the 1780s, the crisis was resolved by a major restructuring of the institutions of government, requiring substantial compromises on the part of the states; in the other instance, civil war resulted. The first solution seems impractical for Canada, and the latter is unthinkable. Those Americans who sympathize with the plight of their northern neighbor can only hope that there remains a sufficient reservoir of goodwill within Confederation to accord some modest prospect of success to a House of the Provinces and to similar structural reforms.

NOTES

1. See Garth Stevenson, "Federalism and the Political Economy of the Canadian State," in Leo Pantich, ed., *The Canadian State: Political Economy and Political Power* (Toronto: University of Toronto Press, 1977) pp. 92-93.

2. See, for example, Elliot J. Feldman, "Expanding Vancouver

International Airport: The Politics of a High Technology," Occasional
Paper Number 12, Center for Transportation Studies, University of
British Columbia, p. 26, for an account of the inability of two
divisions of the Ministry of Transport to coordinate airport plans in
Vancouver. The efforts of the Ministry of Transport to employ
rational planning in the development of major air facilities in
Montreal, Toronto, and Vancouver are chronicled in Elliot J. Feldman
and Jerome Milch, *Canadian Federalism and Airport Development*
(forthcoming).

   3. Elliot J. Feldman and Jerome Milch, "Coordination or Control?
Federal Initiatives in Canadian Cities," paper presented at the 1978
Annual Meeting of the American Political Science Association, New
York Hilton Hotel, New York, N.Y., August 31-September 3, 1978.
The quotation is from a description of the responsibilities of the
Ministry of State for Urban Affairs in *Organization of the
Government of Canada* (Ottawa: Information Canada, 1975).

   4. For a more detailed description of this problem, see Elliot J.
Feldman and Jerome Milch, "Organizing Disunity: Rational Planning
in Canadian Administration," paper presented at the Conference on
Canada's Major Problems and Prospects, Royal Military College,
Kingston, Ontario, June 18-July 5, 1978.

8 ENERGY, NATURAL RESOURCES, AND THE ECONOMICS OF FEDERALISM

NATIONAL HARMONY OR CONTINENTAL HEGEMONY?

Ian McDougall

"There are only 6 percent of the people of the world living in the United States, and we use 30 percent of all energy. That isn't bad; that is good. That means we are the richest, strongest people in the world, and that we have the highest standard of living in the world. That is why we need so much energy and may it always be that way."

—Richard M. Nixon
1973

Too frequently current regional discontent is viewed in Canada as resulting from the failure of Ottawa to strike the correct cooperative balance between conflicting regional aspirations. This view acknowledges no defect in Ottawa itself. It pays no heed to the next-to-nonexistent federal presence in the sphere of primary resource development. It asks that we accept the proposition that the existing division of legislative competence under sections 91 and 92 of the British North America Act is outmoded. And it requires us to turn a blind eye to the reality that Ottawa has failed to act on its constitutional responsibilities and to call upon the wide constitutional powers that are available to it.

Much of the present regional discontent is rooted in material rather than political or cultural causes. Canada was a richly-endowed country in terms of its primary resource base. Today, as a direct product of federal neglect, many of these primary endowments have been alienated in favor of the U.S. export market, and Canada has imported premature shortages and rising costs. The provinces have been left to act as free agents in terms of across-the-border sales of their indigenous resources, without any obligation to consider the needs of neighboring provinces or the country.

Now Canada must deliberately attempt to exploit the comparative advantages inherent in its primary resource base. Future Canadian needs must be given preference over demands of export markets. Secondary industrial opportunities that may exist as a result of having such resources must be secured. And continuing exports must be priced in such a manner as to insure fair returns to Canadians as the ultimate resource owners. In this regard the federal government alone, with its jurisdiction over international and inter-provincial trade, has the legislative competence necessary to meet the challenge.

The disposition of our conventional reserves of petroleum, natural gas, and hydroelectric power-generating capacity amply illustrates both the costs of failing to come to grips with the need to develop and implement effective national policy, and the now-urgent necessity of coming to terms with the problem. As a matter of sentiment alone there has never been doubt as to the desire of Canadians to keep the country independent and whole. But past failure to realize our potential for prosperity has shaken the virtue of the federal system in the eyes of many Canadians. It is now time to put federalism and the country as a whole back to work and in this way to offer a tangible demonstration of its worth to its citizens in all regions.

Defining the Federal Crisis

The future of federalism is clearly a central preoccupation of many Canadians. But to date, the problem has been characterized as one of simply cultural accommodation, unrelated to the overall economic viability of a Canada unified under a federal structure. This is something of a mystery in view of the full decade of public concern about economic nationalism that preceded the current crisis.

Conventional political wisdom appears to be that earlier concerns about inadequate federal resource policies and the problems stemming from foreign domination in the economy should be attended to only after the Quebec challenge has been resolved. This is perhaps an unfortunate simplification. It has in addition produced an enormous paradox.

It is a matter of general belief that to reunite Canada the terms of Confederation will have to be rewritten so as to allow the provinces, and Quebec in particular, an increased share over matters that are today questions of exclusive federal jurisdiction. At the same time, Canada must resolve basic economic difficulties that arise from premature and largely unanticipated shortages in the primary extractive sectors, a task that necessitates vastly increased rather than reduced central authority over what are today traditionally fields of intra-provincial jurisdictional competence.

A Byzantine interpretation of the federal preoccupation with the Quebec crisis would suggest that it came as a welcome relief to the federal government because it simultaneously diverted attention from the economy and diminished the public's belief in central government authority as a suitable means of coming to terms with economic problems. A better case, however, might be made for the proposition that the linkages between current regional discontent and an effective centrally-directed federal economic strategy have yet to be recognized.

The federal government could have—and can yet assume—a far greater say, under the British North America Act, over the development and commercial exploitation of the country's primary resource base. Through a nationwide rationalization of production and sale of primary assets, Canada has had the potential to secure a broad range of comparative advantages that could do much to stimulate greater domestic development of secondary industry and thus national wealth. In this fashion, Canada's capacity to come to grips with regional income disparities would be increased, and to the extent that such disparities have spawned discontent and disillusionment with Confederation, regional confidence might yet be restored.

In this context, the history of Canadian energy resource development both offers a rich example of a dismal federal track record, and illustrates an area where future federal assertiveness might yet prove highly productive.

Energy Resource Development: Federalism's Loss Leader

Since 1973 a great deal of ink has been spilled over the so-called "energy crisis." Depending on one's persuasion, the Western industrial economies are either teetering at the brink of complete collapse, or alternatively, are the victims of a global hoax carefully animated by an intricate collusion between the Organization of Petroleum Exporting Countries and the infamous Seven Sisters—the world's major oil companies. But apart from any controversy regarding the true state of remaining world petroleum and natural gas reserves, there is cause for unease about the very term "energy crisis." More specifically, this phrase fails to describe the breadth of the ultimate economic and social implications so far as Canada in particular is concerned.

Canada's oil and gas supply prognosis is now clear. The warnings about dwindling oil and gas potential, which a few short years ago were cursorily dismissed as sheer uninformed hysteria, proved ultimately optimistic. For example, in 1974 one commentator summed up Canada's prospects as follows:

> The empirical odds against the three provincial frontier areas of Canada all containing the oil reserves required to justify future projections are approximately 1 in 2,750—1 in 14. Only one explored basin in the world out of 14 has more than 5 billion bbl of reserves and this amount would be required to justify the projections being made by major oil companies in Canada. No entrepreneur would expect these odds, and the possibility of this production being achieved is nil.
>
> The projections of the NEB staff report of December 1972, which required an infusion of frontier oil beginnings in 1979, are impossible to achieve as no new oil has been discovered. So all the major oil companies have postponed the steep rise in frontier production until 1985....
>
> I am satisfied that most of the major oil companies no longer believe the statements they were making in 1969, 1970 and 1971. Several have written off large parts of the frontier regions. H.R. Warman, Exploration Manager, B.P. Oil (the principal operator at Prudhoe Bay) stated to an industry group in England in September 1973 that it is now likely that the Canadian Arctic does not contain a prolific oil basin.[1]

This same spokesman went on to suggest that Canada would

become a net importer within a three to five year period. In fact, Canada moved into net import status as he wrote, and reliance upon offshore supplies has been increasing steadily since that date. As Western production continues to decline the market reach of crude imports will move progressively westward.[2]

The natural gas picture, if not attended to, may end up being equally dismal.[3] Thus, in a purely physical sense, Canada is faced with the possibility of extreme shortfalls in terms of both oil and gas production, with few prospects of relief for a generation or more. To this degree, Canada indeed has an "energy crisis."

But Canada's energy difficulties have both causes and consequences that give the lie to the notion of a technically defined problem that can be limited to a discussion of kilowatts, barrels, or million cubic feet. Since the late 1950s, there has been very little central direction with respect to provincially-inspired resource development projects. As a result, Canada has seen two decades of massive exploitation in the energy sphere which has in large measure resulted from export opportunities. In the cases of gas, oil, and hydroelectric power, this exploitation has produced both a. rapid cost and price increases in domestic markets, and b. foreseeable shortages that are so severe that they may permanently alter the standard of living enjoyed by most Canadians.

There are at least five elements that go towards explaining Canada's failure to develop effective national controls over the exploitation of these resources, including: 1. federal Constitution constraints, 2. immature regulatory traditions, 3. limited public perception and participation in the formation of central resource exploitation policies, 4. the failure to develop comprehensive regional economic development policies at the federal level, and 5. U.S. domination.

Constitutional Constraints

It was the undisputed intent of the Fathers of Confederation to create a strong and highly centralized federal structure, in complete and deliberate contrast with the American constitutional model. A broad range of factors, including concern about the sheer geographical breadth of the country, the small indigenous population, the U.S. history of state rights controversies, and genuine fear that Canada might be absorbed into the Republic, all combined to support a strong central government. As one leading author noted, the British North America Act gave the provinces:

... only enumerated powers to make laws, giving the residue of power to the federal Parliament. This was a departure from the American precedent where residuary power had been left with the states. And the list of specific heads of federal power included several topics left to the states in the United States. Thus, the Canadian federal Parliament was given, by Section 91 (2), the power to regulate "trade and commerce" without qualification, while the United States Congress had been given the more limited power to regulate "commerce with foreign nations and among the several states and with the Indian tribes" ... the federal government was envisaged as fiscally dominant. The federal Parliament was given, by Section 91 (3), the power to levy indirect as well as direct taxes while the provinces were confined, by Section 92 (2), to direct taxes; in the 1860s the indirect taxes of customs and excise accounted for 80% of the uniting colonies' revenues, and so a system of federal grants to the provinces was established from the beginning in recognition that the provinces' tax-raising capacity would not be adequate for their needs.

Not only did the B.N.A. Act's distribution of powers contemplate a more centralized system than that of the United States ... the provinces were actually made subordinate to the center in violation of the principle that in a federal state the regions should be coordinate with the center.[4]

But, since 1867, a series of Privy Council decisions moved reality far away from the intended direction of the British North America Act. The wide interpretation given the provincial jurisdiction over Property and Civil Rights constrained the early evolution of a tradition of federal regulatory intrusions in the field of primary resource development:

> The Judicial Committee of the Privy Council was the final court of appeal for Canada in constitutional cases until appeals were abolished in 1949. Two figures dominated the course of decision in Canadian constitutional cases: Lord Watson, who was a Law Lord (and thus a member of the Privy Council) from 1880 to 1899, and Lord Haldane, who was a Law Lord from 1911 to 1928. They believed strongly in provincial rights, and they established precedents which gave a narrow interpretation to the principal federal powers (the residuary power and the trade and commerce power) and a wide interpretation to the principal provincial power (over

Property and Civil Rights in the province). The decisions of the Privy Council—the "wicked stepfathers of Confederation," as Foresy calls them—were much criticized in English Canada (although not in French Canada) for their provincial bias.[5]

The ultimate implications of this hitherto unchecked traditional provincial power over resources were not fully realized until the engineering capability to harness entire river systems and to pipeline petroleum and natural gas over vast distances was acquired. Beginning in the late 1950s, major undertakings were being considered in most of the provinces that were to have substantial impact upon neighboring provinces, and ultimately the entire country. The twenty-year period between 1956 and 1976 bore witness to a series of massive developments that included the hydroelectric development of the Columbia and Kootenay rivers in British Columbia,[6] the development of Alberta and British Columbia petroleum and natural gas reserves,[7] the construction of major north-to-south pipeline facilities, and harnessing of vast power reserves in the Churchill and Nelson river systems of Manitoba,[8] the beginnings of development of the James Bay power reserves in the province of Quebec, and the Churchill Falls hydroelectric project in Labrador.[9]

In almost all of the above cases:

1. the development initiative came primarily from the individual province concerned;
2. federal involvement in the basic decision was decidedly peripheral;
3. in almost every case the opportunity to develop arose principally from market opportunities in the United States and not Canada;
4. in virtually every case the value of the assets that were being exploited, and the cost of development were both grossly understated, and later became the source of profound regret in many regions of the country.[10]

These projects, as the following map illustrates, are not isolated cases; to the contrary, every known major power and fuel reserve within commercial reach of the U.S. frontier is either exploited or slated for development.

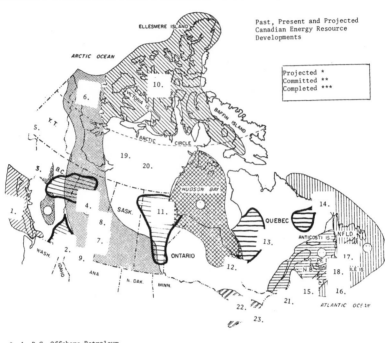

Past, Present and Projected
Canadian Energy Resource
Developments

Projected *
Committed **
Completed ***

```
  *  1. B.C. Offshore Petroleum
 *** 2. Columbia River Treaty
 *** 3. B.C. Oil and Natural Gas
 *** 4. Peace River Development        * 16. Stoddard Island Plant
  *  5. Yukon Taku Rivers              * 17. Maritime Offshore Petroleum
  *  6. MacKenzie Valley Petroleum     * 18. Canso Strait Superport
 *** 7. Southern Alberta Petroleum     * 19. North American Water & Power Alliance
  *  8. Prime Plan                     * 20. CENAWP
 *** 9. Kaiser Coal Development        * 21. Lorenville Superport
  * 10. Arctic Oil and Gas          *** 22. Essex County Petroleum
 ** 11. Nelson-Churchill Power Project *** 23. Niagara Power Export
  * 12. Grand Canal Plan
 ** 13. James Bay Project
 *** 14. Churchill Falls Project
 ** 15. Lorenville Thermal Plant
```

In addition, the north-to-south orientation of all of these developments has given rise to substantial capital investment redundancies within Canada. For example, Alberta and Saskatchewan power consumers, who might have benefited from surplus hydroelectric capacity in British Columbia, have instead been forced to develop their own. Ontario Hydro today might well be capable of absorbing power surpluses in Quebec, thus offsetting the need to develop a massive thermonuclear program. Churchill Falls power, if available in Quebec, could have permitted deferment of the James Bay project for an extended period of time. More natural gas from Alberta delivered at reasonable cost to Manitoba might have allowed that province to delay the need to undertake the massive Churchill-Nelson diversion scheme.

Beginning with the Columbia River Treaty controversy, the provinces consistently have adopted the position that there is no constitutional obligation to give priority to the energy requirements of neighboring provinces as opposed to American consumers hungry for Canadian oil, gas, or hydroelectric power. The federal government appears never to have challenged the validity of this position. As a result, while current Canadian energy production is substantial, transmission flexibility between provinces is severely restricted. To reverse this situation at this late date would necessitate an unprecedented federal assertion of jurisdiction over primary resource deployment, backed by a massive capital commitment in new inter-provincial pipeline and electric transmission facilities. From the perspective of the provinces that are currently the major producers of petroleum, natural gas, and hydroelectric power, so dramatic a federal intervention would in all probability be regarded as a fundamental and intolerable breach of constitutional tradition. And there can be no doubt that it would indeed represent a complete 180-degree change from the customary federal position, essentially one of uncritical accommodation of provincial wishes.

Undertakings of this magnitude have had a pronounced long-term economic impact upon the country. The welfare of Canadians is a concurrent federal and provincial jurisdiction. Under the Peace, Order and Good Government[11] and the declaratory provisions[12] of the B.N.A. Act the federal government has both the right and the obligation to insure that the resources of the provinces will be exploited in a fashion that is compatible with long-term national interests. The federal government could take steps to insure that James Bay power surpluses move into Atlantic Canada; it could establish greater Canadian access to oil and gas reserves rapidly being exported from Alberta; and it could redevelop transportation, communication, and environmental policies on a nationwide scale. Since 1957, however, federal officials have preferred to fall back upon what is described as "cooperative federalism." Its underlying premise, according to its proponents, is the notion that because the original terms of Confederation are "outmoded" and "inadequate," a passive federal stance is more appropriate than strict adherence to the existing central-

residual powers under the Constitution.

Individual provinces have interpreted this doctrine to mean that everything is up for grabs in federal-provincial negotiations, including such matters as jurisdiction over international trade,[13] external relations,[14] resource agreements,[15] and so on. In short, provincial expectations of the concessions that could be expected of Ottawa were aggrandized beyond all proportion with the introduction of cooperative federalism. And the federal government unnecessarily established a Constitutional tradition that made it impotent with respect to using the basic and fundamental curbs that it possessed under the British North America Act.

Regulatory Traditions

The evolution of federal regulatory controls over Canadian energy resources development and marketing has been less comprehensive than in the United States, which in part reflects the constitutional standoff described above. The federal tribunal responsible for interprovincial and international movements of petroleum, natural gas, and hydroelectric power is the National Energy Board (NEB), created in 1959[16] largely in response to a protracted political controversy over the building of the Trans-Canada natural gas pipeline from Alberta to Montreal. The NEB was to facilitate a more systematic and politically dispassionate examination of future pipeline decisions.

When the NEB was created, it was widely believed that Canada possessed an overwhelming wealth of gas and oil. Indeed, as recently as 1970, the then federal Minister of Energy Mines and Resources, J.J. Green, publicly proclaimed that Canada possessed a potential stock of oil amounting to 923 years' supply, and natural gas that approached 400 years' worth of supply. With such thinking, no level of government took serious account of the possibility that Canada might experience shortages within two decades. Representations brought to the NEB were, almost without exception, from an industry uniformly optimistic, and there was little non-industry involvement in Board proceedings until the early 1970s. Perhaps more importantly, the Board did not receive strong representations from the major utility and consuming provinces to counter the tribunal's preoccupation with maximizing production rates.

The industry believed that a policy maximizing production would create the cash flows necessary to enable producers to delineate the purportedly vast deposits that otherwise remained unidentified. The

Western economic base would receive the benefit of a petroleum and natural gas sector advanced far beyond what the Canadian market would by itself justify. Possible doubts about Canada's ultimate petroleum and gas budget for the long haul were not considered seriously until late 1974. Nor was there wide concern as to the low border prices being paid for Canadian natural gas, and the consequently retarded net return to Canada (after all deductions) from the sale of this valuable commodity. The NEB simply and uncritically assumed the merit of substantial export of Canadian oil and gas. It developed no protection formula for Canadian petroleum sales until after 1973, and employed a highly conservative gas export formula that provided minimal protection for Canadian requirements. At no time has the Board expressed any concern with respect to pricing and to the fact that cheapest sources, being developed in favor of export customers, might cause (and indeed have caused) prices to rise rapidly for future Canadian consumers who have to depend upon more distant, smaller, and more costly sources of supply.

The NEB has failed to protect Canadian market needs, paid no attention to potential development advantages from an oil and gas endowment beyond immediate short-term returns to the producing sector, and made no attempt at evolving comprehensive regulatory/marketing policies such as have been undertaken by the U.S. Federal Power Commission. Indeed, since 1974, its major preoccupation has been the examination of the domestic implications of shortages and cost increases that have been the direct product of its own neglect.[17]

Public Interest

Canadians have been unwilling to accept even the possibility of resource scarcities, and there has been until now a fundamental complacency about economic issues. Canada is experiencing the start of a "public interest" vanguard in the regulatory process, as in the Northern Pipeline Hearings of the National Energy Board and the Northern Pipeline Inquiry of Mr. Justice Berger, which attracted broad participation from public interest groups. But, to date, there is little evidence of a desire by either the federal government or the regulatory tribunals to encourage the growth of a public interest tradition, and there continue to exist substantial barriers that deter effective public involvement.

Nor is there, for reasons already discussed, much public dissension concerning government policies in the primary resources sectors. The implications of our current and projected supply difficulties are technically complex, and they ramify in forms that are often not immediately traceable to a single cause. Similarly, a large number of small secondary industries, dependent upon petroleum and gas products, have been added to the Ontario bankruptcy lists. In both cases, labor costs have been cited as the major difficulty, and not energy. Food costs have also risen, a fact usually blamed on the farmer rather than on the actual evidence, which once more implicates petroleum cost increases.[18]

Most Canadians rely on the tax-paid "experts" in government to deal with these complex issues, a matter of trust rather than consensus. Unfortunately, history and current developments give little reason for confidence that the broader public interest will in fact prevail.

Regional Economic Disparity

Canada has been characterized by substantial regional economic disparity since Confederation. However, the original areas of depression have changed over the last hundred-odd years. The Western prairie provincial economies have, as a result of improved transportation, expanded agricultural markets, and through the discovery of oil and gas, experienced steady expansion and diversification. Atlantic Canada, on the other hand, entered Confederation during a minor economic zenith with the shipbuilding and port commerce that was mainly a residue of the earlier West Indies' trade. After 1867 the Maritimes experienced a hundred years of recession, and today are the most depressed provinces in the country.

To a very significant extent most of the provinces have at one time or another expressed serious concern that the benefits of Confederation have tended to concentrate in favor of the Province of Ontario, which indeed has experienced more or less unabated growth since the 1860s. The answers to this criticism are perhaps predictable. First, attention is often drawn to the obvious proximity enjoyed by Ontario to large U.S. markets. Second, its large base of agricultural production has allowed for the growth of a large indigenous population. Third, its commanding position with respect to the Eastern Seaway traffic has made it the logical clearinghouse for Western raw materials. And fourth, Ontario transfers large sums to the less developed provinces through its tax contribution towards

Equalization, and is a proportionately larger contributor towards other federal regional development programs.

This reasoning does not answer all grievances concerning federal policies, such as freight rates which clearly have simultaneously served Ontario's need for raw materials and yet deterred the development of a competitive manufacturing base outside of the province. Nor does it answer the criticism lodged against Ottawa that preferential treatment has been accorded Ontario needs in trade discussions and agreements with other countries, most notably the United States. In short, some provinces, if indeed not all, view Ottawa in much the same way that some Canadian economic nationalists have often perceived the United States; namely, that federalism is artificially preventing regional economic diversification in order to guarantee that Ontario will have unrivalled access to the country's raw materials, and enjoy domination over the finished goods markets in Canada.

The debate on both sides probably presumes too much coherency on the part of federal planners. It is true that Ontario has fared rather better economically than the rest of the country since Confederation. It is also true that federal policies often have reflected some bias in favor of Ontario's needs. But there are outstanding examples to the opposite effect. Recent federal commitments to price domestic gas and oil at "world commodity levels" have clearly been weighted in favor of Western interests. More significantly, the history of federal support given primary resource trade flows to the United States was in large part justified in the name of greater economic development in the West, and so far as oil and gas are particularly concerned, has proved to be very much to the long-term disadvantage of Ontario. Nonetheless, it is abundantly clear that federal policy makers have at no time attempted to take stock of how Canada might plan its economic future with a view to obtaining maximum benefits from its resource base through which the power to redistribute in favor of the depressed regions would be enlarged.

U.S. Domination

An overwhelming preponderance of foreign ownership, especially American, is a Canadian fact of life,[19] but the long-term influence of U.S. investment in the formation of federal energy and resources policy is not highly visible. Still, the present primary trade flows are observable and, in the oil and gas sector, Canada has found it difficult to extricate itself from export trade that has ominous implications for future secondary industrial and household consumers who will confront potential shortages and dramatically rising costs. Indeed, the major producers, most of whom are U.S. owned and controlled, argued before the National Energy Board in 1975 that exports should continue as a matter of policy, notwithstanding the potentially adverse effect upon domestic consumers.[20]

Whether it is possible to extrapolate from this major illustration and generalize about the entire primary sector is perhaps debatable. It is, however, clear that no industry, having once established markets, will willingly let government take measures to close off or reserve production. This reaction may result from the nature of private ownership, argued with equal vehemence by capital holders of any nationality. Nevertheless, Canada has permitted the establishment of private domination in the primary sectors, with the export of primary commodities flowing mostly to the United States. Indeed, one prominent American student of this history, George Ball, is hardly tentative in his observations that Canada:

...is fighting a rearguard action against the inevitable ... the Canadians recognize their need for United States capital; but at the same time they are determined to maintain their economic and political independence ... the desire to maintain their national integrity is a worthy objective. But the Canadians pay heavily for it and, over the years, I do not believe they will succeed in reconciling the intrinsic contradictions of their position. I wonder, for example, if the Canadian people will be prepared indefinitely to accept, for the psychic satisfaction of maintaining a separate national and political identity, a per capita income less than three quarters of ours. Meanwhile, there is danger that the efforts of successive Canadian governments to prevent United States economic domination will drive them towards increasingly restrictive nationalistic measures that are neither good for Canada nor for the health of the whole trading world....

Sooner or later, commercial imperatives will bring about free movement of all goods back and forth across our long border; and when that occurs, or even before it does, it will become unmistakably clear that countries with economies so inextricably intertwined must also have free movement of the other vital factors of production—capital, services and labour. The result will inevitably be substantial economic integration, which will require for its full realization a progressively expanding area of common political decision.[21]

Putting Federalism Back to Work

Canada has two choices. Ottawa can offer a wholesale surrender of federal power over trade and commerce, external affairs, communications, and so on in favor of the provinces, a policy which will no doubt in the short run placate Alberta and Quebec, but at the same time will ultimately denude Canada of meaningful sovereign capacities. Alternatively, Canada can attempt to develop a federal system within the existing Constitution which systematically generates enough economic wealth to eliminate permanently the present indecision between provincehood and independence—a federalism that is capable of "selling itself."

To achieve the second alternative, Canadians must recognize that the battle to reestablish unity has more than one front. Quebec's regional challenge may be only symptomatic. The sentiments of regionalism also infect provinces and territories that do not claim a separate cultural identity, for many of the problems of unity relate to material causes that cannot be improved, let alone resolved, by Constitutional change. The proponents of federalism face an awesome task in attempting to achieve an acceptable balance between the French and English cultures; but if one adds vexing constraints imposed by fundamental weaknesses in Canada's economic structure, the dilemma cannot be resolved without swift remedial federal action.

Federal action cannot fail to have an impact upon the international community in general and the United States in particular. President Carter has expressed support for a unified and whole Canada, and the selection of a joint session of Congress for Prime Minister Trudeau's first formal address following the Quebec election was significant: at an emotional level, American expressions of support for the cause of unity hold much meaning for Canadians. But at the same time there is a slight air of unreality present in the U.S. attitude, for the steps necessary to preserve Canadian unity and to build a new and more credible federalism may prove to be inimical to U.S. interests.

It would be an error for Washington to assume that Canada can cope with an economic recession and placate regional discontent simultaneously. The economy is the potential reserve of strength that will be called upon to the fullest extent if Canada is to succeed in the coming years. But in order to draw upon this reserve a number of major steps must be taken to restore the economy's health; first and foremost, more central control must be secured, a step which will cut against short-term regional interest and may also reduce some of the advantages hitherto enjoyed by the United States. More precisely, Canada will have to be far more conscientious in securing higher domestic returns from natural endowments, both in the form of increased indigenous industry and in higher export net backs (i.e., returns on exports after all deductions). Dealing with Canada's rapidly protracting energy problems appears to be a logical jumping-off point.

The Need for New Energy Resources Policy

The preservation of adequate stocks of energy is a first principle of any industrial society. No other factor of production has a more decisive effect upon the potential for economic growth. The relative cost of energy supplies is often the most critical determinant in trading competition among two or more economies.

The federal government has for so long turned a blind eye to the need to manage our energy assets that all simple options have disappeared. The crisis is not merely an "energy crisis" concerning how much oil or gas might be available in future. The real problem is to be found in the growing unemployment rolls, the ever-increasing bankruptcy lists, the declining value of the Canadian dollar, and lowered investor expectations regarding the country's future. The ultimate stakes are to keep Canadian industries competitive, maintain existing employment levels, hold the line on domestic living standards, and generate the wealth necessary to unify the country. Put simply, if the costs of energy rise faster in Canada than they do in Detroit, or Buffalo, business will suffer. If the finished cost of glass, bricks, plastics, cement, pharmaceuticals, resin-based construction products, and petrochemical products generally increases, so too will the Consumer Price Index, and shortly thereafter wage rates. Canada today, more than ever before, needs secondary industrial growth and the employment and income that comes with it. The rate of secondary growth is completely dependent upon the quantity of energy available and, even more importantly, on the price at which it can be delivered.

The laws of physics have now begun to assert inexorable precedence over the treasured myths of abundance held by our politicians. There is belated recognition that Canada does have a problem. But to date federal actions have hardly inspired confidence. On the pricing issue, for example, the government has accepted the proposition that indigenous supplies of cheap natural gas and petroleum should be sold at a level set by the most powerful cartel in modern history, i.e., the "world commodity price," which the current Energy Minister publicly calls the "fair market price." This policy represents reward to the same corporate interests that are substantially to blame for Canadian difficulties in the first instance, and thus, while the Canadian economy has been faltering, the asset value of the multinational petroleum subsidiaries in Canada has experienced a rate of growth that is without precedent.

To take a second illustration, in answer to the allegedly urgent need for access to additional supplies and the growing concern about raising the necessary capital for developing energy requirements (estimated by the Ministry of Energy, Mines and Resources at more than $120 billion until 1985 in 1975 constant dollars), the federal government has committed the country to the largest private capital undertaking in the history of man, the "ALCAN Pipeline." This project's main, and possibly sole function, is the delivery of Alaskan gas to consumers in the lower 48 states. Canadian gas production connected to the mainline in the future is largely hypothetical, expensive in the extreme, and will necessitate the construction of an enormously difficult and expensive spur line up the Mackenzie Valley. The more or less simultaneous signature of the new Panama Canal Treaty and the conclusion of the Alaska Pipeline negotiations was in this context something of an irony, for Canadian negotiators appear not to have considered that they were negotiating the beginnings of the very situation the Panamanians were trying to end. And Canada made many serious mistakes that any self-respecting student of Panamanian history would have avoided.[22]

Despite such a depressing record, there are still productive steps Canada can take in particular: a. a national stock-taking of present and potential energy supplies; b. a cost options review; c. a pricing options review; d. a Federal Energy Marketing Board.

National Stock-Taking of Present and Potential Energy Supplies

At first blush the notion of undertaking a national inventory may seem obvious. Oil and gas are to the economy what topsoil is to a wheat farmer, and it is no answer for either government or industry to contend that the risky calculus of available supplies can lend justification to Canada's massive over-commitment to the U.S. export market.

Canada without doubt has long passed the turning point for conventional oil from Alberta and British Columbia. The bulk of productive potential has been exported, and reserves are now in a state of irretrievable depletion. There is no hope of developing conventional productive capacity sufficient to satisfy national demands to the east and west of the Ottawa Valley Line; nor will an alteration of the current export flows materially improve this situation. The gains to be achieved from modification of exports are too slight to warrant a great deal of effort.

Provided steps are taken quickly, the situation may be considerably better for natural gas. The principal future difficulty relates to deliverability rather than straight quantity. As of this moment, Canada possesses two prime sources of the utmost importance for future domestic market requirements: Waterton and Kaybob gas fields, at present under contract to the Alberta and Southern export system which proposes to sell them ultimately to consumers in California. These reserves, if made available for future domestic market needs, would on the basis of current market projections, forestall a deliverability deficiency until close to the turn of the century.[23]

In addition, in the late 1970s there have been encouraging discoveries in Alberta. These new natural gas finds are for the most part deep and of marginal quality, but they nonetheless represent a potentially important contribution to the stock of reserve energy provided they are retained in the country and are produced in combination with the revised mix of fields suggested above.

Canada is healthy in existing hydroelectric power production. There are the vast power reserves of the southerly river systems (the Columbia, Kootenay, St. Lawrence), as well as the more northerly systems, such as the Nelson and Churchill rivers, the James Bay inflows, and the Churchill system in Labrador. Here again, any future difficulties will result from the premature commitment to the United States of a significant proportion of the output of these developments, coupled with inadequate east-to-west transmission capacity. And over the longer term, Canada has the much-touted potential of the McMurray Tar Sands,[24] the heavy oil deposits of Saskatchewan, the vast coal reserves of both the Western Provinces and Atlantic Canada, unknown supplies of uranium, and the potential of the Bay of Fundy tides, the Skeena, Laird, Yukon, and other river systems.

In short, Canada on paper has ample supplies of energy. Unfortunately, it has created artificial shortages through the misallocation of the least expensive reserves of gas, petroleum, and hydroelectric power.[25] Domestic requirements can be satisfied only by reducing exports or by developing new sources of supply, which would push domestic prices far above prices elsewhere.

In theory, petroleum, natural gas, and electric power exports are all conditional upon the existence of surpluses relative to foreseeable domestic requirements.[26] On this basis there is clearly no surplus, and present exports contradict federal policies and statutes. At the same time, closing all the pipe valves and cutting all the north-to-south transmission lines is unrealistic and unnecessary. Again, Canada lacks the east-to-west transmission capacity necessary to derive immediate advantage from such a step. Second, even with such capacity, present markets could not absorb the sudden surge in power supplies. Third, American consumers would quite properly be more than a little offended. Fourth, Canada would lose all of the foreign exchange earnings resulting from such exports which would, in the short term, upset its balance of payments. Finally, in the case at least of natural gas, there is plainly no need for such a drastic step, given the ability to partially maintain needed export flows without depleting the prime sources of high pressure supplies.

A sensible first step, then, would be to inventory those sources of energy worthy of ultimate repatriation, reorganize existing non-renewable export production so as to prevent depletion of needed deliverability potential, and undertake the investments necessary for the development of greater east-to-west transmission flexibility that will permit the country to attain a higher level of domestic self-sufficiency from existing sources of energy production in the future as present export licenses expire and/or are subject to statutory termination.[27]

Energy Cost Options Review

A major thrust of any large-scale rationalization of Canadian energy supplies should involve the rededication for domestic needs of as much of the presently developed sources as possible. Developed supplies are many times more cost-efficient than undeveloped synthetics, frontier sources of natural gas and petroleum, or untapped hydroelectric sites that are distant from major load centers.

If energy policies are to encourage economic growth, the central objective of any future reallocation program must be the minimization of average domestic production costs. There are obvious reasons for this. First, preservation of low-cost sources of supply will allow

Canada the flexibility to establish a rational price structure. Until now, Canada has reacted to price pressures without any rigorous attempt to analyze whether costs are in fact increasing, at what rate, and why. Second, wherever there exists a differential between domestic energy production costs and the relative price at which energy is sold, there equally exists surplus value which might alleviate the price impact of the new sources as they are brought on stream (by way of price-averaging). The more substantial the basic cheap production, the greater will be the power to "average down" high-cost supplies. And the more successful this effort, the less the transition from the era of cheap energy will strain the economy.

Pricing Options Review

A wholesale effort should be made to evaluate systematically implications of various available pricing options. Such a task is not simple. The range of considerations must include the fair distribution of economic payments between producing and consuming regions, the net effect upon per capita consumer buying power, primary and secondary employment, the structure of federal and provincial fiscal expenditures, and conservation incentives. Still, some effort must be devoted to sorting out the complexity.

Unfortunately, there is no indication that the Ministry of Energy, Mines and Resources has considered these issues. Conservation *qua* conservation has no independent virtue. The chief objective of moving toward "world commodity pricing" in Canada is not merely conservation, for conservation objectives can be achieved in entirely the wrong way; stimulating a depression that rivals the stature of the 1929 experience is arguably "conservation-oriented." Yet there is absolutely no danger that the country will ever use more energy than it has. Demand and supply will always be in balance. The real concern is whether that balance will be achieved in a fashion which obliterates the standard of living that Canadians have come to expect, or whether careful programming, aimed at preventing a material disruption of the overall welfare of the country, will prevail.

At the present time, any petroleum that is saved by way of price increases in Canada immediately becomes available for export to the United States. Similarly, proposals for further export of natural gas from Alberta are now well advanced, and, given concerns over the financing of the Alaska Pipeline, appear likely to be given government approval.[28] But forcibly cutting back Canadian demand by prematurely exporting limited supplies is not conservation.

Canada does need a massive conservation program. But it must be extremely careful about the type of conservation program put into effect. To employ unstudied price increases as the mainstay of a conservation program is to invite rather large problems. Higher prices can mean economic downturn; welfare demands upon the federal treasury then tend to increase, leaving government less able to commit large sums of money for the stimulation of better energy conservation technologies. Such calculations will depend on a great deal more information about the comparative elasticities of demand in the various energy consumption sectors, and more information about the potential for natural gas as a temporary substitute for oil, or hydroelectric power for gas, and so on. And much more information is needed about the changes in employment and income resulting from price increases already in place.

The relative merit of any conservation program lies in its overall costs and benefits, i.e., the value of what is saved as opposed to the cost associated with the savings.

A Federal Energy Marketing Board

Canada's power to control its future position derives from having *first*, adequate stocks in reserve, *second*, complete flexibility in transportation, and *third*, the power to exert some control over price structures. All of these factors argue in favor of one overall solution: namely, establishment of a Federal Energy Marketing Board.

Canada must make full use of its present jurisdictional tools under the Constitution if it is to take advantage of the few choices that remain. The Energy Marketing Board should be given a general mandate for research and analysis. In addition, it should be able to implement a price-averaging system between least-cost conventional and frontier or synthetic sources of supply, with all private producer revenues put on a fixed rate of return basis. Payments reflecting differentials between cost and price should be collected to pay for upgrading transmission flexibility; a national power grid extending into the import-reliant regions (Atlantic Canada) should be a fundamental priority.

All renewable power supplies should be repatriated as existing export licenses expire. Nonrenewable energy, and most particularly natural gas now being produced for export, should be reorganized to preserve deliverability capacity for future Canadian use. And all export prices should be reviewed and where necessary increased to reflect rough replacement costs. Export producers should, like their domestic counterparts, be put on a utility-based return basis, with all differentials between costs and export prices centrally taxed and shared between producing provinces and the federal government.

Towards a New Primary Resources Policy

The earlier action is taken to exert control over primary production and pricing decisions, the higher the rewards. From the point of view of the primary sectors, there is thus a strong case for asserting a higher degree of central control.

In the case of energy, Canada's present predicament warrants the exercise of broad federal powers of intervention under the Peace, Order and Good Government provision of the British North America Act. But for primary resource extraction, the constitutional solution may be more complex, involving as it must, the cooperative exercise of provincial and federal legislative jurisdiction. At the federal level it is clear, however, that there is jurisdiction to regulate interprovincial and international sales of primary commodities. The following steps might be worthy of consideration.

Primary Supply Assessment

An assessment, resource by resource, of domestic requirements and trends in domestic delivery cost requires the delineation of a broad industrial growth strategy so that foreseeable domestic requirements can be predicted. It also requires, in face of uncertain technology, an assessment of cost trends in primary production, again resource by resource.

International Market Assessment

Export should depend somewhat on the export market's "willingness to pay," as demonstrated in the extreme by OPEC. Canada must be completely assured that (a) returns are at a fair level, and (b) that returns are at least in parity with replacement costs inside Canada; then, and only then, is it safe to enter into export trade. In addition, Canada should be assured of a "reserve bank," like the one theoretically employed for natural gas, but with higher protection levels than employed by the NEB.

Crown Marketing Boards

Because the buyer has in many instances been able to set prices, to submit to "world market forces" is naive. Some countries have employed market quotas or import quotas to bolster their domestic markets. With uranium, the United States set up an embargo and then subsequently complained about the encouragement of a cartel, a classic irony that underscores Canada's shortsightedness as a primary exporter. Nevertheless, international cartels are horrendously difficult to police, involving both substantial conflicts of laws and the extra-territorial reach of foreign laws into Canada.

Because the major difficulty with international cartels lies in characterizing their development as a proper "act of state," all doubt ought to be eliminated: the export of such commodities should be put under the jurisdiction of Crown Corporations. I am not suggesting nationalization, but some degree of central control to generate domestic and foreign market conditions that serve the best interest of the Canadian people. These Crown Corporations need not be oriented towards bludgeoning the export customer, but they must guarantee that on balance Canada will do as well as it resonably can in all primary exports.

Public Stockpiling

Public stockpiling is a device that has worked very well in other countries such as the United States. Obviously, larger countries are capable of absorbing vast stockpiles which smaller countries, such as Canada, could never consider. However, it may be possible to bolster the ability to stockpile without loss. Such stockpiling would smooth out vagaries in the market place and insure even returns over time, which would afford some measure of stability to the primary sectors.

Federal Export Taxing

The primary sector ought to make a much more substantial contribution to general revenue than at present. Returns could be divided into two main streams: towards the creation of a workable and substantial stockpiling system (see above), and into a general equalization system. More substantial returns could then be guaranteed to the Province of Quebec and Atlantic Canada through higher returns on indigenous production, and, in those cases where a province was not a major. primary producer, it would receive the benefit of the federal tax on exports from the richer provinces.

Creation of a Two-Price System

If Canada is to make full use of its primary endowments and encourage secondary processing, a two-price system favoring domestic consumers would be advantageous. Predatory pricing in the export market is not necessary to subsidize domestic consumers, but if Canada enjoys a competitive edge in some primary sectors there would seem little point in importing world commodity pricing standards.

Summary

There is a case to be made for deliberate attempts at preserving comparative advantages that would be of benefit to the secondary sectors of the economy; the economy then might be left more or less alone to prosper without either government aid or interference. Primary producers are increasingly advocating the adoption of "world market prices" that will ultimately undermine the competitive viability of Canada's most important secondary producers. This trend may be consistent with the principle of noninvolvement in the private economy, but if it continues it will reduce the level of overall economic activity in these sectors most decisive for the generation of employment and national health.

Conclusions

Canadians are, as the Chinese proverb aptly puts it, condemned to live in interesting times. If Canadians fail to take initiatives, there may well be a catastrophic restructuring of the way of life all have come to expect. To date, federalism has failed to capture maximum advantage from Canada's natural heritage.

Given the current constitutional debate, to argue in favor of greater central authority may at first blush seem extreme. Nonetheless, many of our present difficulties trace back to Canada's failure to foster and develop an effective tradition of central resource management, a failure to utilize the federal constitutional authority conferred under the British North America Act. At the risk of appealing to no higher authority than common sense, it would seem that Canada's capacity to make meaningful concessions to various regional interests is tied critically to overall wealth. Much wealth is, in turn, dependent upon primary endowments. Canada is not Switzerland or Japan. Comparative advantages are not generally the product of ingenuity or personal habits of industry. Canada is first and foremost a primary producing economy. Secondary industries have located in the country only because of primary cost advantages that outweigh a depressing array of disadvantages, including an underproductive and overpaid work force, a burdensome tax system, and small markets. The key to future wealth creation, then, lies in carefully programmed exploitation of remaining natural endowments to insure maximizing national returns from export and the attraction of as much secondary investing in Canada as possible.

Had Canada exercised more care in the past, had it prevented each province from losing resource development programs at the first opportunity—or worse still, underbidding one another for the opportunity to serve the American export markets—and had Canada judiciously tailored regulatory power to tax and control export and interprovincial flows of commodities, it would be a much richer and happier place today. As matters now stand, it is perhaps hard for Quebec to appreciate the millions spent on federal bilingualism programs when over one in ten in the province are unemployed. It is hard to conceive of a new federalism acceptable to Nova Scotia, where for many people home-heating costs exceed monthly rental or mortgage payments. And the growing rolls of the unemployed in Canada will not be convinced easily of the need to ignore their plight in favor of multimillion dollar National Unity Task Forces.

As a first step, response to the energy crisis is perhaps the best of all National Unity Projects. Here Canada has the opportunity to demonstrate in a tangible fashion that federalism not only can work, but in the long run is worth literally billions of dollars in economic benefits. It is only through such steps that the tedious debate, and the ever-present national sense of inadequacy, may belatedly be put to rest.

NOTES

1. F.K. North, "Viewpoint," *Chemistry in Canada*, November 1974, p. 3.

2. The trends since 1972 of petroleum imports and exports, expressed in average barrels per day are as follows: Canada: Imports and Exports Crude Oil (exclusive of product flows)

	Exports		Imports		Surplus (Deficit)	
1972	956,832	Bld	769,600	Bld	187,232	Bld
1973	1,138,243		897,400		240,843	
1974	910,915		797,600		113,315	
1975	707,548		818,000		(110,652)	
1976	465,147		766,300		(300,153)	

Bld = barrels per day, Canadian std. Barrel = 35 imperial gal. Sources: National Energy Board, Annual Reports, 1972, 1973, 1974, 1975, 1976.

3. See *Canadian Natural Gas: Supply and Requirement*, National Energy Board, April, 1975, and discussion *infra*.

4. Peter W. Hogg, *Constitutional Law of Canada*, (Toronto: The Carswell Company Limited, 1977), pp. 37-38.

5. *Ibid.*, p. 36.

6. See Ian McDougall, "The Development of International Law with Respect to Trans-Boundary Water Resources: Co-operation for Mutual Advantage or Continentalism's Thin-Edge of the Wedge." *Osgood Hall Law Journal*, Vol. 9, No. 27.

7. Ian McDougall, "The Canadian National Energy Board: Economic Jurisprudence in the National Interest or Symbolic Reassurance?", *Alberta Law Review*, Vol. II, 1972.

8. Ian McDougall, *The Churchill Diversion: An Examination of its Implications with Respect to the Development of a Legal Framework for the Management of Canadian Water Resources*. Department of the Environment (Ottawa) 1971.

9. See generally, Philip Smith, *Brinco: The Story of Churchill Falls* (Toronto: McClelland and Stewart Ltd., 1976).

10. See Philip Sykes, *Sellout: The Giveaway of Canada's Energy Resources* (Edmonton: Hurtig Press, 1973); Ian McDougall, *Canadian*

Energy Development and Trade: The Last Hand of the Poker Game, Protecting the Environment (Toronto: Dividi, Copp Clark, 1974).

11. "91. it shall be lawful for the Queen, by and with the Advice and Consent of the Senate and House of Commons, to make laws for the Peace, Order and Good Government of Canada, in relations to all matters not coming within the classes of subject by this Act assigned exclusively to the legislatures of the Provinces ...."

12. "92 (10) local works and undertakings other than such as are of the following classes:—... (c) Such works as, although wholly situate within the Province are before or after their Execution declared by the Parliament of Canada to be for the General Advantage of Canada or for the Advantage of two or more of the Provinces."

13. For example, the recent lobbying of Alberta for more favorable U.S. Tariff structures with respect to western Canadian petrochemicals.

14. For example, Quebec relations with France, and Quebec's participation with sovereign states at an international conference in Gabon.

15. For example, British Columbia's position with respect to the terms of the Columbia River Treaty.

16. The National Energy Board, R.S.C. 1970, C.N.-6.

17. See Ian McDougall, "The Canadian National Energy Board," *Alberta Law Review, op. cit.*

18. According to one authority, the processes employed to bring food to the table account for 12-15% of Canada's total energy consumption. See the Retail Council of Canada Report, *Energy and the Consumer Budget*, Toronto, November 3, 1977.

19. See Walter L. Gordon's discussion in this volume and also his *Storm Signals: New Economic Policies for Canada* (Toronto: McClelland and Steward Ltd., 1975).

20. National Energy Board Gas Requirements Hearings, 1974-75. See the submissions of Shell, Gulf, Imperial, and Canadian Arctic Gas Study Limited.

21. George Ball, *The Discipline of Power* (Boston: Atlantic-Little Brown, 1968), pp. 42-43.

22. Major criticisms of the agreement include: (1) calculation of the cost-of-service; (2) financing and insurance against cost overruns; (3) the cost of service that may apply to movement of Canada gas through the line in the future; (4) Canadian content in the construction of the line; (5) Northern environmental effects; (6) delivery capacity and flexibility with respect to the movement of any future gas

production connected to the mainline in Canada.

23. See maps 2 and 3 in Appendix.

24. Consider, however, the sheer magnitude of the capital requirements for tar sands production and output: the last minimum syncrude cost estimate was approximately $2 billion, which at 10% interest equals $200,000,000 per annum. Estimated annual production: 100,000 barrels per day—36,500,000 barrels per year. Cost of oil on a per-barrel basis attributable to interest equals $200 million divided by $36,500,000—$5.46. At 35 gallons per barrel, interest alone will account for a 15 cent per-gallon levy. Additional investments and debt for transportation and refining (although less than for crude oil in relation of naphtha, kerosene, etc.), will increase cost dramatically.

25. At some point in the future, long before, technically speaking, Canada runs out of gas and oil, recovery costs will begin to exceed the amount the economy can reasonably afford. From this perspective, Canada's limited recovery capability may suggest the wisdom of assuming much smaller petroleum and gas potential than is usually assumed. The post-syncrude withdrawals suggest that this may be the ultimate lesson of the tar sands. Vast physical potential is of itself a slight comfort.

26. The National Energy Board Act provides: "83. Upon an application for a license ... the Board shall satisfy itself that (a) the quantity of gas or power to be exported does not exceed the surplus remaining after due allowance has been made for the reasonably foreseeable requirements for use in Canada having regard, in the case of an application to export gas, to the trends in the discovery of gas in Canada; and (b) the price to be charged by an applicant for gas or power exported by him is just and reasonable in relation to the public interest. 1969-70, c. 65, s. 28.

27. The NEB's export authorization mandate has been clear from the outset: gas for export must be surplus to the reasonably foreseeable requirements of the domestic market (bearing in mind discovery trends; a safeguard to allow the Board sufficient power to recommend to the Cabinet that existing exports be varied ex post facto in the general interest of protecting the domestic consumer is in section 17: "(1) Subject to subsection (2), the Board may review, rescind, change, alter or vary any order or decision made by it, or may rehear any application before deciding it. (2) The Board may change, alter or vary a certificate or license issued by it, but no such change, alteration or variation is effective until approved by the Governor-in-Council."

28. Discussions between Canadian and American officials have centered on the possible export of reserves to defray the cost of leaving the southern portion of the Alaska Highway Pipeline idle while the northern component is completed.

_____APPENDIX*

*Maps 2 and 3 are from *An Assessment of Canada's Conventionally Producible Crude Oil and Natural Gas Resources and a Forecast of Additions to 1995*, JLJ Exploration Consultants, Ltd., August 1974.

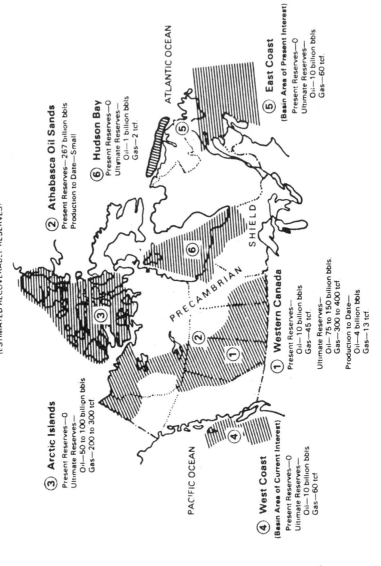

CANADIAN SEDIMENTARY BASINS
(ESTIMATED RECOVERABLE RESERVES)

③ Arctic Islands
Present Reserves—0
Ultimate Reserves—
  Oil—50 to 100 billion bbls
  Gas—200 to 300 tcf

② Athabasca Oil Sands
Present Reserves—267 billion bbls
Production to Date—Small

⑥ Hudson Bay
Present Reserves—0
Ultimate Reserves—
  Oil—1 billion bbls
  Gas—2 tcf

⑤ East Coast
(Basin Area of Present Interest)
Present Reserves—0
Ultimate Reserves—
  Oil—10 billion bbls
  Gas—60 tcf

① Western Canada
Present Reserves—
  Oil—10 billion bbls
  Gas—45 tcf
Ultimate Reserves—
  Oil—75 to 150 billion bbls.
  Gas—300 to 400 tcf
Production to Date—
  Oil—4 billion bbls
  Gas—13 tcf

④ West Coast
(Basin Area of Current Interest)
Present Reserves—0
Ultimate Reserves—
  Oil—10 billion bbls
  Gas—60 tcf

PRECAMBRIAN SHIELD

ATLANTIC OCEAN

PACIFIC OCEAN

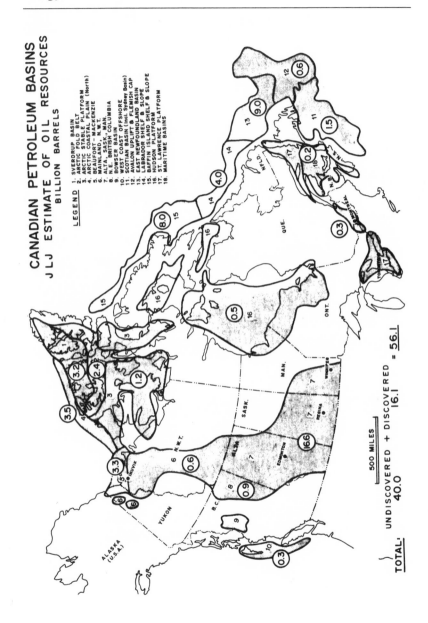

CANADIAN PETROLEUM BASINS
JLJ ESTIMATE OF OIL RESOURCES
BILLION BARRELS

LEGEND
1. SVERDRUP BASIN
2. ARCTIC FOLD BELT
3. ARCTIC STABLE PLATFORM
4. ARCTIC COASTAL PLAIN (North)
5. BEAUFORT - MACKENZIE
6. MAINLAND, N.W.T.
7. ALTA., SASK., MAN.
8. N.E. BRITISH COLUMBIA
9. BOWSER BASIN
10. WEST COAST OFFSHORE
11. SCOTIAN BASIN (incl. Sydney Basin)
12. AVALON UPLIFT & FLEMISH CAP
13. EAST NEWFOUNDLAND BASIN
14. LABRADOR SHELF & SLOPE
15. BAFFIN ISLAND SHELF & SLOPE
16. HUDSON PLATFORM
17. ST. LAWRENCE PLATFORM
18. MARITIME BASINS

TOTAL: UNDISCOVERED + DISCOVERED = 56.1
          40.0   16.1

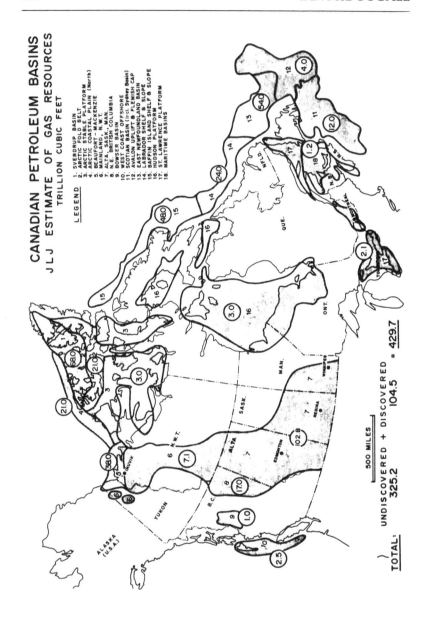

CANADIAN PETROLEUM BASINS
JLJ ESTIMATE OF GAS RESOURCES
TRILLION CUBIC FEET

LEGEND

1. SVERDRUP BASIN
2. ARCTIC FOLD BELT
3. ARCTIC STABLE PLATFORM
4. ARCTIC COASTAL PLAIN (North)
5. BEAUFORT - MACKENZIE
6. MAINLAND, N.W.T.
7. ALTA, SASK, MAN.
8. N.E. BRITISH COLUMBIA
9. BOWSER BASIN
10. WEST COAST OFFSHORE
11. SCOTIAN BASIN (incl. Sydney Basin)
12. AVALON UPLIFT & FLEMISH CAP
13. EAST NEWFOUNDLAND BASIN
14. LABRADOR SHELF & SLOPE
15. BAFFIN ISLAND SHELF & SLOPE
16. HUDSON PLATFORM
17. ST. LAWRENCE PLATFORM
18. MARITIME BASINS

500 MILES

TOTAL: UNDISCOVERED + DISCOVERED = 429.7
            325.2   104.5

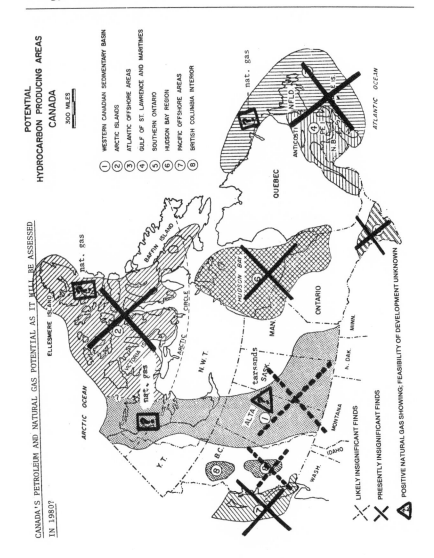

CANADA'S PETROLEUM AND NATURAL GAS POTENTIAL AS IT WILL BE ASSESSED
IN 1980?

POTENTIAL
HYDROCARBON PRODUCING AREAS
CANADA

300 MILES

① WESTERN CANADIAN SEDIMENTARY BASIN
② ARCTIC ISLANDS
③ ATLANTIC OFFSHORE AREAS
④ GULF OF ST. LAWRENCE AND MARITIMES
⑤ SOUTHERN ONTARIO
⑥ HUDSON BAY REGION
⑦ PACIFIC OFFSHORE AREAS
⑧ BRITISH COLUMBIA INTERIOR

LIKELY INSIGNIFICANT FINDS

PRESENTLY INSIGNIFICANT FINDS

POSITIVE NATURAL GAS SHOWING; FEASIBILITY OF DEVELOPMENT UNKNOWN

8 ENERGY, NATURAL RESOURCES, AND THE ECONOMICS OF FEDERALISM

COMMENT

Stewart L. Udall

There are so many facets to Ian McDougall's essay that I have elected to eschew an essay of my own in favor of pointed comments on those theses embodied in his argument which I find most provocative.

Thesis I: One way to help Canada resolve its constitutional crisis is by stronger, not weaker, federal leadership—particularly in the management of Canada's resources.

This is an attractive and timely argument. If Dr. McDougall is correct (and I find his position persuasive) and the British North America Act gives the national government powers it has not exercised in the past by default, the door is wide open to vigorous federal leadership which might promote unity and strengthen the ties between the provinces and the national government. In my dealings with Canadian officials on resource issues in the 1960s (primarily relating to petroleum exports and the Columbia River treaty), I was always told that the Canadian constitution assigned the primary role in resource development to the provinces.

I remember well a Western political campaign trip I took with President Lyndon Johnson in the late summer of 1964. The main purpose of the appearances in Montana and Washington and British Columbia was to celebrate the beginning of construction work on the upper Columbia, and Johnson invited Prime Minister Pearson to join him at ceremonies in these states. I distinctly recall my puzzlement at the

difference between the seeming degree of involvement of the two
leaders: President Johnson was in high spirits because his administration was responsible for what had happened and he was in a position
to take credit for the benefits which would accrue to the U.S. as the
various projects were completed. By contast, in his comments and
attitudes Mike Pearson seemed like a spectator who was detached
from the real action. I now understand the differing stances of the
two leaders, for the U.S. role in resource development was dominant;
the role of the government of Canada was passive and secondary.

My own experience would suggest that if the government of Canada
provided stronger future leadership in energy and resource development, it inevitably would enhance its prestige and standing at home.

Thesis II: Canada "was" a nation richly endowed with natural
resources.

I must dispute this point. By comparison with the United States
(which is rushing hellbent to become the first industrial have-not oil
country in the world!) Canada has endowments and advantages
which are considerable. On a per capita basis, unless Canada
squanders its proven reserves, it has oil and natural gas stocks in place
which will last twice as long as those possessed by the U.S. And
Canada has many other built-in advantages as it faces a future in
which energy efficiency will be a prime determinant of national
power. To name just two of these advantages, Canada has a superior
railway system and most of its cities are much more compact (i.e.,
efficient) than those in the U.S. Economically, when one looks ahead
at the next two or three decades, the energy crisis is much more acute
and threatening to the U.S. than it is to Canada.

Thesis III: By formulating a farsighted national energy policy, the
government could reinvigorate itself and enhance the future of
Canada's economy.

This is, to me, the crux of Dr. McDougall's essay, and it is a thesis
with which I emphatically concur. As I read contemporary trends, the
imperatives of the energy crisis will be the great shaping force in the
next few decades. I am likewise convinced that this is an area of
policymaking where national governments can—indeed must—play a
predominant role if satisfactory solutions are to be achieved. Insofar
as Canada is concerned, the forging of a national energy policy could
do more to unify the nation—and improve Canada's prospects for
economic prosperity—than anything which will emerge in the years
ahead. It was not an accident that the one harmonious interval at
Prime Minister Trudeau's economic conference with the provincial

premiers in February 1978 came when an agenda of future energy projects was discussed. The report in one U.S. newspaper which covered the conference contained the headline: "Canadians Concur on Energy Projects: Political Bickering Stilled as Premiers Discuss Development of Resources." Plainly energy cooperation is a topic which induces cohesion and emphasizes positive feelings of nationalism.

Thesis IV: As a corollary to Thesis III, Dr. McDougall makes the point that Canada should put "federalism back to work" and be rigorously nationalistic in all energy matters, i.e., it should put Canada's future in the forefront and reassess its export and development policies accordingly.

He summarized this thesis in the cogent sentence: "The preservation of adequate stocks of energy is a first principle of any industrial society." I do not see how any fair-minded U.S. spokesman could quarrel with this principle. After all, "energy independence" has been the openly proclaimed goal of the last three American presidents. On what rational grounds could U.S. officials object if the government of Canada takes action to conserve its remaining petroleum, and to protect its consumers and the present and future industries which will need petroleum as a feedstock or raw material? On what national grounds could any U.S. group object if Canada elects to build much needed East-West electric power interties—or extend its natural gas pipeline system to its energy-starved Eastern provinces? Patently, the best way for Canada to keep its industries competitive and its economy healthy is to assure that it has adequate supplies of relatively low cost energy for the long run. The axiom that the health of the national economy must come first has long been a *sine qua non* of public policy in all industrial countries.

Having made these observations, I am puzzled by one of Dr. McDougall's examples. He objects to the building of the ALCAN pipeline—and implies that somehow it might set the stage for a Panama Canal situation between our countries. I confess to a bias (as a lawyer I have rendered services to the Canadian pipeline companies who won the license to build the ALCAN line), but I fail to see how it can possibly harm Canada to provide a land route—and build facilities which will be paid for entirely by U.S. consumers— to help the U.S. to bring its Alaska natural gas to market in the most economical way possible. I see nothing but economic pluses for Canada in the implementation of the project. It is not an energy exportation project; it is rather a service project in which both countries should reap substantial benefits.

To conclude, I share Dr. McDougall's conviction that where Canada is concerned (and the U.S., too, I would add) the times demand bold initiative. Moreover, I believe he has not only laid down a provocative blueprint for action, but is eminently right in identifying the resolution of the energy crisis as "the best of all national unity projects."

8 ENERGY, NATURAL RESOURCES, AND THE ECONOMICS OF FEDERALISM

COMMENT

Robert E. Stein

Although Professor McDougall concentrates on energy issues, they are but one of the many transborder natural resource questions that require close attention. Some energy systems, such as hydroelectric power, have long been both a source of contention and a basis for cooperation between the United States and Canada. They have also been a bone of contention between both the provinces and the federal government in Canada as well as between the states and the federal government in the United States. In this sense, there are parallels that should not be overlooked. Nor is hydro power the sole water or water resource-related question which has arisen over the period of U.S.-Canadian cooperation. Water levels of such mammoth bodies as the Great Lakes, dams for flood control, pollution control, and entrophication have all been issues needing resolution between the two countries. Water quality, and the use of water for a variety of consumptive purposes—such as agriculture and as a potable resource—also affect bilateral relations. Indeed, water and, more broadly, international environmental quality, may come to be as important as some energy issues in relations over resources between the U.S. and Canada.

Financial Advantage or Environmental Protection?

Looking at Canada from the United States, one does not get the impression that Canada has been outclassed and outmanned. In many instances, the United States believes it has surrendered more than it should have in order to secure hydroelectric power and water use, because of shrewd provincial negotiating. Admittedly, this view comes from one side; the Canadian perspective may be different. However, I think it is important to see that there are different perspectives.

Let us look at some of the issues involved: The Columbia River Treaty[1] and the treaties that flowed from it yielded British Columbia substantial sums of money. These sums, although the Canadian government may consider them to be insufficient for the long term, provided Canada a large front-end payment which enabled the United States to develop the hydroelectric potential of the Pacific Northwest. It was an example of cooperation between one side that had a commodity and another that had capital, and the problem may have been less financial than whether the environment and ecology of the area was protected.

The International Joint Commission and Canadian Advantages

Transborder water and air pollution problems continue to involve considerable negotiation between the United States and Canada. The International Joint Commission (IJC),[2] established by the Boundary Waters Treaty of 1909, has been for the past 69 years the most advanced binational body concerned with the management and partial regulation of natural resources shared by two states. It is responsible for transborder water and air pollution. The two governments submit problems of environmental pollution control to the Commission for recommendations; the Commission also has jurisdiction over cases involving the obstruction and diversion of waters; it has the right to pass upon changes in levels and flows; and it must agree on construction of remedial or protective works or dams on boundary waters or waters running across the boundary.

Article IV of the Boundary Waters Treaty, with uncommon prescience, states:

> It is further agreed that the waters herein defined as boundary waters and waters falling across the boundary shall not be polluted on either side to the injury of health or property on the other.

This provision has not won compliance in its letter nor certainly its spirit in dealing with problems of water pollution of the Great Lakes and other boundary waters. It is this provision, however, that led to the 1972 Great Lakes Water Quality Agreement between the two countries.

With 80% of its population living along the Great Lakes, Canada regards boundary water relations as much more important than they appear to the United States; although there are eight states along the Great Lakes, the U.S. pays less attention to the Lakes than does Canada. The consequences of this imbalance are contrary to the implications for transborder relations in Dr. McDougall's essay. First, as for the IJC itself, the Canadians often have been able to outman the U.S. side, especially in personnel assigned to follow the work of the Commission and actually to work on Commission staffs. Second, the Congress of the United States has been less willing than Canada to give priority to the Great Lakes. The U.S. House of Representatives, for example, appropriated monies for the Federal Water Pollution Control Act by stating specifically that priority funds should not be given to waste treatment facilities for Great Lakes states.

IJC Weakness

Because the IJC has power only to make recommendations to governments, it has not dealt satisfactorily on all levels with disputes involving natural resources. The Commission's recommendations usually are accepted, but there are some disagreements that governments cannot solve, whether for political reasons or because of insufficient technical competence. In part, the technical boards of the Commission, composed of individuals from the federal, provincial, and state governments of both countries, help the Commission gain acceptance by doing the principal work. Although they serve as individuals, board members often reflect the attitudes of their respective governments and can insure the presentation of a government interest—which a government subsequently may support. However, such political influence can also involve later disagreement between a board and the Commission itself. This kind of controversy probably will continue.

Some Commission decisions or recommendations may not provide final resolution for resource problems. From the 1920s through the mid-1930s, the IJC considered the problem of a smelter at Trail, British Columbia. The smelter was emitting fumes that crossed the border into the state of Washington where farmers claimed damages to crops and livestock. The Commission recommended that the

governments submit the dispute to arbitration; the subsequent
Tribunal decided in 1942 that there was damage which should be com-
pensated, and further—in a remarkable decision for that time—the
Tribunal established a monitoring regime for the smelter, limiting the
kinds of emissions in order to provide more safety for U.S. victims.[3]

Nothing like the Trail smelter dispute has happened since 1942, but
one can envisage a number of situations involving transborder pollution (as a result of a siting of power plants, for example, or switching
in the United States from oil to coal in the Northeast, or problems
involving water pollution, or the siting of pipelines across borders).
These problems might not be suitable for decision by the IJC and may
require submission to other independent arbitration or to some form
of mediation.

The Future of Water

In the western part of the United States, water is a very, very
important part of a person's livelihood and way of life. The drought of
1976 and 1977 may for the moment have been forgotten, but it is clear
that the drought and the intensive use of water in California (where
80% is used for agriculture) have made irrigation more important
than ever before. Like a secure supply of energy, a secure supply of
water is something for which individuals, corporations, municipalities, and states will be willing to pay. Western Canada has abundant
water which, for the time being, is not being used. In the next ten
years the uses of that water will become an important issue between
the United States and Canada. Will the Canadian government or the
provinces export water to the United States? Will it be sold too
cheaply, whatever that may mean, or will it be sold for a price which
will compensate Canada for the loss of its use? As with the Columbia
River, will it be a question of price, or will the importance of the
resource itself be considered? This issue has raised its head before and
it is certainly going to be of direct concern. It will, I believe, replace
some of the energy issues as a very significant sticking point between
the United States and Canada.

Will the U.S. and Canadian governments rely on traditional
methods for conflict resolution (diplomatic negotiations and the
commissions), and will old decision-making tools, used in the past for
energy and water source questions, continue to shape choices? Or,
will new devices be used? What will be the respective roles of the
provinces and states in the two countries? It is, after all, groups far

from the domestic capitals which will feel the need for clean water. The resistance to strong federal control that Professor McDougall felt in the energy field may be even stronger here, with states of the U.S. joining the provinces of Canada for a "western solution." Is "Canadian water" a resource which should not be used but which should be "preserved" for the use of Canada for all time? Or is water a resource in which the good to both countries will be enhanced by its sale to the United States? The future of federalism in Canada and the United States will depend as much on water as on extractable energy supplies, and water as much as energy will determine whether in the future there will be national harmony or continental hegemony.

NOTES

1. Signed in Washington January 17, 1961.

2. Boundary Waters Treaty between the United States and Canada (1909). See, for example, works cited in Bilder, "The Settlement of Disputes in the Field of the International Law of the Environment," 1975, I Reveil des Cours of the Hague Academy of International Law, 139.

3. The Trail Smelter Arbitration BUN Reports Int'l. Arb. Awards, 1938 (1942). See also Read, "The Trail Smelter Dispute," 1 Can. Yb. Int'l. L. 213 (1963).

9__THE FEDERAL BUREAUCRACY AND CANADIAN DISUNITY

Gordon W. Stead

It has long been assumed that the federal bureaucracy in Canada is neutral, able to serve political masters of whatever political stripe the public chooses to elect. There has been a good deal of ideological flexibility, but the federal bureaucracy cannot be expected to weigh regional interests equally with national ones. In this respect, the bureaucracy is not neutral.

As the ongoing portion of the government system, the civil service has reflected interests established in the political arena. The rise of the bureaucracy in recent years has made it into a force in its own right for projecting these dominant interests. The political arm, however, has been unable to check this independent thrust, which itself has become a divisive factor in Canada's present stage of development.

Internal Colonialism

The central government in Ottawa tries to treat all parts of the country the same way. In so doing, this "federal" government acts as a unitary state on the British model.[1] The metropolitan core of a unitary state naturally exerts a disproportionate influence on policy, reducing the periphery to colonial status. Coupled with overriding power, this domination invites struggle in an organically growing country.

In Canada's present stage of development, there is effectively but one metropolitan core, Toronto. Here are centered most of the oligopolistic banking and financial institutions, corporate headquarters, industry, population, and personal wealth. As the center of gravity shifts westwards, obedient to the long-term trend, the influence of Montreal declines relatively. Although Calgary is rising fast, Vancouver is still the leading Western city; nonetheless, it is essentially a branch plant operation, and other urban areas along the East-West axis have even less influence. The Maritimes were left behind almost from the beginning. It is a situation strikingly different from that in the United States, where there are many important urban centers.

National policies decided at the center often have unwelcome impact on the regions. Immigration criteria, for example, which are set for industrial or occupational needs, determine cultural and demographic patterns. The results are frequently at variance with the wishes of the regions where the immigrants settle, often imposing burdens on local governments. The customs tariff encourages economic concentration and penalizes the hinterland which must sell on world markets. Railway freight rates favor movement of raw materials and inhibit economic diversification in resource areas. Transportation subsidies reduce the natural barrier of distance and constitute a negative internal tariff, thus extending the reach of core area industry to sources of supply and to markets that would otherwise be regional. Jealously guarded banking and finance legislation supports strong, large central institutions. Foreign relations are controlled in Ottawa, even when they involve explicit provincial functions.

When oil prices rose precipitously, Alberta found itself selling below the world market to ease the blow on Eastern Canada in the interest of "national unity," a term too often a euphemism for Ontario dominance. The same philosophy gives primacy to central values in the federal management of the television system and in support for publishing. The list of illustrations is long. The 1977 Report of the Western Premiers' Task Force lists nearly 60 instances of existing or impending federal incursions into provincial fields: consumer and corporate affairs; resources; housing, urban affairs and land use; economic development; trade; communications; demography and immigration; manpower, training and labor; the administration of justice; and federal court interventions against provincial statutes.[2]

The federal government has come to represent the central core area and hence to stand for the *status quo*. It is conservative in its response to organic change and yet genuinely puzzled by the restiveness of the colonials, only seriously inquiring as to causes when shaken by Quebec separatism or the clout of Alberta's oil. The response to restiveness has been band-aid policies applied to "regional disparities," which treat the symptoms but fail to reach the cause. The public tends to think that federal politicians, even those from outside the core area, are contaminated by the Ottawa atmosphere. Federal bureaucrats are seen as the authors, administrators, and interpreters of centrist policies. And nowadays, bureaucrats have more contacts with the public in more intimate ways than do politicians.

Avenues of Influence

The interests of southern Ontario permeate the thinking behind federal policy making. The avenues for this influence are the Ontario representation in the House of Commons, the preponderance of civil servants from Ontario, and direct pressure upon Ottawa by core interest groups located conveniently close to the capital. One-third of the members of the House are from Ontario. This substantial bloc stands for a single set of interests and looms large over the Ottawa scene. The Senate is not organized for geographic representation to the degree it is in the United States; it is appointed by the government rather than elected and provides no counterweight.

Data on the origins of civil servants are not publicly available. According to one estimate, 36% of all federal officials in the senior executive classes in 1975 were from Ontario. This percentage is in proportion to population, and even this share could be controlling. Only in the case of Ontario does the share even equal the province's proportion of population, because 16% of the total originated outside Canada.[3] Hence, of those officials in these classes who were of Canadian origin, 43% were from Ontario.* Many of those from abroad are known to have come directly into the federal service from other unitary states. It is not known how many of these immigrants lived outside the central area of Canada for a suffcent length of time to have acquired an extra-centrist point of view before joining the public service. Unless some of them did, the effective centrist component could be as high as 52%, and it is safe to assume it to be almost half. With such a proportion, the atmosphere is set, and many of those originating elsewhere take on the coloration of the dominant group.

This dominant presence does not take the form of an Ontario juggernaut that in every issue bars the way to rational discussion. Such tactics would be incompatible with civil service traditions and are hardly necessary in the circumstances. Rather, it sets the tone and tacit assumptions of policy consideration. Policy consideration is

---

* The 16% includes naturalized immigrants and, exceptionally, individuals in the process of fulfilling citizenship requirements.

already overweighed by the strong Ontario voice in the House of Commons and the easy input from nearby core interests. In any event, sheer economic arithmetic implies an abiding concern for the core area, to the point where it seems that what is good for Ontario is good for Canada.

Federalism in Flux

The philosophy behind the Canadian federal system is that the center should take the lead in those things in which the country faces the rest of the world as well as those which go to make the whole greater than the sum of the parts; the provinces may respond to particular needs which inhere in their territory or population. Federal and provincial governments are each sovereign in certain areas of jurisdiction, and they have legitimate constituencies which, in total, are the same.

If this much is agreed, its application is less certain. There came to be but 10 provincial governments to share power with the central government compared with 50 states in the American Union. Many of the functions assigned to the provinces, such as education, health and welfare, resource development and urban matters, were minimal or nonexistent as government responsibilities 100 years ago. They have now become predominant politically and financially. The resulting shift to the provincial level has encouraged the central government to encroach on provincial jurisdiction to maintain its concept of a nation-state.

The growth in relative significance of the provinces *vis-à-vis* the central government has not been steady. In times of crisis, such as wars and depressions, the swing is to the center; in calmer times, the trend to the human and regional end of the scale resumes. The operation of the system thus involves constant adjustment in the sharing of rights and responsibilities. Constant adjustment requires constant and effective consultation, particularly since functions within one jurisdiction commonly impinge on functions in another.

In the Ottawa bureaucracy, on the other hand, the "nation" is perceived as the supreme entity, with the regions somewhat unruly junior subdivisions imprecisely represented by the provinces. Such an attitude may be right for a world power like the United States which may feel it needs a standard patriotism, but it is neither relevant nor accepted in much of Canada. The bureaucracy tends to share the views of centrist propagandists who bemoan the lack of a "Canadian identity," when the whole point of being Canadian is freedom to be different. Canada is more like a modern family than a melting pot.

Bureaucrats and Politicians

The place of the civil service within the federal structure has changed materially over the past 25 years with expansion of the federal role. Senior civil servants once confined themselves to the supervision of ministerial policies. In those simpler times, it was possible for a minister to get his mind around the activities of his department and to direct his staff. As government came to touch many more aspects of life, however, it became more complex in an increasingly interdependent and technical society. Ministers were obliged to narrow the range of questions they could handle and the bureaucracy necessarily emerged to fill the vacuum over a growing span of problems.

Civil servants came out of the back room to become accountable in their own right before parliamentary committees, to receive delegations on behalf of their minister, and to act as spokesmen for government. Cabinet committees were set up as the effective decision-making instrument of government over a decade ago; civil servants have taken an active part in meetings of these committees in company with their Ministers, and sometimes even in their absence.[4] They have been obliged to take more initiative in policy formulation. Prime Minister Trudeau, especially, has expected them to be more innovative.

Ministers in the Canadian Cabinet are selected to represent regions and cultural groupings. Nurturing their constituencies and attending to the popularity of their party is essential to survival. Once selected for the Cabinet, they are assigned to portfolios but rarely stay in one for more than two years. With one essential interest and one transitory responsibility, they are prone to give departmental business low priority. While once they could do both tasks, they have now become obliged to abdicate much departmental decision-making to their permanent staff in order to focus on imperious political demands.

Civil Service Growth

The shift of policy initiative to the civil service developed gradually but was becoming evident to those within the system in the late 1960s.

At the same time that civil servants were being asked to be more innovative, politicians were lamenting publicly that policy formation was being taken out of their hands. Despite this contradiction, the government approved the expansion of the service that was the inevitable bureaucratic response to the new demands.

From the early 1950s, the rate of growth of the civil service as a whole exceeded that of the population it served, reflecting expansion in government activities. Growth accelerated after 1970. Between 1970 and 1976, the population of Canada increased by about 8%,[5] while the civil service grew by 30%, excluding the armed forces and crown companies such as Canadian National Railways.[6] The upper echelons grew even faster. In the same period, the number of senior executive officers increased from 538 to 1,223,[7] or by 127%, more than four times the rate for the bureaucracy as a whole, which was itself growing at nearly four times the population rate.

The growth in the senior executive classes was not caused by mere wage inflation. Salary levels, grade for grade, increased mightily at the same time. Much of this growth, together with the addition of support staff, went into newly created "policy" or "planning" units. The Government Telephone Directory now lists many of these units that did not exist less than a decade ago. Formerly, the word "policy" was used most sparingly in the titles of such analytical units as did exist, as its use implied an infringement on the prerogatives of ministers. The process of expansion, concentrated at the top, and the assumption of a policy role for civil servants, produced a bureaucratic momentum. Ministers complained that they were losing control of their departments.

It may not be mere coincidence that all but a few of the long list of alleged federal intrusions enumerated by the Western premiers have arisen within the last three or four years.[8] While it is hard to unscramble cause and effect, it may be noted that this encroachment came hard upon the heels of the spectacular expansion of the policy levels of the bureaucracy. These developments occurred in a period of relative calm in which the functions of prime public interest were those originally assigned to the provinces.

The Complication of Technology

Bureaucratic growth could not be balanced. Our technological society encourages the production of specialists, and technical departments increasingly need "experts." The generalists of the earlier dispensation, the "mandarins," have become an endangered species. Mandarins and ministers receive staff recommendations in which questionable assumptions can be buried in technological imperatives.

The effect of burying assumptions so they are not challenged is to confuse political priorities by making staff proposals appear more urgent than they are.[9] Confused priorities dull the feel of the minister for the public will and raise the chances of popular objection. The resulting clamor for public dialogue cannot be met effectively as the few generalists available cannot be sprung often from their supervisory positions at headquarters. Hence, technologists are assigned to take part in the dialogue, but their dedication to a single function only serves to alienate those with whom they have been sent to negotiate.[10]

The Politician and the Public

Under the parliamentary system, the minister is at once a member of the House of Commons and the head of his department. He is thus the critical bridge between the elected representatives and his ministry. It is the duty of the minister to sense the public will. When government was more remote from the public, the minister could handle the trickle of submissions with little help. As the scope of government activities expanded, touching many more people more intimately, as the scale of government projects grew, often uprooting whole communities, and as the impact of industrial development caused demands for extensive regulation, public comment grew to an unmanageable flood. Ministers became unable to sense the public will in all the issues before them. Perforce, they delegated public dealings on departmental business to senior civil servants. The critical bridge became the weak link.

The consequence of insulating the minister from departmental issues, and the miscalculations that resulted, set off a protest movement. Actions taken within the narrow confines of departmental terms of reference, or lack of action in the face of changing circumstances, periodically provoked public outcry. The weak link could be strengthened if public forces could be channelled so as to convey to the minister the public will on particular issues. Ministers recognized the potential for avoiding confrontations with references to "participatory democracy," although they often saw the reality of participation as a challenge to their authority.

Results of Greater Bureaucratic Influence

Under fire from increasing public protest and inclined to have the issues fully aired, ministers have sent civil servants to put out the fires. In a few cases, government has financed public participants, often including vocal opponents of government policies. Civil servants have been cast in the role of politicians, for which many have not been fitted.

A few civil servants could make this transition into politics, and some anticipated the new trend to more public consultation. The political role sat better on those generalists who could be made available. Others found it difficult to transfer their allegiance from the minister to the public and did not see that keeping the public happy also served to secure their minister's position. In high technology departments there is a greater chance that specialists will reach the top, yet their tunnel vision disqualifies them for the political role. Long, unquestioning public acceptance of an agency creates an arrogance that inhibits consultation. On the other hand, the work of some technical departments charged with new tasks not yet established fully in the public mind, such as conservation of energy or protection of the environment, induces a softer approach. The result is unevenness in handling public comment. Unevenness creates public uncertainty and tarnishes the whole bureaucracy with arrogance and bias.

Civil servants who are purveyors of the core view are unable to resolve local problems, particularly if they are technologists, as they themselves are parties to the dispute. Thus their entry onto the local scene aggravates the problems more often than it solves them. If they fail to join the fray, the problem festers and brings charges of lack of interest by a remote Ottawa.

The result is public alienation and a tendency to blame the civil service for all the ills of the system. As ministers have abdicated much of their function as sensors of the public will on departmental business, they have blamed the bureaucracy for their troubles. Although the civil service has emerged as a force in its own right, espousing the macro view in a high technology society, it alone is not to blame. Bureaucratic influence is a symptom of deeper maladjustments that need to be addressed in more basic political and constitutional terms.

Public Consultation

The need for public consultation has not gone unrecognized in Ottawa. Several forms were tried as thought appropriate to different situations.

Regulatory commissions have long been used to control specific functions. Their terms of reference provide for hearings, so public feedback can be obtained, usually by way of objection to proposed rulings. Most of them also advise the government on policy, hence their rulings often involve interpretation of policies they themselves have recommended. The commissioners and staff are based in Ottawa, where they are part of the establishment, and their terms of reference are defined by the federal government.

Royal Commissions, now called Commissions of Enquiry, are also of long standing. Originally they were used to examine questions of broad policy when special staff were needed to do research beyond the capacity of departments with continuing responsibilities, and when a tangle of conflicting interests called for public soundings. More recently, the device has been applied to individual projects encountering resistance, such as pipelines and airports. Their terms of reference are laid down by the government appointing them. In many cases, federal civil servants are seconded to commissions to serve on their research staffs for the duration of their studies.

A unique mechanism known as a joint planning committee was set up to consider expansion of the Vancouver International Airport. Not so much a joint planning process, it was rather a negotiating instrument and a body to direct relevant research. The terms of reference were negotiated by the original parties and the membership was drawn from all levels of government and all interests, including public participants, although staff support was dominated by the federal civil service. With all parties otherwise on an equal footing, it was unable to reach consensus and produced three alternative sets of recommendations for political decision.[11] This particular issue was, as of mid-1978, not yet resolved.

A number of departments have set up advisory committees, typically to deal with matters that are not crucial for government policy, such as marine safety measures or the allocation of research funds. Representation is by invitation of the department.

Special meetings have been convened to discuss particular questions with local or interest groups. Some have been extensive in subject coverage, but most are brushfire operations dealing with a single point. Whether open or by invitation, such meetings are generally representative of the interests affected. In addition, federal officials often attended conferences organized by nongovernmental groups to explain, if not defend, government policies. These methods afford an opportunity for public feedback and constitute an aspect of the emergence of the bureaucracy into public view.

Since 1970, federal property acquisitions have been made subject to public hearings. Although legally circumscribed, such hearings have had the political effect of bringing basic issues into the open.

These devices for public consultation have several common features:

1. Their terms of reference and personnel are determined unilaterally by the federal government even when there may be substantial provincial or local impact. The Vancouver case is an exception that is unlikely to be repeated.

2. They generally involve the use of Ottawa bureaucrats at key points in the process, so that the central influence is prevalent in the back room where the conclusions are reached.

3. They provide for consultation and advice, but no real involvement in decision-making. In the rare case of the Vancouver airport, where participation of other levels of government and public groups was specifically included, there was no resoultion of the problem. In all cases, the effective decision-making power remained where it started, with the central authority.

4. Even when anything has come out of the process that could be thought of as breaking new ground, the superficial changes recommended have mesmerized the public into believing that something really had happened; basic questions, in fact, had not been seriously examined.[12]

Thus, while attempts to resolve problems through consultation have blunted comment on the particular issue and turned aside political flak, they have not altered the power relationships which caused the problems in the first place. Ministers have failed to sense the public will on regional concerns, sometimes even within their own regions. They have delegated to the civil service the politicians' responsibility for political sensitivity; civil servants are ill-equipped to insure meaningful communication between the public and the minister. The critical ministerial bridge remains the weak link.

Structural Change

The civil service may be able to serve governments of different ideologies respecting policies applied across the country, although it has not really been tested. However, on the other axis, the federal bureaucracy cannot be expected to balance the aspirations of the regions with the interests of the country as a whole. That is not its job, although the need becomes important when federal actions affect those aspirations.

Ministers' advisers influence assumptions and attitudes underlying policy, and this influence becomes more subtle as issues become more intricate. When civil servants are used to sense the public will, they constitute a filter through which the expression of regional concerns must pass. Thus, through increased technical complexity and greater regional divergence in a changing country, the impact of the civil service is enhanced. As the civil service is oriented nationally rather than regionally, the exercise of its influence intensifies the strains within Confederation.

The federal bureaucracy is, of course, responding to its environment. If cohesive balance between national and regional concerns is to be achieved, the environment must be altered. Even though bureaucratic momentum has outrun political initiative as a factor in current tensions, both have a common source in the dominance of the single central core. Political forces, shaped by the present structure, have set the present pattern of power; thus, the way to start reform is to change the structure of political relationships.

The problem of the federal bureaucracy is thus a part of a larger issue which goes beyond the scope of this essay. Elsewhere in this volume, Gordon Gibson and Flora MacDonald have advanced many proposals for reform. Any set of proposals has three essential elements. The most obvious is the reaffirmation and, perhaps, extension of provincial jurisdiction. Machinery for effective consultation between equal partners must be created, whatever the division of powers. However, the basic purpose of reform should be to dampen down the dominance of the central core *within the federal government.* It would serve no long-run purpose merely to increase the stature of the provinces. Unless the federal government itself can be made responsive to fundamental regional concerns, any new or restated division of powers *vis-à-vis* the provinces would be merely the prelude to another process of erosion.

The Civil Service in a New Confederation

In the past, bureaucracy has been examined almost entirely in terms of administrative structure, competence, and process. In the particular context of Canada today, there is a need to look also at the bureaucrats themselves and the influences acting on them.

More should be known publicly about the policy-making levels of the civil service in order to illuminate the bureaucratic aspect of the current political debate. What are the origins of its members, their academic backgrounds, career patterns, and attitudes? What influences are acting on them from interest groups and peers? What public good has come out of the recent sudden surge in numbers: measurably better staff work, more effective liaison or, conversely, schemes for encroachment on the provinces, or mere busy work? Much of the personal data is already in the government's computers, but it will need elaboration for this purpose.

It is hardly conceivable that any viable restructuring of Confederation would not result in some transfer of functions from the federal government to the provinces or, at least, the elimination of present duplication by consolidation primarily at the provincial level. It is equally probable that greater intergovernmental and interdepartmental liaison will be required. These likely consequences of political realignment can be expected to involve reassignment of civil servants both between and within governments. The information needed now to throw light on the present problem would also point the way to this part of the solution.

While restored provincial authority and a more amenable federal power would contain the federal bureaucracy within narrower limits, means should be considered for insuring that the civil service falls into line and stays that way. Such means might include measures to encourage better regional balance within the higher civil service grades, exchange arrangements between levels of government, and the placing of provincial nominees on federal panels from the Supreme Court down through regulatory commissions to commissions of enquiry. Ways should be worked out for injecting provincial interests into departmental policy-making.

The Coming Crisis

Quebec is the cutting edge of regional discontent. It has been, until recently, the only province doing useful thinking about the future of Confederation. Language and cultural survival have given Quebec reason to think; social cohesion has given its thinking focus; a substantial minority position and geographic location have given it clout.

Language is not the only issue, and most other provinces are discontented, too. Complaints about the working of the system have been general for many years, becoming more strident with extending federal encroachment, but until recently Ottawa has not listened. Now, with the publication of new constitutional proposals, Ottawa at last has recognized the existence of a problem. But Ottawa cannot solve it because the problem is Ottawa itself.

A good part of the Ottawa problem is bureaucratic influence, extended in recent years in two directions. The civil service, a proxy for the country's central core, has been impelled to reach *out* to interpose between government and public, and to reach *in* to the decision-making center of the parliamentary system.

Federal assertiveness has escalated, and the provinces, emerging from a colonial mentality, have responded by demanding that their new maturity be respected. The federal constitutional proposals result from an awareness of this political confrontation, but they are essentially defensive; they do not recognize at all the contribution of the bureaucracy to the perpetuation of conflict.

NOTES

1. Michael Hechter, *Internal Colonialism: The Celtic Fringe in British National Development* (Berkeley: University of California Press, 1975).

2. *Report of the Western Premiers' Task Force on Constitutional Trends* (Victoria, B.C.: Queen's Printer, May 1977). Finance, welfare, education and health were not covered.

3. The profile from which these figures have been taken is unattributed, but it has been obtained from a reliable source.

4. For an official description of the Cabinet Committee system, see the *Canada Year Book*, Statistics Canada, Ottawa, 1974, p. 70.

5. Estimated mid-1970 population: 21,297,000 (*Estimated Population of Canada by Provinces*, Statistics Canada, Cat. 91-201);

mid-1976 census: 22,992,604 (*Census of Canada*). Census years were 1971 and 1976.

6. From 239,577 in 1970 to 312,465 in 1976 (annual *Estimates*). The strength of the civil service cannot be traced consistently from published sources due to changes in definition and coverage from time to time. Past growth rates can be determined from the several series available for succeeding periods.

7. *Annual Reports* of the Public Service Commission of Canada, Ottawa.

8. *Western Premiers' Task Force*, op. cit., Part II, p. 17ff. *passim*.

9. For an example from American experience, see "Inverted Pyramids: The Use and Misuse of Aviation Forecasting," by Jerome Milch, in *Social Studies of Science*, 6 (1976), pp. 5-31.

10. For an elaboration of this argument, see Elliot J. Feldman and Jerome Milch, "Organizing Disunity: Rational Planning in Canadian Administration," paper presented to Duke University Canadian Studies Seminar, Royal Military College, Kingston, Ontario, June 1978.

11. *Final Report*, The Airport Planning Committee, Vancouver International Airport, March 1976.

12. The Royal Commission on Transportation (the MacPherson Commission) of 1961 is an example. Its report was substantial, well received and largely acted upon, yet complaints that rail freight rates inhibit economic diversification in the West continue. See *Western Premiers' Task Force, op. cit.*, p. 13.

9__THE FEDERAL BUREAUCRACY AND CANADIAN DISUNITY

COMMENT

Robert J. Art

What is unique in the Canadian national bureaucratic experience? I shall comment on Gordon Stead's perceptive essay and seek to answer this question by comparing Canada with the United States. The utility of the comparative approach, after all, is to locate and then put aside the similarities between entities in order to pinpoint and thereby highlight that which is unique to each.

I would like to compare the national (central) bureaucracies of each country along the following four dimensions: (1) the degree to which each central bureaucracy holds a presumptuous attitude towards the nation's major political subdivisions (states or provinces); (2) the extent to which each country's national political executives can control their bureaucratic subordinates; (3) the prevalence or absence of a mandarin class in each central bureaucracy; and (4) the effects of the central bureaucracy's operations on each nation's political cohesion.

Canada and the United States are alike in the first two dimensions, different in the last two. The two similarities stem largely from characteristics inherent in the powerful, large-scale national bureaucracies of today's centralized, democratic nation-state. The contrast between Canada and the United States with regard to a bureaucratic mandarin class stems from differences in the political traditions of each nation. The contrast in the fourth dimension derives from differences in political structure, political development, and regional evolution within each nation.

Bureaucratic Arrogance and Political Control

Both the Canadian and American national bureaucrat share the "there-are-only-bumpkins-in-the-boondocks" complex. The high-handedness of the Washington-knows-best attitude is familiar to Americans. Revenue sharing has returned some untied monies back to the states and cities, but the conflicting welter of federal regulations, the seeming insensitivity to local needs and regional differences, and the detailed involvement of Washington in state and local decision-making remain. From afar, the "feds" are usually seen as arrogant and presumptuous; up close, they often are. It is some small comfort to an American, though not to a Canadian, to know that Ottawa views the provinces much as Washington views the states and cities.

This is so in both nations because of the lure and pitfalls of the metropole. For many years the best brains interested in public service went to Washington and Ottawa because that was where the power was and hence where the reputations and fame could be made. Once ensconced, the ambitious bureaucrat and politician alike partook of the rarefied atmosphere. People in the metropole develop an inflated view of themselves in good part because of the importance of the work they do. The questions dealt with are incredibly complex: the decisions made, of great consequence. The lure of power is clear ("Power is the ultimate aphrodisiac," Kissinger is reputed to have said). So, too, is the pitfall. The importance of the work done is transferred to the people who do it by those very same people. To realize that what one does is central to the nation and yet to retain a sense of humility and perspective about oneself is a fine balance hard to strike. Politicians probably strike the balance better than bureaucrats because they are comparatively more vulnerable to the wishes of the people than the career civil servants.[1]

Canada and the United States are also alike in a second sense. Cabinet officers, whether appointed by the Prime Minister from among elected Members of Parliament as in Canada or by the President from the country at large as in the United States, must work hard at controlling their bureaucratic subordinates, though the reasons why officers in each nation must do so are not totally the same. I would single out three factors in the American case: (1) the sheer number and technical complexity of the matters that Cabinet officers must deal with; (2) the enduring Congressional subcommittee-executive bureau alliances; and (3) the "untouchability" of the federal civil service employee. The first is straightforward. Any political executive must rely on his staff, but he can become its captive if he lacks the technical expertise necessary to deal with the myriad issues brought to him. He gets more of what he wants from his subordinates than they from him when he has the ability to cope with the technical complexity of the issues. Bureau-subcommittee networks are a hall-mark of America's decentralized national government. "Separated institutions sharing powers" has produced close ties between Congress and the permanent bureaucracy. Each component needs the other because neither can dictate policy. Congress needs executive policy initiatives in order to perform its legislative role effectively; the executive bureaucrat needs Congress's goodwill if he is to obtain his preferred policies and implement them effectively. Years of working with the relevant subcommittee enables the canny careerist to forge potent political links. Harried and transient political appointees can find their policies undercut by subordinates who know they can count on Congress for support. Finally, the leverage of the Cabinet officer over his department is diluted when he can neither fire nor discipline his careerists. The spoils system was thrown out for good reasons, but quality work and merit promotion have not flowered sufficiently because the careerists have been *too* insulated from political control.[2] Under President Carter's proposed civil service reforms, the United States may strike a better balance between too little and too much political control.

Mr. Stead tells us that Canadian ministers have the same problem of control. There is the familiar technical complexity of the issues with which Cabinet ministers must cope. But the Canadian parliamentary system appears to magnify the problem in two important ways. Ministers are selected, not for their substantive expertise, but for their ability to represent the nation's major regional and culture groupings within the Cabinet. (In the United States, regional representation is less important for a Cabinet post than compatability with Presidential views and substantive expertise, with the former the more important.) If substantive expertise is not taken seriously in selecting ministers, the ability of the permanent bureaucracy to capture the minister is enhanced. The political duties of the minister, moreover, interfere with his departmental duties. Forced to "nurture constituencies" and "attend to party popularity," he has that much less time to attend to his departmental garden. The result of all these factors has been to produce a significantly, if not inordinately, large policy-making role for the ministry careerist. And the rapid turnover of ministerial portfolios, reminiscent of the Third and Fourth French Republics, makes a bad problem worse.

In the final analysis, however, though some of the particulars differ, Canada appears much like the United States. In both cases, the proliferation of substantive specializations and technical staff assistants outpaces the ability of any one individual to keep up. In both cases, political exigencies, whether of the congressional-executive or parliamentary-representative variety, complicate the Cabinet officer's task of controlling his department. In both cases, political executives must fight hard to keep on top of their departments. In both cases, the job appears nearly impossible. In short, it seems to me simply that Canada has come of age. Those simpler times to which Mr. Stead fondly refers, when a minister could "get his mind around the activities of his department and direct his staff," will probably never return. For Canada clearly has entered the age of the technological society, of mass interest group democracy, and of heated politics, with all the attendant headaches for politicians. What is surprising, in retrospect, is not that Canada has arrived, but that it took her so long to get here.

Mandarins and Political Unity

In the third respect—the way they treat their highest civil servants—Canada and the United States differ. The contrast is a product of differences in political traditions. More in the British mold, Canada early developed a bureaucratic mandarin class, a group of elite, senior civil servants who possessed a generalist and elitist education and skills, long years of experienced operation at the top, and a fierce dedication to protecting the minister of the day. Before 1950, with the exception of the Treasury, where, as in England, the very best of the best went for a period of training and then moved out into other departments, the careerist would generally move up in the department in which he was originally recruited. Since about 1950, Canada has tried to promote generalists in the careerist ranks by encouraging movement among departments. Vacancies in a department's senior posts are now advertised all through the government if there is a dearth of good candidates within the given department. Movement to the top of the careerist ranks is now aided by competitive movement among departments. Canada holds the sensible view that, although proven substantive expertise in one area does not translate into expertise in another, administrative and decision-making skills do. Good experienced generalists easily carry in their heads knowledge of how to manage almost any large-scale public bureaucracy.

We in the United States have not taken this approach. As Hugh Heclo has written, here there is "an absence of any government-wide career structure for civil servants" and hence a great deal of "organizational immobility" among the elite civil servants.[3] In the United States successful careers in the bureaucracy for the upwardly mobile are made by remaining in one's department and even in one's bureau. Once having attained success, individuals are reluctant to try new fields, understandably so the older they become. This natural reluctance is enhanced by the civil service provision that rank and pay generally attach to the job, not to the individual. Effective direction over an individual's civil service career, moreover, lies at the bureau rather than at the departmental level. The lower into the bowels of the bureaucracy one proceeds, the narrower becomes the perspective. Promotion depends upon pleasing one's immediate superior. Moving to another bureau within the agency, much less to another agency, carries with it the danger of setting one's career back. Thus, in the American civil service, the career incentives to move out of one's niche are low and the risks high. As a consequence, bureaucratic generalists are not numerous; and senior careerists do not freely and easily move at the top among the bureaus and departments.

In another fundamental sense there is less incentive for American careerists to move than for their Canadian counterparts. In Canada, the third and usually the second highest (the deputy minister) positions within a ministry are filled by careerists. A career structure that puts a premium on lateral movement for broad experience, that offers the chance to sit at the power pinnacles of policy-making, and that offers job security to boot (except for the deputy minister of a department, whom the Prime Minister can fire), obviously promotes the development of career generalists. The United States has chosen differently. There, the first (or top) five policy-making tiers (Secretary, Under Secretary, Deputy Undersecretary, Assistant Secretary, and Deputy Assistant Secretary) are left open for presidential appointment. Civil servants can and do often compete successfully for these positions, but they generally lose the security of their civil service status if they win the job. With the bulk of the senior policy posts reserved for the "inners and outers" and with the high risks of losing careerist status by occupying such a post, the American structure does not encourage a cadre of career generalists among its senior civil servants.

Virtues and Vices: The Systems Compared

Which system is better? Clearly, the answer is not clear. The virtues of the American system easily can become its vices. The ability that a new president has to pack the senior levels of the executive branch with his men and hence quickly make the bureaucracy (to the extent that it can be made so) amenable to his political mandate brings with it this danger: a period of fumbling because of lack of experience and continuity by the political appointees. The wheel must be rediscovered by every new administration. And, yet, rediscovery of the wheel can be healthy because fundamental assumptions can always use periodic reexamination. The virtues of Canada's system can also become its vices. The reservoir of expertise provided by the career civil service can make for stability and continuity of policy. It can also lead to rigidity, much conservatism, and lack of political control. Perhaps each nation's careerist system best fits its larger political system. With rapid ministerial turnover and with ministerial selection by political needs rather than by substantive expertise, Canada may be well served by a career service that reaches almost to the very top of government. With a large reservoir of inners and outers to draw upon in order to fill the policy-making pinnacles, the United States may be well served by its system.

And, yet, there is reason to reconsider this final judgment. Canada asks too much of its senior civil servants, while the United States both asks too much and receives too little from its careerists. According to Mr. Stead, the Cabinet ministers make too many demands upon the senior civil servants by asking them to be that which they are not. Instead of being simply senior advisers and permanent administrators, they are now too often asked to be surrogate politicians. Witness, for example, the practice of sending senior civil servants out into the provinces to put out political fires. If this trend continues, the Cabinet risks the very essence and legitimacy of the civil service—its reputation for professionalism and neutrality, both of which are already under attack for other reasons. Given Canada's current intractable political problems, this practice seems to an outsider to be foolhardy.

The United States, on the other hand, receives too little from its senior civil servants because it has not yet found a way to create a cadre of career generalists in order to tap their expertise for government-wide service. But it also asks too much from them because it requires that they give up their career status and assume the high risks of the political arena in order to move closer to the top tiers of power. In short, even though each country has a different personnel structure, both are producing the same result: more politicization of senior civil servants than is healthy.[4]

Canada and the United States, finally, differ in regard to the effects that each central bureaucracy's operation has on the nation's political cohesion. The Ottawa bureaucracy reinforces the disintegrative trends rampant in Canada today. The Washington bureaucracy at its best reinforces and at its worst does little if any harm to the national cohesiveness. The United States had its Civil War and New Deal, both of which legitimized a powerful federal government. In the United States today the federal government can be viewed as the adjudicator and adjustor among the competing claims of the nation's major interest groups, states, regions, and cities. The decisions of the federal government do not generally and consistently penalize or reward one group, state, city, or region for the benefit or at the expense of all others. The decentralized structure of the federal government makes for multiple points of access so that political pressures can always find a hearing somewhere in Washington. Interest groups are spread over many states and usually over at least two major regions so that no consistent and clear convergence between group and regional interests obtains. All major interest groups are well organized so that they make their influence felt on issues of central importance to them. The demographic and economic developments within the nation have produced many powerful regions and geographical groupings, none of which clearly dominates. In short, power is shared by many structures in Washington and dispersed among many groups throughout the nation. There is no consistently winning coalition. As a consequence of all these factors, Washington can be viewed by the cities, states, and regions as presumptuous, overbearing, and meddlesome, but, paradoxically, not also as arbitrary, discriminatory, or vengeful.

Sadly, this is not so for Canada. Not yet resolved are the original ambiguities of the 1867 British North America Act. Ottawa is aggressively encroaching in the growth areas of governmental activity—education, health, welfare, land and natural resources, all of which were originally miniscule, privately run, and mandated by the 1867 Act to the oversight of the provinces. Consensus about the minimum proper role and legitimate spheres of activity of the federal government do not yet exist. For too many years, one region—Ontario—has far surpassed all others in population, economic wealth, and political influence. There has been a clear convergence of interests between the nation's major industrial, commercial, and financial groups and one particular region. The federal government, which has been Ontario-centric in its outlook and policies for so long, is now aggressively fighting to maintain its centralizing role amidst the ascendant provinces. The proper functions of a federal government thus have become hopelessly entangled politically with Ottawa's Ontario-biased policies. In comparison to the United States, Canada possesses neither a legitimized powerful central government nor a pluralism of strong regional power centers. If governmental power is both shared at the federal level and dispersed nationally in the United States, in Canada it is highly concentrated at Ottawa. Washington could never dominate the United States. Ottawa, until recently, has been able to rule Canada. Ottawa, as a consequence, appears to the rest of the nation to be both presumptuous *and* discriminatory.

Canada's political structure and unique internal development have thus spawned a central bureaucracy that is, not surprisingly, reflective of the larger political system. The Ottawa bureaucrat understandably thinks that what is good for the metropole is good for the periphery, or, perhaps, even worse, he is not even aware that he thinks in such a fashion. Clearly, the Ottawa bureaucracy is not the problem in Canada's political troubles today. Rather it is a clear manifestation of the problem. Mr. Stead, therefore, has it exactly right when he states that "the federal bureaucracy is responding to its environment" and hence that "its environment must be altered" if its behavior is to change.

After reading this wise essay, I am left with only one nagging doubt, which neither Mr. Stead nor anyone else can presently resolve. If the political will is mustered to restructure the environment, how quickly will the Ottawa bureaucracy respond? Bureaucracies are not noted for their quick reaction times. That the Ottawa bureaucracy will respond in time is assured. But how long will it take, and how much time does Canada have?

NOTES

1. Recently in the United States, the arrogance of the metropole towards the "peripheries" has probably lessened. A great explosion in

governmental employment has occurred in the last 15 years, and it has come not at the federal but at the state and local level. The increased respectability of non-Washington governmental service was enhanced by Watergate, but the trend predates it. From the tone of Gordon Stead's comments, I suspect that provincial work in Canada has been held in comparatively lower repute than is state and local work in the U.S. But I also suspect that this statement will shortly no longer be valid, if indeed it now is, as the complaints of the provinces against Ottawa-centric policies continue to gain even greater political legitimacy. For with legitimacy comes respectability.

2. In his *A Government of Strangers: Executive Politics in Washington* (Washington, D.C.: Brookings, 1977), Hugh Heclo offers a contrary view. He asserts that the upper levels of the bureaucracy in Washington have become overly politicized. But the manner in which bureau chiefs have become politicized since the early 1960s cuts both ways. Bureau chiefs became more pliant to presidential political wishes, or less pliant by becoming better politicians *vis-à-vis* Congress. I am more impressed with the latter than the former. See pages 64-83.

3. *A Government of Strangers, op. cit.,* chapters 4 and 7.

4. The politicization of the senior civil servant is one of Heclo's major themes (*op.cit.*). He is more concerned, however, with presidents manipulating the civil service in order to make political appointments *within* its career ranks.

10___QUEBEC SEPARATISM IN COMPARATIVE PERSPECTIVE

Peter Alexis Gourevitch

Comparing countries involves finding contrasts and similarities. In some respects, all countries are unique; in others, they are alike. The point of comparing is to help clarify just what is unique and what is not. Canada at present attracts considerable attention as an advanced industrial country with a serious chance of breaking apart. Some aspects of Quebec's relation to the rest of Canada are certainly unique and help explain this possibility: there are no other groups of six million francophones on the North American continent, let alone with Quebec's complex history of defeat, *survivance*, and assertion. The phenomenon of culturally-based challenges to existing nation-states is not, however, unique to Canada. Similar movements exist in Scotland, Wales, Brittany, Catalonia, the Basque provinces of Spain, Flanders, and Croatia, to name but a sample of culturally distinct regions who challenge their relationship to the central government of each country.

While each of these movements has its unique features, they also have features in common, an examination of which may help shed light on the phenomenon as a whole as well as on each case. This essay seeks to expose the similarities in one aspect of contemporary nationalisms in Western Europe and North America—economics and its relationship to the politics of separatism. In this attempt, I do not by any means intend to "reduce" nationalism to economics. On the contrary, I shall suggest that economic disparities do not by themselves create such movements: without some ethnic or cultural

I am deeply indebted to David Bloom, Tom Naylor, Harvey Rishi-kof, Michael Stein, and James de Wilde, who have encouraged my comparative speculations and tutored me about Canada, but who are in no way responsible for my essay.

I also appreciate the assistance of Milton Esman, Michael Hechter, Lisa Hirschman, James Kurth, Martin Shefter, Theda Skocpol, and Aristide Zolberg.

soil the seeds of economic discontent do not sprout into a "nationalist" tree. Economics is frequently neglected in discussions of nationalism: the focus tends to be on constitutional and cultural issues, explanations, and solutions.[1] While important, constitutional and cultural variables are insufficient.

The Comparative Framework

All over Europe, the construction of the modern nation-state involved the destruction of potential nations and the subordination of certain cultures and languages to others. In some cases, these cultures have become virtually extinct (Provençal in Southern France), or if not extinct, politically quiescent or weak. This situation prevails in Britany, French Occitania, the French Basque provinces, and in Italy. Culturally based demands for decentralization, autonomy, or separation do exist, but they are comparatively feeble.

In other cases, such movements have long been, or have recently become, politically strong: Scotland, Catalonia, the Spanish Basque provinces, Flanders, Croatia, Quebec. What accounts for the difference between these two groups of regions? What distinguishes ethnic regions with strong autonomist movements from ethnic regions with weak ones?

One line of reasoning looks at the geographical distribution of economic activity in each country. This approach is suggested by the contrast between Britain and Spain on the one hand, and France on the other. In Britain, a distinct Scottish identity has always been present: there have always been identifiable Scottish institutions, traditions, customs, linguistic habits, religious practices, and so on. There have always existed groups dedicated to the defense of Scottish culture, Scottish autonomy, and even Scottish independence. But the translation of that identity into a powerful political movement is recent. The strength of the Scottish National Party coincides with the discovery of large oil deposits off the Scottish coast at a time when the English economy has been faltering. In Wales, where the incidence of Welsh-speaking is much higher than of Gaelic in Scotland, but where there is no oil or its functional economic equivalent, the Plaid Cymru is much weaker. The combination of an economic trump for Scotland and a poor hand for the traditional economic center clearly has boosted the fortunes of the Scottish National Party.[2]

In Spain, autonomist movements in the Basque provinces and Catalonia have been strong throughout the 19th and 20th centuries.

Throughout this period there have also been serious economic imbalances: Castile (the area around Madrid) unified the country politically and tried to centralize it. Industrial development, however, occurred outside Castile, in Catalonia and the Basque provinces. The political leader, Castile, soon found itself in constant conflict with the economic leaders. The grievances of the latter were repeatedly expressed in cultural terms through nationalist movements demanding greater autonomy.[3]

In France, by contrast, political leadership and economic leadership have coincided geographically for most of the 19th and 20th centuries. The area of the "langue d' oïl" (stretching from Lille to Lyon, centered on Paris) led integration of the country around the crown, then spearheaded French industrialization. The areas of the "langue d'oc," in the South and West, and Brittany, were integrated into the system as subordinate farming regions. Movements of cultural defense exist in those regions, but they remain politically weak.[4]

These patterns suggest that where economic strength and political leadership coincide, ethnically or culturally distinct regions acquiesce in their integration into the larger unit. Where the two functions do not coincide, the chances of a region expressing its grievances in ethnic or cultural terms increases. This "non-congruence" may arise where: a) the original "core" or leadership region falters, as in England today; or b) the peripheral region improves its economic position, or acquires the prospect of doing so through the development of some resource or some other economic advantage (location, labor supply), as in the case of Scottish oil.[5]

These generalizations may be put another way. Imagine three over-lapping transparent maps for each country to be analyzed for regional movements. One map shows the geographic location of the region which was and is the political leader; a second map highlights the region which was and is the economic leader; the final map shows the geographic concentrations of ethnic or cultural distinctiveness. If the regions in the first two maps coincide (if the same region is both political and economic leader), strong autonomist movements in the third are unlikely. If the first two do not coincide, and significant economic activity occurs in a region with a distinct culture and/or ethnicity, political discontents in that region are likely to use ethnicity to express those discontents. By itself, economic disparity does not produce *culturally based* expressions of discontent. The North of England, for example, is as badly off as southern Scotland. There is no "North National Party" there. Why?—because there is no distinct culture available to nourish the "nationalist" seed. (These generalizations are grouped in tabular form in the Appendix.)

Canada-Quebec

What happens when this line of reasoning is applied to Canada and Quebec? It calls attention to certain economic-political relationships which are familiar to Canadians and Québécois, but whose importance to an understanding of current developments is frequently neglected in favor of emphasizing cultural grievances and constitutional issues. We must look to the historical relationship of national economic and political centers, and to the relationship between the distribution of economic and political power and the distribution of francophone and anglophone cultures. What changes in these relationships have occurred since Confederation?

The Confederation Deal and the Distribution of Power

Canadian Confederation was founded on an alliance among shipping, banking, manufacturing, and agricultural interests in Montreal and Ontario. Confederation offered these groups several economic advantages. Industrial tariffs helped push goods along an East-West axis, resisting the North-South pull of the United States. The income from these duties financed railroads and canals, extending the transportation link from coast to coast. Transportation improvements in turn opened the West for development, encouraging industrial growth behind tariff walls. The stronger finances of the larger federal unit reassured foreign, especially English, investors.

Confederation served imperial needs as well. The transcontinental railway provided an alternative route to the Far East for a Britain always concerned about its link to India. Extending the rail lines from Montreal to Halifax without going through Maine would provide an alternative to Portsmouth (N.H.) as a warm water port at a time when British-American relations were strained by the American Civil War.

The long economic downturn in world agricultural and industrial markets after 1873 produced new tensions inside the Confederation between industry and agriculture, between East and West. Industrial tariffs obliged farmers to sell their products in open world markets (whose prices were dropping in the period 1873-96) and to buy manufactured products in protected and costly domestic markets.

Deflation—falling prices, tight money—hurt debtors, especially farmers, to the benefit of bankers located in Montreal. Manipulation of freight rates worked against users, especially those in the West, to the benefit of the owners of the railroads, again Easterners.[6]

The grip of banking, shipping, and manufacturing interests in Ontario and Quebec was never threatened, but Quebec was internally diverse, and the anglophone industrialists were not the only force in the province. While economically weak, francophones had some political leverage. Anglophone entrepreneurs had to persuade the majority of the population of their definition of provincial interests if they were to secure Quebec support for industrial policies at the federal level.

The great majority of francophone Québécois lived in the countryside, only marginally connected to dynamic Montreal. The lifelines of Canada passed down the St. Lawrence through the francophones, but not with their active involvement. Relations between the anglophone core and the mass of inhabitants were mediated by a traditional pre-industrial elite composed of the clergy, large landowners, and members of the traditional middle class (lawyers, doctors, apothecaries). In exchange for an anglophone "hands-off policy" on cultural and religious matters, this francophone elite supported industrial Montreal's needs in Ottawa; Quebec Members of Parliament voted to support high tariffs, railroad construction, freight rates, and bond markets. Thus, Quebec politics expressed a compromise between two groups of unequal bargaining strength—in economics, the province would support the interpretation of the province's interests put forward by the Montreal-based industrialists, who were largely anglophone; in culture and religion, francophone elites were permitted autonomy.

Quebec in the Twentieth Century

All these relationships have altered dramatically since World War II. Francophones are no longer isolated. People have moved from the countryside to the city, from farming to industry. The influence of traditional elites, most notably that of the Church, has dropped off sharply. Education provides increasing numbers of francophones with the training needed for the new professions and management. With such training have come aspirations. Francophones have become increasingly dissatisfied with the subservient positions offered them in the industrial economy. They want better jobs. Life in the countryside helped defuse the consequences of having two cultural groupings in the same territory; life in the city, a new economy, makes the old relationship unacceptable.

The ability of anglophone interests in Montreal to satisfy rising francophone demands has decreased. Montreal has lost its central place in Canadian economic life as activity and control have shifted westward, or to other countries. Banking, manufacturing, resource extraction and development, agro-business—these have moved steadily to Ontario and beyond, to resource-rich Alberta, British Columbia, and the prairie provinces. This geographical shift in the economic center of gravity has many causes: direct access to the Great Lakes bypassing Montreal (because of the St. Lawrence Seaway), the location and development of natural resources in the West, the shift of American economic activity southward and westward, and the proximity of southern Ontario to American manufacturing and markets.

Québécois nationalism frequently is cited as a cause of these shifts, particularly of the flight of head offices from Montreal. Such national-ism can instead be seen as a consequence of the westward shift. Had the massive investments in the West gone instead into the province of Quebec, the economy would be booming. It would need labor of all kinds. Private business, providing it showed some willingness to accommodate French (which many companies have done under pressure from Liberal and Union Nationale governments), would have been in a position to forge a stronger coalition with some segment of the francophone community interested in preserving a federally-oriented society and economy.

Although many francophones favor a larger economy, beyond Quebec, many others prefer a strategy of economic development which is province-centered rather than federal or even international, which is public rather than private, and which is francophone rather than anglophone. These three preferences in economic development—Quebec, public sector, and francophone—are interrelated. They embrace much of the strength of the nationalist movement.

Only an independent, or highly autonomous, Québécois state, it is argued by some separatists, can achieve economic growth in a way which promotes French culture. The private economy, in this view, seeks to extract profits without creating the infrastructure for a modern economy. In public hands, resources can be exploited following Québécois, rather than foreign or federal, imperatives. Since private capital is not interested in such a strategy, and is in

Canada largely anglophone , the state must be the leader in development.[7] Because a Québécois state would be controlled by francophones, development of the economy through the state sector makes it possible to insure that francophone culture will be favored in compensation for its historical neglect by the private sector. The nationalization of Hydro-Quebec exemplifies these links between political power, economic power, and cultural defense: before nationalization, most engineers were anglophones as the companies claimed there were no qualified francophones; after nationalization, the production of electricity took place in French.

The vision of an independent strategy for Québécois development is sustained by resource wealth, which has a political impact comparable to that of North Sea oil on Scotland. Hydroelectric power, asbestos, wood, pulp and paper, aluminum processing plants, iron ore, uranium—with these, argue the separatists, Quebec has the base for an autonomous future. Although this independent strategy is hotly debated in the province, were Quebec much poorer, or much less developed, the argument would be less credible among various elites and the mass electorate.

Quebec and the Rest of Canada

Change in the geographical distribution of economic activity not only encourages separatism in Quebec, but also increases limits on the federal government's ability to deal with it. Economic conflicts of interest among the provinces, always a major fact of Canadian politics, have worsened. This is visible in the domains of tariffs, monetary and fiscal policy, taxation, foreign investment policy, transfer payments, profit flows, and so on.[8] Alberta clashes with Eastern provinces over the distribution of oil revenues. Alberta resents the federal tax which takes part of the profits from Albertan oil sales and uses them to subsidize oil imports into Quebec and the Maritimes. Restrictions on foreign investment attract support in Ontario (where manufacturing is already developed) but provoke opposition in Alberta and British Columbia (which want to develop their resources) and in the Maritimes (which hope foreign investment will help them out of a long-term structural depression). Prairie farmers oppose, as they have for a long time, tariffs on industrial goods and discriminatory freight rate structures which make feed grains and other agricultural inputs cheaper in the East than in portions of the Western provinces where they are grown. The principal beneficiaries of both policies are residents of Ontario and Quebec.

Government equalization payments siphon money from Alberta and Ontario to the other prairie provinces, Quebec, and the Maritimes. Monetary and fiscal policies set in Ottawa are tuned largely for industrial interests in Ontario. An economy stoked up to keep the Maritimes warm would make Ontario boil; modulated for Ontario, it leaves the Maritimes (and to some degree Quebec) badly underemployed. The flow of profits, perhaps the hardest to quantify, probably funnels money into the head offices of Ontario, Alberta, and Quebec, and from there much of it goes to the United States and elsewhere.

This tangle of tensions does not polarize the provinces in any single direction: Quebec and Alberta both demand more autonomy from Ottawa, but disagree over oil. Quebec and Prince Edward Island both benefit from the oil policy, but residents of Prince Edward Island could buy cheaper textiles on open world markets rather than pay more for Quebec goods in the protected Canadian one.

The clash which dominates the news—Ontario vs. Quebec— obscures a convergence of interests between the two which has persisted since the emergence of the National Policy one hundred years ago. Most manufacturing in Canada still takes place in Quebec and Ontario, shielded behind tariff walls. Conceivably, in the long run, these provinces, and Canada as a whole, might have higher incomes were they to specialize in an open international economy, as a recent report of the Economic Council of Canada recommended. Any such change, though, would require stupendous adjustments, involving massive shifts of capital, of entrepreneurial activity, and of populations—and for that reason such ideas have had little resonance in the two provinces.[9]

Much of Quebec-based manufacturing is especially vulnerable. It is labor-intensive (textiles, furniture, clothing) and uncompetitive in world markets. The Parti Québécois Government is acutely aware that Confederation shelters markets provided by the Maritimes, Ontario, and the West. Hence the notion of sovereignty-association, which seeks to marry the advantages of independence with the advantages of membership in a larger economic unit. Everyone wants to know, of course, just how sovereignty-association will be defined. Those inside the provincial government who are especially worried about Quebec's economic vulnerability support a definition which permits the fullest possible integration of Quebec into the Canadian economy—common currency, common tariffs, free flow of all factors of production. The sovereignty dimension would come from giving Quebec a greater share in decision-making on economic issues. Others in the government blame the economic development led by anglophones for Quebec's vulnerability; they demand a sharper break, whatever the consequences.

In Ontario, manufacturers of protected goods, and the work force employed by them, continue to have a strong interest in keeping Quebec inside Confederation in a form which maintains the representation of Quebec in the House of Commons. Tariff walls, taxation, banking laws, government spending, regulation of investment—these policies require the preservation of majorities in Parliament, and Quebec continues to be Ontario's principal ally in the defense of these policies. Without Quebec votes, Ontario would have a harder time shaping the policies of Canada as a whole. It would face the rest of the provinces alone, as the one manufacturing region—six million people out of seventeen, rather than twelve million out of twenty-three.

Will Ontario's elite and public make concessions to Quebec in order to maintain it as an economic ally, or will they defend a political and cultural vision of Canada which is more unitary? If they are prepared to make concessions, will they be able to persuade the rest of Canada to go along? Will Alberta support Quebec to get greater provincial autonomy for both, or will it support Ontario to prevent special treatment for Quebec?

And what does Quebec want? Quebec is divided by competing visions of its future. One vision is protective, seeking to preserve existing businesses and present markets, growing according to the logic of a greater Canada. The other vision is transformative, seeking to shift the Quebec economy to new activities, more competitive in world markets. To some degree, this divergence overlaps with two other cleavages: private vs. public, and anglophone vs. francophone. At the core of federalist sentiment in Quebec stand private businesses tightly linked to a Canadian economy, whose owners and managers are still disproportionately anglophones and to which a large francophone population is oriented, whether by interest or by aspirations.

At the core of separatist sentiment in Quebec stand civil servants and professionals, overwhelmingly francophone and rather more involved in the provincial economy than their federalist brethren, whose links are to the Canadian economy. The economic connection is not necessarily prior to the political one. Individuals make a choice of career partly out of their ideals about the type of society they wish to have. It may be that they avoid private careers, with anglophone and federalist links, *because* they are *separatiste*, and not simply that they are *separatiste* because they have no private, anglophone links. The choice is personal. The options are shaped by economic developments.

Conclusions

The argument here seeks to clarify where significant demands for separatism and/or autonomy are likely to be strong and where such demands are likely to be weak. It suggests we examine the relationship between political union and economic activity. Where there is a discrepancy in the geographic location of each, we are likely to find strong regional consciousness. Where that regional consciousness has some ethnic soil, it may well take root in ethnic terms; that is, the regional discontents may use ethnicity or cultural distinctiveness as a medium for the articulation of many grievances. Economic interests *per se* are not defended against the center—culture is defended, of which economic independence is one component.

In this respect, the case of Canada-Quebec is not unique. It bears a strong resemblance to the situation in Great Britain, Spain, Belgium, and Yugoslavia in contrast to France, Italy, and Germany. In the former set of countries, significant economic activity occurs in regions with cultural distinctiveness: Scotland, the Basque Provinces of Spain, Catalonia, Flanders, Croatia. In Britain and Belgium, the traditional economic cores (England and Wallonia) have in recent years lacked the dynamism which once supported their dominance. In France, Germany, and Italy, by contrast, economic and political cores historically coincided, and continue to be dominant. Nationalist movements exist but are weak compared to their counterparts in other countries.

Why does congruence/non-congruence have this effect? Congruence structures the resources available to the political core with which to integrate its culturally distinct elements. A political and economic core, committed to a particular nation-state, has many incentives to offer peripheral elites and masses: jobs in business, positions in the bureaucracy, prestige, security. In Italy and France, civil servants and politicians have come disproportionately from the south of each country to the center, while poorer people migrate north to jobs. The system becomes staffed by people from the peripheries, but they run it along lines shaped by the center. The result is acquiescence to the center's domination. When and if the core declines economically, its ability to offer these inducements and to shape the system declines; autonomist strategies of regional defense are likely to increase.

The features of the Canadian situation which help account for the present form of Québécois nationalism are the relative decline in the Montreal economy and its shift westward at a time when masses of francophones were pouring into the economy. In these new conditions the traditional strategy of cultural defense in Quebec was no longer possible—that is, acquiescence to anglophone domination in exchange for isolation and elite mediation. Mobilization into the modern economy makes for higher living standards, but also for cultural vulnerability through exposure and demands for participation in the majority culture. In this sense, separatism may be seen as a new way of achieving a goal of long standing. When the Church and conservative elites lost their influence over the electorate, autonomy became possible politically; when loss of opportunity in the private sector combined with the prospect of state economic development, autonomy became plausible economically.

Why does cultural distinctiveness, or nationalism, become a vehicle for the articulation of a regional strategy? Why not other appeals, based on religion, for example, or class? In Scotland the electorate always expressed a separate identity, but through the idiom first of religion (as non-Conformists they supported the Liberal Party against Anglican Conservatives) and then through class (supporting Labor against the Conservatives).[10] Both modes of expression, religion and class, show orientation to the nation as a whole: they constitute dimensions of choice common to the entire country. They therefore indicate the power of the center, its ability to define the political cleavages to which the periphery must relate. When that center weakens, the possibility of an alternative definition of issues arises, in particular one which pits region against region.

Nationalist appeals stress the unity of all members of the region or province, obscuring the conflicts of interest or outlook among them. Quebec, Scotland, Catalonia, Flanders, and Croatia are, after all, diverse territories with complex social structures. The nationalist argument is that all these groups have something in common with each other that differentiates them from their social counterparts in other parts of the existing nation-state. The defense of culture acts as a glue; it structures the debate in such a way as to convey the need for solidarity among potentially conflicting elements of society.

Economic, cultural, and political grievances reinforce each other. Neither cultural grievances without an economic component, nor economics without a cultural component would have the capacity to threaten so fundamentally the present distribution of power in Canada and in other countries. Ambition and ideals are stronger together than either is alone.

Economics is but one dimension, and economic reality is ambiguous. Much of the dispute has to do with vision and values: what kind of society is sought and what kind of risks are worth taking? The positions of Lévesque and Trudeau are asymmetrical, giving each an advantage and a disadvantage. Lévesque must convince the electorate of a vision of what could be; vested interests and caution work against him. Trudeau can appeal to prudence, restraint, and immediate interests during a difficult and uncertain period; he has difficulty finding a moral vision of Canada, and of Quebec's place in Canada, which is both attractive to francophones and not alienating to the rest of Canada.

There may be some trade-off between these two dimensions: the stronger the cultural grievances, the less "economics" it takes to produce a given level of political opposition to the status quo; the stronger the economic dimension, the less cultural grievance is required. Scotland, in which the sense of cultural deprivation is far weaker than in Quebec, has a stronger economic trump in the form of North Sea oil and a dragging, stop-go, crisis-ridden English economy. In Quebec, where the economics of the argument are more ambiguous, the cultural tensions are far more severe, and the Parti Québécois appears stronger than the Scottish National Party.

The future of nationalist movements in all these cases will be affected by international developments. A relatively open world economy may encourage autonomist and separatist movements by lessening the importance of belonging to larger economic units. Should present protectionist tendencies around the world increase dramatically, fear of breaking away may increase. Similarly, in Western countries, the traditional defense functions of the large nation-states have diminished. The NATO shield will protect Scotland and Quebec regardless of their formal membership in the United Kingdom or in Canada, but a sharp increase in international tensions or a change in their character could alter these defense calculations.

Finally, the speculation as to whether Quebec will actually separate should not be divorced from a more important question: What will Quebec and Canada each be like if separation does occur? And what will they be like if it does not occur? Will the process of discussion produce polarization and radicalization? Is radicalization more likely in Quebec if the Parti Québécois succeeds or fails? Which segment of the PQ will predominate—left, center, or right? What party system would form in Quebec and in the rest of Canada? It is far from clear that the defeat of the PQ would produce the results many who want a defeat expect. On the cultural issue, the opposition parties do not differ profoundly from the PQ, nor do they on many aspects of the economy—former Premier Bourassa's comments in this volume suggest remarkably little divergence, and we might also note the Quebec Liberal Party's support of the PQ's response to the federal government's sales tax policy in April 1978.

At present, the Parti Québécois is tempered by the responsibility of governing, by the need to make things work, by the imperative of finding allies and of expanding its base in order to win its promised referendum, or at a minimum to stay in office. The English language press in the United States and Canada understandably has focused on threats to individual rights and to economic stability. It has neglected a significant aspect of the Quebec scene since November 15, 1976: the enthusiasm, pride, and commitment among some sectors of the Québécois population which never before have been able to identify with the tasks of governance. Uncreative radicalization—alienation, apathy, dispair—might be far greater among people consigned, without hope, to the opposition.

NOTES

1. See, for example, the chapters in this volume by Robert Bourassa, Walter Gordon, and John Roberts.

2. Harry Hanham, *Scottish Nationalism* (Cambridge: Harvard University Press, 1969); Michael Hechter, *Internal Colonialism* (Berkeley: University of California Press, 1975); Milton Esman, "Scottish Nationalism, North Sea Oil and the British Response," Waverly Papers on European Political Studies, No. 6, series 1, April 1975, Edinburgh University; and E.J. Hobsbawm, "Some Reflections on The Break-up of Britain," *New Left Review* No. 105 (1977), 3-23, which reviews Tom Nairn, *The Break-up of Britain* (London: New Left Books, 1977).

3. Juan Linz, "Early State-Building and Late Peripheral National-isms against the State," in S.N. Eisenstadt and Stein Rokkan, eds., *Building States and Nations* (Beverly Hills: Sage, 1973), 32-112; Juan Linz, "Politics in a Multilingual Society with a Dominant World

Language," in Jean-Guy Savard and Richard Vigneault, eds., *Les Etats multilingues* (Quebec: Presses Universitaires de Laval), 1975, 367-444.

4. Robert Lafont, *La révolution régionaliste* (Paris: Laffont, 1967); Robert Lafont, *Décoliniser la France* (Paris: Laffont, 1971). The creation of regional government in France has had little to do with peripheral nationalism and much more to do with party politics, bureaucratic rivalries, and economic imbalances. See Peter Gourevitch, "Reforming the Napoleonic State: the Creation of Regional Government in France and Italy," in Luigi Graziano, Peter Katzinstein, and Sidney Tarrow, eds., *Territorial Politics in Industrial States* (New York: Praeger, 1978); also Sidney Tarrow, *Between Center and Periphery* (New Haven: Yale University Press, 1977). Note that Corsica and Alsace do not fit the model—it would predict more nationalism in Alsace because the province was economically advanced, and less in Corsica which was behind.

5. For a well-known statement of the mobilization argument, see Karl Deutsch, *Nationalism and Social Communication* (Cambridge: MIT Press, 1953); Aristide Zolberg, "Culture, Territory, Class: Ethnicity Demystified," International Political Science Association, Edinburgh, August 16-21, 1976; Aristide Zolberg, "Les nationalismes et le nationalisme québécois" in *Le nationalisme québécois á la croisés des chemins* (Québec: Choix, 1975). For a fuller statement of my own arguments focusing on the European cases, see Peter Gourevitch, "Politics, Economics and Nationalisms: Some Comparative Speculations," in *Comparative Studies in Society and History* (forthcoming).

6. Similar tensions occurred in industrial countries everywhere. For a comparative discussion of the impact of changes in the international economy on domestic politics see Peter Gourevitch, "International Trade, Domestic Coalitions and Liberty: Comparative Responses to the Crisis of 1873-96," *Journal of Interdisciplinary History*, (Autumn, 1977).

7. The pressure for the state to play an active role in Quebec has sources other than culture. Several authors have argued that in countries which develop an industrial economy relatively late (in comparison with Britain), of which Quebec is one, the state is propelled into an important position. For a classic statement of this theme, see Alexander Gerschenkron, "Economic Backwardness in Historical Perspective," in *Economic Backwardness in Historical Perspective* (Cambridge: Harvard University Press, 1963). For further discussion of Gerschenkron's theme, see James Kurth, "The Political

Consequences of the Product Cycle: Industrial History and Comparative Politics," in *International Organization* (forthcoming), also Kurth, "Delayed Development and European Politics" (mimeo, 1977); and Peter Gourevitch, "The Second Image Reversed: The Impact of International Relations on Domestic Politics," *International Organization* (Fall, 1978).

8. Richard Simeon, "The Regional Distribution of the Benefits of Confederation: A Preliminary Analysis," Queen's University, Institute for Intergovernmental Affairs, draft mimeo, December 1976; Rodrique Tremblay, Minister of Industry and Commerce, "Présentation des comptes économiques du Québec, 1961-1975," (Québec: Gouvernement du Québec, 1977); Gérard Bélanger, "Why do the Balances Differ on Federal Receipts and Expenditures in Québec?" C.D. Howe Research Institute, Montreal, October 1977; Antal Deutsch, "The Political Economy of Québec Libre," *Canadian Economic Problems*, 407-418; Richard Caves, "Economic Models of Political Choice: Canadian Tariff Structure," *Canadian Journal of Economics* (May, 1976), 278-300; Garth Stevenson, "Federalism and the Political Economy of the Canadian State," in Leo Panitch, ed., *The Canadian State: Political Economy and Political Power* (Toronto: University of Toronto Press, 1977); Richard Simeon, ed., *Must Canada Fail?* (Montreal: Queen's University Press, 1977).

9. *Looking Outward: A New Trade Strategy for Canada*, Economic Council of Canada (Ottawa: Information Canada, 1975).

10. See Hechter, *Internal Colonialism, op. cit.* Also, Stein Rokkan and S.M. Lipset, *Party Systems and Voter Alignments* (New York: Free Press, 1966).

Appendix

Strength of Peripheral Nationalisms and the Congruence of Political and Economic Leadership Functions for Regions with "Ethnic Potential."

Degree of Congruence	CONGRUENCE	NON-CONGRUENCE
Political Intensity of Periphery Nationalism		Britain-Scotland Spain-Catalonia, Basque Provinces Canada-Quebec Belgium-Flanders
STRONG		Yugoslavia-Croatia
WEAK	France Italy Britain pre-WWII Belgium pre-WWI Germany	

10___QUEBEC SEPARATISM IN COMPARATIVE PERSPECTIVE

COMMENT

François-Pierre Gingras

Professor Gourevitch proposes a model for the development of national independence movements. This model emphasizes the distribution of economic and political strength, and it is tested through the examination of Quebec nationalism compared to a number of other national cases.

Until recently, many students of nationalism have neglected its economic dimension, especially in the independence movements of industrialized states. The Gourevitch model represents a challenging change, for Professor Gourevitch demonstrates that cultural distinctiveness is a prerequisite for culturally based independence demands, but that demands are likely to increase within a state when economic and political leadership do not coincide geographically.

Unfortunately, the Gourevitch model suffers from two substantial deficiencies. First, it fails to define key terms; second, the model neglects the difference between structural cleavages and social strain, as well as the gap between aspirations and expectations.

The Need for Definitions

The absence of adequate definitions inhibits making the model operational. We have little idea of what, precisely, Professor Gourevitch means by "political leadership," "economic strength," or even "national potential." Economic strength is relatively easy to measure, and the model would benefit from testing with such indicators as the regional (or provincial) shares of the gross national product, or of the assets of industries, or of corporate profits, or of personal incomes, of unemployment, etc. One might also examine, for example, inter-regional (or inter-provincial) exports. "Political leadership" seems in Professor Gourevitch's essay to refer to the location of a country's capital, yet surely it must include such elements as the distribution of legislative jurisdictions, the regional or provincial or ethnic orientations of the political elite, and so on. Professor Gourevitch offers neither careful definition nor empirical examples for these key concepts, nor does he provide explanation for the concept of "nation," which is so fundamental to any analysis of independence movements.

Relative Deprivation

Professor Gourevitch is correct in arguing a relationship between cultural (or ethnic) considerations and the geographic location of economic and political leadership, but these factors are not a sufficient condition for the emergence of strong national independence movements within multi-cultural states.

The mechanism which spawns these movements involves perceptions of relative deprivation. When a people hope for more yet expect less, they incline toward independence. This principle is particularly applicable when consideration is given to Professor Gourevitch's analysis of congruence between political and economic centers. Political power and economic strength are each an essential factor in national status. When these two factors are not congruent, when people perceive that political and economic strength is not matched, the relative deprivation increases dissatisfaction with the political order, which is held responsible for inhibiting the improvement of economic or political strength. If institutions are perceived as responsible for the non-congruence, they may emerge as manifestly illegitimate, and there may be demands for the creation of a new and distinct national political order.

Hence, we might extend the Gourevitch model by focusing not merely on the geographical location of strength, but rather on popular perceptions of relative status. If political or economic status declines, it must regain congruence with the other factor; similarly, if either economic or political status should be perceived to improve, the other must rise to meet it. When social strains caused by such incongruence take the form of long-term political or economic grievances, national independence movements are likely to last a long time. Their durability will depend on the severity of the grievances, the gap between aspirations and expectations, and the gap between economic and political status.

Testing the Model: Quebec and Other National Cases

Professor Gourevitch proposes a comparative test of his model, which inevitably involves discussing the concept of "nation." Undoubtedly the cases he cites (Scots, Welsh, Bretons, Catalans, Basques, Flemings, Croatians, and Québécois) conform to the broad assertion that these groups consider themselves members of communities enclosed within states which are led by different communities. However, do they conceptualize themselves as nations? Such self-conceptualization is the best indicator for the existence of a nation, and nationhood is commonly used by communities to legitimize collective actions such as the quest for national independence. To what extent are the test cases similar in their "national perceptions?" Professor Gourevitch offers no answer to this crucial question.

In the case of Quebec, the Quiet Revolution of the 1960s provided a new impetus for the independence movement. However, the economic improvements associated with the Quiet Revolution were relatively less spectacular than one might suppose. Largely due to access to higher education, vertical mobility improved and so did popular aspirations and expectations for economic status. Nevertheless, it is not statistically demonstrable that Quebec's economy strengthened sufficiently to match economic growth in Ontario, Alberta, and British Columbia. More and more French-speaking Québécois came to resent this relative deprivation. Their aspirations rose, but economic conditions prevented them from entertaining the expectation that they would enjoy economic improvements comparable to their English Canadian counterparts (Maritimers excepted). It could even be argued that in the economy of the 1970s, with prevailing unemployment exceeding 10% and inflation often reaching double digits, the econ- omic expectations of many Québécois have declined at the same time that their aspirations have risen.

We can also appreciate the disparity between aspirations and expectations regarding political strength. During the past twenty years, Québécois have turned increasingly to their "national" (i.e., Quebec) government, making Quebec easily the most "interventionist" of all provincial governments in Canada. Québécois political strength, both provincially and federally, is apparent, but appearances can be deceptive. The Canadian Constitution and a century of practice have given the Québécois an influence roughly commensurate with their 30% of the country's population. However, occupation of the Prime Minister's office (Laurier, St. Laurent,

Trudeau) does not guarantee policy favorable to Quebec; indeed, there is strong evidence of a pressure to over-conform to the Canadian national myth and to resist Quebec's national assertiveness. Hence, the Quebec government appears more the champion of Quebec's national opportunity, and the federal government, even (and perhaps, especially) when led by French Québécois, may be perceived to exacerbate the gap between political aspirations and expectations. Combined with relative economic deprivation, there is a strong inclination to reject the legitimacy of the Canadian political community.

In sum, the kernel of a model which helps us understand Quebec is offered here by Professor Gourevitch, but it is important to recognize more the cultural—the "national"—relationship to economic experience. Because Quebec's political and economic grievances are deep and of long standing, and because the Quiet Revolution widened the gap between aspirations and expectations, the national independence movement will last until the gaps are closed...or independence is achieved.

Part Four

COMPETING SOLUTIONS TO THE UNITY CRISIS

11_____THE WEST IN THE CANADIAN CONFEDERATION

Gordon F. Gibson

Our problems these days are generally cast in terms of French vs. English, Quebec vs. the rest—a misconception even in Canada. In fact, there are other important currents and other important players in the game—as was true at the time of Confederation, and has been the case ever since. The West is at least as important in what the world thinks of as "Canada," as is Quebec—and the West has equally persuasive reasons for dissatisfaction with the existing confederal deal.

The basic issue we Canadians grapple with now refers to Prime Minister Mackenzie King's famous remark: "Some countries have too much history. Canada has too much geography." Do we have more geography than one country can handle? The question is basic, especially because of our particular history, during which our geography was simply stitched together by the relatively weak ties of uneconomic transportation systems and tariff barriers, and a common concern about the power of our neighbor to the south.

Nature of the Canadian Union

The relative looseness of these confederal ties is an important starting point in attempting to understand our problems of national unity. The American union was forged in a crucible of revolution and emotion and a dedication to high principles, and eventually was cemented with a tremendous quantity of blood.

The Canadian union was entered into much more as an exercise in convenience—the convenience both of the English colonial power and of several colonies that had trade, defense, transportation, and in certain areas, cultural problems that could be dealt with better in an association than individually. It was a deal worked out in relative calm, and maintained by reason and inertia and habit, rather than conviction. There were dreams, there was emotion, but Canadians have above all been sensible.

In the language of business the Canadian union was, and is, a deal. The American union has more of the characteristics of a merger. The parties to the Canadian deal have, to a considerable extent, retained their identity and therefore the ability to vary or even terminate the deal itself. That realization is an essential starting point.

For a time there were some—largely in English Canada—who fought this kind of analysis on the grounds that it would be economically impossible for the various regions of Canada to do anything other than continue the confederal deal—in other words, that Canada is really a merger, too. To show why that is not so, consider a few figures. The population of the enormously wealthy land mass of Western Canada is about 6,200,000. The population of the rich land mass of Quebec is almost exactly the same. Both of these areas economically, culturally, and every other way, have the capacity to be nations in their own right, as could indeed even my own province of British Columbia by itself, with some two and one-half million people. One has but to look at the Scandinavian countries, or some of the other smaller developed members of the United Nations, to understand this clearly.

So let us take, as a starting point, the following in the interests of realism: a Canadian union is a reversible arrangement, unlike the American one, and the reversal is economically feasible, though with tightened belts for a time. It is also politically feasible, and the politics of a continued Confederation is what I want to discuss.

Long History of Western Alienation

As usual, while the politics of the West in Confederation have come into prominence almost overnight in historical terms, Western feeling about Confederation has been a long time abuilding. Latent strains and grievances, and feelings of alienation from central Canada, have existed over the years. They center around the concept that both in the original deal and the ongoing interpretation of it, Western Canada has received less than its due in terms of political influence and economic benefits, and more than its due in terms of the cost the West has to pay for membership in Canada measured by dollars and by federal restrictions on our abilities to work out our own destinies. The seeming inability, year after year, to do anything about these concerns is well illustrated by the story of a Western wheat farmer's reaction to the quintessential symbol of central Canadian authority, the Canadian Pacific Railway. It had been a bad summer for the farmer, with drought and pestilence, which had reduced most of his crop to no value, and he was coming to his wit's end. Just before the time for harvest of what grain was left, an enormous hail storm came along and flattened the whole crop. The farmer went out into the hail storm and shook his fist at the sky and yelled, "God damn the C.P.R.!"

But, more often the Western sense of alienation is latent. It has been muted by a number of things—first and foremost, perhaps, a "what's the use" feeling of helplessness and inertia and history—a failure to realize our own strength.

It has been muted as well by certain ties of sentiment, whether to the concept of one Canada from sea to sea, or residual loyalties to the common British Crown. There has also been an inevitable softening that comes out of affluence, because compared to the rest of the country, the West is doing very well economically, and it perhaps seems a little ungracious to complain in such circumstances.

And, partly the articulation of alienated feelings is dampened by a simple ignorance; there is a lack of concrete specified detail relating to Western problems.

Quebec as a Western Catalyst

All of these factors are changing as the West becomes more self-conscious, more strongly led, less sentimental, and worried by greater economic problems. But the single greatest influence in the development of the latent Western image is unquestionably the impact on the Western consciousness of political emanations from the province of Quebec over the last decade or so. Quebec has made us look at ourselves.

The first reaction of Western Canadians to the newly aggressive Quebec, as exemplified by the Quiet Revolution of the early 60s, was probably, "Who do those Frenchmen think they are?" We had a lot of problems out west, but still the Canadian union was good enough for us. Quebecers, according to prevailing Western wisdom, had had the inside track on Confederation benefits for years and had no right to be complaining.

As the years went by and the linguistic and cultural problems and aspirations of French Canadians in Quebec, and elsewhere in Canada, became better understood by English Canadians, the reaction by many Westerners turned around to the stage, "Well, maybe they've got a point," but impatience was still the major mood.

Then, on November 15, 1976, all of that became prologue—a government was elected in the province of Quebec with the avowed intention of ending the Canada to which the West had become accustomed. Let no one doubt that the potential for the secession of Quebec is very real. The province has the unquestioned physical ability—short of armed force, which will not be used—and the economic ability to do so as well.

The desire to separate is held by many of the citizens, though by no means yet a majority, and the desire to restructure arrangements with the rest of Canada is held by a good many more. In advancing this cause, the province is led by an extraordinarily capable catalyst and political leader in the person of Premier Lévesque.

As these facts have begun to seep into the consciousness of Westerners, a new realism is emerging—the realism that says that whether we like it or not, there is a situation here that we have to deal with; it could have very great consequences for our lives, and it seems not to be very much within our control.

At another level, the Quebec experience has had a profound effect on the West in this sense: the forcefulness of Quebecers in articulating their problems and aspirations has given us Westerners the strength and motivation to articulate ours.

Western Reaction

That is being done effectively these days, and a sense of Western regionalism unquestionably has been fostered by the Quebec example. We even have our own Western separatist parties, particularly in Alberta and British Columbia, though they, as yet, remain numerically small.

Ironically, while Westerners on the one hand express profound shock at the prospect that Quebec might leave Canada, we turn right around and express outrage at the possibility that the federal government might concentrate all of its attention on solving this difficulty with Quebec and ignore what we perceive to be real problems out west. We have, thus, in the very recent past advanced a giant step towards political maturity—the long suppression of the aggressive articulation of Western alienation has ended, and aggressive measures to do something about it have begun.

We now have to deal with the possibility that we live in a country that might come apart; from that has to flow a genuine study of what price the country is worth for us, as Westerners, to keep it together, if the paying of prices is what it comes to; on the other hand, what will be our future if the Canada, as we know it, disappears?

I believe that in this situation of incredible national turmoil, a solution agreeable to all is more likely to be found with articulate, aggressive Western representation at the bargaining table—just as a solution of the deadlock between Upper and Lower Canada, at the time of the 1867 Canadian Confederation—required the additional factors brought in by the Maritime provinces to enable a deal to be made. In the current context, we have much in common with Quebecers, some things in common with the federal government and with the central provinces, a warm feeling for the Maritimes, and perhaps enough trade-offs, if possible, among us all to put together a new and useful Confederation arrangement.

British Columbia's Hesitant Entry into Canada

Western Canada came into Confederation either with serious misgivings (as was the situation with British Columbia), or with very little say on the terms, as was the case with the prairie provinces. In the case of British Columbia, many of the misgivings were realized, and in the case of the prairies, lack of local participation in the setting of the terms (which were basically dictated from Ottawa and the older provinces) resulted in conditions that give real substance to the sense of Western grievance.

One of British Columbia's most respected politicians of the day, Dr. Helmcken, said in debate on the Confederation proposals that:

> It would be absurd for us to sacrifice our interests in order that laws may be made for us by a people who know little of our condition and wants, and who, in fact, must necessarily legislate for the greater number—the people of the Atlantic provinces. It is dangerous to place ourselves at the disposal of superior numbers.
>
> It is absurd to suppose that the same laws, whether civil, commercial or industrial, will be found equally advantageous to all parts of this great continent. It manifestly cannot be so; the conditions are different. We know what is best for ourselves, and are able to legislate to affect that. We have no wish to pay Canada to do our legislation....

No union between this colony and Canada can permanently exist, unless it be to the material and pecuniary advantage of this colony to remain in the union. The sum of the interest of the inhabitants is the interest of the colony. The people of this colony have, generally speaking, no love for Canada; they care, as a rule, little or nothing about the creation of another empire, kingdom or republic; they have but little sentimentality, and care little about the distinctions between the form of government of Canada and the United States.

Therefore no union on account of love need be looked for.[1]

Advocates of the union were no more sentimental—they proposed it and advanced it in terms of material advantage. Amor de Cosmos, who would later become Premier of British Columbia, stated:

I am in favour of Confederation, provided the financial terms are right in amount.....if we cannot get favourable terms, which I believe we can, it will then be for the people of this country to say whether we shall remain in isolation or seek some other more favourable union.[2]

Surely this was not a marriage made in heaven, but rather in the counting house!

The Prairies and Confederation

British Columbia, at least, had a say in the matter—the three prairie provinces did not. Their land had been controlled by the British Crown and the Hudson Bay Company; it was simply transferred to Canada. One of the largest transfers of sovereignty in history was done largely in the nature of a real estate deal. The territories then were sparsely populated, and their regional governments were imposed by the federal government.

The Alberta writer James Gray says:

We are all prisoners of our history and none of us more so than the people of Western Canada. At the time of Confederation, central Canada covered one million square miles inhabited by three million people, two million spoke English and one million spoke French. New Canada [which is Gray's description for the prairies] was populated by five million buffalo, a few thousand French and Scottish half-breeds, a sprinkling of Ontario Orangemen, a tiny handful of Québécois, the remnants of the Selkirk settlers and a few thousand

Anglo-Saxons in British Columbia. Between the Red River and the Rockies were several thousand stone-age aborigines who lived with, and off, the buffalo. To wit, another one million square miles of empty wilderness.[3]

Between 1896 and 1915 this emptiness was populated by one of the most amazing movements of immigrants in history, most of them simply dumped on the railway platform. The bulk of these settlers came, not from Europe or central Canada, but from the United States, with American ideas. Gray traces this influence on the farmers' cooperatives and wheat pools, the populist movement, and the progressive movement on the prairies. He traces the American melting pot that was deplored in central Canada but became a main feature in the West, one of the lasting reasons for the difficulty of Western Canadians in understanding why French-speaking Canadians chose not to assimilate with the English-speaking minority. To British, Germans, Ukranians, Scandinavians, Poles, and many others on the prairies who have melted at least into one language pot (if not one community), the Quebec French example stands almost as an indictment; if the francophones are right to insist on their language and culture, other people have been wrong to melt theirs. That is a difficult message to accept.

While this vast emptiness was being settled and the populations were blending, Western Canadians noted the phenomemon equally obvious to Western Americans—the financial control by the Eastern part of the country. Western Canadians had an additional burden not known to Americans, in terms of the tariff, and the prairie catchphrase of "twenty percent more for everything we buy and twenty percent less for everything we sell."

But out of all this a certain consensus was formed as well, which brings us to Western sentiment today. There is, in fact, a great deal more to Canadian identity, as it is understood in the West, than simply the classic Canadian definition that we are not American.

A Western Identity

In fact, Westerners feel a sense of identity partly Western, partly Canadian. The West is large enough that we can be proud of size in a geographical unit, and appreciate the merits of something even larger than ourselves, namely the vastness of Canada and the advantage of the free movement of people and goods through such an area.

There remains a considerable degree of sentiment towards Great Britain and the Crown and a concept of a country for which many Westerners fought in the war. And, of course, nowadays in Canada, many Westerners are former Easterners, so they bring with them a sense of old Canada. Still, the former Easterners become Westerners very quickly. A study of Western grievances over the decades shows that they have changed hardly at all, while the population has changed enormously in its composition.

The West has one crucially different perception of the role of its political institutions, as distinct from Quebecers. Westerners do not conceive of themselves as being members of a minority, and consequently can afford to pay more attention to the elaboration of individual destinies. For Westerners, government properly done is seen as an agency that makes individual development possible. It is less of an instrument for the achievement of collective goals, and that applies even to the strong socialist strands in Western political thought.

Western political thought tends to be less left or right than populist. As was pointed out by Michael Webb in his Alberta report to the Western Commission of the Liberal Party:

> It is important to emphasize that despite current indications to the contrary Western alienation in Alberta at least has not been historically a right wing phenomenon—on the contrary, it is possible to discern in many of the powerful political movements such as the United Farmers of Alberta, the Progressives and the original Social Credit, a truly liberal concern for the freedom of the individual and an almost prophetic obsession with the tyranny of large power structures which is so current and topical an issue today.[4]

The West as a Subordinate Region

The Role of Provincial Governments

Thus, up until recently, Westerners did not see their provincial governments as speaking for them, in a national sense, because Westerners did not conceive of themselves as part of a minority. With the new regionalism and the new understanding of the Western condition, a sense of Western minority is very definitely developing, and provinces are taking on a far stronger moral authority in terms of speaking for their people to the rest of the country than has been the case in the past.

Quebecers, on the other hand, always have seen themselves as a minority, in Canada and in North America. (English-speaking Quebecers, until very recently, saw themselves not as a minority, but as part of the larger majority, with all of the privileges attendant thereto.) From that perspective, the regional government—the government of the province of Quebec—became more than simply a regulatory instrument, but in fact an instrument for the expression of a people, which gave rise to the sterile controversy in Canada as to whether our country is one or two "nations." Claude Morin, the Quebec Minister charged with his party's move of the province towards separatism, speaks for many French Canadian nationalists in commenting on the cultural effects of centralist tendencies:

> When one considers that the Quebec government is the only major political instrument to be easily controlled by us, it becomes clear that the present tendencies are equivalent to a gradual lessening of our political power and significance, as Quebecers.[5]

There is an unquestioned sense in which the government of the province of Quebec has had a larger mandate from its people than have the governments of the Western provinces. That difference—through the enlargement of the Western mandate—is starting to diminish.

Confederation Economics

There are extremely important aspects related to the economics of the West in Confederation. Put simply, the West has had a bad economic deal. First and foremost is the fact of the tariff. Western Canadians sell the produce of their labor on world markets—they buy what they consume or the goods used in production on protected markets. The cost of this—basing my judgment on studies done in British Columbia and in Alberta and by the Economic Council of Canada—probably runs about $500 per capita per year, applying to all Westerners in a greater or lesser degree, depending on their level of affluence.

The West is clearly a strong contributor to the country's balance of payments, probably the only regional contributor on a net basis, and the West is a heavy contributor on balance to the rest of the country through transfer payments. The situation here is mixed, however, for transfer payments to the rest of the country by British Columbians and Albertans, on a net basis, run something like $250 to $300 per capita per year, while residents of Saskatchewan and Manitoba are net recipients, though on a much smaller basis. Nonetheless, Westerners consider transfer payments, especially for social security, a part of their duty to fellow Canadians, rather than a grievance.

Transportation is the most famous Western economic grievance, and probably the most difficult to sustain, since in fact the Canadian transportation system is heavily subsidized, with much of that subsidy being expended in the West. That, however, does not prevent transportation being the usually cited complaint of the West toward central Canada—transportation loosely based on freight rates which encourage Westerners to ship their raw materials eastward, or out of the country for processing, rather than processing in the West.

In addition to the pure economics, the membership of Western provinces in Canadian Confederation has implications for cultural development. Speaking of Canada as a whole, the authors of the report investigating the impact of foreign investment in Canada referred to the Canadian economy as "truncated"—the higher functions of foreign-owned multinational enterprise tend to be located outside of the branch plant economy of Canada.[6]

That applies in an even stronger fashion to Western Canada. Our "head offices" and owners tend to be in central Canada, if not in the United States or elsewhere. We have seen little of the California shift of industrial, technological, and financial enterprise that has occurred in the United States. Where this shift has taken place, it has resulted from governmental action, with the province of Alberta having been by far the most effective in this regard.

Our communications, arts, and finance tend to be controlled in central Canada. Typically, this control has not bothered us Westerners, not seeing ourselves as a cultural minority—an essential difference compared to Quebec, and one of the reasons why we were not stirred up as soon as they were. We have lacked an identifiably Western cultural mirror. In part this has been an outgrowth of the Western inferiority complex; and in part it has been a Western feeling—analogous to the common sentiment in the United States—that it probably does not make that much difference where cultural control is located, as long as it is within the national political unit.

Western Politics

The realities of confederal politics in Western Canada turn on questions other than those of ideology.

Traditionally, Western Canadian politics have been parochial; apart from the continuing shouldering at the federal public trough, provincial governments have dealt with local questions, not the great national questions of the day.

Western provincial politics, and the Western branches of federal parties, have been characterized by a lack of influence in the national government. The West in the past has not been sufficiently important in numerical terms to make a distinct difference in the balance of power of the national capital, especially because the West historically has not acted as a unit. The parliamentary system actively suppresses such tendencies.

Moreover, the West has tended to be under-represented in the party in power in Ottawa. The West has typically not returned a large number of Liberals; in fact, the Liberal Party has governed but 15 years of the 20th century. This trend has been heightened in recent years, as in the last two elections, when the Liberal Party in Canada has not had a single representative from the province of Alberta. (The Conservative Party suffers from the same problem in the province of Quebec.) Thus, the federal institutions that we do have to provide for regional influence are handicapped because Western voters do not often choose Western representation in the government party of the day.

Structural Imbalance

The British Parliamentary System in a Federation

The problem goes a good deal beyond party representation. Canadian federal mechanisms for regional brokerage are entirely inadequate. Under the British system, worked out several hundred years ago between the monarchy and the aristocratic establishment for the upper class governance of a small unitary state, the government controls both the legislative and executive branches. There is no check or balance, save elections at intervals of no greater than five years. In most of our provinces and at the federal level, there is usually an insufficient contest, or people vote out of fear of the alternative; the result then is insufficiently responsive to public opinion.

Since 1940, looking at the Western provinces of Canada, a right-wing coalition has been in power in British Columbia for all but three years, in Alberta, continuously though with a change of name, and in the poorer provinces of Saskatchewan and Manitoba, left-wing governments have been in power all but eight years in Saskatchewan and for most of the past seven in Manitoba.

In Ontario, the pivotal province of English Canada, the Conservative Party has been in power for 35 years. When one considers that these effective one-party states, and virtual four-year elected dictatorships, control not simply the executive branch, but the legislature as well, one begins to understand the way particular governments may be enabled not only to build up enduring strength, but enduring prejudice as well. Since elections rarely turn on constitutional issues, constitutional prejudices have exhibited a remarkable degree of continuity; each side, federal and provincial governments respectively, is convinced it has the one true way.

The important result for Canadian federalism is that national instruments, because of the parliamentary system, are not seen as powerful and suitable voices for regional interests. The provinces, almost by default, thus enjoy their astonishing moral primacy in this area.

Regional Brokerage

American regional brokerage takes place much less in the single-party executive branch and much more in the two-party—really multi-party—legislative branch. That does not happen in Canada. Regional brokerage takes place in the federal cabinet, occasionally in the federal caucus, and never in the federal parliament, which, like the provincial legislature, is a eunuch except at times of minority government. In the United States, federal-state brokerage and regional interest logrolling take place in a federal institution, the U.S. Senate, which is designed for that purpose. In Canada, the important regional brokerage takes place in a federal-provincial institution, a federal-provincial conference.

The federal-provincial conference has grown into one of the monstrosities of Canadian politics. At its highest level, it is a meeting of the Canadian prime minister with his provincial counterparts—a meeting of plenipotentiaries who completely control their executive and legislative branches. The decisions they make are binding and enforceable. As a group, they are accountable to no legislature and no electorate; many of their meetings are in private. That, on the face of it, is an extraordinary situation.

The position of the federal government in this system is also notable. In psychological terms, it often appears to be ten against one. Language often tells us a good deal about reality. Communiqués emanating from federal-provincial conferences often refer to "the eleven senior governments." It is, of course, unthinkable in the United States that the President would meet with a group of governors and issue a communiqué referring to "the fifty-one senior governments." In the United States there is one senior government. In Canada, in 1978, there is not. That is both our strength and our weakness.

Failed Attempts at a Brokerage Mechanism

Other brokerage possibilities have been tried and have failed. The first attempt was the Canadian Senate, which was Lower Canada's (Quebec's) guarantee in the original confederal deal against the tyranny of majority rule. The Senate had two fatal flaws. First, it was appointed and therefore lacked the legitimacy of an electoral base; second, it was appointed by the federal government and therefore lacked the legitimacy of a provincial base. It has become an institution which has a certain charm and value, but it relates little to problems of national unity.

A second mechanism, which endured for many years and probably failed more as a result of personalities than of institutional characteristics, was the federal Cabinet, which is where all that matters happens within the Canadian government. Prime ministers were always at great pains to appoint appropriate representation from each region, and the ministers for regions were charged with regional responsibility. For the first half of this century, persons from Saskatchewan or British Columbia or Quebec who had business with the federal government or regional interests could be certain that the interest would be carried by their regional minister and that they would be well represented. That system broke down—in part because prime ministers started paying more attention to premiers, in part because of the personalities fulfilling the roles, and in part because the system was secret in a problem area that increasingly needed public solutions publicly arrived at.

At the same time, provincial governments became stronger (or, more properly, started to realize their own strength). They began balancing Ottawa's competence with salaries and personnel. The contest then became one of political will, and the provincial governments, with their closer contact and their more simple and homogeneous identification of interest, had a distinct advantage.

Moreover, provincial governments are now working together. The four Western premiers, for example, have a close working relationship and an agreement to clear with each other any constitutional initiatives that any of their number might take. Meetings of provincial premiers across the country used to be social get-togethers; they are now significant political events. A second Confederation, based on provincial association, is being formed, in political terms, to contest the authority of the Ottawa government. These changes are not as dramatic as war or revolution, but a major shift in the balance of power has, for the time being, been effected; for Canada, these changes are extraordinary.

Crisis

A Cultural Crisis Point in Quebec

Into this situation, both as catalyst and beneficiary, comes a powerful Quebec. Confluence of demographic, technological, and cultural currents led the French Canadian leadership in the province of Quebec to feel, in the early 60s, that it was "now or never"—and that the place of the French Canadian in North America had to be established or disappear.

Leadership disagreed over how to secure this objective. One group, now represented by Prime Minister Trudeau, took the position that Quebec by itself would be an isolated backwater, inevitably and quickly to be overwhelmed by the English-speaking North American culture; the only safety, they reasoned, lay in the tolerant arms of a much larger Canada predisposed to be protective of its French-speaking minority.

Another group, now led by Premier Lévesque, took the view that all of the powers of a sovereign nation necessary to preserve the French culture in the province of Quebec (i.e., complete control over communications, economy, transportation, and so on, all now subject to federal primacy) were required to allow the French-speaking

Canadians not only to realize their destiny within North America, but to secure it as well.

Mr. Trudeau sees a Canada where the francophone and the anglophone may move, at their pleasure, the two greater for membership in a larger club. Mr. Lévesque sees the francophone as being lost in that club and wants to form a smaller club of his own.

These competing solutions are not new, but the forces now at work in the second half of the 70s almost guarantee that the answer will be new. The result will turn on the response of Canadians, and particularly Quebecers, to these arguments. The dialogue has been well and truly joined.

An Opportunity for New Arrangements

In the meantime, the fact that a new deal is required by Quebec offers an opportunity for Western Canada. There are few contracts in this world that do not need renegotiation after a hundred years. It is time for a new set of arrangements. The rigidity of the Canadian Confederation has been rendered fluid by the insistence of Quebec, which poses not only a challenge to the West, but an enormous opportunity as well. It is difficult to see how, in objective terms, the West can end up the loser in the current confusion. If Canada breaks up, the West will do very well,* freed at last from some of the very serious economic constraints and costs brought about by membership in Confederation. If Canada stays together, the resulting reconfiguration will be one in which the West will have a chance to request and require a better deal for its citizens.

Truly, it is a time of incredible excitement and opportunity for Canada. It is, at the same time, a moment for a good deal of concern in the United States. There are legitimate worries, particularly related to trade and defense. However, there is no conceivable reconfiguration of the Canadian Confederation, up to and including fragmentation into several parts of the nation now known as Canada, that would result in any change of trade and defense relations in the

---

* In economic terms only, not necessarily psychic, and in the long run only. In the short run, the disruption of separation would adversely affect the West economically, as it would every other part of Canada.

northern half of this continent. Perhaps there will be two or more treaties where now there is one. The content and the friendship will hardly be different.

The Consequences of Disunion

What are some of the things that might come out of the present turmoil? In my opinion, that depends to a considerable extent on how it comes about. If Canada's constitutional development now occurs by means of crisis—specifically, a unilateral and successful decision by the province of Quebec to separate—we will end up with a long period of estrangement between Quebec and the rest of Canada, and a considerable lack of cooperation. There will be economic loss, though not necessarily any greater than the economic losses which are attributable to current circumstances of uncertainty. Relations would, in due course, improve and mellow, and at no time would they be so unreasonable or uncivilized that either party would seek in the areas of either security or defense to cut the throat of the other.

Once what was left of Canada got over the initial shock and negotiations with Quebec, we would probably see an evolution towards a *de facto* separation of the remaining parts, with perhaps a maintenance of some nominal ties, ironically in the form of "sovereignty association," which is the name given to the preferred solution of the present government of Quebec. There probably would be strong economic consequences for the Atlantic provinces with decreased assistance from the rest of Canada; the possibility of a movement for annexation to the United States would grow and people would emigrate.

For Ontario, the result would be considerable economic disruption, particularly arising out of necessary adjustments to tariff and commercial policy. Ontario's main business relationships, however, would continue to be, as now, inside the province and across the border with the United States. A movement for merger with the United States would be unlikely, at least in the short term.

For Western Canada, the results would be psychologically distressing, but probably on balance, of considerable economic benefit. It is likely that the Western Canadian provinces would remain linked together in some reasonably strong kind of association, and almost certainly independent of the United States, with perhaps some residual links to the previous components of Canada.

Alternatives to Crisis

A "No Crisis" Possibility

The second possibility, of course, is that there may be no crisis. The question might be settled short of *de facto* separation, however named. This could come about for any of several reasons, including a successful federalist counter-campaign in the province of Quebec or a failure, successively, of referenda attempts by the separatists or an undermining and failure of the separatist party in control of the provincial government through events unrelated to separatism, as was the case with the scandals that hit Mercier's government in 1890, when a similar challenge to Confederation seemed imminent.

The separatist party is in control of the referendum apparatus and the propaganda apparatus of the state. It is the Parti Québécois that will frame the question and will set the ground rules under which the battle will be fought. Those ground rules thus far indicated in a white paper on the subject give ample scope for rigging the balance against the federalist forces within Quebec and for virtually excluding influence from those outside of Quebec. Those who look simply to repeated referenda failure for the future continuation of Canada are taking a huge gamble.

The possibility remains of a strong federalist counter-offensive within Quebec, but with all the good will in the world it is not clear at this moment how that would proceed. Federalist forces are in disarray. The provincial Liberal Party was disgraced by the previous administration that was thrown out more for its excesses than for any love of its successors. Moreover, the provincial Liberal Party faces strong competition from another federalist party at the provincial level, the Union Nationale.*

A federal counter-offensive might, in theory, be mounted by "federal Quebecers," French Canadians from Quebec who have gone to Ottawa, made their mark there, and believe in Canada, starting with the prime minister and working on down. This is the most likely option, and it has worked before. Its most marked success was at the

---

* In both cases it should be noted, the adjective "federalist" is not necessarily the *status quo,* and to paraphrase Mackenzie King again, probably necessarily not the *status quo.*

beginning of World War II; a national crisis of a similar dimension currently exists.

A Federalist Initiative?

Unfortunately, a federalist initiative is fragmented between the federal and provincial arenas; furthermore, because there is no agreed definition of what a new form of Confederation should look like, or whether the *status quo* should be preserved, there is no stable resting point currently in the federalist option. It is mainly an amorphous concept that "we should stay in Canada for the good of the French Canadian community, but exactly what this Canada should look like we aren't certain." The separatists labor under no such difficulty, for while specifics of their separation program may shift and change, the general outlines are quite clear, or appear so to the ordinary person.

Moreover, the separatists feel that they have time on their side. They feel that theirs is an idea whose time has come and that they can afford to lose battle after battle and return to the fray refreshed. The federalists, they feel, can only afford to lose one battle and the war will be over.

In a situation of this kind there is a very real danger that national unity will be lost through simple impatience. Quebecers may eventually grow impatient with the problem—which after all is taking a serious emotional and economic toll as long as uncertainty continues—and simply opt for the one precise new option they have been offered.

English Canadians, on the other hand, may well tire of the problem, gain the feeling that there is nothing that is going to convince Quebecers, and give up trying. This double impatience will then be reinforced until the medicine of separation, which at least ends the uncertainty and pain, may be seized upon gladly by both sides.

The only other real possibility, in my mind, is that of bold federal initiative. One of the curious features of the existing situation is that almost everybody outside of Ottawa sees the federal government as part of the problem, rather than as part of the solution. Clearly there has been something lacking in terms of the perceived success of the federal government with respect to its most sacred charge of all, namely, national unity: but this is the quarter from which federalist leadership would most logically come.

Curiously, too, given the perception of Ottawa as part of the problem, the political conditions exist for exactly that sort of leadership, because for most Canadians the very personification of Canadian unity and its reaffirmation is Prime Minister Trudeau. His stature in matters of national unity at this moment, both in French and English Canada, is of such dimension that he has at least one shot at a major federal initiative to resolve the crisis. I think this initiative is the most likely outcome of current circumstances; my guess is that this initiative (of which the draft Constitutional Bill is the first component) is unlikely to come to completion until we are so close to the crisis of separation, or so frustrated by disagreement, that most Canadians will be persuaded that they are going to have to accept some kind of a new deal or see the end of their country.

Provincial governments are likely to be most reluctant to see a federal reform package. They are not likely to favor proposals which would increase the legitimacy and usefulness of federal institutions for the voicing of regional interests, and direct constitutional guarantees for citizens, both at the expense of provincial governmental power. For that reason, a time close to crisis will be the psychologically best time to put forward a new deal. And naturally, in any case of such delicate timing, it will also be a very dangerous situation.

Elements of a New Federal Arrangement

There is an almost infinite variety of the new kinds of arrangements that might be proposed. Detailed proposals for constitutional reform have been made at federal-provincial conferences, but they are unlikely solutions. Any dressing up of historic proposals will be seen at this stage as mere tinkering. Something grander and also less dangerously specific will be required.

The proposals with the best chance of success would be based on a reform of federal institutions for regional brokerage, some changes in the division of powers, and an increased reliance on the Constitution as the guarantor of individual and minority rights. The proposals would have to provide sufficient scope to the national government to maintain an enduring national fabric, while at the same time providing sufficient guarantees to linguistic, cultural, and regional minorities.

A partial list of elements I believe will end up in the final package includes:

Political

— Continuation of a single sovereign entity with constituent parts known as Canada.
— Retention of common security arrangements, a common monetary system, a common market, and internal freedom of movement of goods, people, and capital.

Regional

— Enhanced regional influence over immigration and monetary policy.
— A strong bias to local and neighborhood services, with some constitutional provision for them.
— A regional brokerage system at the national level directly elected by the people, and/or appointed by the provinces, and/or appointed by the regions, with powers analogous to those of the U.S. Senate.
— A sophisticated system of information and cooperation between levels of government.

Cultural

— Concurrent jurisdiction in cultural fields, with provincial primacy.
— Constitutional guarantees for very broadly based rights in the two official languages in all parts of Canada.

Economic

— Continuation of our present system of a mixed economy, but probably with clearer rules and control systems.
— Continuation of the equalization system for transfers of revenues between richer and poorer regions of Canada, supplemented with an individual equalization system similar to the guaranteed annual income concept.
— A commitment to a gradual elimination of tariffs. Social security programs will be brought more under regional control.

Constitutional

— Recognition of the sovereignty of the people (as distinct from that of Parliament) in such nationally enforceable enactments as a Bill of Rights, and freedom of information laws, applicable to all levels of government.
— A constitutional court and an amending formula for the constitution, both giving great strength and protection to provinces and minorities and perhaps with some particularly important

guarantees being more "deeply entrenched" than others.
— The possibility of new kinds of government, not excluding the parliamentary system, but not excluding congressional forms either, and probably providing for some shifting of the balance of power from the executive to the legislative branch and some separation of powers. (This shift is almost a necessity once one moves to a genuinely independent second chamber with regional interests. Agreed means will be required to handle deadlock.)
— A possibility of new forms of voting, such as proportional representation or the transferable ballot. (Some form of proportional representation is one way of ensuring that the long-standing and extreme regional imbalance in political party representation is brought into better harmony with local political sentiments. The West votes over 25% Liberal; Quebec polls show around 25% Conservative. Our current voting system fails miserably to reflect these minorities, to the detriment of national unity.)
— A widespread use of concurrent jurisdictions, rather than an attempt to demarcate them specifically, but with indications of primacy to federal or local governments in various fields. (As an example, in communications the federal government might have primacy in assignment of frequencies, the local government might have primacy in terms of cablevision, and both might have the right to license broadcast stations.)
— Limitations on the federal spending power, which has been a constant irritant to regions and in some ways has been subversive of the British North America Act.

Methods of Proposal

The federal package might be proposed by the federal government to the provinces, or it might be proposed directly to the people, particularly if an atmosphere of crisis were to exist and the possibility of provincial agreement seemed unlikely.

The proposals, were they presented directly to the people, whether in a general election or as a referendum in some other fashion, would have to obtain decisive support in all parts of the country, not simply in the country overall.

In all likelihood, at the time of these amendments, other basic changes in the Canadian federal system would be overlooked because

of the controversy they might cause with existing provincial governments—such possibilities as the division of Canada into small
provinces (and therefore less important focal points for the challenge
to federal interests) or the subdivision of Canada into four or five
regions (with the opposite effect). The thrust, I suspect, will be to
reach over the heads of the provinces and the federal government to
consolidate more effectively basic power in the hands of the people
through such devices as a Bill of Rights, a stronger constitutional court
system, and constitutional recognition of municipalities and other
local government units.

The Role of the West in Forging a New Union

And what of the West in this process?

A couple of leading questions are in order. First: Why have the
players in the Canadian deal retained their identities? In the U.S. those
identities have been merged. What is the difference here?

Constitutional factors have played an important part. The
parliamentary system, for example, centralizing power in a small
executive, militates heavily in favor of the maintenance of local
empires. Also, in the relatively large size of our provinces we differ
markedly from the United States.

More importantly, however, in Canada the original players and
their successors have not trusted the deal. Hence, they have never let
down their guard, and the various regions of the country and their
inhabitants have found it necessary to stay vigilant, watching their
relationships.

The second fundamental question, when talking about re-drafting a
constitution, is: Who should the players be? Should the players, as
now, be the federal and provincial governments, proven failures at
reform or even serenity in the Canadian Constitution of the past one
hundred years? Should there not be an element of popular
opportunity in terms not only of the adoption and approval, but also
the formulation of Canada's new Constitution? Some kind of constitutional convention, working with basic ground rules is a distinct
possibility and may in the end form a part of the successful initiative.

The role of the West will be both popular and governmental. On the
citizen's side, we see very yeasty developments in Western Canada
these days. The separatist movements are only the tip of the iceberg.

Numerous and influential national unity movements have sprung up in every province, as the dimensions of our current problems are becoming apparent. These forces will be working with groups all across the country and interacting with the federal government and with local governments to try to shape events of Western sentiment.

Western governments also have a very definite role to play. At the time of the original Canadian Confederation, Upper and Lower Canada (Ontario and Quebec) were deadlocked. To make the deal work, it was necessary to bring in third parties and their interests, which added enough counters to be moved around the table until it was possible to put things together to satisfy everyone. The West has a similar role to play today. The Canadian national unity problem at the moment is being cast as a sterile confrontation of English against French, and Quebec against the rest. As long as that false perspective exists, there is a good chance we all may lose.

Western Canada, by a thoroughly vigorous advocacy of its own case, can enter the game as a player that is firstly powerful, desirable to the others as a continuing associate; is secondly neither English nor French, more of an alloy of all kinds of peoples; and is thirdly neither Quebec nor Ontario, but has regional interests distinct from either—and probably far more in common with Quebec than with Ontario.

In this context, the West has finally come into its own. The West will be, or can be, a new strong player at the table, the player that perhaps has enough new counter-balances to satisfy some of the needs and to quiet some of the fears of the other partners who are about to break up the game.

To make this contribution, we in the West must be aggressive, not only in our own interest, but also in the interests of all of Canada. We must let Quebecers know that we are not only sympathetic to their problems, but share many of them as well. We must let the Maritimes know we will work with them to save the Union. We must let Ontario know that we expect the economic needs and muscle of the West to be respected, particularly in regard to the tariff. And we must let Ottawa know that while we expect leadership and constitutional reform, it must serve the interests of the West as well as any other's.

At the formulation of the original Confederation deal, the West was not consulted at all. British Columbia entered only later and with misgivings; the prairie provinces were simply ordered into being on central Canada terms. The new Confederation will be, to a much greater extent, shaped by James Gray's "New Canada." The result will be an Old Canada—renewed.

An Old Canada renewed is my hope. But is would be a disservice to suggest that that hope has a 100% probability of success. The continuation of a Canada somewhat as we know it today, over a period of greater than say the next five to ten years, is definitely in question. That is not a statement of doom, but an acceptance of difficulty, which is the first step to doing something about it.

Moreover, the advantage to Canadians in various areas, and of various sorts, for one result or the other, is not wholly clear at this time. We all have our faiths, we all have our catechisms, but we are, thus far, a little short of mutual understanding. As we gropingly attain it, we will be more able to see where the interest of each of the parties lies. I believe it will be found to be in a continuing union, but the next decade in Canada will not be dull, in the West or anywhere else.

NOTES

1. British Columbia Legislative Council, "Debate on the subject of Confederation with Canada," *Government Gazette Extraordinary*, (March 1870, Government Printing Office, Victoria, B.C.), p. 5 (Reprint of Legislative Debates of March 9, 1870).

2. British Columbia Legislative Council, "Debate on the subject of Confederation with Canada," *Government Gazette Extraordinary*, (March 1870, Government Printing Office, Victoria, B.C.), p. 19 (Reprint of Legislative Debates of March 10, 1870).

3. James Gray, speaking at York University Conference, "Destiny Canada," June 1977.

4. Liberal Party of Canada, *Report of the Alberta Commission*, Western Commission 1976-77, March 1977.

5. Claude Morin, in *Quebec at a Glance*, Special Section, Government of Quebec, May/June 1977.

6. *Foreign Direct Investment in Canada* (Ottawa: Government of Canada, 1972). See also John Fayerweather, *Foreign Investment in Canada* (White Plains, N.Y.: International Arts and Sciences Press, 1973).

THE WEST IN THE CANADIAN CONFEDERATION

COMMENT

David C. Smith

More regional strains to the Canadian Confederation have developed, as Mr. Gibson reminds us, than those related to Quebec. He is not highly optimistic—but he is hopeful—that the country will avoid a two-fold and, subsequently, at least a four-fold division. With the future of Confederation seriously in question, if not a toss-up, he is clearly a persuasive spokesman for the West's bargaining case that it should benefit, however the die is cast. (Notably, whereas many people in Quebec have emphasized political independence while retaining an association of considerable economic dependence, he suggests a greater value to economic independence in Western Canada, but a desire to retain political dependence.) He is perceptive in his analysis of weaknesses in the present federal mechanisms for regional brokerage and imaginative and positive in his proposals remedying them. Yet, informative, stimulating, and wide-ranging as his essay is, important aspects of the underlying reasoning need to be examined critically. In particular, I shall comment on, first, Mr. Gibson's argument that in economic terms the West has suffered from Confederation and would benefit from separation and, second his conception of a renegotiation of Confederation based on regional power brokers.

The Economics of Confederation

Regional cost-benefit measurements of membership in and separation from Confederation are extraordinarily difficult to make, despite their current popularity; they leave a substantial residue of uncertainty. Measurements of factors such as fiscal transfers and the impact of tariffs are easier, but nevertheless they are subject to dispute. How to value public goods and services common to various regions is not at all clear. Does Canada's unified bargaining position in international relationships achieve more benefits than a separate regional state could achieve? How does one compare the past indirect returns from regional specialization and trade with those of a hypothetical regional state whose policies are unknown, as are those of its trading partners? (One cannot, of course, rely on an assumption that a new state would achieve an ideal set of economic policies to replace imperfections in the current state.) Such issues leave me much less certain than Mr. Gibson that: 1. the West has had "a bad economic deal" out of Confederation (even though "relative to the rest of the country, the West is doing very well economically"), and 2. in the event of a breakup of the country and apart from some psychological distress and short-run disruption, the "West will do very well, freed at last from some of the serious economic constraints and costs brought about by membership in Confederation."

The evidence does tend to confirm strongly his point about the cost of the tariff to the West (and to the Maritime Provinces). The tariff is a cost to all consumers in the country, not just to those in the West. However, since there are regional differences in the location of business activity protected by tariffs, a regional redistribution of the effects of the tariff occurs. Would the West's separation solve this problem? Although the structure might change, it is by no means clear that the West alone would be more successful in ridding itself of tariffs; economic interests in the West have apparently been as vociferous as in other parts of the country in pressing Ottawa for tariff protection. Such representations are not unimportant. A recent study by R.E. Caves suggests that the Canadian tariff structure has responded more to pressures of economic interest groups than to conceptions of a national industrial strategy or voting patterns.[1] Also of relevance for the popular notion that Ontario has always had most to lose from lower tariffs is the earlier research by R.J. Wonnacott; for example, that of all regions, Ontario would be in the best competitive position to gain from a move to free trade with the United States.[2]

The differential impact of the tariff on individuals within a region should remind us of the dangers of assuming homogeneous interests within regions. Canada may have too much geography, but so may the great Canadian Confederation debate. Individuals can be classified into many groups according to age, sex, level of income, occupation, region of residence, and so forth. The greater ease of organizing political power on a regional basis in Canada gives great weight to this particular classification. But how powerful do people want representatives of this particular classification to be in altering the basic constitutional rules of political and economic organization which affect their other interests? At this time, the people of Canada have rights and obligations to all parts of it. Individuals can move freely—as they do in great numbers—among regions; they can enjoy pride of ownership in all parts and are entitled everywhere to a minimum standard of public services. Along with this scope for greater choice are the obligations which the people have undertaken collectively in order to assist individuals and institutions (the province of Alberta, for example, only a few decades ago) and which, when classified regionally, may happen to show a transfer sometimes to one part of the country and sometimes to another. The approach to welfare that I suggest has appealed to most Canadians is that of maximizing individual welfare (however imperfect policies may have been in this respect), rather than some aggregate indicator for the state or region.

New Bargains

The depiction, then, of regional units coming together to sit around the bargaining table to renegotiate the basic rules of the game has disturbing aspects. Regional bureaucracies have not unnatural economic and political incentives for aggrandizement of their power. Nor do they represent individuals outside their jurisdiction who, nevertheless, feel entitled, regardless of where they currently live, to be represented by all the regional players. Moreover, given the incentives, is it likely that provincial governments, or regional groupings of provincial governments, will regard changes in the "regional brokerage" political institutions in Ottawa as favorably as changes that preserve or enhance the power of provincial governments?

Mr. Gibson is not unmindful of these dangers. He speaks of the present federal-provincial conference as "one of the monstrosities of Canadian politics," of the distinct possibility of a constitutional convention to supplement the negotiations of the federal and provincial governments in redrafting a constitution, and of the likelihood of constitutional changes reaching "over the heads of provinces and the federal government to consolidate more effectively basic power in the hands of the people." Yet, given his political experience and insights, more attention to problems of determining the longer term will and interests of the people would have been particularly illuminating and helpful. At this time of possible fundamental changes in the constitutional arrangements, how does one determine the long-term will?

A New Constitution?

Various new brands are being proposed, but the constitution is not toothpaste or soap powder. People are not used to expressing their preferences on such major and irreversible matters, and brands X, Y, and Z cannot coexist to satisfy different tastes. Mr. Gibson thinks a major shift in brand is needed; he rejects what might be seen as "mere tinkering" and advocates "something grander" in constitutional reform. Exciting and important as it is to discuss proposals for major change, there are several issues in the process of selecting one which he has not discussed.

First, in his bargaining game, there will be an understandable tendency for regional players to exaggerate the extent to which current economic grievances are due to the present constitution (instead of due to the C.P.R.!) and to claim great remedial powers for the region from a particular new brand. Whatever the final compromise solution, is there not likely to be considerable frustration and political disillusionment because people have been misled to expect much more in order to strengthen the hand of the regional players?

Second, one problem of a complex, major package of constitutional reform is that many voters will find some fault with different parts of it; consequently, it could be rejected even though there were wide support for key elements of it. Might it be better, therefore, to resolve only one or two basic issues first that provide agreement on mechanisms for further evolutionary change?

Third, given the number of options and the well-known inconsistencies that can emerge over time in the expression of people's preferences, should the procedures for reform have major checks and rechecks—even though they slow the process—because they reduce the danger of instability in the process? As Mr. Gibson states, "there are few contracts in this world that don't need renegotiation after a hundred years," but a primary function of a constitutional contract remains that of reassuring people of stability (without rigidity) in the basic rules governing their political, social, and economic environment.

NOTES

1. Richard E. Caves, "Economic Models of Political Choice: Canada's Tariff Structure," *Canadian Journal of Economics* (May, 1976), pp. 278-300.

2. On this and related points, see T.K. Shoyama, "Comment" in symposium on Conflict and Consensus in Canadian Confederation, *Canadian Public Policy* (Autumn, 1977), p. 442.

12_____QUEBEC'S ECONOMIC FUTURE IN CONFEDERATION

Robert Bourassa

In November 1976 the election of the Parti Québécois (P.Q.) appeared to change the future of foreign investment in Quebec. The circumstances of the election, and the policies of the new government, are central to any judgment of Quebec's economic future.

The Election of the Parti Québécois

The election of the P.Q. can be analyzed according to five distinct categories: 1) economics; 2) labor relations; 3) language; 4) federal-provincial relations, and 5) the general atmosphere of the Province of Quebec.

Economics

Economic difficulties during the three years prior to the election resulted in unemployment and inflation rates of 10 percent and 8 percent respectively. Anti-inflation measures initiated jointly by Ottawa and Quebec imposed a ceiling on wages (a step which was unpopular in many sectors). Restrictive federal agricultural policies were poorly received by Quebec farmers.

Labor Relations

Continuing labor disputes resulted in massive strikes in both the public and private sectors. Official statistics revealed that Quebec lost more work days proportionately due to strikes in 1976 than any other industrialized nation. In part, this condition could be explained by the Olympic Games, where labor difficulties brought about a further deterioration in government-labor relations. Anti-inflation legislation by both the federal and provincial governments contributed to labor difficulties.

Language

The adoption of a law making French the official language of Quebec brought about increased tensions between the franco-phone majority and the anglophone minority. This tension helped split the federalist vote, which benefited the P.Q. The anglophones' reaction to the provincial language law (Bill 22) was more emotional than the provincial government had expected. On November 15, 1976, between 30 percent and 40 percent of the anglophone voters supported the Union Nationale; most academics considered such support a "protest vote" against the Liberals. The divided anglophone vote allowed dozens of P.Q. candidates to capture their respective ridings.[1]

Federal-Provincial Relations

Two particular issues marked a worsening of Quebec-Ottawa re-lations: a) the threat by Prime Minister Trudeau to patriate unilater-ally the Canadian Constitution, without a formula for Quebec approval, and b) the problem of French-Canadian pilots who desired to communicate in French within Quebec air space but were denied permission by federal regulations. In an address to a Toronto audience several months after the election, Mr. Trudeau pointed to English Canada's attitude on the pilots issue as a major factor in the P.Q. victory. However, he appeared to forget that his administration, under pressure of a strike, had been supporting the federal regulations.

General Atmosphere

In Quebec, like in other Western democracies in the last few years, people were preoccupied with a number of pseudo-scandals. During the 1976 campaign, M. Lévesque accused the Bourassa government of "lax practices" concerning the James Bay hydro-electric project. How-ever, after attaining power, the P.Q. admitted that the previous government had made a wise decision in going ahead with James Bay. The P.Q. even applauded the project's administration, especially the individual most responsible for the project, Robert Boyd, who was promoted by M. Lévesque to the presidency of Hydro-Quebec.

Developments since November 15

It is important to compare the climate in March 1978 with the situation prior to November 15, 1976. First, the state of the economy had deteriorated further, reflected in an unemployment rate of about 12 percent and an inflation rate of almost 9 percent. Illegal strikes (particularly in the utility, hospital, and police sectors), continued to plague provincial labor relations. Most of the collective agreements within the public sector had been signed before November 1976, in some cases for the first time without need for government decrees. A second linguistic law, in many ways more restrictive than the original one, is now in existence. With the emergence of the P.Q. administration, federal-provincial relations have become more strained.

It is in light of the deteriorating economic situation, and the new policies of the P.Q. government, that serious consideration must be given to prospects for Quebec's economic vitality. Foremost in this area of concern must be foreign investment.

The Value of Foreign Investment

First, one must establish the need for additional foreign investment in Quebec. There is no doubt that with such an extremely high unemployment rate, investment is necessary, not solely for the purposes of economic growth but also for reasons of social stability. As a domestic investor, the state can and does play a significant role. However, one must realize that there are limits to public investment. The increasing investment levels in the province are due primarily to the exceptional rate of public investment, particularly in the case of the James Bay project.

Public expenditure growth as a percentage of Gross Provincial Product is comparatively high, (approximately 45 percent compared with the Canadian average of 41 percent). Even by the standards set in a study commissioned by the Organization for Economic Cooperation and Development, listing the general government expenditure levels of 14 member states, the Quebec public expenditure rate of 45 percent would have placed the French-speaking province fourth (Holland was recorded highest at 51.2 percent).[2] Consequently, it is difficult to foresee further great increases in public expenditure.

There is a substantial private entrepreneurial sector. It, too, is limited in its ability to provide all the jobs which are required. Therefore, Quebec is receptive to foreign (particularly American) investment. However, investors avoid sectors which seem precarious.

The size of American portfolio investment in Quebec is also important. Consider, for example, the loans made to the Hydro-Quebec agency for development of the James Bay project. The outstanding Hydro-Quebec debt to U.S. investors is now about $5 billion (U.S.). There is no doubt that the need for large-scale capital in the energy field will continue to grow, thus increasing Quebec's dependence on the American financier. Due to the sheer size of the amounts involved, however, at some level the debtor has potentially as much bargaining power as the creditor. Foreign investors become sensitive to the overall success of their ventures, for if a certain project is not finished they stand to lose heavily. Hence, they will still be inclined to contribute additional funds to insure completions.

P.Q. Government Policy toward Foreign Investment

The present government's attitude toward multinational corporations is at variance with its campaign rhetoric for the simple reason that foreign investment is so important. For example, in late 1977 competition developed over a substantial provincial government contract between the American-based General Motors and the Quebec-based firm Bombardier. Despite popular support for the Quebec firm, and the P.Q.'s official policy of preference for Quebec firms, the contract was awarded to G.M.

A second illustration of government policy toward multinationals is the contract signed with Alcan outlining the details to furnish hydro-electric energy. During the 1976 electoral campaign the P.Q. took a hard line toward Alcan, but the agreement was considered surprisingly acceptable by Alcan officials.

The government's observed actions are relatively moderate. M. Lévesque, officially expressing the new government's policy at the Economic Club of New York, said that any policy of nationalization was the exception and not the rule, and the only exception thus far concerns asbestos. "We are not against foreign investment as such," he said, "and we have no intention of picking fights with private enterprise, for the Parti Québécois approach is essentially pragmatic." He also mentioned that the present government is ready to accept and welcome foreign enterprise so long as it respects the majority language and culture. Finally, M. Lévesque stated that Quebec obviously needs and will continue to need new investment and technology, from both domestic and foreign sources.

P.Q. Provincial Policy

One can also observe prudence in the provincial budget. The first budget of the Parti Québécois government was relatively conservative. Even the President of the Provincial Employers Association labelled the budget "too conservative." Although it was obviously popular with the business sector, the public was highly critical, particularly of such provisions as taxing children's clothing. The second budget, however, renewed the Liberal policy of emphasizing tax reductions for low wage-earners and was more popular. Here, once again, P.Q. campaign rhetoric, critical of Liberal indexing formulas, had been modified in the practice of power.

In other areas (social, labor relations, and language) policies seem to have a more harmful effect on small and middle-sized business than on the traditionally large U.S. subsidiaries where the impact has been moderate. Criticism by the business community has been directed mainly at the manner and short period of time in which all these policies were adopted, particularly as the economy was already deteriorating. The further deterioration of the Quebec economy, in comparison with Canada, can at least in part be attributed to the timing of the new policies as well as to the political uncertainty which still prevails.[3]

The application of language policy, too, is moderate toward business. Indeed, for business, language policy largely conforms to the Liberal Bill 22. Multinational corporations are used to working in different languages. As long as the language legislation is applied in a rational manner, no apprehension on the part of American investors should be expected.

Options for Quebec's Political Future

What is more important to the American investor is the Quebecer's determination of his political future. Investors must know whether political decisions will change existing economic institutions. The P.Q. Government, in order to reduce the economic consequences of its secessionist policies, is proposing what it calls the "sovereignty-association" formula.

What are the options for the P.Q. formula? There are three possibilities, among which only one is to be taken seriously. First, there is the "free trade association" (meaning that goods could circulate freely within the territories of the two states, Quebec and

Canada, but that these two states could have separate external tariff policies). This option would harm Quebec's exports to Canada (which in 1974 amounted to almost $7 billion). Moreover, if Canada were to choose a lower external tariff, Quebec's trade to other provinces would be hurt seriously.

The second option, a customs union between Canada and Quebec, implies a common external tariff but not necessarily a free movement of manpower and capital. It would require controlled borders. Due to the highly integrated capital movements which already exist throughout North America, there is no known control which could be very effective in regulating these intense flows, and control would be burdensome.

Regulations could be undertaken to control the movement of manpower, but the consequence would be a disproportionate distribution of labor throughout the regions. Under Canadian federalism one significant structural problem is the already inefficient allocation of manpower resources. Any added restrictions would aggravate the present problem.

Finally, there is the common market alternative, which operates without border controls and allows for the free movement of produced goods within the market. A common market without a monetary union, however, is more and more difficult to establish, especially when one takes into account the level of commercial transactions between Quebec and the rest of Canada. In fact, the latest statistics reveal that Quebec was the only region in which the percentage of goods exported to other Canadian provinces (55.9%) exceeded exports to external markets (44.1%).[4] Successful trade depended on the non-tariff barriers imposed by the Canadian Government.

Today's European Common Market reveals the difficulty of different currencies. I do not need to elaborate on problems of the "green pound" or the "green lira." The fact that the "agricultural currencies" in many cases are not in line with the real currencies of the E.C. severely hinders the practical functioning of the Common Market, and there are tensions amongst the European Community states over the Monetary Compensatory Payments procedure. Exchange rate shifts are producing a negative effect on the participating countries' balance of payments accounts by magnifying the surpluses and deficits of the various states. Monetary union would lead to a transfer of power from individual central banks to a European Central Bank, logically accountable to the European

Parliament, and it would strengthen the European economy by reducing regional disparties and by reducing the speculative mobility of capital. A successful common market, then, requires monetary union, which means a reduction in the sovereignty of member states.

The currency question is ultimately pragmatic: Given the high degree of exchanges between the French-speaking province and the rest of Canada, how would a separate currency affect the hundreds of thousands of Quebecers who travel annually outside Quebec and thus need foreign currency? Quebec is heavily endowed with hydro-electric power, but it still relies on external energy for 75% of its requirements. What will be the attitude of energy-producing states to Quebec's new currency?

The answers to such questions are very complex. Still, a separate currency will affect Quebec's present standard of living. At present, the P.Q. has not committed itself to the establishment of a separate currency, and there would be little chance of public support for a sovereign Quebec if it entailed economic separatism. Eleven years ago I first raised these questions of a "separate currency"; it seems the P.Q. has yet to make any progress in dealing with the issue.

There still are P.Q. members who advocate a separate Quebec currency, arguing that devaluation could be an efficient instrument in combating unemployment. However, in the last 25 years most devaluations have been unsuccessful in acting as a real stimulant to the domestic economy. Successive devaluations of the British pound, for example, led to one of the poorest economic performances in the free world. Devaluations meant higher levels of inflation, which in turn raised wages, leading to a lower level of productivity. "Open" economies, such as Quebec's, are even more prone to these effects.

In the absence of a Quebec currency, the common currency must be maintained. The protection of a common currency requires complementary fiscal powers, and the application of those powers requires a democratically-elected institution. One could hardly expect technocrats, instructed by two different governments, to have the final decision in monetary and fiscal policy. The absence of an elected central body would imply different governments trying to agree on common economic policies through respectively selected civil servants.

A true common market, then, implies a monetary union. An economic union, which requires a significant degree of political integration, is necessary to maintain the Quebecers' high standard of living.

I believe that since Quebecers are already accustomed to a high standard of living, they will refuse to give up economic union with the rest of Canada. Quebec requires the immense natural resources existing outside the province (oil, gas, uranium, and in the long term, especially with population growth, wheat). There is already exceptionally great commercial and financial integration. Finally, we must note the established economic and fiscal advantages of Canadian federalism, including (to name only two) equalization payments and federally-funded economic development programs.

The Timetable for Decision

The next few months will witness some significant events. First, federal elections will have been held, but at the time this is written it is obviously too early to make any prognostications regarding the effects the elections will have on the fate of Quebec within the Canadian Confederation.

Second, the Parti Québécois will hold a provincial referendum on Quebec's status before too long. In the Summer of 1978 it seemed that moves favoring Quebec independence will be soundly defeated. The contemporary economic situation, the administrative efficiency of the P.Q. government, and the state of Ottawa-Quebec relations all could influence the outcome. M. Lévesque declared in a November 1977 interview that a high unemployment rate would help him in the referendum, since people will be inclined to blame Ottawa. That may be true, but it implies an abdication of responsibility for the reduction of unemployment.

The final determinant of the future will be the Quebec provincial elections of 1980. It is too early to predict what will be the outcome, but one cannot ignore the fact that if Quebec voters strongly support the reelected Liberals at the federal level and again support the federalist position in the referendum, some could possibly be disposed to balance federalist inclinations by voting the P.Q. into a second term in office. (Under these circumstances, the Provincial Liberals could be vulnerable, too, if the P.Q. were to abandon suggestions of a second independence referendum.) This was the situation throughout the 1950s, when Quebecers continuously supported M. St. Laurent on the federal level while simultaneously electing his political opponent, M. Duplessis and the Union Nationale, on the provincial level.

Continuity and Change

Whatever the future of Canada and Quebec, there are some changes which seem necessary because of the special cultural situation in Quebec. The economic system, however, seems relatively inelastic. The Canadian problem is complex. There is no simple solution, as there is no simple solution in any multi-lingual state. Belgium, for example, in order to achieve cultural peace, has recently changed its political structure; there soon will be seven assemblies and four executive institutions for that small country. We can easily observe cultural decentralization in other states, including Germany and Switzerland.

For many people, the "One Canada" and the "Quebec Independence" concepts seem simple and therefore desirable, but in light of the complexities of the Canadian situation, such as the existence of minorities in both English Canada and Quebec, these approaches are too simplistic. In addition, the French-speaking population is declining within Canada. There is now in Ottawa a strong French political contingent which developed during the early 1960s (following the first wave of terrorist activities), and the existence of a strong independence movement in Quebec certainly has aided the acceptance of the growing French-speaking presence within the country.

Canada requires a political system sensitive to its complexity. Quebec's economic needs and Quebec's cultural problems are pulling in opposite directions. No easy solution exists. The *status quo* is not acceptable. Neither is "sovereignty-association," as we have understood it so far. It is clear to me, however, that Quebec's sovereignty in cultural affairs must be achieved for the maintenance of Quebec's identity in a greater Canada.

NOTES

1. It is worth noting that after the November 15 election, the Union Nationale changed its position on the linguistic issue. Its only anglophone member in the Assembly, Dr. William Shaw, then resigned.

In my mind, there is no doubt that had the format of the election been one of two rounds (as, e.g., exists in the French electoral process), the anglophones would have voted Liberal in the second round. Thus, one may conclude that voters behaved inconsistently with their own objectives.

2. Economic Policy Committee of the O.E.C.D., February, 1978.

3. Although the recent increase in the minimum wage is a practice with which my administration also complied (at an even greater percentage increase), the economic climate then was strong and there was no political uncertainty.

4. Suggested by Professor C. Nappi in a symposium at the University of Montreal, Hautes Etudes Commerciales, May 16, 1978.

12_____QUEBEC'S ECONOMIC FUTURE IN CONFEDERATION

COMMENT

Michael Parenti

I could not hope to comment on all of the interesting points raised by M. Bourassa. Let me be satisfied with some observations on the central question of today's discussion: U.S. investments in Quebec, or more generally, the pattern of overseas U.S. investments. I believe that Quebec faces the same dilemma as does most of the non-socialist world. Suffering a capital shortage and needing capital investments to solve economic problems, many countries do their utmost to lure multinational corporate investments, only to discover that such investments do not solve and usually worsen economic conditions within their lands.

There are several reasons for this problem. First, the function of private investment is not to build up the economic infrastructure, nor to develop native talent, nor to advance the education, health, and income of the populace, nor to improve social services or increase the native food supply. The function of corporate investment is to make the highest possible profit for the investor, to extract more capital than is invested.

While investment leads to new jobs and new consumer products for a small portion of the indigenous population, especially concentrated in the more developed urban areas, there are other spin-offs of a harmful kind. The investment is usually capital-intensive, creating less employment than hoped for, and far less than needed, with most of the choice jobs going to the corporation's own personnel, that is, to persons other than those drawn from the needy populace. The investments are usually concentrated in extractive industries or in cash crop exports or in mass-produced durable goods intended for foreign markets. These jobs and goods do little to develop the economy of the recipient nation in ways that will solve its problems of want and underemployment. Quite the contrary, such investments lead to a maldevelopment of the local economy, a destruction of indigenous modes of production and local food supplies without putting anything in their place, and a dislocation of the entire economy around some few capital export industries such as asbestos, hydro-electric power, coal, tin, rubber, sugar, and petrochemical products.

The results can be seen most dramatically in such places as Northeast Brazil, Appalachia, and elsewhere: rich regions which have made fortunes many times over for outside investors, inhabited by poor people whose labor was part of the raw materials exploited by the corporations. Faced with such poverty what do local political leaders do? They ask for more. They look around at the unemployment, poverty, illiteracy, and hunger and they decide that what is needed is capital investment that would create jobs and supposedly bring prosperity.

In addition, the countries that invite capital investments and loans get caught in a cycle of indebtedness until a kind of financial alcoholism sets in. New York City provides an internal colonial example, having to borrow vast sums from the banks in order to pay off past loans, thereby going deeper into debt and having to demonstrate its fiscal responsibility to its creditors by cutting back on expenditures, specifically in the area of human services, including welfare, education, firemen, aid to the handicapped and the elderly, and other such "frills."

With some countries, the situation is so bad that the greater portion of their export earnings is used to pay off their creditors. Far from being a solution, multinational investment is a central part of the problem.

Does Quebec fit into the picture I have drawn? I think so. U.S. investments are high in Quebec and the debt is great, some $7.4 billion according to M. Bourassa, and with this goes an increasing dependence on U.S. financing. At the same time, as M. Bourassa notes, there is a troubled economic situation in Quebec, an increasing inflation, one of the highest unemployment rates of any modernized nation and the worst labor unrest in the world (as measured by the number of strikes). One might add that Quebec, as compared to the rest of Canada, has more than its share of poverty, poor housing, and insufficiencies in human services.

The record of private enterprise, as measured by the social conditions mentioned above, is hardly an inspiring one. Yet M. Bourassa calls for more of the same, more private investment which might have some short-term benefits but which eventually will lead to greater economic disruption, deprivation, and dependency for

Quebec. He advocates financial alcoholism, believing it will work for Quebec rather than for the investors.

M. Bourassa points out that the public sector cannot be called upon to rescue Quebec, since the public sector is already growing at an abnormally high rate. The public sector in a capitalist society is used (1) to perform services which offer no profit to private industry, or insufficient profit, and (2) services necessary for private production (e.g., building roads, harbors) and (3) for insuring social order (police, welfare). The public sector, however, could be expanded dramatically to move into areas of production that are normally monopolized by private firms, thereby providing jobs, goods, and services that the private sector is expected to provide, and thereby building a capital reserve which could be used for further socially useful economic growth. Such a step would no longer be state-supported capitalism. It would be socialism. And neither major political party in Quebec seems willing or able to entertain moves in that direction.

Here I agree with most of M. Bourassa's criticisms of the Parti Québécois (although he is attacking the P.Q. from the right and I from the left—there being a difference between those of us who pursue revolution and those who pursue re-election). The P.Q. has focused on the highly emotional issue of autonomy for the French-speaking population. It has won some cultural victories but it has brought no solution to Quebec's economic problems. The P.Q., as M. Bourassa pointed out, had certain pretensions to being something of a "leftist government." But it is running into the same dilemma faced by any political group that tries to solve socio-economic problems by working within the very system that is creating these problems. The party's first obligation must be to improve the economy—but this means the capitalist economy doing what the capitalists need to insure profitability—rather than what the populace requires to serve social and productive needs. Thus, the P.Q. wins office by promising a change and ends up doing pretty much the same as the Liberal Party.

The only solution, I would argue, is for the P.Q. or the more populist and socialist elements within it to concentrate on building a mass organization, a social movement, that could provide the support for a new social order in Quebec. An electoral party cannot transform the society. Its concern is with taking office and working within the class and social structure as is. The promise is that it will do the same thing but better. What Quebec needs is not just a better way but a *new* way, the development of massive, non-profit investment and public control of production for purposes of social need rather than private greed.

A discussion of how that could be accomplished would take us beyond the boundaries of the present discussion. Let me just point out that I do not believe the economic crisis in Quebec is due to a recent decline in public morality as M. Bourassa seems to argue. It may be that some workers will begin to manifest the same narrow self-interested greed that one finds in the average multinational corporation. But usually workers strike and commit acts of disruption and even violence because they feel compelled to by the conditions of their labor, by inadequate wages and benefits, by work conditions that are dangerous, unhealthy, or in other ways demoralizing and unjust. I would conclude that the labor problems of Quebec, like others of its problems, are systemic and not so very different from the problems created by the multinationals in other exploited regions of the world.

13___TOWARDS A REVITALIZED CONFEDERATION

Flora MacDonald

Since the Quebec election of November 1976, Canadians have begun a grand national search for the "solutions" to their complex political and constitutional problems—a search greatly complicated by the simultaneous existence of a severe economic crisis, which itself has deep roots. During this period, national unity groups have sprung up all over the country. The ten provincial premiers have met in annual conclave and the leader of the opposition has convened his own federal-provincial conference. The prime minister went on a round of visits to provincial capitals with a view to proposing constitutional amendments in early 1977.

In this rush of activity, it is hard now to find many people who ardently defend the *status quo*—whatever that is—and terms like a "renewed federalism," a "third option," and so on are being bandied about everywhere. Except for the most naive or unconcerned of Canadians (and there are some of those), the matter of constitutional reform has become one of great urgency and immediacy.

There is a sense that if we just look hard enough, we will discover a package of constitutional and political changes; that there exists a new constitution, just waiting to be unearthed, a Canadian version of the Holy Grail, pulsing away with an eerie light, probably deep in some cave on Baffin Island.

But to talk of a single grand solution is misleading and maybe even dangerous. First of all, there may, indeed, be no solution, at least none which preserves the essentials of the united Confederation. It may even be impossible to resolve the multiple conflicts and cleavages which now divide Canadian society.

Secondly, different groups vary widely in what they would consider an acceptable solution, just as they differ widely in their diagnosis of the problems facing the country, and in their images of what they would like the country to be.

Thirdly, any solution is not likely to be a single neat package—a new British North America Act, for example. Instead, it is likely to be made up of a large number of diverse elements, including constitutional changes, changes in policy, and changes in attitude.

Lastly, and most importantly, it is misleading to talk of a solution as being one grand resolution of all our discontents, after which harmony would prevail far into the future. Politics does not work that way. In thinking about solutions, Canadians instead must realize that the goal should be to provide a *framework* and a set of rules within which the continuing debate and dialogue between regional and national interests, and between French and English, can go on in a civilized way. It is dangerous to put too much stock in search of a grand once-for-all solution. We also have to realize that, in the short run at least, a new constitution cannot change old attitudes and cannot alter fundamental realities. What it can do is recognize and reflect those realities, and make it possible to engage in a continuing search for accommodation and reconciliation.

Interpreting the Crisis

Any solution that one proposes must depend greatly on one's diagnosis of the nature and causes of the current political crisis in Canada, and of the longer-term dissatisfaction that has developed over many years as the federal system has grappled with the twin problems of reconciling the interests of French and English-Canadians, and of accommodating growing regional discontent. It also depends on one's values, and on the kind of Canada one wants to create.

The problem facing us at the present time is one of reconciliation of three fundamental images which have dominated Canadian political, economic, social, and cultural life throughout its history. Indeed, our history is one of a constant tension and dialogue between these three images, in which now one, now the other, tends to be dominant.

The first image is regionalism, or province building, the recognition of the unique historical, cultural, and economic attributes of each region, and of the desire of each to develop itself to the fullest extent possible.

The second is the search for a truly pan-Canadian development, building on shared values and attitudes, the common desires for national services, the desire to create an independent, integrated Canadian economy, and the need to develop an equitable sharing of resources among all regions of Canada.

The third might be called two-nation building, the recognition that sociologically Quebec is a distinct society and culture which exists alongside a less clearly defined English-Canadian nation. This drive reflects itself in the desire for equality between the two nations, and in the search for a distinct political role for the Quebec government.

So we have in Canada one country, a partnership between two language groups, five regions, ten provinces, and vast northern territories. Somehow, our institutions must reflect and accommodate all of them, and be flexible enough to respond to changes in the underlying situation—as in the change from dominance of national aspirations and feelings during and after World War II, to the contemporary dominance of and preoccupation with regionalism and even, by some with two nations.

Regionalism

Mackenzie King's statement that while some countries have too much history, Canada has too much geography, has a great deal of wisdom. Geographical factors account for many of our differences and for many of our problems. There is another aspect of Canadian regionalism, however, which cannot be attributed to geography, belonging more properly to history. The different regions of our country were settled at different times by peoples whose values and attitudes were shaped in diverse societies. These values and attitudes in turn have helped shape the political and social cultures of the regions, and thus of the country.

The Maritimes, for example, have been influenced heavily by the clan system of the Scottish settlers. This influence is manifested in the Maritimers' strong sense of community and cooperative effort as well as an almost mystical attachment to their home province, no matter where they may wander.

The culture of Quebec, besides being different because it is predominantly French, is also different because it reflects the influence of the first settlers who emigrated at a time when the doctrines and practices of absolutism held sway in France. This influence is reflected in a history of authoritarian, paternalistic institutions in the province of Quebec, a pattern that remained unchallenged until the Quiet Revolution. As a result, Quebecers have been far more prone than other Canadians to allow their government and their bureaucracy to manage their affairs.

By contrast, the people of Ontario are highly individualistic, demanding a voice in running the province, resenting the interference of governments, and feeling strongly about individual rights and responsibilities. It is no coincidence that these attitudes should prevail in a region where the first influential wave of settlement took place in the wake of major reform and civil rights movements in Britain at the beginning of the nineteenth century.

Equally remarkable is the consistency with which radical political thinking, of both the right and the left, has dominated the politics of the Western provinces. One can trace the influence of immigrants who arrived from the United Kingdom in the post-Fabian period, or from Europe, after periods of oppression or persecution had literally driven them from their lands. Westerners are highly politicized and when the contemporary political setting has not met their needs, they have had no hesitation in creating third parties to represent them.

Thus, it can be seen that aside from the very obvious geographical factors which create regional pulls, there are very strong historical and social factors and influences that have contributed to the emergence of different value systems in the various regions.

These value systems affect patterns of voting behavior, citizen participation, attitudes towards government, and even ideological tendencies in a way that simply cannot be explained by geographic or economic factors. I firmly believe that until we truly understand these regional modes of thought and sets of values, until we really understand how they have come about and what makes them persist, we will continue to concentrate on the problems of regionalism rather than on the potential it offers to a creative restructuring of confederation.

The Federal Alternative to Regionalism

Canadian political debate has tended to concentrate almost entirely on the negative side of the regional dimension, stressing the grievances of every region against the federal government, stressing what it is that divides Canadians from each other rather than what unites them. That is a healthy and interesting development, but if it is carried too far, stressing how many pieces Humpty-Dumpty has broken into, we run the risk of simply not being able to put him back together again.

While regionalism is one of the major impulses in Canadian federalism, the quest for a sense of national community is another. This pan-Canadian impulse remains strong, even in areas such as Alberta which have led the drive for greater attention to regional problems.

Canadians have sought to weld their diverse economic regions into a single national economy, and increasingly they are worried about the need for effective national economic planning to deal with common economic problems, and with such common concerns as foreign ownership. Similarly, since World War II, Canada has created an advanced welfare state, with substantially similar programs and standards across the country—something that provinces acting alone probably could not have done, and which could only be achieved through the leadership and financial support of the federal government. Canadians do not appear willing yet to sacrifice these goals of building a strong, independent country.

Moreover, Ottawa need not necessarily ride roughshod over the regions. Indeed, the existence of a strong federal government is, in some areas, a precondition for *regional* development. Through equalization, shared cost programs, and programs like unemployment insurance, Ottawa transfers large amounts of resources from the richer to the poorer regions. Currently, the beneficiaries of these programs are Quebec and Atlantic Canada, but it is sometimes forgotten that the present division of prosperous and less prosperous regions has not always held.

Thirty-five years ago, Alberta was near bankruptcy, its agricultural base shattered by soil erosion and low prices. Today, it has an economy as prosperous as any in the world. It was able to build up that economy in large measure because the national government recognized its obligation to see Alberta through its lean years with direct financial assistance. Who is to say that 35 years from now, the industrial base of Ontario might not experience a similar crisis and this province desperately require the aid which would come to it under revenue equalization? Indeed, if offshore oil, mineral and fish resources match some optimistic projections, that aid to central Canada might well be subsidized by taxpayers in Newfoundland or Nova Scotia. Only a federal government committed to a concept of equalization can achieve that balance within our national community.

Consequences of Competing Images

Each of the three images (regionalism, pan-Canadianism, or two-nation building) tends to be associated with a distinct set of proposals for change in Canada's constitutional arrangements. A two-nation image leads us in the direction of recognizing a distinct role for the Quebec government, as the only government in which French-

Canadians constitute a majority, and which has a special role in promoting Quebec's development. Hence suggestions have been made that Quebec should have more freedom and autonomy than other provinces.

A regional image tends to lead to the call for decentralization, for weakening the powers that Ottawa holds, and for strengthening the roles of the provinces. Some proposals for decentralization are mainly cosmetic—giving greater say to the provinces over cultural policy or immigration, for example. Others are much more drastic, suggesting that the federal government greatly reduce its role in many areas of social and monetary policy, becoming perhaps little more than a balance wheel of the federal system.

Many who argue for decentralization are also concerned with the growth of big, complex bureaucratic government in today's society. One reason for that in Canada is the incredible overlapping of federal and provincial activities in most areas. Hence decentralizers also call for disentanglement, for a more rational sharing of responsibilities in which each government will get out of the other's hair, and citizens will know which government to praise or blame for what gets done.

On the other hand, growing provincial power, and especially growing provincial concern with how the federal government makes and implements fiscal, transportation, tariff, energy, and many other policies—all of which have a major regional impact—have led to calls for greater sharing of responsibilities, for an explicit recognition of more areas of concurrent jurisdiction in the constitution, and for creation of more effective bodies for coordinating federal and provincial policies in place of the wrangling which now characterizes federal-provincial relations. Many of these demands are legitimate and can be met if Ottawa were to accept the true nature of federalism, in which the provinces are partners and not necessarily adversaries.

Decentralization is the current catchword, but is has its dangers. It suggests we have failed to build a common sense of community in the past, and probably cannot do so in the future. It opens the door to many forms of interprovincial competition. It suggests that it will be much harder to deal with problems like foreign ownership; and if Canada is now highly vulnerable to manipulation by large multi-national corporations, it could become even more so if federal economic powers are weakened. It suggests the poorer provinces would become even more vulnerable in the future, especially if in a regionally fragmented country citizens of the richer areas decided they no longer shared enough sense of community with those in the poor areas to be willing to redistribute wealth to them.

Any new constitutional arrangements are almost certain to involve some elements of decentralization. That is the way the tide is running, and not only in Canada. The provincial governments will be central participants in the renegotiation, and we can expect them to fight well for their interests.

Federal Failures

As a federal politician, and one who was brought up in Cape Breton and now represents an electoral district in central Canada, I want to focus on another set of changes, changes which rather than weakening the central government, rather than giving up on the dream of a Canada of shared interests and mutual responsibilities, try instead to build on them. This strategy does not deny the value and importance of regionalism. Nor does it deny the impulse of Canada-building. It seeks to reconcile them *within* the institutions and processes of the central government itself. Rather than having the provinces as representatives of the regions, and the federal government as the representative of the whole, with both of them constantly at logger-heads, the question is: Can Ottawa rediscover its ability to respond to regional diversity and, at the same time, more effectively discover and implement those interests which Canadians have in common?

The answer may be no. Over the last few years there has been a tremendous erosion of the support and legitimacy of Canadian central political institutions. Ottawa is almost universally regarded as part of the problem rather than part of the solution. There are many elements to this alienation. In part it lies in the failure of federal policies—the lack of leadership in economic matters, the combination of arrogance and disarray of a government too long in power. In part it stems from noble policies badly executed: policies to promote bilingualism have failed to stem the growth of separatist feeling in Quebec, while stirring up deep resentments among many English-Canadians.

In part it stems from a sense of unfairness in federal policies over a long period: the view in the Maritimes, for example, that however big federal welfare payments have been they have not ended the long economic stagnation of a region which in 1867 was one of the most prosperous. In the West there is a sense that federal policies, especially in transportation and the tariff, have worked systematically to the advantage of central Canada and imposed heavy costs on the outlying regions. In Quebec there is the sense that, historically, federal policies have served the interests of the English-Canadian majority, and imposed their values on Quebecers.

The failures are also the result of institutions unable to accommodate regional diversity. Along with growth in provincial jurisdiction and the emergence of highly skilled and effective provincial leaders and bureaucracies, federal failure has meant that regional discontent has been channelled through provincial governments, rather than through Ottawa.

The classic model of Canadian brokerage politics suggested that political parties were to be able to appeal to, and win support from, all regions. Party leaders would have strong regional bases and strong regional lieutenants. The federal cabinet would then be the arena in which these leaders expressed their regional interests and hammered out compromises. That model no longer applies.

First, both Canadian major parties have failed to win national support. My own party, for a variety of historic reasons, remains a small minority voice in Quebec. The governing Liberals have been more successful, but they, too, have been frozen out for a very long period in Western Canada.

Party failure in turn is partly the result of the effects of our electoral system. The number of seats a party wins is, more often than not, a poor reflection of its popular strength or weakness. My party usually wins about 20 percent of the vote in Quebec—not much, maybe, but our caucus would look very different if we had 20 percent of the Quebec seats. The same is true for the Liberals in the West.

Moreover, the growth in complexity of federal policy and the exaggerated role of the leader in an age of television heroes have greatly reduced the ability of members or cabinet ministers to act as regional representatives or spokesmen in the national government.

The result is that a semi-permanent loss of representation in the governing party reinforces a sense of alienation, of governmental insensitivity and unfairness. It means that the views of important regions are not effectively represented within each major party.

This same lack of regional sensitivity and awareness pervades the bureaucracy, and the host of federal regulatory agencies—the NEB, CTC, CRTC and others—which are playing an increasingly important role in our lives.

Ottawa, therefore, seems increasingly cut off from its roots. It cannot reconcile diverse interests at the center. Nor can it develop those truly national policies which all Canadians might have in common.

Major Proposals for Confederation

If we wish to preserve the essentials of a national community, the question becomes, how can we improve it? How can we remake the central government? How can we relegitimize federal institutions? Many suggestions have been made, all of which need further thought, but the outlines can be sketched now.

The Senate

Canada's Senate is perceived as something of a joke. Appointed solely by the party in power in Ottawa, it has largely become a refuge for worthy party supporters, exercising little power and almost no role in regional representation. It could be changed to become a veritable House of the Provinces. At one extreme it could become a forum for constant federal-provincial bargaining, if it were set up like the West German Upper House with its members directly appointed and responsible to provincial governments. A less drastic change would be to have the provinces given a voice in appointments to the Senate, or to have senators elected by provincial electorates at the same time as provincial elections were held.

Such a revised Senate would have to have more real power, and would certainly challenge the hallowed principles of cabinet government responsible to the House of Commons. But it would mean, and this point is crucial, that whatever the results of elections and the party system in the House of Commons, each region would feel that its voice was being expressed in the councils of federal decision-making, through a Senate whose structural reforms were not merely cosmetic.

The Electoral System and Parties

A second major institutional change would be to reform the electoral system, giving up the first-past-the-post system, and electing members on the basis of some form of proportional representation. Then, even with only a small proportion of the vote in a given province, a party could still count on having members from that region. This change, too, could have drastic effects on traditional cabinet government, since it would lead almost certainly to permanent minority governments, perhaps to frequent coalition governments on the European model, and perhaps as well to a proliferation of small parties.

A third direction would be to relax the importance of party discipline in the House of Commons, to move toward the American system, in which members are more free to represent their local interests and to form alliances with members of other parties on specific issues.

One can see immediately the potentially far-reaching effects of such changes, and certainly there would be powerful resistance to them, both because of the reverence for the British model in Canada, and because the consequences for other aspects of our political system would be hard to predict. But I believe that we must now begin to think seriously about such changes if Ottawa is to regain its role as a center for reconciliation of the Canadian community.

Minor Proposals for Confederation

Along with these major changes could come minor ones. The Supreme Court of Canada is now appointed entirely by the federal government, even though it must adjudicate between federal and provincial interests. While charges of systematic bias do not seem well founded, decisions which can pit the three Quebec judges against the other six lend credence to the Parti Québécois argument that Quebec loses out in the federal system.

Similarly, the federal regulatory agencies make many decisions which have a significant impact on the provinces, even though the provinces have no special standing in arguing before these tribunals. Again, a very strong case can be made for structuring them on more regionally sensitive lines and for allowing a provincial voice in appointments.

The massive Ottawa-based bureaucracy also needs to be structured to represent regional needs more adequately. Recently, the federal government has undertaken a program of decentralization of administration by transferring some government offices to slow-growth areas. This move should be supplemented by the delegation of real decision-making power to regional field offices so that national policies can be made to reflect regional influence.

My purpose here is not to argue the case of any particular proposal from this catalogue of proposed changes in our national institutions; it is, rather, to show the many possibilities which exist, and which might revitalize the federal political process.

The Future Through Reform

Professor John Meisel of Queen's University points out that if regional or provincial representation were included in national institutions, those institutions

> would thus...act as brokers of distinct regional and ethnic interests, and the decisions of such bodies, while applicable nationally, would result from the reconciliation of various provincial interests...Federal policies would more likely respond to regional interests; but also the regional interests represented in Ottawa would begin to perceive the national dimensions to be their concerns.[1]

What I propose constitutes some of the possible elements, not of a solution which will instantly bring forth unity and harmony, but of a new framework for creative debate and flexible adaptation to changing circumstances. Canadians must engage in a great act of creative political imagination, encompassing a number of changes.

1. We must change our national political institutions, to provide effective representation and leadership.

2. We must recognize the drive for more provincial autonomy, first by decentralizing some powers, and second, by providing a clear provincial voice in those areas of primarily federal jurisdiction—transportation, economic policy, cultural policy—which have particular implications for regional development, yet which may clash with provincial development plans. We require more explicitly concurrent powers, clear rules for which level of government predominates when there is a clash, and more effective machinery for intergovernmental negotiation.

3. We must give greater recognition to Quebec. None of these changes goes to the heart of the demands made in Quebec, not only by the Parti Québécois, but also by every Quebec government in power since 1960. Quebec's demands precipitated the present crisis and it is silly to think we can avoid grasping the nettle. Noble as it is, the strategy of making Canada the homeland of all French-Canadians and denying a special role and responsibility to the Quebec government clearly has failed. This does not mean that we should not move immediately to entrench minority language rights, but that Quebec must have more autonomy, real and symbolic, in any revised constitution. Perhaps that autonomy could also be offered to the other provinces, so as to avoid the clear implication of "special status," a word that in Canada has become the graveyard of politicians.

4. We must resolve the incredible anomaly that the Canadian Constitution is in fact no more than an Act of Parliament of a foreign government; we must therefore provide for its patriation. That in turn requires that Canadians agree at long last on a procedure for its amendment. The question is whether that agreement will precede, or flow from, agreement on the broader issues.

5. Finally, we must strengthen the relatively weak elements of popular representation in Canadian political life. A new constitution should be open and democratic. That means such things as entrenching the Bill of Rights and a parallel right to information. Senate, electoral reform, and other changes might also open up what is now a highly centralized and executive-dominated political system.

Truly, the situation is one that demands the best of all Canadians. There are many who question that a solution is possible. There are many who are amazed, not that the country may break up, but that it ever held together for so long. This attitude is destructive since it suggests that the whole idea of Confederation was a mistake.

I, for one, will never be convinced that Canada is a mistake. There are tensions and strains in our union. They run deep. And the sense of grievance is strong, not only in Quebec, but in all regions and communities. The problem is not new. It has been there from the beginning. Arthur Meighen stated it succinctly in 1925:

> The main problem with Canada is a spiritual problem. It's a problem of getting all our people to see that we have only one country, that we have not a collection of unrelated sections. It's a problem of getting our people to see that the objective of all is to help each and that the success of one does not mean the failure of another.[2]

It may well be impossible to reconcile the different interests of the regions of Canada. But it is my firm belief that, given the proper attitudes, our regional differences could, and should, work for us and not against us. They could prove to be our strength and not our weakness. To control our differences and not to be controlled by them is our challenge at this time. It is a large task and I hope, with all my heart, that we are up to it.

NOTES

1. John Meisel, "J'ai le gout du Quebec but I like Canada; Reflections of an Ambivalent Man," in Richard Simeon, ed., *Must Canada Fail?* (Montreal: McGill-Queens University Press, 1977), p. 302.

2. Debates of House of Commons 1925, p. 3808.

13___TOWARDS A REVITALIZED CONFEDERATION

COMMENT

Walter Dean Burnham

In her essay, Flora MacDonald has given us one insider's view of the tensions which are building up within Canada. These tensions actively threaten to produce the disintegration of the Canadian Confederation in the not too distant future. Ms. MacDonald's essay reveals how keenly aware this leading member of the Progressive Conservative Party is that this threat may become a reality. But she is determinedly optimistic about the future, provided that certain reforms are undertaken in the Canadian political structure.

Ms. MacDonald would increase the power of the Canadian Senate and convert it into a "congress of ambassadors" from the provinces, very much as the American constitution-makers contemplated the functions of the Senate which they created. She proposes as well the adoption of such changes as proportional representation in parliamentary elections and a movement away from the responsible-party pattern inherited from the British and toward the more loose-jointed American model of legislative politics.

All of these proposals reflect an acute perception that the specific kinds of fissiparous pluralisms which dominate the Canadian social structure are accommodated poorly by a British parliamentary system of government. No doubt this is so. And for Canada, even more than for the United States, as Herbert Agar and other pluralists have seen it, rampant pluralisms and the ability of any group to thwart the will of the majority in the political process may literally be "the price of union."[1]

Yet one may legitimately wonder whether any reforms of the political structure may suffice any longer, or whether there still remains any determinate price of union to be paid by the parties to it. As Ms. MacDonald points out, there is a single country, two language groups, five regions, and ten provinces. Canada is also a country in which many social and political problems of the gravest character coexist. The one which is most salient, obviously, is the "problem of

Quebec," a problem which now appears to be coming to a head. But this particular problem, fundamental as it is, cannot be wholly understood in isolation from the others.

The Imperial Legacy

Canada cannot be understood apart from the political problems—some of immensely great age—which are produced by imperialism. In an earlier and more innocent time, when imperialism was not the dirty word it has become, it was accepted as applying to Canada—next, perhaps, to India, the brightest jewel in Victoria's imperial crown. The French in Canada were conquered by a nation whose language, religion, and culture were wholly alien to those of the original *habitants*. This experience of conquest has, in one way or another, been a central part of Canadian political and social existence since the first granting of self-government by the imperial power. It surfaced explicitly (and with permanent damage to the Conservative Party in Quebec) in the conscription crisis of the two world wars. Historically, its chief political manifestation within Quebec was a culturally preservationist isolation from the outside world. This isolation was reflected in the age-old ascendancy of the Catholic clergy as a political and opinion-forming elite, and in the generation-long rule of Maurice Duplessis and the Union Nationale during the second third of this century.

Experiences of this kind—imperialist conquest of populations with cultures different from those of the conquerors, densely occupying a large, contiguous, and rural territorial base, are not unique to Canada. Conspicuous parallels are to be found in the history of Ireland (the first and least successful of all Britain's imperial conquests) and of Poland. In both countries, as in Quebec, the modal response to conquest was the development of a very special role for the Catholic clergy. These countries, from the conventional Protestant point of view, were (and still are) all "priest-ridden" to a degree not found by any means in other countries with Catholic majorities.

The underlying reason for this peculiar quality of social life—the authoritarian tradition to which Ms. MacDonald refers—is obvious. A peasant population, stripped for whatever reason of its "natural" secular leaders by alien conquest, turns to its religious leaders to perform *the* essential role required of them for cultural defense. This role is to construct a hermetically sealed social order among the vanquished, cutting it off so far as possible from cross-pressures emanating from the conquering power and its culture: passive resistance and pattern-maintenance until the time when political independence can be wrested from the conquering power.

A common complaint was voiced among British political elites dealing with Ireland at the turn of this century: "What do the Irish want? They wanted land reform, we gave them land reform; they wanted emancipation, we gave them emancipation. Yet nothing seems to be enough." In such cases, very typically, nothing *is* enough, since the primordial objective—often adhered to not merely for years or decades, but centuries—is independence. And along the way, it almost always seems to happen that a great and impassable gulf of understanding between people who belong to the dominant culture and those who belong to the subject culture develops and widens—even with the best will in the world.

But to this intractability must be added another. Canada is in some respects an almost unique case of multiple-layered "imperialisms." Ontario has profited most from Confederation. It is the powerhouse and center of Canadian capitalism. It has the most to lose if the Confederation breaks up. Both the Western provinces and Quebec have resented and attacked this dominance of the "center" over the "periphery" for many years. Its existence, and local reaction to it, is the prime reason for the existence of Western "populism" in electoral politics, as C.B. Macpherson has demonstrated.[2] Yet this domination of a "metropole" over the internal "colonies" is in itself a subset of the overwhelming American domination of the Canadian economy as a whole. In many respects, this penetration is unique among economic imperialisms, for it coexists with very high levels of technical, industrial, and social well-being in the "colonized" country. One of the implications to be derived from this experience is that—unlike situations in the Third World—the number and variety of Canadians who have an economic stake in the existing pattern of control is relatively large. This state would appear to preclude—though we cannot be wholly sure—any very major effort within Canada to attack the foundations of the country's "special relationship" with the United States.

The Impact of the Quiet Revolution

There is yet more to the story. The most decisive sociological fact about Quebec, apart from its enduring particularity, has been its abrupt transition from the country to the city, its industrial development squeezed within the space of a single generation. Not surprisingly, the role of the priests has declined, and quite new intellectual and political elites speaking for the "nation" of Quebec have arisen. It is precisely this process which has provided the fuel for the drive toward national independence for the heartland of French Canada. Why? Of course, there are general processes of social disruption which occur during the transition to industrial capitalism, and the more rapid the pace of industrialization the greater these disruptions are likely to be. The literature of "political development" is replete with analyses of this kind of problem. But there are also things specific to Quebec in this stormy development of economy and society. These, I believe, tell us something not only about the current Canadian problem but also about the recrudescence of national devolution movements throughout the Western world today, from Scots nationalism in Britain to the "rise" of French Occitania and Spanish Catolonia in the Mediterranean.

Late capitalism, like all other forms of social domination in history, has a hegemonic ideology which supports, rationalizes, and legitimates it. This ideology may be described as managerialist, bureaucratic, scientistic, and dedicated to the supremacy of instrumental rationality in socially-relevant thought processes. A major objective of the "organic intellectuals" (as Gramsci calls them[3]) who espouse this ideology is to convert all political issues into administrative issues, all substantive conflicts within society into debates over the proper technique of social engineering to be used in the particular case. This ideology is encountered in a myriad of forms and in the consciousness, writings, and speeches of a very wide variety of elites whose manifest partisan or other differences may appear to loom large. It is found among economists who assure us that free trade is the only rational way to organize international economic relations, among political scientists who are worried about the "governability problem" in contemporary Western societies, and among political leaders concerned with managing the "free world" and providing rational, comprehensive, nonpartisan, schemes for legislation to cope with issues such as the energy crisis.

This ideology shapes consciousness to accept instrumental rationality as the only valid thought process in dealing with questions of society and politics. In the end, its ineluctable tendency is to create a society of smoothly functioning and interchangeable parts, social atoms who can fit into organizational needs of the giant bureaucracies which dominate our lives. It is, consequently, fundamentally opposed to any solidaristic impulses arising from social communities or other collectivities which are not yet under bureaucratic control. Naturally, there is no space within this ideology for accepting the legitimacy of nationalist movements based on such collective social solidarities, least of all if the consequence of the rise of such solidarities is to increase the costs of doing business and to multiply the error terms in econometric equations.

Imperialism, Capitalism, and Canada's Future

So far as the Quebec-Canada situation is concerned, this reality has two chief implications. The first is that cultural defense—the *permanent* objective of the "nation" and its elites, however differently expressed symbolically at different times—requires and obtains new exigency. Hermetic isolation within the Confederation is no longer enough: Quebec is penetrated at every point by the cosmopolitan, collectivity-dissolving cultural instruments of the new economic order. Independence thus becomes the rallying cry. For their part, the "organic intellectuals" of the "nation" draw heavily on paradigms and slogans developed by the Left of Europe and the Third World in fulfilling their appointed role of mobilization. In the end they, too, will probably be drawn into the maw; but that is a discovery which, it seems, every national movement must make for itself.

The second implication of this argument is that the gulf of incomprehension between Quebec and elites in the rest of Canada can be expected to grow. The ideology of late capitalism is as widely, one may say unquestioningly, accepted in Ontario as it is among cosmopolitan elites and organic intellectuals in the United States. But to a French-Canadian national consciousness, it must be rejected as the work of the Devil himself (religious or secular). Thus, arguments made in the vein of instrumental-rational thought on behalf of the Confederation (it "pays," the economic/financial consequences to Quebec of separation will be disastrous, etc.) can only produce the opposite of their intended effect. Yet what other categories of social understanding do English-speaking cosmopolitan elites and organic intellectuals possess? How does one build bridges across this chasm?

I greatly admire Ms. MacDonald and the valiant effort she has made in her essay to provide a way out of the Canadian dilemma short of disunion. All of us who are well-wishers to both anglophones and francophones in Canada—and I count myself one—continue fervently to hope that goodwill and hard thinking about political structure will result in a restructuring of Canada short of dissolution. But I am bound to say, for reasons I hope have been made clear in these comments, that their task is vastly more formidable than that assumed by the American constitution-makers of 1787.

NOTES

1. Herbert Agar, *The Price of Union* (Boston: Houghton Mifflin, 1950).
2. C.B. Macpherson, *Democracy in Alberta* (Toronto: University of Toronto Press, 1953).
3. Antonio Gramsci, *The Prison Notebooks* (New York: International Publishers Co., 1971).

14_____THE LIBERAL APPROACH TO A RENEWED CONFEDERATION

John Roberts

Canadians are deeply ambivalent about the United States. In fact, the origins of this deep-rooted ambivalence are not difficult to find. Canada was formed and maintained by those who for one reason or another, good or bad, decided that they did not want to be part of the United States. Or, in many cases, people who decided to leave it. One original strong impetus to the formation of Canada came, for instance, from what we call the United Empire Loyalists—often called royalists or Tories in the United States—who decided after the Revolution that they did not want to stay in the new American experiment but wished to leave the United States in order to continue to live under the British Crown. They joined French-speaking Quebecers with deep roots in their land who, in spite of all the blandishments of Benjamin Franklin, resisted what they saw as a secular and peculiar society to the south of them.

Our differences were heightened by the war of 1812, and by the continuing raids across the border in the 1840s. Indeed, some of the motives for the establishment of the present constitution of Canada in 1867 can be traced directly to apprehension of American intentions— to the decision of the United States to end free trade with the British colonies, and the consequent Canadian search for economic security in union; and to the concern in Canada for what the United States, with the largest standing army in the world after its Civil War, might choose to do with that army in the pursuit of manifest destiny. This sense of difference between the two countries has been maintained by Canada's commitment in two world wars to enter the battle for freedom and democracy, in both cases at an earlier stage than that at which the United States saw fit to become involved.

If we look at the past of our two countries it must be confessed that while geography has made us neighbors, history has not always made us friends. But this sense of resistance to the United States—and it is deep within the Canadian character—takes place within a very strong context of friendship. We are both countries which have treasured and developed the tradition of British representative institutions. We adopted, and adapted, the form of federal government which you invented. We both were frontier societies which rejected the class structures of Europe, societies which still hold the ideal of the classless society, and therefore emphasize strongly the desirability of equality of opportunity.

The formation of the Canadian nation state in 1867 was a practical step devised to maintain Canadian peculiarities, to provide the basis for economic growth and to solve the immediate administrative, financial, and defense problems of the British colonies.

The classic conditions for the establishment and development of a federal state were described by K.C. Wheare:

> A federal government is appropriate for a group of communities if, at one and the same time, they desire to be united under a single independent general government for some purpose and to be polarised under independent regional governments for others.[1]

The future of the Canadian federation depends on our ability to sustain the existence of such a general, common interest shared by its constituent communities—especially its francophone and anglophone communities. It depends on the *perception* of that common interest, a *recognition* that common institutions are the best means for furthering that common interest, and an *act of will* to ensure that common institutions operate.

The first question then is: What is the common interest of anglophone and francophone Canadians in the Canadian federation? Its historic roots in the 19th century are clear. To simplify, they might be summarized briefly under two headings, as *negatively*, a concern for absorption by the United States, and *positively*, a desire to achieve material benefits through the establishment of a common market. The result of these two factors was a political arrangement whereby all benefited economically while preserving the integrity of their community and their culture.

These two motives have, as a foundation, sustained the Canadian federation for over a century, and with great success. The accomplishment in economic terms is great—the expansion and exploration of a continental economy. Though some may squabble over which region has benefited most—the fact is that *all* regions have benefited, and all would certainly suffer from its disruption.

Federalism—the federalism of Canada—has not caused the social and economic problems of Quebec. It has not been a conspiracy to keep Quebec as an internal colony, as Premier Lévesque described it in this volume, feeding the economic and social development of other regions of Canada. After the conquest, when Quebecers were abandoned—except for the Church—by the establishment which had come from France, Quebec consisted of 55,000 inhabitants. After two centuries of living together in Canada with an English-speaking population—after, as separatists would argue, two centuries of frustrations and neglect, if not oppression—look at present-day Quebec. Here is the description of one of the contributors of this book:

> ...now, at long last, Quebec is a fully developed society. It has over 6 million people, 82 per cent of whom are French by descent, language and cultural heritage. Montreal, our metropolis, is the second largest French city in the world. Our gross national product would make us twenty-third among the nations of the world, and eleventh on a per capita basis.

So spoke René Lévesque on January 25, 1977, to the Economic Club of New York. Federalism seems not to have been as bad for Quebec as some would have us believe. A few score thousand people settled on the banks of the St. Lawrence, poor, rural and withdrawn, have succeeded in transforming themselves into an important population, into a developed society which has attained a high level of well-being.

But if Quebecers have, within the center of Canada, built a strong society, what is the cause of the present discontent? Why do a significant number of Quebecers want to leave Canada? The reason is simple. For all their success in creating a durable community in North America, French-speaking Quebecers now feel faced with stronger pressures for assimilation to the North American anglophone society than has ever been the case in the past.

Various factors account for this sense of insecurity. The advent of modern technology and the development of an integrated North American communication and transportation system have threatened the integrity of the French language and culture. Urbanization has further eroded the solidarity of the French-Canadian identity. Fundamentally, the quiet revolution has "opened" up Quebec. It has provided an opportunity for Quebec to develop economically, socially, and materially. But it has "plugged in" Quebec more strongly than ever before to the economic and communications forces of North

America. In ending its isolation—a natural and advantageous step—Quebec risks losing the language and culture which are its personal heritage.

It is true that many French-speaking Quebecers perceive their English-speaking compatriots as the source of the threat to the survival of their language and culture. I would argue, however, that it is much more accurate to perceive that threat as emanating from the context of an English-speaking North America and that the real danger lies in the complete integration of Quebec into a North American economy.

In the age of multinationals, it is difficult to see how independence of action could be better achieved in a separated Quebec market than in a larger Canadian one. The fact is that the more fractured the economy of Canada becomes, the less power its constituent parts will have in determining their economic future, especially in the face of the pressures from the United States' economy and the interests of large multinational enterprises.

If there still is a common interest among francophone and anglophone Canadians based upon our concern over North American economic and cultural absorption, the question remains: Can this interest be met effectively outside a Canadian federal system?

I think the answer is clearly "no." The Parti Québécois answers, of course, "yes," and suggests now that "sovereignty-association" is a better formula for meeting the interests of French-speaking Quebecers. But "sovereignty-association" is a flim-flam formula. Association is not precisely defined. Moreover, it is not within the capacity of the government of Quebec even to obtain. It is hope with fingers crossed—a wish to be achieved, not a policy that the provincial government can deliver. To regions outside Quebec, "sovereignty-association" is simply the desire to throw out the cake and have it again the next day.

It would be a tragic mistake for French-speaking Quebecers to underestimate the strong emotional commitment of English-speaking Canadians to the idea of one Canada "from sea to sea." The traumatic effects of shattering that dream would be enormous. In the face of this trauma it is very unlikely that they will retain a desire to maintain a "common market." Very rarely in life do divorced couples preserve a joint banking account.

I am not, of course, alone in this view. The premiers of a number of provinces have already gone on record, saying clearly the same thing. If you shatter the *political* and cultural idea of Canada, then the counterpoise to American absorption will be gone, and the net effect will be that the powerful north-south forces in our economy and culture will assert themselves very strongly.

It is true that the remnants of Canada, after the separation of Quebec, would be driven to find association in larger markets. But let us be clear. It will not be with Quebec. Western Canadians would certainly prefer, with the collapse of Canada, free-trade arrangements with the larger United States market, and southern Ontario, with its manufacturing infrastructure and its close ties to United States industry and markets would probably follow the same path.

There is, I believe, another more important reason for arguing that the maintenance of the federal structure is essential for the common interest. It is that the protection of the French language and culture is *more strongly assured* within a Canadian federalism that makes concern with language and culture a central concern of politics.

The reality of Quebec in Canada has made us sensitive to, or more accurately, obsessed with, the question—how can a political system maintain its structure while at the same time acting to preserve the linguistic duality and cultural diversity of its constituent parts? In Canada we have wrestled with this problem for over 111 years. We have devised some solutions, such as the provincial role in education, the Languages Act, and the endorsement of multiculturalism as objectives for our society.

In our present crisis we do not lack suggestions—from associations, from businessmen, from politicians—on what new steps should be taken to overcome our discontent. Some have been presented in this book.

The most common suggestion is that the Canadian federal system should be further decentralized. "Decentralization" is not the magic wand which will resolve all our problems. There are those who confuse the "status quo" with "static." The federal division of powers has not been static. There has already been—at least since the mid-60s—a strong trend to decentralization in Canada. We now have one of the most decentralized countries in the world. There is no need to illustrate this in detail. One statistic will suffice. In 1966 the provinces and municipalities collected 20% of taxes; eight years later the figure was 42%. I do not condemn this past decentralization. Given Canada's social and cultural diversities, I think it is essential. But I am certainly not under the illusion that the decentralization of the past decade has diminished the forces of separation. There seems little basis in historical record to believe that further decentralization would retard forces of separation.

If we follow the direction of decentralization blindly, we risk undermining the capacity of the federal government to perform its essential tasks. We must maintain a viable federal authority in order to provide a national direction and a national capacity to address and solve the problems of managing our economy.

If we are to resist the forces of assimilation and integration into the North American continent, if Canada is to retain its own identity in the face of natural American influence, then all Canadians, including Quebecers, have an interest in preserving a strong federal government which has the capacity to protect that identity. To sap federal economic power would not lead to a strengthening of regional identities, but rather a weakening of our capacity to withstand the pressures for integration into the North American market. The separate provincial economies, or five regional ones, or even two shattered economies, would be in a situation of such disproportion that they would become mere appendages to the economy of the United States, and our national resources would be less likely to be exploited with Canadian interests first in mind.

Many of the real problems we face in Canada can only be solved if we maintain an ability to use federal power to coordinate economic strategies. In the modern world, economic policy cannot be made effectively by small-scale municipal or provincial units. National governments are the most effective mechanisms we possess to develop strategies for economic policy or to endeavor to make multinational corporations serve the national interest.

Another suggestion which has been presented to you is to change the Canadian Senate into a "House of the Provinces" through appointment by provinces or elections or some combination of the two. Let me say a few things about that.

Any structure of government is a captive of its own history: it is a complex of formalized rules, traditions, practices, and convenient adjustments. Any change in one part can have vast ramifications for the rest of the structure. A "House of the Provinces" will have major effects upon the nature of parliamentary government as it is practiced in Canada. The real question of a reformed Senate involves not its method of selection but its powers. If it is reformed to give it substantial and not simply formal powers it will undermine the basis of Cabinet responsibility to the Commons which is the key to parliamentary government. If it is not given substantial powers it is unlikely to be credible as a representative of provincial interests.

I have addressed two suggestions for the solution of our problems. A third relates to language and culture. One of the challenges to Canada is to find a way of giving an assurance to French-speaking Canadians of the future of their language and its culture. That is at the heart of their concerns over the future. It is the root of the uncertainty over the future of our country. It is the fuel which feeds separatism in Quebec.

If we are to make the case honestly that a Quebec in Canada is more likely to protect the language rights of French-speaking Canadians than a Quebec outside Canada, it can only be done if we agree that their rights to language are protected within a state of 23 million people—in Canada as a whole, not just in one part of it. Otherwise, French-speaking Quebecers will look inward, relying only on their own society.

On the whole, in spite of some errors, this policy has been successful; but in spite of our success we need to do more: we must overcome the sense of insecurity which French-speaking Canadians experience by enshrining language and cultural rights within the constitution. This is a difficult area because in order for it to be effective, we must persuade provincial governments to accept the principles of our official Languages Act within their jurisdictions. The onus for the achievement of those principles cannot fall on the federal government alone.

National unity is not just a question of language rights—it is also a matter of making regional voices heard effectively in the national government. And it is a question of ensuring that the economic benefits of the Canadian union are shared throughout the country.

But the issue of language rights is fundamental to national unity. I believe that those rights, along with the other fundamental individual freedoms, should be entrenched in our constitution—entrenched against the interference of federal and provincial governments alike.

I have suggested that enshrining language rights within a new constitution is one concrete act the federal government should now undertake. I have also mentioned the need to provide for greater regional representation and sensitivity in federal institutions.

All too often we think of the Canadian situation as sets of problems. The relationship of French-speaking Canadians to English-speaking Canadians is a problem. "Problems" are in some ways reassuring. They are neat, tidy, and definitive. A problem has a "solution," an answer, one answer which settles the matter forever. It is utopian to believe that many of our "problems" are capable of such definitive resolution.

Tensions between French-speaking and English-speaking Canadians, tensions between the provinces, the federal government, tensions among the economic regions of Canada, tensions between Canada and the United States, have been the stuff of Canada politics for two centuries, they will be the stuff of it for the next two centuries, they will never be "solved." They are tensions which can be fruitful as well as, occasionally, constraints. They are an opportunity as well as an obstacle.

NOTES

1. Kenneth C. Wheare, *Federal Government* (New York: Oxford University Press, 1963).

14____THE LIBERAL APPROACH TO A RENEWED CONFEDERATION

COMMENT

Elliot J. Feldman

There are three central, interrelated points in John Roberts' essay on a renewed Canadian Confederation. First, the Secretary of State attributes Canada's constitutional crisis chiefly to Québécois dissatisfaction. Second, he explains Québécois dissatisfaction in terms of forces internal to Quebec—the Quiet Revolution—and external to Canada—North American technology and culture, "North American" being a code term for the Untied States; Ottawa, he implies, is in no way responsible for Quebec separatism. Third, he identifies the common interests of anglophone and francophone Canadians as the need "to resist the forces of assimilation and integration into the North American continent."

These points constitute a message to Quebec. Your unhappiness, the Secretary of State tells Québécois, is due to pressures on your language and culture from the United States; Canada will protect you from these pressures and from the United States-based multinational corporations. Furthermore, Confederation has delivered you economic growth but other provinces will not negotiate a new common market with you. Therefore, your economic well-being depends upon continuation in the present system.

Mr. Roberts' essay, in presenting this argument, is at odds with the other essays in this volume. Gordon Gibson, Flora MacDonald, Richard Simeon, and Gordon Stead all regard Ottawa as an important cause of the present crisis, and none of them isolates Quebec as a lone challenger to Confederation; Frank Peers and Ian McDougall both perceive a threat from the United States, but they explain failures to protect Canadian culture and resources more in terms of Canadian decisions than in terms of aggressive pressure from U.S. multi-nationals or "North American" technology. Neither the former Premier of Quebec, Robert Bourassa, nor the present Premier, René Lévesque, expresses any anxiety over potential assimilation into

North America, nor do they indicate any desire to be protected from the United States economy. Mordecai Richler expressly denies John Roberts' suggestion that anglophone and francophone Canadians share a common identity.

Competing Perceptions of History

Many of the apparent disagreements between the Secretary of State and other contributors to this book arise from competing interpretations of history. Mr. Roberts tells us that the Confederation was founded "to maintain Canadian particularities." Gordon Gibson, however, calls Confederation a "business deal," and Walter Dean Burnham implies that Confederation confirmed the conquest of the French. Mr. Roberts emphasizes the "desire to achieve material benefits through the establishment of a common market," yet Peter Gourevitch emphasizes Quebec's desire to protect its own institutions. Mr. Roberts insists that Quebec has reaped great economic benefits from Confederation, yet François-Pierre Gingras illustrates a gap between Québécois aspirations and expectations, and he blames Ottawa for encouraging social mobility without economic improvement relative to the rest of Canada.

Mr. Roberts' history is the history of Canada as seen from Ontario. He recognizes only the Ontario incentives for Confederation. He understands disruption in an efficient system as originating in the backwaters of Quebec, out of ignorance. If the Québécois understood what central Canada had done for them, if they appreciated how they have been protected and nurtured so that their once-tiny settlement could flourish on an inhospitable continent, they would not behave so ungratefully. Indeed, the history of Canada, Mr. Roberts suggests, involves well-meaning anglophones in Ottawa laboring for the greater good despite selfish demands from citizens elsewhere.

Responding to Criticism

Although several authors in this volume are prominent critics of present federal arrangements, Mr. Roberts addresses none of their criticisms because he rejects their analyses. Consequently, his proposals for the renewal of Confederation do not seem to correspond to the challenges.

Ms. MacDonald and Messers. Gibson, Simeon, Stead, and Gourevitch all suggest that the federal establishment has encroached on provincial authority. Mr. Roberts replies that Canada is perhaps the most decentralized country in the world, offering the same lone statistic as Prime Minister Trudeau at the Economic Club of New York in March 1978.[1] However, tax collection data reveal nothing about the federal guidelines which, until this past year at least, have governed provincial expenditure. Nor do they reveal the constitutionally-determined shift from Ottawa to the provinces in the costs of governmental responsibilities. Even then, using data of this kind, Sweden, for example, relies much more heavily on local taxation than does Canada. More importantly, taxes do not of themselves constitute power. As Gordon Stead points out, the parliamentary system is a centralizing force which defines power on a unitary model. In my own research on airport development in Canada and in four other advanced industrial Western countries, I have found Canada easily the most centralized in its organization and management of vital decisions.[2] France, commonly considered the quintessential centralized system, has no concentration of power to rival Ottawa's.

Messers. Gibson, Lévesque, and Gourevitch all suggest that portions of Canada might be better off economically as separate states. Mr. Roberts replies that "all would certainly suffer from [the Confederation's] disruption." No one denies an immediate economic dislocation, however. Rather, the other authors indicate long-term benefit; they also tend to deny, along with Gingras, Parenti, Smith, MacDonald, and Burnham, the primacy of the economic issue.

What's in Confederation for Quebec?

Confederation must stand, Secretary Roberts says, as a "counterpoise to American absorption." He says Canada provides Quebec with a shield against the multinational corporation. Walter Gordon, however, the former Liberal Minister of Finance, writes in this volume that the federal government has failed totally to defend Canada against the impact of the multinational corporation. Robert Bourassa, the former Liberal Premier of Quebec, favors foreign investment in Quebec and in Canada. Prime Minister Trudeau told the Economic Club of New York, "Let it be quite clear that foreign investment is welcome in Canada, that we need it, that we want it, and that we hope it will come." The Foreign Investment Review Agency may have changed the investment atmosphere, but it has not changed the balance of foreign investment. Indeed, as Prime Minister Trudeau also told the Economic Club, "The fact is that we are the industrialized nation with the highest percentage of foreign investment of any." Mr. Roberts contends that small units, or a fragmented Canada, would fare less well, but Sweden, Norway, and Switzerland all compare favorably with the larger and more heavily populated Canada.

The issue is not size, then, but ideology. The desire to increase the presence of foreign capital is, as Michael Parenti implies, characteristic of a lesser developed country. The Trudeau-Roberts position is, on the one hand, to resist the impact of the United States while, on the other hand, to encourage American investment. This ambivalence, a practical outcome of the uncertainty noted by Mr. Roberts at the outset of his essay, is ideological. Canada, it would appear, wants (with the exception of economic nationalists such as Walter Gordon) an ambivalent position in world capitalism: to be treated both as an advanced industrial country and as a member of the Third World. Moreover, Premiers Bourassa and Lévesque do not appear so concerned about the influence of foreign capital, although the Canadian Secretary of State thinks they should. If they indeed were concerned, the present record of protection against the intruding multinationals would not be very heartening.

The social side of this economic picture involves Canadian identity. Mr. Roberts suggests that there is a Canadian identity derived, in part, from the presence of francophone Quebec. Like Prime Minister Trudeau, Mr. Roberts asserts that this identity needs to be preserved against the United States. However, the distinguished Canadian sociologist John Porter has observed:

> Non-French Canadians, at least at the level of political rhetoric, and sometimes intellectual inquiry, search for what is essentially Canadian in the fact of biculturalism and a bi-national state. Something new supposedly is generated by the two major groups, but in effect the cultural division is so great that neither group breaks through the barriers of its own culture. The French struggle to retain their identity, while the non-French are looking for one.[3]

In suggesting that the French should rally to the defense of a pan-Canadian identity, Mr. Roberts asks the French to sacrifice the very thing for which he says they are fighting.

Proposals for Unity and the Constitutional Amendment Bill

Quebec has neither an economic nor a political complaint,

according to Mr. Roberts, and the complaint over language and culture is the consequence of being North American, despite Canada's efforts to provide protection. Mr. Roberts therefore psychoanalyzes Quebec in seeking a solution to the present crisis: "We must overcome the sense of insecurity which French-speaking Canadians experience," he writes, "by enshrining language and cultural rights within the constitution." He insists that language and culture constitute the "heart of the issue."

The Constitutional Amendment Bill (1978) followed logically from Mr. Roberts' analysis of the Canadian crisis, and his comments on certain proposed reforms are particularly revealing of the apparent intentions of the Bill. He wants to enshrine language and cultural rights, even though such rights are already protected in Article 133 of the British North America Act. He appeals for "greater regional representation and sensitivity in federal institutions," yet beyond the House of the Federation and the selection of Supreme Court judges, neither he nor his government offers a single proposal for the achievement of either representation or sensitivity.

Gibson, Simeon, and MacDonald call for Senate reform and so does Secretary Roberts, but the institutions they have in mind have little in common. Other authors here perceive a need for revision in the locus of fundamental decision-making authority; the Liberal government, however, intends to increase representation at the expense of power. Decentralization is bluntly rejected; the new Senate, perhaps more representative, would have even less power than the discarded institution which is already, in Flora MacDonald's words, "a bit of a joke." Participation in government may take the form of advice; consent remains confined, however, to federal authorities, especially the Cabinet.

Conclusion

What John Roberts has attempted here is a fusion of Canada's two post-World War II crises. The first crisis came with growing independence from Great Britain and the rise of technology. On the one hand, as Willis Armstrong, Joel Rosenbloom, and Alan Henrikson point out, more identity with the United States improved Canada's economy and Canada's international status. On the other hand, as Walter Gordon and Frank Peers argue, the removal of economic and commercial decisions to the United States robbed Canada of sovereignty. The result was what Mr. Roberts calls "ambivalence," but he translates this ambivalence into a rallying cry for the preservation of Canadian Confederation. He adopts the position of the Canadian nationalist.

The second postwar crisis stems from the growth of government responsibilities and functions, the profound geographic and ethnic shifts of Canada's population, and the emergence of a more confident and assertive Quebec. After World War II, when governments assumed greater responsibility for activities such as welfare, health, and education, the provinces accepted responsibilities allocated to them under the British North America Act and stepped in. But the federal government, eager to protect its status as the superior authority in the Canadian system, encroached upon provincial prerogative. Municipalities, for example, are strictly within the jurisdiction of the provinces, according to Article 92 of the British North America Act, yet the Liberal government created a federal Ministry of State for Urban Affairs in order to influence municipal decision-making.[4] Economic development lay within provincial jurisdiction (also according to Article 92), but the Liberal government created a Department for Regional Economic Expansion with the express purpose of affecting economic development choices through public works and the federal purse. As Robert Art points out in this volume, Canada came of age—with an arrogant bureaucracy and a highly visible and forceful central government.

The shift of power westward, discussed by both Peter Gourevitch and Gordon Stead, and this developing conflict between the provinces and Ottawa, created the conditions for a constitutional crisis. At the same time, Québécois perceived the Quebec state as a viable vehicle for their economic, political, and social—their national—aspirations. The Quiet Revolution sharpened a consciousness of class conflict[5] and, according to Dale Posgate and Kenneth McRoberts, "the emancipation of the [francophone workers] involves the emancipation of Quebec from Canada."[6] Today's crisis emerged out of the collision of these forces.

The United States did not figure among the forces of the second postwar crisis. Indeed, it has been in the midst of the present crisis that relations between Canada and the United States have warmed as never before.[7] While Mr. Roberts sounds the alarm against North American homogeneity, his Prime Minister calls for greater investment and tourism, more contact and exchange. If the two postwar crises can be related, it would not appear to be in the manner Mr. Roberts perceives. Rather, it may be that federal authorities look to the United States as a most important and likely ally in the crisis of unity.

By reducing the present disagreements to language, culture, questionable economics, and Quebec, Mr. Roberts understates the concerns of his fellow Canadians. As Walter Dean Burnham warns, such functionalist arguments gravely misread the depth and complexity of the situation. If the common interest should prove little more than a common resistance to the United States and a common desire for a chicken in every pot, there may be little of a Canadian nation to save. And Ottawa must confront criticisms more directly in order to save what there is. Admirers of Canada, and I count myself one, look to Canadian imagination and ingenuity so that union may be preserved.

NOTES

1. Address of Prime Minister Pierre Elliot Trudeau to the Economic Club of New York, March 22, 1978.

2. The study included airport planning in Italy, France, Great Britain, the United States, and Canada.

3. John Porter, *The Vertical Mosaic* (Toronto: University of Toronto Press, 1965), p. 35.

4. Elliot J. Feldman and Jerome Milch, "Coordination or Control? Federal Initiatives in Canadian Cities." Paper presented to the Annual Meeting of the American Political Science Association, New York, September 1, 1978. The ministerial effort failed and the government abolished the Ministry of State for Urban Affairs, effective March 31, 1979.

5. See discussions in Sheilagh Hodgins Milner and Henry Milner, *The Decolonization of Quebec* (Toronto: McClelland and Steward, 1973); Marcel Rioux, "Remarks on the Socio-Cultural Development of French Canada," in Marcel Rioux and Yves Martin, *French Canadian Society, Volume 1* (Toronto: McClelland and Steward, 1969); Richard Hamilton and Maurice Pinard, "The Bases of Parti Québécois Support in Recent Quebec Elections," *Canadian Journal of Political Science*, March 1976, pp. 3-26; Leo Pantich, ed., *The Canadian State: Political Economy and Political Power* (Toronto:University of Toronto Press, 1977).

6. Dale Posgate and Kenneth McRoberts, *Quebec: Social Change*

and Political Crisis (Toronto: McClelland and Stewart, 1976).

7. Lily Gardner Feldman, "Canada and the United States in the 1970s: Rift and Reconciliation," in *The World Today*, December 1978, pp. 484-492.

Part Five

CONCLUSION

15____NATIONALISM, STATES, AND NATIONS

Neil Nevitte

The theme of nationalism is present in nearly all the preceding essays, yet there is very little explicit discussion or debate about its role in the Confederation crisis. Quebec's status in Canada, the potential for Western independence, the competing interests of Canada and the United States—all are subjects involving assumptions about nationalism and its relationship to the nation-state. The elaboration of this theme can provide a useful framework and give coherence to the diverse diagnoses and prescriptions offered in this volume and in constitutional debates throughout Canada.

Definitions

Nationalism

Successive rounds of debate over the concept of nationalism have dispelled some important myths.[1] One myth concerns the perceived consequences of nationalism, rather than nationalism itself. Some argue, for example, that nationalism entails "militancy,"[2] "exaggerated or unjustified behavior,"[3] and that nationalism should be regarded as "a source of grave abuses and evils."[4] Generally, however, scholars now recognize that nationalism does not necessarily entail extremist, pathological, or unreasonable behavior.

A second general area of agreement is related to the first. It used to be argued that nationalism involves a particular ideological coloration or regime style. Carlton Hayes, for example, connects fascism with nationalism in coining the expression "integral nationalism,"[5] which is later linked to "totalitarian nationalism." For the most part, this perspective, too, has fallen into disrepute. A comparison of many contemporary nationalist movements shows that nationalism may be appropriated by many regime styles with widely different ideological

frameworks. Unless nationalism itself is taken to be a discrete ideology (and some think that it is),[6] Elie Kedourie's point of view seems
to make the most sense: "It is a mistake," he says, "to ask whether
nationalism is politics of the right or politics of the left. It is
neither."[7]

These broad areas of agreement reflect a consensus about what
nationalism is *not*, rather than what it *is*. Still, there are reasons to
suggest that the context, consequences, and intensity of nationalism
are variable dimensions of a phenomenon which has a more general
character. Because many of the current definitions of nationalism are
lengthy and complex, brevity and simplicity may be significant
advantages.

Here, in its minimal form, nationalism is taken to mean *the making
of claims in the name or on behalf of the nation*. First, this definition
emphasizes a process by focusing on the activity of claim-making. It is
not sufficient to view nationalism as a state of mind or simply as
loyalty to the nation because these formulations imply that
nationalism may be understood as only a latent or passive phenomenon.

Second, this formulation does not attempt to specify the content,
scope, or mode of expression of the national claims. In addition, it
does not try to limit nationalism to any particular individual or group;
nor does it restrict its origin to the advent of nationalist political
parties. While these parties may dominate the formal avenues of claim-
making, the origins of nationalist movements often can be traced
to artists, poets, and others who create and transmit the national
idea. Literary guilds, language societies, religious associations, for
example, commonly precede nationalist political parties as the
creators and articulators of the nation, and they frequently have
provided the first national elites.[8] In short, this definition allows individuals or groups to be nationalists under one set of circumstances but
not others; they may be nationalists at one moment but not another,
over one issue but not over all. But the preeminent and distinguishing
feature of nationalism is, of course, that the claim-making activity is
necessarily and logically linked to the nation.

The Nation and the State

The terms "nation," "state," and "nation-state" should not be used
interchangeably. Essentially, the state consists of a legally defined

relationship between a governing body and a social group which, together, are delineated territorially. The *International Relations Dictionary*, for example, refers to the state as "a legal concept describing a social group that occupies a defined territory and is organized under common political institutions and effective government."[9] Alternatively, "the state refers to the sovereign political organization which governs people encompassed by a particular territory."[10] There is little disagreement about the boundaries and the essential characteristics of the state.

The nation is much harder to define. Scholars frequently suggest that common language, geography, race, religion, etc. are usually useful ways to recognize a nation.[11] Such objective socio-structural indicators are ultimately, however, an inadequate basis for a definition of the term nation'. Ernest Renan argued as early a 1882 that none of the conditions of common geography or territory, language, race, or religion meets the critical test of being either necessary or sufficient conditions for the existence of a nation.[12] He reckons that if none of these socio-structural characteristics is necessary to establish the existence of the nation then they must be distinct from it. The conclusion, by default, is that we should pay attention to the subjective character of the nation.[13] Thus Max Weber, continuing in Renan's tradition, posits that the nation cannot be stated in terms of empirical qualities common to those who count as members; rather, the concept belongs to the sphere of values.[14]

Scholars who focus on the subjective dimension speak of the nation as embodying "common sentiments," a "collective consciousness," or "shared assumptions." But specification of the precise dimensions of the nation has proved as difficult as the problem faced by anthropologists in elaborating the concept of "culture"; the similarity, moreover, may be more than coincidental. John Plamenatz, for one, fashions an explicit association between culture and nation:

> I say national or cultural, for what distinguishes a people from one another in their own eyes consists of ways of thinking, feeling and behaving which are, or which they believe to be, peculiar to them.[15]

The nation may be viewed as the political dimension of culture. But membership, for Renan and others, involves more than latent sharing of a common culture; it has a voluntaristic dimension. It is for this reason that Renan speaks of the nation as a "daily plebiscite"[16] and Hans Kohn, emphasizing the collectivity, refers to the nation as a "corporate will."[17]

Distinguishing Nation from State

Because the nation and the state are different we should not expect the boundaries of the nation and the state to coincide. In fact, one scholar has calculated that nations and states coincide, i.e., form "nation-states," only about ten percent of the time.[18] The corollary is that membership in the nation should not be equated with membership in the state. Variations in the dimensions of the national constituency derive from the subjective choice involved in identifying with the nation. People can and do assume, learn, accept, and reject different national identifications. Indeed, as Weber and others have noted, nationalists, especially radical nationalists, are often of foreign descent.[19]

Secondly, because the nation is substantially different from the state and because the nation, logically, is the only referent of nationalism, definitions such as Kalman Silvert's, which identify nationalism as the "acceptance of the state as the impersonal arbiter of human affairs,"[20] are fundamentally misleading. It is only by maintaining the distinction between the nation and the state that the disintegrative potential of nationalism can be appreciated: the claims of nationalists can be directed *against the state.*

The central assumption of all nationalists is that their nation is different from others and that those differences are worth preserving. The essays in this volume refer to alternative strategies for enhancing and preserving national differences; they are concerned with the process of nation-building, and nationalism may be a part as well as a result of that process.

The nationalist debate in Canada is especially complex because the two dominant images, Canada as "One Country" and Canada as "Two Nations," involve two different sets of assumptions about the most significant unit of analysis. On the one hand, "One Country" theorists like to equate the nation with the state; they emphasize the differences between Canada and the United States. On the other hand, "Two Nations" theorists, especially Québécois, are interested in upholding the distinction between the nation and the state and emphasizing that national differences exist within Canada. Nation-building and national integration hold very different meanings for each perspective. Thus the two dominant images of Canada appear incompatible; they suggest that Canada's present conflicts may be insoluble.

Canadian Nation-Building and the United States

The process of Canadian national development has taken place in the context of a powerful, outward-looking, unified nation-state—the United States. It is not surprising that the claims made on behalf of the Canadian nation are directed frequently against the United States.

Many similarities and differences between Canada and the United States are played out in the arena of foreign policy. According to Allan Gotlieb, Canadian foreign policy initiatives in Latin America, sub-Saharan Africa, China, Western Europe, and elsewhere are manifestations of peculiarly Canadian interests. For Gotlieb these interests are rooted in historical, structural, and geopolitical factors that set Canada clearly apart from the United States. For example, Canada's link to the Commonwealth "has no parallel in the context of American foreign policy." The uniqueness of Canada's foreign policy is, he says, a measure of Canada's autonomy from the United States. But in the final analysis, the "fundamental political contrast between the United States and Canada," according to Gotlieb, stems from "the quantitative and qualitative difference between a superpower and a middle power."

Perhaps Gotlieb doth protest too much. Despite all of the emphasis on differences, Gotlieb admits that Canada shares in the United States' "vital culture, powerful economy, and cornerstone role in Western security." The Third Option policy orientation reflects Canada's need for networks and associations to act as political counterweights against the pull of the United States.

Unconvinced by Gotlieb's attempt to show that Canadian foreign policy flies free of the U.S. orbit, Alan Henrikson counters by arguing that Canada's foreign policy, "even in its far-flung manifestations, is a function of Canada's proximity to the United States." Henrikson is unimpressed by Gotlieb's claims about Canada's "moral autonomy." Indeed, he implies that Gotlieb indulges in sleight of hand by ignoring the nice but crucial distinction between "what Canada can achieve on its own and what it can only accomplish in partnership with the United States." Canadian "leadership" in the case of China is an example, Henrikson contends, for Canada acted like a waiting room for an emerging Sino-American courtship.

The second component of Henrikson's position relates to how others see Canada and the U.S. To others, Henrikson argues, "the images projected by Canada and the United States are often indistinguishable." Moreover, he adds, "both governments are unlikely to

be able to reduce this perceived identification." A realistic determination of Canadian-U.S. relations augmented by the external perceptions of that relationship, Henrikson argues, logically calls for a
"systematically developed" North American diplomacy with "greater
coordination," which would make American as well as Canadian
diplomacy "more reliable" and "more effective" and would open up
"new vistas" for both countries.

According to Henrikson, there are two options open to Canada. It
can remain doomed to live with the "faint image of a neutral" and
"stand alone" as a "moderating moderated middle power." Alternatively, Canada can submit to reason, take advantage of its relationship with the United States and, Henrikson promises, "step to the
front as a leading power."

There are perhaps two options, but is there a real choice? Henrikson
argues that a North American partnership in diplomacy "need not
detract from the identity of either." At the same time he says "one
cannot deny the risk in the suggested program to Canada's wonted
freedom of action," its "distinctiveness." Henrikson artfully implies
that there is no necessary contradiction in these views; Canadians are
to some extent reluctant Americans.

Is foreign policy a true reflection of Canada's autonomy from the
United States? There is no question that comparing foreign policies
provides a useful sketch of the different aspirations and capabilities of
Canada and the United States, but the extent to which Canadian
foreign policy is a measure of Canada's national development is
equivocal at best. Foreign policy is about the interaction of states; it
has a centrist bias which deflects from the crucial distinction between
the nation and the state. Moreover, because Ottawa is responsible for
Canadian foreign policy, it is in the arena of foreign policy that
Canada appears most united. The federal government promotes ideals
that have been unobtainable at home. While we cannot rest
exclusively on foreign policy as a reliable yardstick of Canada's
national development, the Gotlieb-Henrikson exchange thus fixes the
broad perimeters for more detailed debate.

One Country?

Given the nationalism framework, the central question is not
whether Canada, as a state, is separate from the United States; it is
whether a Canadian nation exists independently of the United States.
Because this question cannot be answered by comparing foreign

policies, we must consider the progress of nation-building within Canada.

Through Culture and Commerce

The process of collective self-differentiation is usually the domain of cultural elites who articulate the national idea. Mordecai Richler points to important changes in the orientations of such a cultural elite—Canadian writers—in this role. The 1950s, he says, were years of "internationalism" when Canadian writers looked to advance their careers under "foreign skies." The war for Canada's "cultural integrity," when Canadian *literati* first started to react against the cultural spillover from the United States, only began in earnest in the 1960s. Thus, it is not surprising that Canadian literature, in Richler's estimation, is still linked to the U.S. literary tradition and that Canada is still a "cultural branch plant" of the United States.

But how could such a cultural battle for the nation be won? Protectionism, calling for one set of standards for Canadian artists and a different set for others, Richler warns, is false strategy. "Hysteria is no shield," he says, "and chauvinism an unacceptable armor." Protectionism can mummify as well as incubate fledgling national cultures.

The commercial power of the United States is another major factor that has conditioned the Canadian collective character. Foreign investment, of course, is a mixed blessing, and most economists, Walter Gordon included, acknowledge that U.S. investment helped to develop the Canadian economy more rapidly than would otherwise have been the case. But Gordon argues that the cost of this early and rapid development has been too high. First, the presence of foreign corporations tends to reduce job opportunities while increasing the deficit in the Canadian balance of payments, and second, the scale of U.S. commercial penetration threatens Canadian autonomy, encouraging the idea that Canada is "just another state of the Union" rather than a "separate sovereign nation."

The Role of Ottawa

The scope of American cultural and economic penetration into Canada leads several authors in this volume to focus on Ottawa's ability to generate and execute policies which protect and nurture the Canadian national identity. According to Walter Gordon, the commercial solution is for Ottawa to persuade foreign-owned enterprises to sell their assets to Canadians. This remedy is calculated, in part, to contribute to the process of self differentiation from the U.S. Frank Peers, similarly, outlines how Canada's communications system developed with the goals of forging a national identity and protecting it from the vital culture next door. So much for theory. According to Peers, the track record of Canada's communications policy has been littered with inconsistencies. And—Catch-22—these inconsistencies may be "a product of the ambivalence of Canadians themselves and the continuing influence exerted on them by American institutions, American values, American culture, and American success." The problem is, in part, that communications networks carry messages between the United States and Canada just as efficiently as between Canadians. More than that, Canadians often prefer the messages that come from the U.S.

Although Canadian nationalists may look to Ottawa to promote identity, Joel Rosenbloom contends that, rather than protecting Canada's cultural soul by fending off U.S. values, the Canadian federal government has gone out of its way to encourage the reception of American broadcast stations in Canada. Indeed, he says, "the CRTC has licensed Canadian cable systems not only to carry American signals but, where necessary, to reach out for those signals by means of microwave, over hundreds of miles." For Ottawa, Rosenbloom charges, "national identity has been nothing but a fig leaf of principle to cover their naked desire for gain."

As Walter Gordon looks to Ottawa to promote a pan-Canadian national economy and Frank Peers looks to Ottawa for leadership in communications, so Ian McDougall concentrates on Ottawa's role in natural resources. The astute management of Canada's natural resources, the country's greatest asset, might have provided a firm anchor for national unity. Instead, McDougall argues, Ottawa's policies have been haphazard and the federal government has stood by while the provinces underbid each other for the opportunity to serve American export markets. McDougall concludes that the national identity is obscure because national unity is endangered—and both because "Ottawa has failed to act on its constitutional responsibilities" by "not calling upon the wide range of constitutional powers that are available to it."

Of course, the central government's power is determined by more than formal constitutional authority. Canada's crisis, some argue, is caused by the inability of "national" institutions to perform their integrative tasks and produce nationwide, or Canada-wide support. Flora MacDonald, for example, points out that neither of the two major federal political parties can claim a national constituency: the Liberals have little support in the West, and the Progressive Conservatives have virtually none in Quebec. Her solution, like Richard Simeon's, is to harness the provincial political systems to the service of the national cause. This solution, of course, admits that the provinces are the true center of political gravity.

The bureaucracies of central governments are often considered important national integrators; they are supposed to combine expertise and other resources for a broad national purpose. According to Gordon Stead's diagnosis, however, the Canadian federal bureaucracy has failed to live up to these ideals. Several factors are involved: the changing role of the ministers, new responsibilities foisted upon senior bureaucrats, and the lack of public accountability which produces a weak bridge between the public will and policy initiatives. But Stead's argument goes even further. He contends that because Ontario has greater access to the avenues of influence in Ottawa, the values that are promoted by the federal bureaucracy are not national values at all; they mostly reflect the interests of the core, Ontario. And Jerome Milch, pursuing Stead's argument one step further, suggests that the organization of the bureaucracy precludes an integrative role regardless of regional orientation. Both Stead and Milch warn that Ottawa is an unlikely source of conflict resolution.

Gordon Stead's argument provides support for a more general hypothesis advanced by Peter Gourevitch. Gourevitch argues that when the economic and political centers of gravity coincide, peripheral nationalism is unlikely. Quebec's peripheral nationalism occurs as a response to the progressive divergence and dislocation of the economic center from the political center, or vice versa. Specifically, as Canada's economic center of gravity has shifted westward, decreasing Ontario's economic dominance, it becomes increasingly disruptive to promote an Ontario-centric view as if it represented the interests of the Canadian state. In short, institutions which might have been marshalled to forge "one country" have not only failed—they have sometimes intensified the forces of disintegration. It seems that Canada is still in the early stages of nation-building, and the image of one Canada remains more goal than reality.

Two Nations

The "Two Nations" interpretation of Canada, commonly is posed as an alternative to the "One Country" image. From this perspective Canada is pictured as a binational state and the implication is that Canada has two national histories, two sets of national symbols, two groups of national elites and two of all of the other things necessary for maintaining two distinct national societies.[21] The dominant assumption is that the two national identities correspond to Canada's two founding cultures, the British and the French.

A Quebec Nation

Members of the majority culture sometimes express impatience, even rancor, with the "Two Nations" interpretation.[22] After all, it represents a radical challenge to the legitimacy of the Canadian state. The burden of proving the existence of a distinct Quebec nation seems to fall into the lap of the cultural minority, the French Canadians.

Many of the authors in this volume summarize the basic distinctions between Québécois and other Canadians. Prime Minister Lévesque explains that cultural differences mean more than just language; culture is expressed through institutions, symbols, and traditions which become transformed with time. The buoyancy of national feeling can be inferred from the victory of the Parti Québécois and other data which specifically explore the subjective orientations of Québécois.[23] According to most of those criteria, the Quebec nation is alive and well.

The vitality of the Quebec nation stems from the success of past nation-building efforts. But why has Quebec succeeded where, to date, Canada has failed? History shows that Quebec has enjoyed important advantages over the rest of Canada in the nation-building process. First, Quebec has been in the business of nation-building longer. French Canadians were cut off from Europe, "abandoned," as John Roberts would have it, right from the start. As a result, French Canadians had to become self-reliant; they had to develop on their own, and early weaning led to early maturation. Quebec produced its own national leaders and its own distinct national institutions.

Second, Britain's style of colonial rule encouraged the cohesion of French Canadian society. Britain's goal of cheap and effective administration was achieved by utilizing the existing infrastructure of indigenous elites. The Roman Catholic Church filled this role; it was the only institution capable of administering French Canadian society effectively. In return for insuring French Canadians' loyalty to the Crown during Britain's conflict with the United States, clerical elites secured guarantees for the protection of French Canadians' religious rights. This protection found broad interpretation in a society where the Church controlled education, welfare, health, and other important social and economic institutions.

The colonial administration purposely drew the boundaries of Lower Canada to coincide with, and therefore contain, the great concentration of French Canadians. It was in this religiously and culturally homogenous milieu that the extension of religious rights was the functional equivalent of extending national rights.[24]

In short, the initial bargain between the colonial and the clerical elites established the pattern for future bargains. The mechanisms for French Canada's cultural survival became crystallized with the evolution of Canada's constitution, particularly with the Quebec Act and later with the British North America Act. Maximizing provincial rights became the best way to guarantee the cultural integrity of French Canadians, at least in Quebec.

Of course, there have been many obstacles confronting Quebec nation-builders. Being a numerical minority in a democratic political system poses obvious disadvantages. Demographic forces have worked to integrate French Canadians into the majority culture. The structure of economic rewards has favored the anglophone culture, thereby providing French Canadians incentives to become more anglicized. Nevertheless, Québécois have resisted total assimilation. As a result of this history, Quebec is not just a province or a region: it is a unique and politically potent fusion of three out of the four images described by Flora MacDonald: Quebec stands as a province, a region, and a nation.

Quebec's leaders, of course, acknowledge, that some factors, such as economics, are crucial variables in determining the future of the province. Both Robert Bourassa and René Lévesque foresee a Quebec that will continue to be integrated into the North American economy and, notwithstanding Michael Parenti's warnings of economic dependence, they want to attract more foreign investment into the province. Bourassa is persuaded that as long as Quebec is tied economically to the rest of Canada the forces for functional integration will override the impulse for cultural disintegration and help keep Quebec inside Confederation; Lévesque seeks more foreign investment for Quebec, in part because he is confident that Quebec's national identity is strong enough to withstand assimilation into the majority culture. The strength of the Quebec nation, in one sense, is a measure of the weakness of the Canadian nation.

The "Other" Nation

Demonstrating the existence of the Quebec nation is sometimes considered adequate justification for endorsing the "Two Nations" image of Canada. But some of the authors in this volume, along with a handful of other scholars,[25] challenge the logic which automatically links the majority culture with the "other nation." This reasoning underplays the significance of the divisions within the "other nation." There are several.

First, there are important geopolitical cleavages. Whereas Quebec has fused territory, culture, and political organization to produce a relatively cohesive national unit, the "other nation" has not. The rest of Canada consists of four regions, nine provinces, and two territories, and each element has retained a measure of cultural distinctiveness.[26] More importantly, there are no functional symbols distinct from the apparatus of the state which fuse those regions into a cohesive, separate national unit.

Second, it is a mistake to equate "the other nation" with the British ethnic group. At the time of Confederation, two out of three Canadians were of British origin, but the balance among the ethnic groups has shifted. According to 1971 census data, fewer than 45% of Canadians are of British origin.[27] The "other nation" is becoming more divided along ethnic lines; in this respect, it is becoming less, rather than more coherent.

Can we say, thirdly, that the other nation, perhaps as a result of habit or common history, has developed the perception of a "common interest" that John Roberts considers essential to the definition of a national community? Gordon Gibson, for one, thinks not. In Gibson's politics of realism there is little room for sentimentality. The calculus of Confederation, he says, "should be measured by dollars and by federal restrictions on our abilities to work out our destiny." The Canadian union is a reversible arrangement and the reversal, according to Gibson, is economically and politically feasible. "The parties to the Canadian deal," he asserts, "have to a considerable extent retained their identity." The Western provinces, even British Columbia, "have the capacity to be nations in their own right."

Gibson's message to Ottawa is loud and clear, but it is not delivered in the unified voice of the "other nation." Indeed, one could conclude that the "other nation" is too fractured to be considered a nation at all. Perhaps rather than being second best, the "Two Nations" image is an interpretation that actually flatters the Canadian state.

Conclusions

This elaboration of nationalism focuses squarely on the nation as a crucial, though often elusive, object of analysis and gives special weight to the problems of national integration and national development. In one guise or another these problems have been recurring themes in Canadian history.

In 1873, Edward Blake predicted: "The future of Canada depends very largely upon the cultivation of a national spirit."[28] A little more than fifty years later, Arthur Meighen figured that the main problem with Canada was spiritual: the problem of getting all Canadians to see that they have only one country.[29] In 1978, Prime Minister Trudeau told Canadians that it is "A Time for a Change"—"we must renew ourselves." "This test must begin," Trudeau declared, "with a form of exorcism. Our national mythology must come to reflect the realities of contemporary Canada." And this whole challenge "requires of us a new openness of spirit, a new dedication."[30] More than one hundred years after Confederation, the same theme is struck, the same urgent problem given the highest priority. The goal remains unfulfilled and, according to some, it is a serious mistake to cling to it.

Canada's distinctiveness, and *raison d'être* as a nation-state, is challenged by the economic and cultural penetration of her North American neighbor, a powerful and relatively unified nation-state which does not suffer from similar crises of identity. Moreover, one of Canada's potentially unique attributes, its cultural duality, can no longer be touted convincingly as a firm anchor of a pan-Canadian identity, for many French Canadians reject the One Canada image. Without a French Canadian contribution to the pan-Canadian identity, differences between Canada and the United States fade.

If national self-determination provides the impetus for Canada's independence from the United States, then it is understandable that nations, like Quebec, borrow the same logic to advance their own goals. It is unlikely that any lasting solution will be reached by insisting that all Québécois are Canadians and that they should be content with the condition defined by Canadian law. Such a perspective disregards the fundamental distinction between the nation and the state. Laws, the language of the state, are defined by the majority. Therefore, to pose Canada's difficulties in legal terms feeds French Canadian suspicions that the state, an instrument of the majority, represents a threat to the future of the cultural minority.[31]

The debates about Canada's structural, institutional, and policy problems can be interpreted in relation to the central government's efforts to fashion an integrated nation-state. But when the obstacles to that goal are laid out for all to see, it is difficult to be optimistic about prospects of reaching that goal in the near future. The political solutions proposed in this volume do not presume a non-existent consensus, nor do they require an uncharacteristic change of heart. The proposals involve demystifying, not disbanding the state; they involve sober calculations about different institutional umbrellas. That, surely, is an important first step.

Some authors, like Gordon Stead, view Canada as a place where different cultures can, and should, co-exist—*e pluribus plures*. However, the compelling reason for jointly celebrating that communal diversity in the same state hinges upon whether the present configuration of the state provides the best framework for the effective articulation of regionally and provincially defined interests. The role of the state in guaranteeing diversity, in turn, depends upon the locus and exercise of power. Ian McDougall argues for the full use of existing central powers to make resource management more profitable, thereby serving federalism; Frank Peers looks for an Ottawa-based communications policy, and Walter Gordon wants more "Canadian" control of the economy. Whereas John Roberts looks to the maintenance of the central state as an essential instrument for dealing with multinational corporations, Richard Simeon, like Gordon Gibson and Flora MacDonald, calls for greater decentralization: all three say the provinces can choose their priorities, protect their interests, and exploit their resources better than Ottawa.

Discussion, obviously, has shifted its focus away from the elusive national spirit and towards the functional efficiency of the state. The Canadian state precedes the Canadian nation; the evolution of Canada's larger national identity refuses to be hurried. Meanwhile, tuning the apparatus of the state is necessary. Federalism will cleave to the hearts of Canadians, Québécois included, if each unit of the Confederation, Quebec included, is convinced that it pays. That, probably, is the surest footing for any liberal political system. In the end it may also provide the firmest ground from which a national identity can evolve.

NOTES

1. Anthony D. Smith, *Theories of Nationalism* (London: Duckworth, 1971), Konstantin Symmons-Symonolewicz, *Modern Nationalism: Towards a Consensus in Theory* (New York: The Polish Institute of Arts and Sciences in America, 1968); and L.L. Snyder, *The Meaning of Nationalism* (New Brunswick, N.J.: Rutgers University Press, 1954), contain useful summaries of the literature.

2. F.O. Hertz, *Nationality in History and Politics: A Study of the Psychology and Sociology of National Sentiment and Character,* (London: Kegan Paul, 1944), p. 34.

3. Quoted in Hans Kohn, "A New Look at Nationalism," *The Virginia Quarterly Review,* XXXII, 1956, p. 322.

4. Carlton J. Hayes, *Essays on Nationalism* (New York: Macmillan, 1926). p. 258.

5. Carlton J. Hayes, *The Historical Evolution of Nationalism* (New York: R.R. Smith, 1931), p. 221; and then Carlton J. Hayes, *Nationalism: A Religion* (New York: Macmillan, 1960).

6. As does David Cameron in *Nationalism, Self-Determination and the Quebec Question* (Toronto: Macmillan, 1974), p. 70; and Roger Gibbins, "Models of Nationalism: A Case Study of Political Ideologies in the Canadian West," *Canadian Journal of Political Science,* June 1977, 10:2, pp. 341-373.

7. Elie Kedourie, *Nationalism* (London: Hutchinson, 1960), p. 70.

8. For example, see Patricia E. Mayo, *The Roots of Identity* (London: Allen Lane, 1974)

9. J. Plano and R. Olton, *The International Relations Dictionary* (New York: John Wiley and Sons, 1969), p. 30.

10. F.A. Sondermann, W.C. Olson and D.S. McLellan (eds.) *The Theory and Practice of International Relations,* Second Edition (Englewood Cliffs, New Jersey: Prentice Hall, 1970), p. 12.

11. Dankwart Rustow, "Nation," *International Encyclopedia of the Social Sciences* (New York: Macmillan, 1968), Vol. 2, pp. 7-14.

12. Ernest Renan, "What is a Nation?" reprinted in *Poetry of the Celtic Races and Other Studies,* (London: Kenikat Press, 1970), pp. 61-83. For a more recent statement, see Rupert Emerson, *From Empire to Nation* (Boston, Mass: Beacon Press, 1959), pp. 102-104.

13. Of course, as Karl Deutsch has noted, the difficulty lies in assigning precise meaning to subjective terms. See Karl W. Deutsch, *Nationalism and Social Communication: An Enquiry into the Foundations of Nationality* (Cambridge, Mass: M.I.T. Press, 1972), p. 172.

14. H.H. Gerth and C. Wright Mills, *From Max Weber: Essays in Sociology* (New York: Oxford University Press, 1973), p. 24.

15. John Plamenatz, "Two Types of Nationalism," in Eugene Kamenka (Ed.), *Nationalism: The Nature and Evolution of an Idea* (Canberra: Australian National University Press, 1973), p. 24.

16. Ernest Renan, "What is a Nation?", op. cit. p. 80.

17. Hans Kohn, *The Idea of Nationalism*, op. cit., p. 15.

18. See Walker Connor, "Nation-Building or Nation-Destroying?" *World Politics*, 24 (April 1972).

19. Gerth and Mills, op.cit., p. 173.

20. See K. Silvert in Silvert (Ed.) *The Expectant Peoples: Nationalism and Development* (New York: Random House, 1963), p. 19.

21. Hugh McLennan's *Two Solitudes*, (Toronto: W. Collins Sons & Co., 1945) of course is the best known statement of the cultural divisions in Canada. The *Two Nation* thesis, counterpart to the two solitudes, received renewed attention among scholars following Eugene Forsey's presidential address at the 1962 meeting of the Canadian Political Science Association. For the text, see *Canadian Journal of Political Science*, November 1962, pp. 485-501.

22. See Hugh Thornburn's "Needed: A New Look at the Two Nations Theory," *Queen's Quarterly*, Summer 1973, vol. LXXX, pp. 268-273; and David Kwavnick's "Quebec and the Two Nations Theory: A Re-examination," *Queen's Quarterly*, Autumn 1974, vol. LXXXI, pp. 357-376; as well as the *Journal of Canadian Studies*, July 1977, vol. 12, no. 3.

23. For example, see the data presented in Neil Nevitte and François-Pierre Gingras, "The Religious Factor in Quebec Politics Reconsidered," Paper presented to the annual meeting of the Canadian Political Science Association, May 1978.

24. I make a more detailed argument in "Religion and the 'New Nationalisms:' The Case of Quebec," unpublished Ph.D. dissertation, Duke University, 1977, chapters four and five.

25. For example, Donald V. Smiley, *Canada in Question: Federalism in the Seventies*, Second Edition (Toronto: McGraw-Hill Ryerson, 1976), pp. 220-224.

26. See Richard Simeon and David J. Elkins, "Regional Political Cultures in Canada," *Canadian Journal of Political Science*, VII, September 1974; also Mildred A. Schwartz, *Politics and Territory: The Sociology of Regional Persistence in Canada* (Montreal: McGill-Queens University Press, 1974).

27. Richard Arès, *Les positions ethniques, linguistiques et*

réligieuses-Des Canadians francais á la suite du recensement de 1971 (Montreal: Bellarmin, 1975), p. 31.

28. Pierre Elliott Trudeau, *A Time for Action: Toward the Renewal of Canadian Federation* (Ottawa: Government of Canada, 1978), p. 4.

29. Quoted by Flora MacDonald in this volume.

30. Pierre Elliott Trudeau, *A Time for Action*, op. cit., p. 2.

31. But, as Weber suggests, it is natural for "those who wield power in the polity to provoke the idea of the state," Gerth and Mills, op. cit., p. 176.

FURTHER READING*

This brief reading list, which supplements the bibliographies contained in the Notes at the end of most chapters, consists of recent monographs and articles on the major subjects discussed in the essays. The list is classified under four broad headings: Canada-United States economic relations, Canada-United States intergovernmental relations, Canadian federalism, and Quebec nationalism.

CANADA-UNITED STATES ECONOMIC RELATIONS

Abdel-Malek, T., and Sarker, A.K. "Analysis of the Effects of Phase II Guidelines of the Foreign Investment Review Act." *Canadian Public Policy* 3 (Winter 1977): 33-49.

Brown, R.D., ed. "United States Tax Reform Proposals—Threat to Canada?" *Canadian Tax Journal* 26 (January-February 1978): 68-84.

Canada. *Foreign Direct Investment in Canada* (The Gray Report.) Ottawa: Information Canada, 1972.

Canada, Laws, Statutes, Etc. *Foreign Investment Review Act* (SC 1973-74, c. 46). Ottawa: Information Canada, 1973.

Canadian-American Committee. *Keeping Options Open in Canada-United States Oil and Natural Gas Trade: A Statement.* Montreal: Canadian-American Committee, 1975.

Clement, Wallace. *Continental Corporate Power: Economic Linkages between Canada and the United States.* Toronto: McClelland and Stewart, 1977.

Dickey, John Sloan. *Canada and the American Presence: The United States Interest in an Independent Canada.* New York: New York University Press, 1975.

Fayerweather, John. *The Mercantile Bank Affair.* New York: New York University Press, 1974.

Freeman, Susan. "Canada's Changing Posture Toward Multinational Corporations: An Attempt to Harmonize Nationalism with Continued Industrial Growth." *New York University Journal of International Law and Politics* 7 (Summer 1974): 271-315.

Goldman, R.K., et al. "North American Market? U.S.-Mexican-Canadian Perspectives on Terms of Trade and Rationalization of Production; Antidumping and Countervailing Duties." *American Journal of International Law. Proceedings* 68 (1974): 92-117.

Lamont, Douglas F. "Emerging Neo-Mercantilism in Canadian Policy Toward State Enterprises and Foreign Direct Investment." *Vanderbilt Journal of Transnational Law* 8 (Fall 1974): 121-44.

Munton, D., and Poel, D.H. "Electoral Accountability and Canadian Foreign Policy: The Case of Foreign Investment." *International Journal* 33 (Winter 1977-78): 217-47.

"The Regulation of Foreign Investment in Canada: Experience and Prospects." *Journal of Contemporary Business* 6 (Autumn 1977): 31-51.

Stevenson, G. "Foreign Direct Investment and the Provinces: A Study of Elite Attitudes." *Canadian Journal of Political Science* 7 (December 1974): 630-47.

Trooboff, P.D., et al. "Should Investment Capital Stay Home? A Canadian-U.S. Dialogue." *American Journal of International Law. Proceedings* 68 (1974): 16-38.

United States Congress, Joint Economic Committee, Subcommittee on Inter-American Economic Relationships. *Canadian Procedures and the Role of Foreign Investment in the Canadian Economy: Hearings 16 December 1975-25 January 1976.* 94th Congress, 1st and 2nd sessions, 1976.

Vickery, E. "Exports and North American Economic Growth: Structural and Staple Models in Historical Perspective." *Canadian Journal of Economics* 7 (February 1974): 32-58.

* The reading list was prepared by the Director of Publications, Institute for Research on Public Policy, Montreal.

CANADA-UNITED STATES INTERGOVERNMENTAL RELATIONS

Alper, D.K. and Monahan, R.L. "Bill C-58 and the American Congress: The Politics of Retaliation." *Canadian Public Policy* 4 (Spring 1978): 184-92.

Canada, Parliament, Senate, Standing Committee on Foreign Affairs. *Canada-United States Relations, vol. 1: The Institutional Framework for the Relationship.* Ottawa: Information Canada, 1975.

Dickey, John. *Canada and the American Presence: The United States Interest in an Independent Canada.* New York: New York University Press, 1975.

Dwivedi, O.P. "The International Joint Commission: Its Role in the United States-Canada Boundary Pollution Control." *International Review of Administrative Sciences* 40 (1974): 369-76.

English, H. Edward, ed. *Canada-United States Relations.* New York: Praeger, 1976.

Fox, A.B.; Hero, A.O., Jr.; and Nye, J.S., Jr., eds. *Canada and the*

United States: Transnational and Transgovernmental Relations.
New York: Columbia University Press, 1976.

Gilpin, R. "Integration and Disintegration on the North American Continent." *International Organization* 28 (Autumn 1974): 851-74.

Heintzman, Ralph, ed. "Thinking about Separatism: les conséquences de l'élection du 15 novembre 1976." *Journal of Canadian Studies* 12 (July 1977).

Hillmer, Norman, and Stevenson, Garth, eds. *A Foremost Nation: Canadian Foreign Policy and a Changing World.* Toronto: McClelland and Stewart, 1977.

Holmes, J.W. "Impact of Domestic Political Factors on Canadian-American Relations: Canada." *International Organization* 28 (Autumn 1974): 611-35.

Leach, Richard H., *et al.* "Province-State Trans-Border Relations." *Canadian Public Administration* 16 (Fall 1973): 468-82.

Leach, Richard H. "Canada and the United States: A Special Relationship." *Current History* 72 (April 1977): 145-49.

Litvak, I., and Maule, C. *Cultural Sovereignty: The Time and Reader's Digest Case in Canada.* New York: Praeger, 1974.

LoGalbo, John R. "The Time and Reader's Digest Bill: C-58 and Canadian Cultural Nationalism." *New York University Journal of International Law and Politics* 9 (Fall 1976): 237-75 (published 1978).

Manning, B., *et al.* "Entente cordiale? Divergence and Accommodation: Approaches to Multilateral Issues." *American Journal of International Law. Proceedings* 68 (1974): 204-25.

Redekop, J.H. "Reinterpretation of Canadian-American Relations." *Canadian Journal of Political Science* 9 (June 1976): 227-43.

Rickerd, D.S., *et al.* "Power to the People: U.S.-Canadian Energy Policy." *American Journal of International Law. Proceedings* 68 (1974): 76-92.

Ross, C.R., and Cohen, M. "International Joint Commission: United States-Canada." *American Journal of International Law. Proceedings* 68 (1974): 229-39.

Roy, J.L. "French Fact in North America: Quebec-United States Relations." *International Journal* 31 (Summer 1976): 470-87.

Rubin, A.P., *et al.* "Perils of Proximity." *American Journal of International Law. Proceedings* 68 (1974): 1-16.

Smedresman, Peter S. "The International Joint Commission and the International Boundary and Water Commission: Potential for Environmental Control Along the Boundaries." *New York University*

Journal of International Law and Politics 6 (Winter 1973): 499-531.

Swanson, Roger F. "Canada and the United States: The Range of Direct Relations between States and Provinces." *International Perspectives* (March/April 1976): 18-23.

Watkins, M. "North American Triangle." *Canadian Forum* 56 (February 1977): 14-17.

CANADIAN FEDERALISM

Astrachan, A. "Obsession with Unity." *New Republic* 177 (August 20, 1977): 21-23.

Black, Edwin R. *Divided Loyalties: Canadian Conceptions of Federalism.* Montreal: McGill-Queen's University Press, 1975.

Blackman, W.J. "A Western Canadian Perspective on the Economics of Confederation." *Canadian Public Policy* 3 (Autumn 1977): 414-30.

Cairns, A.C. "Governments and Societies of Canadian Federalism." *Canadian Journal of Political Science* 10 (December 1977): 695-725.

"Conflict and Consensus in Canadian Confederation. Proceedings of a Symposium Held in Conjunction with the Learned Societies Meetings and Sponsored by Canadian Public Policy, Fredericton, New Brunswick." *Canadian Public Policy* 3 (Autumn 1977): 409-78.

Cuneo, C.J. "Education, Language, and Multidimensional Continentalism." *Canadian Journal of Political Science* 7 (September 1974): 536-50.

Drouin, Marie-Josée, and Bruce-Briggs, B. *Canada Has a Future.* Study prepared for the Hudson Institute of Canada. Toronto: McClelland and Stewart, 1978.

Frechette, P. "L'économie de la Confederation: un point de vue québécois; with replies by Thomas K. Shoyama and Antal Deutsch." *Canadian Public Policy* 3 (Autumn 1977): 431-48.

Frye, N. "National Consciousness in Canadian Culture; Address." Royal Canadian Society Transactions 4th series 14 (1976): 57-69.

Gibbins, R. "Models of Nationalism: A Case Study of Political Ideologies in the Canadian West." *Canadian Journal of Political Science* 10 (June 1977): 341-73.

Gonik, C.W. "Is Canada Falling Apart?" *Current* 191 (March 1977): 38-47.

Gordon, Walter O. *What Is Happening to Canada.* Toronto: McClelland and Stewart, 1978.

Harbron, John D. *Canada without Quebec.* Toronto: Musson, 1977.

Harney, J. "Clearing the Constitutional Mist." *Canadian Forum* 56 (February 1977): 6-12.

Mallory, J.R. "Canadian Federalism in Transition," *Political Quarterly* 48 (April-June 1977): 149-63.

Meekison, Peter, ed. *Canadian Federalism: Myth or Reality.* 3rd ed. Toronto: Metheuen, 1977.

Morin, Claude. *Quebec vs. Ottawa: The Struggle for Self-Government, 1960-72.* Toronto: University of Toronto Press, 1976.

Pentland, Charles. *The Canadian Dilemma.* Paris: Atlantic Institute for International Affairs, 1973.

Rotstein, Abraham. "Canada: The New Nationalism." *Foreign Affairs* 55 (October 1976): 978-1118.

Schwartz, Mildred A. "The Social Make-up of Canada and Strains in Confederation." *Canadian Public Policy* 3 (Autumn 1977): 458-78.

Simeon, Richard. *Must Canada Fail?* Montreal: McGill-Queen's University Press, 1977.

Smiley, Donald V. *Canada in Question: Federalism in the Seventies.* 2nd ed. Toronto: McGraw-Hill Ryerson, 1976.

Smith, Burton M. "The United States in Recent Canadian Nationalism." *World Affairs* 140 (Winter 1978): 195-205.

Walsh, Sandra. "Quebec and Confederation: Bibliography." Exchange Bibliography No. 1509. Monticello, Ill.: Council of Planning Librarians, 1978.

QUEBEC NATIONALISM

Bernard, André. *La politique au Canada et au Québec.* 2nd ed. Montréal: Les Presses de l'Université de Québec, 1977.

Bernard, André, ed. *What Does Quebec Want?* Toronto: Lorimer, 1977.

Brossard, Jacques. *L'accession à la souveraineté et le cas du Québec.* Montréal: Les Presses de l'Université de Montréal, 1976.

Creighton, D. "Finies les concessions!" *L'Actualité* 2 (October 1977): 6.

Desbarats, Peter. *René: A Canadian in Search of a Country.* Toronto: McClelland and Stewart, 1976.

Dion, Léon. *Quebec: The Unfinished Revolution.* Montréal: McGill-Queen's University Press, 1976.

Dobell, Peter C. "Quebec Separatism: Domestic and International Implications." *World Today* (London) 33 (April 1977): 149-59.

Fullerton, Douglas H. *The Dangerous Delusion: Quebec's Independence Obsession.* Toronto: McClelland and Stewart, 1978.

Granatstein, J.L. "Canada sans Québec, and Other Options." *Quill and Quire* 44, no. 1:25 '78.

Latouche, D. "Quebec and the North American Subsystem: One Possible Scenario." *International Organization* 28 (Autumn 1974): 931-60.

Latouche, D. "La vrai nature de...la révolution tranquille." *Canadian Journal of Political Science,* 8 (June 1975): 191-234.

Lévesque, René. "Nous sommes des Québécois." par M. René Lévesque, Premier Ministre du Québec devant les membres de l'Assemblée Nationale à Paris (2 novembre, 1977). *L'Action Nationale* (January 1978): 341-50.

Lévesque, René. "For an Independent Quebec." *Foreign Affairs* 54 (July 1976): 734-44.

McKinsey, Lauren S. "Dimensions of National Political Integration and Disintegration: The Case of Quebec Separatism, 1960-1975." *Comparative Political Studies* 9 (October 1976): 335-60.

Moniére, Denis. *Le développement des idéologies au Québec.* Montréal Editions Québec/Amérique, 1977.

Rioux, Marcel. *La question du Quebec.* Montréal: Parti Pris, 1976.

Tetley, W. "Foreign Investment—a Québécois Perspective." *American Journal of International Law. Proceedings* 68 (1974): 24-27.

Trépanier, P. "Les nationalismes québécois." *L'Action Nationale* 67 (January 1978): 388-91.

Usher, D. "The English Response to the Prospect of the Separation of Quebec." *Canadian Public Policy* 4 (Winter 1978): 57-70.

Valliéres, P. "Un Québec impossible." *L'Actualité* 2:14 111 November 1977.

Young, R.A. "National Identification in English Canada: Implications for Quebec Independence." *Journal of Canadian Studies* 12 (July 1977): 69-84.

ABOUT THE AUTHORS

Canadian Identity

Mordecai Richler is the author of *St. Urbain's Horsemen* and *The Apprenticeship of Duddy Kravitz.*

Sylvia Wright is the author of *A Shark-Infested Rice Pudding* and *Get Away From Me With All Those Christmas Gifts.* As a fellow of the Radcliffe Institute (1977-78), she has been writing a biography of Melusina Fay Pierce, a nineteenth-century feminist and writer.

Quebec Independence

René Lévesque is Premier of Quebec and the founder and leader of the Parti Québécois. He is a former journalist and the former Liberal Minister of Public Works and of Hydraulic Resources, former Minister of Natural Resources, and former Minister of Family and Social Welfare.

Canadian Independence

Walter L. Gordon was Minister of Finance for Canada from 1963-1965. He is the former Governor of the University of Toronto and former Chancellor of York University, and he is the former President of the Privy Council. Mr. Gordon is a founder of the Committee for an Independent Canada and is author of *Troubled Canada—The Need for New Domestic Policies; A Choice for Canada—Independence or Colonial Status; Storm Signals—New Economic Policies for Canada; A Political Memoir* (published in 1977), and *What Is Happening to Canada* (1978).

Willis C. Armstrong is former Minister in the United States Embassy in Ottawa and former Assistant Secretary of State for Economic Affairs; he is now a consultant to the International Chamber of Commerce and several multinational corporations.

Tensions over Communications

Frank Peers is Professor of Political Science at the University of Toronto. He is the former editor of the *Canadian Journal of Political Science* and is author of *The Politics of Canadian Broadcasting, 1920-1951,* and *The Public Eye.*

Joel Rosenbloom is a member of the law firm of Wilmer, Cutler, & Pickering in Washington, D.C. He has represented American broadcasting interests before the Supreme Court of Canada.

Power and Vulnerability: Canadian and American Perspectives on International Affairs

Allan Gotlieb is Canada's Under Secretary of State for External Affairs. He holds degrees from Oxford and Harvard and is the former Deputy Minister of Manpower and Immigration and former Deputy Minister of Communications.

Alan K. Henrikson is Associate Professor of Diplomatic History at the Fletcher School of Law and Diplomacy. He is author of "Le Canada Français dans la presse americaine," in Albert Legault, ed., *Le nationalisme Québécois a la croisée des chemins,* and is currently on leave as a Fellow of the Woodrow Wilson International Center for Scholars.

The Future of Federal-Provincial Relations

Richard Simeon is Director of the Institute of Intergovernmental Relations and Professor of Political Studies at Queen's University. He is author of *Federal-Provincial Diplomacy,* and editor of *Must Canada Fail?*

Jerome Milch is Assistant Professor of Political Science at the University of Pittsburgh. He is co-author (with Elliot J. Feldman) of *Canadian Federalism and Airport Development* (forthcoming) and has contributed to numerous scholarly journals on French local government, bureaucracy, and science and technology policies in the United States.

Energy, Natural Resources, and the Economics of Federalism: National Harmony or Continental Hegemony?

Ian McDougall is Associate Professor of Law at Osgoode Hall, York University. He has written extensively on primary resource management issues for numerous government commissions and scholarly journals, and is the author of *Future Canadian Gas Requirements*.

Stewart L. Udall is the former Congressman from Arizona and former Secretary of the Interior under Presidents Kennedy and Johnson. He is author of *The Quiet Crisis*, and *1976: Agenda for Tomorrow*, and co-author of *The Energy Balloon*. He currently practices law in Washington, D.C. with the firm of Duncan, Brown, Weinberg, and Palmer.

Robert E. Stein is Director of the North American office of the International Institute for Environment and Development. He is former legal counsel to the United States-Canadian International Joint Commission.

The Federal Bureaucracy and Canadian Disunity

Gordon W. Stead is former Assistant Secretary of the Treasury Board, former Assistant Deputy Minister of Transport, former Special Adviser for the Constitutional Review of the Privy Council, and former Professor of Community and Regional Planning at the University of British Columbia. He is now a consultant to the federal Ministry of Transport, the Greater Vancouver Regional District, and other governmental organizations.

Robert J. Art is the Dean of Graduate Studies and Associate Professor of Politics, Brandeis University, and Adjunct Research Fellow at Harvard's Center for Science and International Affairs. He is author of *The TFX Decision: McNamara and the Military*, and co-editor of *International Politics* (with Robert Jervis) and *The Use of Force* (with Kenneth Waltz).

Quebec Separatism in Comparative Perspective

Peter Alexis Gourevitch is Associate Professor of Political Science at McGill University. He is former Director of the Center for European Studies at Harvard and the author of numerous articles on French politics, international trade, and comparative political economy.

François-Pierre Gingras is Associate Professor of Political Science at the University of Ottawa and has taught at Carleton, York, Laval, and McMaster Universities. He has been a consultant for the Official Languages Program of the Secretary of State (Canada) as a specialist on Quebec.

The West in Confederation

Gordon F. Gibson is Leader of the Liberal Party in British Columbia and a Member of the Legislative Assembly. He has studied at the University of British Columbia, Harvard, and the London School of Economics.

David C. Smith is Professor and Head of the Department of Economics at Queen's University. He was honorary research associate in economics at Harvard and a member of the Seminar on Canadian-United States Relations.

Quebec's Economic Future in Confederation

Robert Bourassa was elected the youngest Premier in the history of Quebec in 1970 and was reelected Premier in 1973. He holds degrees from the University of Montreal, Oxford, and Harvard and is a former Member of Parliament and fiscal adviser to the Government of Canada. Since the electoral defeat of his government in 1976, M. Bourassa has been lecturing in Brussels, Paris, and Washington, and is currently preparing a book on the Common Market.

Michael Parenti is a political scientist and author of *Democracy for the Few* and *Power and the Powerless.* He writes on the American political system, ethnic politics, and American foreign policy.

Towards a Revitalized Confederation

Flora MacDonald has been the Member of Parliament for Kingston and the Islands since 1972 and is the Progressive Conservative Party's spokesperson on federal-provincial relations and constitutional reform.

Walter Dean Burnham is Professor of Political Science at the Massachusetts Institute of Technology. He is the author of *Critical Elections and the Mainsprings of American Politics* and *The American Party Systems* (co-edited with William N. Chambers).

The Liberal Approach to a Renewed Confederation

John Roberts is Canada's Secretary of State. He holds degrees from the University of Toronto and Oxford, and has taught at both universities before joining the Department of External Affairs.

Elliot J. Feldman is Assistant Professor of Politics at Brandeis University, Research Fellow at the Center for International Affairs, and Co-chairman of the Seminar on Canadian-United States Relations. He is co-author of *Poliscide* (with Theodore J. Lowi, et. al.), *Canadian Federalism and Airport Development* (with Jerome Milch), and author of *White Elephants and the Albatross* (forthcoming).

Nationalism, States, and Nations

Neil Nevitte is a Visiting Lecturer in the Department of Government, Harvard University, Research Fellow at the Center for International Affairs, and Co-chairman of the Seminar on Canadian-United States Relations.

BOOKS WRITTEN UNDER CENTER AUSPICES

The Soviet Bloc, Zbigniew K. Brzezinski (sponsored jointly with the Russian Research Center), 1960. Harvard University Press. Revised edition. 1967.

The Necessity for Choice, by Henry A. Kissinger, 1961. Harper & Bros.

Rift and Revolt in Hungary, by Ferenc A. Váli, 1961. Harvard University Press.

Strategy and Arms Control, by Thomas C. Schelling and Morton H. Halperin, 1961. Twentieth Century Fund.

United States Manufacturing Investment in Brazil, by Lincoln Gordon and Engelbert L. Grommers, 1962. Harvard Business School.

The Economy of Cyprus, by A.J. Meyer, with Simos Vassiliou (sponsored jointly with the Center for Middle Eastern Studies), 1962. Harvard University Press.

Entrepreneurs of Lebanon, by Yusif A. Sayigh (sponsored jointly with the Center for Middle Eastern Studies), 1962. Harvard University Press.

Communist China 1955-1959: Policy Documents with Analysis, with a foreword by Robert R. Bowie and John K. Fairbank (sponsored jointly with the East Asian Research Center), 1962. Harvard University Press.

Somali Nationalism, by Saadia Touval, 1963, Harvard University Press.

The Dilemma of Mexico's Development, by Raymond Vernon, 1963. Harvard University Press.

Limited War in the Nuclear Age, by Morton H. Halperin, 1963. John Wiley & Sons.

In Search of France, by Stanley Hoffman *et al.,* 1963. Harvard University Press.

The Arms Debate, by Robert A. Levine, 1963. Harvard University Press.

Africans on the Land, by Montague Yudelman, 1964. Harvard University Press.

Counterinsurgency Warfare, by David Galula, 1964. Frederick A. Praeger, Inc.

People and Policy in the Middle East, by Max Weston Thornburg, 1964. W.W. Norton & Co.

Shaping the Future, by Robert R. Bowie, 1964. Columbia University Press.

Foreign Aid and Foreign Policy, by Edward S. Mason (sponsored jointly with the Council on Foreign Relations), 1964. Harper & Row.

How Nations Negotiate, by Fred Charles Iklé, 1964. Harper & Row.

Public Policy and Private Enterprise in Mexico, edited by Raymond Vernon, 1964. Harvard University Press.

China and the Bomb, by Morton H. Halperin (sponsored jointly with the East Asian Research Center), 1965. Frederick A. Praeger, Inc.

Democracy in Germany, by Fritz Erler (Jodidi Lectures), 1965. Harvard University Press.

The Troubled Partnership, by Henry A. Kissinger (sponsored jointly with the Council on Foreign Relations), 1965. McGraw-Hill Book Co.

The Rise of Nationalism in Central Africa, by Robert I. Rotberg, 1965. Harvard University Press.

Pan-Africanism and East African Integration, by Joseph S. Nye, Jr., 1965. Harvard University Press.

Communist China and Arms Control, by Morton H. Halperin and Dwight H. Perkins (sponsored jointly with the East Asian Research Center), 1965. Frederick A. Praeger, Inc.

Problems of National Strategy, ed. Henry Kissinger, 1965. Frederick A. Praeger, Inc.

Deterrence before Hiroshima: The Airpower Background of Modern Strategy, by George H. Quester, 1966. John Wiley & Sons.

Containing the Arms Race, by Jeremy J. Stone, 1966. M.I.T. Press.

Germany and the Atlantic Alliance: The Interaction of Strategy and Politics, by James L. Richardson, 1966. Harvard University Press.

Arms and Influence, by Thomas C. Schelling, 1966. Yale University Press.

Political Change in a West African State, by Martin Kilson, 1966. Harvard University Press.

Planning Without Facts: Lessons in Resource Allocation from Nigeria's Development, by Wolfgang F. Stolper, 1966. Harvard University Press.

Export Instability and Economic Development, by Alasdair I. MacBean, 1966. Harvard University Press.

Foreign Policy and Democratic Politics, by Kenneth N. Waltz (sponsored jointly with the Institute of War and Peace Studies, Columbia University), 1967. Little, Brown & Co.

Contemporary Military Strategy, by Morton H. Halperin, 1967. Little, Brown & Co.

Sino-Soviet Relations and Arms Control, ed. Morton H. Halperin (sponsored jointly with the East Asian Research Center), 1967. M.I.T. Press.

Africa and United States Policy, by Rupert Emerson, 1967. Prentice-Hall.

Elites in Latin America, edited by Seymour M. Lipset and Aldo Solari, 1967. Oxford University Press.

Europe's Postwar Growth, by Charles P. Kindleberger, 1967. Harvard University Press.

The Rise and Decline of the Cold War, by Paul Seabury, 1967. Basic Books.

Student Politics, ed. S.M. Lipset, 1967. Basic Books.

Pakistan's Development: Social Goals and Private Incentives, by Gustav F. Papenek, 1967. Harvard University Press.

Strike a Blow and Die: A Narrative of Race Relations in Colonial Africa, by George Simeon Mwase, ed. Robert I. Rotberg, 1967. Harvard University Press.

Party Systems and Voter Alignments, edited by Seymour M. Lipset and Stein Rokkan, 1967. Free Press.

Agrarian Socialism, by Seymour M. Lipset, revised edition, 1968. Doubleday Anchor.

Aid, Influence, and Foreign Policy, by Joan M. Nelson, 1968. The Macmillan Company.

Development Policy: Theory and Practice, edited by Gustav F. Papanek, 1968. Harvard University Press.

International Regionalism, by Joseph S. Nye. Little, Brown & Co.

Revolution and Counterrevolution, by Seymour M. Lipset, 1968. Basic Books.

Political Order in Changing Societies, by Samuel P. Huntington, 1968. Yale University Press.

The TFX Decision: McNamara and the Military, by Robert J. Art, 1968. Little, Brown & Co.

Korea: The Politics of the Vortex, by Gregory Henderson, 1968. Harvard University Press.

Political Development in Latin America, by Martin Needler, 1968. Random House.

The Precarious Republic, by Michael Hudson, 1968. Random House.

The Brazilian Capital Goods Industry, 1929-1964 (sponsored jointly with the Center for Studies in Education and Development), by Nathaniel H. Leff, 1968. Harvard University Press.

Economic Policy-Making and Development in Brazil, 1947-1964, by Nathaniel H. Leff, 1968. John Wiley & Sons.

Turmoil and Transition: Higher Education and Student Politics in India, edited by Philip G. Altbach, 1968. Lalvani Publishing House (Bombay).

German Foreign Policy in Transition, by Karl Kaiser, 1968. Oxford University Press.

Protest and Power in Black Africa, edited by Robert I. Rotberg, 1969. Oxford University Press.

Peace in Europe, by Karl E. Birnbaum, 1969. Oxford University Press.

The Process of Modernization: An Annotated Bibliography on Sociocultural Aspects of Development, by John Brode, 1969. Harvard University Press.

Students in Revolt, edited by Seymour M. Lipset and Philip G. Altbach, 1969. Houghton Mifflin.

Agricultural Development in India's Districts: The Intensive Agricultural Districts Programme, by Dorris D. Brown, 1970. Harvard University Press.

Authoritarian Politics in Modern Society: The Dynamics of Established One-Party Systems, edited by Samuel P. Huntington and Clement H. Moore, 1970. Basic Books.

Nuclear Diplomacy, by George H. Quester, 1970. Dunellen.

The Logic of Images in International Relations, by Robert Jervis, 1970. Princeton University Press.

Europe's Would-Be Polity, by Leon Lindberg and Stuart A. Scheingold, 1970. Prentice-Hall.

Taxation and Development: Lessons from Colombian Experience, by Richard M. Bird, 1970. Harvard University Press.

Lord and Peasant in Peru: A Paradigm of Political and Social Change, by F. LaMond Tullis, 1970. Harvard University Press.

The Kennedy Round in American Trade Policy: The Twilight of the GATT? by John W. Evans, 1971. Harvard University Press.

Korean Development: The Interplay of Politics and Economics, by David C. Cole and Princeton N. Lyman, 1971. Harvard University Press.

Development Policy II—The Pakistan Experience, edited by Walter P. Falcon and Gustav F. Papanek, 1971. Harvard University Press.

Higher Education in a Transitional Society, by Philip G. Altbach, 1971. Sindhu Publications (Bombay).

Studies in Development Planning, edited by Hollis B. Chenery, 1971. Harvard University Press.

Passion and Politics, by Seymour M. Lipset with Gerald Schaflander, 1971. Little, Brown & Co.

Political Mobilization of the Venezuelan Peasant, by John D. Powell, 1971. Harvard University Press.

Higher Education in India, edited by Amrik Singh and Philip Altbach, 1971. Oxford University Press (Delhi).

The Myth of the Guerrilla, by J. Bowyer Bell, 1971. Blond (London) and Knopf (New York).

International Norms and War between States: Three Studies in International Politics, by Kjell Goldmann, 1971. Published jointly by Läromedelsförlagen (Sweden) and the Swedish Institute of International Affairs.

Peace in Parts: Integration and Conflict in Regional Organization, by Joseph S. Nye, Jr., 1971. Little, Brown & Co.

Sovereignty at Bay: The Multinational Spread of U.S. Enterprise, by Raymond Vernon, 1971. Basic Books.

Defense Strategy for the Seventies (revision of *Contemporary Military Strategy*) by Morton H. Halperin, 1971. Little, Brown & Co.

Peasants Against Politics: Rural Organization in Brittany, 1911-1967, by Suzanne Berger, 1972. Harvard University Press.

Transnational Relations and World Politics, edited by Robert O. Keohane and Joseph S. Nye, Jr., 1972. Harvard University Press.

Latin American University Students: A Six-Nation Study, by Arthur Liebman, Kenneth N. Walker, and Myron Glazer, 1972. Harvard University Press.

The Politics of Land Reform in Chile, 1950-1970: Public Policy, Political Institutions and Social Change, by Robert R. Kaufman, 1972. Harvard University Press.

The Boundary Politics of Independent Africa, by Saadia Touval, 1972. Harvard University Press.

The Politics of Nonviolent Action, by Gene E. Sharp, 1973. Porter Sargent.

System 37 Viggen: Arms, Technology, and the Domestication of Glory, by Ingemar Dörfer, 1973. Universitetsforlaget (Oslo).

University Students and African Politics, by William John Hanna, 1974. Africana Publishing Company.

Organizing the Transnational: The Experience with Transnational Enterprise in Advanced Technology, by M.S. Hochmuth, 1974. Sijthoff (Leiden).

Becoming Modern, by Alex Inkeles and David H. Smith, 1974. Harvard University Press.

The United States and West Germany 1945-1973: A Study in Alliance Politics, by Roger Morgan (sponsored jointly with the Royal Institute of International Affairs), 1974. Oxford University Press.

Multinational Corporations and the Politics of Dependence: Copper in Chile, 1945-1973, by Theodore Moran, 1974. Princeton University Press.

The Andean Group: A Case Study in Economic Integration among Developing Countries, by David Morawetz, 1974. M.I.T. Press.

Kenya: The Politics of Participation and Control, by Henry Bienen, 1974. Princeton University Press.

Land Reform and Politics: A Comparative Analysis, by Hung-chao Tai, 1974. University of California Press.

Big Business and the State: Changing Relations in Western Europe, edited by Raymond Vernon, 1974. Harvard University Press.

Economic Policymaking in a Conflict Society: The Argentine Case, by Richard D. Mallon and Juan V. Sourrouille, 1975. Harvard University Press.

New States in the Modern World, edited by Martin Kilson, 1975. Harvard University Press.

Revolutionary Civil War: The Elements of Victory and Defeat, by David Wilkinson, 1975. Page-Ficklin Publications.

Politics and the Migrant Poor in Mexico City, by Wayne A. Cornelius, 1975. Stanford University Press.

East Africa and the Orient: Cultural Syntheses in Pre-Colonial Times, ed. H. Neville Chittick and Robert I. Rotberg, 1975. Africana Publishing Company.

No Easy Choice: Political Participation in Developing Countries, by Samuel P. Huntington and Joan M. Nelson, 1976. Harvard University Press.

The Politics of International Monetary Reform—The Exchange Crisis, by Michael J. Brenner, 1976. Ballinger Publishing Co.

The International Politics of Natural Resources, by Zuhayr Mikdashi, 1976. Cornell University Press.

The Oil Crisis, edited by Raymond Vernon, 1976. W.W. Norton & Co.

Social Change and Political Participation in Turkey, by Ergun Ozbudun, 1976. Princeton University Press.

The Arabs, Israelis, and Kissinger: A Secret History of American Diplomacy in the Middle East, by Edward R.F. Sheehan, 1976. Reader's Digest Press.

Perception and Misperception in International Politics, by Robert Jervis, 1976. Princeton University Press.

Power and Interdependence, by Robert O. Keohane and Joseph S. Nye, Jr., 1977. Little, Brown.

Soldiers in Politics: Military Coups and Governments, by Eric Nordlinger, 1977. Prentice-Hall.

The Military and Politics in Modern Times: On Professionals, Praetorians, and Revolutionary Soldiers, by Amos Perlmutter, 1977. Yale University Press.

Bankers and Borders: The Case of the American Banks in Britain, by Janet Kelly, 1977. Ballinger Publishing Co.

Shattered Peace: The Origins of the Cold War and the National Security State, by Daniel Yergin, 1977. Houghton Mifflin.

Storm Over the Multinationals: The Real Issues, by Raymond Vernon, 1977. Harvard University Press.

Political Generations and Political Development, ed. Richard J. Samuels, 1977. Lexington Books.

Cuba: Order and Revolution in the Twentieth Century, by Jorge I. Dominguez, 1978. Harvard University Press.

Raw Materials Investments and American Foreign Policy, by Stephen D. Krasner, 1978. Princeton University Press.

Commodity Conflict: The Political Economy of International Commodity Negotiations, by L.N. Rangarajan, 1978. Cornell University Press and Croom Helm (London).

Standing Guard: The Protection of Foreign Investment, by Charles Lipson, 1978. University of California Press.

Israel: Embattled Ally, by Nadav Safran, 1978. Harvard University Press.

HARVARD STUDIES IN INTERNATIONAL AFFAIRS*

[Formerly Occasional Papers in International Affairs]

† 1. *A Plan for Planning: The Need for a Better Method of Assisting Underdeveloped Countries on Their Ecomomic Policies,* by Gustav F. Papanek, 1961.

† 2. *The Flow of Resources from Rich to Poor,* by Alan D. Neale, 1961.

† 3. *Limited War: An Essay on the Development of the Theory and an Annotated Bibliography,* by Morton H. Halperin, 1962.

† 4. *Reflections on the Failure of the First West Indian Federation,* by Hugh W. Springer, 1962.

5. *On the Interaction of Opposing Forces under Possible Arms Agreements,* by Glenn A. Kent, 1963. 36 pp. $1.75.

† 6. *Europe's Northern Cap and the Soviet Union,* by Nils Orvik, 1963.

7. *Civil Administration in the Punjab: An Analysis of a State Government in India,* by E.N. Mangat Rai, 1963. 82 pp. $2.25.

8. *On the Appropriate Size of a Development Program,* by Edward S. Mason, 1964. 24 pp. $1.50.

9. *Self-Determination Revisited in the Era of Decolonization,* by Rupert Emerson, 1964. 64 pp. $2.25.

10. *The Planning and Execution of Economic Development in Southeast Asia,* by Clair Wilcox, 1965. 37 pp. $1.75.

11. *Pan-Africanism in Action,* by Albert Teveodjre, 1965. 88 pp. $2.95.

12. *Is China Turning In?* by Morton Halperin, 1965. 34 pp. $1.75.

†13. *Economic Development in India and Pakistan,* by Edward S. Mason, 1966.

14. *The Role of the Military in Recent Turkish Politics,* by Ergun Ozbudun, 1966. 54 pp. $1.95.

†15. *Economic Development and Individual Change: A Social Psychological Study of the Comilla Experiment in Pakistan,* by Howard Schuman, 1967.

16. *A Select Bibliography on Students, Politics, and Higher Education,* by Philip G. Altbach, UMHE Revised Edition, 1970. 65 pp. $3.25.

17. *Europe's Political Puzzle: A Study on the Fouchet Negotiations and the 1963 Veto,* by Alessandro Silj, 1967. 178 pp. $4.25.

18. *The Cap and the Straits: Problems of Nordic Security,* by Jan Klenberg. 1968. 19 pp. $1.50.

19. *Cyprus: The Law and Politics of Civil Strife,* by Linda B. Miller, 1968. 97 pp. $3.50.

†20. *East and West Pakistan: A Problem in the Political Economy of Regional Planning,* by Md. Anisur Rahman, 1968.

†21. *International War and International Systems: Perspectives on Method,* by George A. Kelley and Linda B. Miller, 1969.

†22. *Migrants, Urban Poverty, and Instability in Developing Nations,* by Joan M. Nelson, 1969. 81 pp.

23. *Growth and Development in Pakistan, 1955-1969,* by Joseph J. Stern and Walter P. Falcon, 1970. 94 pp. $3.50.

24. *Higher Education in Developing Countries: A Select Bibliography*, by Philip G. Altbach, 1970. 118 pp. $4.50.

25. *Anatomy of Political Institutionalization: The Case of Israel and Some Comparative Analyses*, by Amos Perlmutter, 1970. 60 pp. $2.95.

†26. *The German Democratic Republic from the Sixties to the Seventies*, by Peter Christian Ludz, 1970. 100 pp.

27. *The Law in Political Integration: The Evolution and Integrative Implications of Regional Legal Processes in the European Community*, by Stuart A. Scheingold, 1971. 63 pp. $2.95.

†28. *Psychological Dimensions of U.S.-Japanese Relations*, by Hiroshi Kitamura, 1971. 46 pp. $2.50.

29. *Conflict Regulation in Divided Societies*, by Eric A. Nordlinger, 1972. 142 pp. $4.95.

30. *Israel's Political-Military Doctrine*, by Michael I. Handel, 1973. 101 pp. $3.75.

31. *Italy, NATO, and the European Community: The Interplay of Foreign Policy and Domestic Politics*, by Primo Vannicelli, 1974. 67 + x pp. $3.75.

32. *The Choice of Technology in Developing Countries: Some Cautionary Tales*, by C. Peter Timmer, John W. Thomas, Louis T. Wells, Jr., and David Morawetz, 1975. 114 pp. $3.95.

33. *The International Role of the Communist Parties of Italy and France*, by Donald L.M. Blackmer and Annie Kriegel, 1975. 67 + x pp. $3.50.

34. *The Hazards of Peace: A European View of Detente*, by Juan Cassiers, 1976. 94 pp. $3.50.

35. *Oil and the Middle East War: Europe in the Energy Crisis*, by Robert J. Lieber, 1976. 75 + x pp. $3.45.

37. *Climatic Change and World Affairs*, by Crispin Tickell, 1977. 78 pp. $3.95.

38. *Conflict and Violence in Lebanon: Confrontation in the Middle East*, by Walid Khalidi, 1979. 180 pp.$12.95, cloth; $6.95, paper.

39. *Diplomatic Dispute: U.S. Conflict with Iran, Japan, and Mexico*, by Robert L. Paarlberg, Ed., Eul. Y. Park, and Donald L. Wyman, 1979. 173 pp. $11.95, cloth; $5.95, paper.

40. *Commandos and Politicians: Elite Military Units in Modern Democracies*, by Eliot A. Cohen, 1978. 136 pp. $8.95, cloth; $3.95, paper.

41. *Yellow Earth, Green Jade: Constants in Chinese Political Mores*, by Simon de Beaufort, 1979. 90 pp. $8.95 cloth; $3.95, paper.

42. *The Future of North America: Canada, the United States, and Quebec Nationalism*, by Elliot J. Feldman and Neil Nevitte, eds., 1979. 378 pp. $13.95, cloth; $6.95, paper.

*Available from Harvard University Center for International Affairs, 1737 Cambridge Street, Cambridge, Massachusetts 02138
†Out of print. Reprints may be ordered from AMS Press, Inc., 56 East 13th Street, New York, N.Y. 10003.